The Modern Stage and Other Worlds

The MODERN STAGE and OTHER WORLDS

Austin E. Quigley

METHUEN
New York and London

First published in 1985 by
Methuen, Inc.
733 Third Avenue,
New York,
NY 10017

Published in Great Britain by
Methuen & Co. Ltd
11 New Fetter Lane,
London EC4P 4EE

Photoset by
Rowland Phototypesetting Ltd
Bury St Edmunds, Suffolk
Printed in Great Britain
at The University Press,
Cambridge

**Library of Congress Cataloging in
Publication Data**

Quigley, Austin E., 1942–
    The modern stage and other worlds.
    Bibliography: p.
    Includes index.
    1. European drama—19th
century—History and criticism.
    2. European drama—20th
century—History and criticism.
    I. Title.
PN2570.Q54 1985 809.2 84-20759

ISBN 0-416-39310-1
ISBN 0-416-39320-9 (pbk.)

**British Library Cataloguing in
Publication Data**

Quigley, Austin E.
    The modern stage and other worlds.
    1. Drama—20th century—History
and criticism   I. Title
809.2'04   PN1861

ISBN 0-416-39310-1
ISBN 0-416-39320-9 Pbk

For Patricia, Laura and Rebecca

Two cultures or technologies can, like astronomical galaxies, pass through one another without collision; but not without change of configuration. In modern physics there is, similarly, the concept of 'interface' or the meeting and metamorphosis of two structures.

(Marshall McLuhan, *The Gutenberg Galaxy*, London, 1967, p. 149)

Contents

Introduction   ix

Acknowledgements   xv

Part I   A critical framework

 1   Theatres and worlds   3

 2   Marking and merging horizons   22

 3   Reconciling worlds   37

 4   Generalizing about worlds   55

Part II   The plays

 5   Pinero: *The Second Mrs. Tanqueray*   69

 6   Ibsen: *A Doll's House*   91

 7   Strindberg: *A Dream Play*   115

 8   Brecht: *Life of Galileo*   142

 9   Ionesco: *The Chairs*   172

10   Beckett: *Krapp's Last Tape*   199

11   Pinter: *Betrayal*   221

12   Conclusion   253

Notes   264

Selected bibliography   304

Index   315

Introduction

The modern period has been one of the most innovative and productive in the history of the theatre. A steadily growing stock of first-rate plays has encouraged, and been encouraged by, widespread building of new theatres. At the same time, there has been extensive reconsideration of the appropriate nature and structure of the performance arena, with the result that renewal of theatre structures has proceeded in close conjunction with renewal of drama structures. Though theatres depend on economic as well as artistic factors and consequently alternate rapidly between periods of hardship and periods of prosperity, the overall importance of the theatre in European and American society has remained markedly high throughout the last one hundred years.

The successes of the theatre in this period have attracted not only large audiences, but also a steadily increasing collection of critical work. Like criticism in most fields, criticism of modern theatre has been somewhat mixed in quality, but there now exist solid and sometimes inspired introductions to the work of individual dramatists and directors, and several helpful summaries of movements in local parts of the field. Books about the field at large, however, have been less frequently produced and, with one or two notable exceptions, less impressive in their achievements. Scholars have frequently preferred to focus on the local rather than the larger domain, on single dramatists and single movements (naturalism, expressionism, etc.), or on such intermediate domains as the Theatre of the Absurd, the Theatre of Commitment, the Theatre of Protest and Paradox, the Theatre of the Marvellous, and so on. The notion of a Theatre of the Whole has seemed more problematic, in part because the field is still developing, in part because the 'theatre' metaphor acquires an uncertain status in this larger context, and in part because the field seems to be characterized more by its variety than by any underlying, overarching, or emerging consistency. Those who have attempted to deal with the field at large have often found themselves forced into selective and reductive generalization if they focus on the field's putative unity, and into piecemeal criticism if they focus on its manifest changes.

The problems inevitably attendant upon attempts to write in general terms about still evolving patterns are made particularly acute when modern playwrights participate so energetically in the widespread modern movement to 'make it new'. Playwrights, it seems, are just as determined as novelists and poets to make their work significantly different from that of their predecessors. There is thus, we must recognize at the outset, an incipient conflict between the desires of the playwrights, who usually wish to emphasize the novelty of their individual contributions, and the desires of those critics who wish to generalize about the shared achievements of a large group of playwrights. The necessary response to this difficulty is not to try to circumvent or ignore it, but to establish appropriate ways of dealing with it—not least because the problem introduced here as a critics' problem has its counterpart in problems confronted by those in theatre audiences who likewise find the diversity of the modern theatre rather daunting.

It is quite understandable that playwrights seeking to establish their place in a competitive profession should insist on the originality and even uniqueness of their own work. There is nothing more likely to make a modern writer bristle than a suggestion that his latest creative efforts resemble someone else's. But the danger, for audiences, readers and critics alike, is that an excessive concern for the novelty of a work can be as misleading as an excessive concern for the common features it shares with other works. There is, of course, the obvious point that anything entirely new would be incomprehensible, but more important is the recurring tendency to see the new as a massive rejection of the old. The playwright's desire to direct attention to the novelty of his work rather than to its accompanying conventionality thus tends to produce an uncertain response to that novelty. A sense of what is being rejected frequently looms larger than a sense of what is being gained. Novelty following upon novelty is thus often dealt with in terms of 'the shock of the new', or in terms of things falling apart, order giving way to anarchy, or disorientation and *Angst* awaiting audiences bold enough to confront the latest products of the *avant-garde*.

Such emphasis on novelty at the expense of continuity has its contemporary place, but it provides the critic with something of a dilemma when he tries to move beyond a rightful recognition of each writer's novelty towards some larger sense of how the various novelties are related. The trouble is that related novelties threaten to forfeit their status as novelties, and generalizations that invite us to focus on common ground tend to lose contact with the very diversity they seek to illuminate. It is, of course, possible to try another tack and attempt to generalize locally about plays in terms of what they commonly question, attack or reject. But criticism needs to move beyond initial concerns about Theatres of Protest, Revolt and the Absurd, towards a recognition not only of the continuities involved in the field as a whole, but also of the positive implications of creativity and change. Change, though frequently appearing initially as a threat, is often also an opportunity, and criticism needs to keep pace with the speed at which playwrights and audiences adapt to and make use of successive changes. Today's experimental goal quickly becomes tomorrow's starting-point; today's invention is tomorrow's convention. Recognition of the diversity of modern theatre is thus as important as, but no more important than, recognition of its principles of continuity; recognition of its role in challenging what preceded it is as important as, but no more important than, recognition of what its novelties make newly possible.

My aim has thus been not to reject the claims of those critics who have emphasized the novelty of individual writers or local movements in the modern theatre, but to place those claims in a larger context, one which can embrace not only novelty and diversity, but also conventionality and continuity, and at the same time demonstrate the varied connections among them. This is not simply a matter of correcting a critical imbalance but of establishing for readers and audiences alike an enabling mode of access to highly experimental and less experimental modern plays. It is important to overcome a tendency to regard innovation as a deliberate and disturbing choice on the part of the dramatist, and imitation as an unthinking, ill-considered, or unrelated accompanying action. We may misunderstand the nature of the novelty if we ignore as 'derivative' elements of plays that are indispensable if their novelty is to function successfully. And we may likewise be misled if our attempts to generalize direct excessive attention to shared rather than singular features. We might do well to regard both innovative *and* conventional aspects of a drama as necessary and deliberate choices – choices made, each in the context of the other, for particular purposes. Whether this is true or not biographically will vary from case to case, but if adopted as a critical attitude, as a working hypothesis, such an approach will help us locate those elements of conventionality that make invention both possible and accessible.

Though novelty and diversity, along with convention and continuity, thus have their places in the field, the difficulty remains of establishing a general mode of discourse that can locate and exploit their appropriate relationships. What is needed is not the excavation of the hidden common ground of modern plays, but the establishment of a mode of discourse within which generalizations can function as instruments of investigation rather than as summations of common underlying truths. Such a mode of discourse will enable audiences and critics to deal with diversity in a way that neither reduces it to an underlying uniformity nor confronts it as an alarming aggregate of unique and unrelated events. An approach less rigid than that of structuralism and more illuminating than that of merely tracing unrelated trends will allow us to generalize, without limiting us to what the generalizations themselves can readily embrace. Unless we establish such a mode of inquiry, one that allows generalizations to operate as a means of renewing rather than terminating our investigations, we run the risk of being seriously misled by premature and unwarranted conclusions.

I have thus sought to establish an investigative context within which generalizations can function without implying the existence of an underlying unity (which is unavailable) or an emerging closure (which is unjustifiable). In establishing the appropriate mode of discourse, I have sought to replace the search for unity with a search for principles of continuity, and the desire for closure with a respect for principles of generative coherence. These steps are necessary because I have wished to avoid writing two kinds of book, both of which offer inviting, but finally disappointing, possibilities – the kind that addresses itself accurately to the field but deals with only a cross-section of it, and the kind that determinedly seeks to deal with the whole field but addresses only a few lines to each of several hundred plays. The former purchases unity and closure at the cost of comprehensiveness, the latter achieves comprehensiveness at the cost of explanatory power. But if we reject misplaced desires for unity, closure and encyclopaedic comprehensiveness, where do we turn, if we wish to deal with the field at large? Comprehensiveness in principle is, I would argue, preferable to comprehensiveness in demonstrated practice, because the latter, no matter how detailed, must always fall short of the task it sets itself. Comprehensiveness in principle is justified if it can demonstrate explanatory applicability by addressing a wide range and a considerable variety of important cases, rather than by seeking to deal explicitly with all extant plays. The selected plays, if sufficiently varied, can substantiate the explanatory power of principles of coherence not by exhausting their application, but by supporting the possibility of their further application.

This book thus has two major sections. Part I seeks to investigate the nature of the field and the difficulties of generalizing about it. From this investigation, there emerges an appropriate mode of discourse and an appropriate means of generalizing about a field characterized by diversity. The series of plays discussed and the patterns of similarity and diversity located suggest, in turn, certain useful principles of continuity in modern drama and certain lines of their potential extension. Part II seeks to demonstrate the comprehensiveness and explanatory power of these modes of continuity and coherence by exploring, in considerable detail, a small number of diverse plays by important modern playwrights. Generalizations established in the first part of the book are tested out in the light of their ability to take us to the heart, and not just to the periphery, of important and varied plays. The plays given detailed scrutiny are selected to exemplify the diversity of modern theatre, but not to exhaust it.

Arguments over the selection of particular plays could, of course, be raised no matter which plays and playwrights were chosen. I wish only to emphasize that there is no implied judgement that these playwrights and these plays are the most important in the period or that they set a limit to the possibilities of the field; my point is simply that they are diverse and important and that discussion of them helps to clarify the importance of others. As I have not sought to establish an encyclopaedic comprehensiveness, nor to establish local patterns of influence, I have not felt constrained, in selecting plays for detailed study, by geographical distribution, chronological sequence or chronological spacing. The continuity of the field is not so much chrono-logical and uni-directional, but methodological and multi-directional. I have thus not hesitated to explore Pinero's work before Ibsen's or to discuss playwrights whose work is contemporary with that of others. In exploring these particular plays, I have simply sought to demonstrate principles in action; if these studies suggest further cases, more obvious examples, and more complex questions, that is all to the good. I have not wished to close off thought about the field or about particular plays, but to open up both to further consideration by others. The interpretations in the second part of the book serve only as examples, not as the final word about the plays or the principles of coherence located in them.

The book is thus, I believe, susceptible to a variety of uses. Those with a major interest in a particular play or a particular dramatist might well prefer to read selected chapters in Part II before reading selectively in Part I. Those more concerned with the field at large might well prefer to read Part I before reading selectively in Part II. Those who read the whole text sequentially, however, will encounter a relatedness in the emerging patterns of continuity that exemplifies certain larger principles of ordering that are widely dispersed throughout the field. They will also recognize that, for reasons already touched on above and elaborated later, the several chapters in Part II are not mere illustrations of points made in Part I. Every application of the principles established in Part I is both a selective replication and a selective extension of what they seem initially to subsume. The mode of inquiry exemplified in Part I is a means of enabling audiences and readers to construct from a variety of traditional and less traditional sources of information a series of interpretative contexts – contexts that facilitate appropriate access to and appropriate participation in the dramatic experience particular plays have to offer. But each construction of an interpretative context is itself a model for further context-creation – context-creation of related but different kinds for related but different plays.

Such context-creation necessarily involves linking the mode of discourse exemplified in this book to those offered elsewhere. Though my book has its own claims to novelty, this novelty, like others, is grounded in the valuable work of predecessors. I have sought, from time to time, to link my arguments to those of other writers in the field, though there can be no question of comprehensiveness here. I have merely sought to provide informative links to other work and occasional suggestions of the usefulness or otherwise of established lines of argument. Such links are provided not simply because it is appropriate to acknowledge one's debts, but because the drama and the theatre exist as community property and it is important that criticism exhibit its appropriate status as one component of an ongoing community interaction with drama and theatre. There should be no radical discontinuity between (a) conversations among audience members leaving a theatre, and (b) conversations among audience members by way of books and articles. Coming to know a play is partly a process that takes place in the theatre and partly a process that precedes and succeeds what occurs in the theatre. Though its opposite ends may be widely separated, the chain of implication that links audience response to interpretative activity and to theoretical discussion is one that should not readily be severed. When these components are radically separated it is usually to the detriment of each stage in the investigative process. It is important in this respect not to overlook how often playwrights and directors become, intermittently at least, practising theorists. They are much more willing than are many journalists and critics to believe that theatre audiences can deal with intellectual challenge. Learning about the theatre is part of the process of learning about ourselves, our society and our individual and collective pasts.

The critic, then, like the playwright and the audience, relies on appropriate response to the continuities that help provide intriguing novelties with their initial importance and their persisting significance. We do well to remember that in the modern theatre, as in any other field of creative endeavour, discovery is often, in part at least, a matter of rediscovery, and innovation a matter of renovation. I have thus sought in the several chapters of this book to investigate the nature of certain problems that arise for audiences and critics in the modern theatre, to confront the difficulties involved in generalizing locally or at large about the diversified domain of modern theatre, to demonstrate important links between invention and convention, and to suggest a way of thinking about the modern theatre that registers appropriate respect for, and facilitates appropriate participation in, the challenges and opportunities so frequently generated by widespread commitments to variety and change. It will, I suspect, be evident to all who take the time to digest what this argument has to offer that it has implications for our understanding not only of modern drama, but also of other genres in the modern era and of plays in eras before our own. I have pursued these implications only as far as this particular study requires. I hope, however, in the formulation of this argument, not only to have shed some light on modern theatre in general, but also to have made available a means by which others may make further discoveries for themselves.

Acknowledgements

My interest in the theatre goes back as far as my earliest memories. As the child of a village schoolmaster, I found myself at an early age behind the scenes of the school's drama productions; as a youth in the north of England, I was quickly introduced to the boisterous worlds of music hall and community theatre; as a university student and subsequently a university teacher, I exchanged the regional theatres of Newcastle, Leeds and Nottingham for the major theatre centres of London, Europe and North America. It has been a varied but fascinating progression in which I have encountered many, too numerous to record here, whose enthusiasm for and ideas about the theatre have served as catalysts to my own.

This book has emerged over many years, and while writing it I have accumulated many debts. Douglas Day gave me much valued encouragement at the outset and has maintained a calm confidence about the emerging results. Conversations with Del Kolve about pictorial and narrative imagery provided a constant source of inspiration. John Ellis, Ralph Cohen and Wolfgang Iser, three brilliant theorists with three contrasting sets of theoretical commitments, united in reminding me that the theorist's greatest virtue, and the critic's, is his capacity to help others to think for themselves. Over the years, conversations with Rick Waswo, Paul Armstrong, Michael Levenson, Darryl Gless and Karen Chase have challenged, refined and improved my thinking in almost every area of conceptual inquiry. When it was close to completion, Jill Levenson and Thomas van Laan read the manuscript and offered invaluable suggestions for revision. Janice Price, Mary Cusack, and Rosamund Howe did likewise, reminding me once again of the importance of a first-rate editorial staff. The task of research and writing was made easier by the enthusiastic assistance of many at the University of Virginia including Lark Hammond, Laurene McKillop, Patti Schroeder,

Rick Barr, Sherry Buttrick and Julie Bates. And thanks are also due to Toby Eady and Ruthe and Martin Battestin whose generous hospitality and lively opinions made the London theatre so much more accessible and enjoyable.

It is a pleasure to acknowledge the generous support of the National Endowment for the Humanities whose award of a Fellowship for Independent Study and Research made possible the writing of the first draft of this book. Subsequent work was facilitated by a Sesquicentennial Associateship at the Centre for Advanced Studies at the University of Virginia. A summer Research Fellowship and a series of smaller grants from the University's Committee on Research helped speed the completion of the final version. I am also grateful to the editor of *Modern Drama* for permission to reprint in chapter six substantial portions of my essay 'A *Doll's House* revisited'.

My warmest thanks go to my wife, Patricia, who makes everything possible.

Charlottesville
September 1984

The author and publisher would like to thank the following for permission to reproduce copyright material:
Grove Press, Inc. and Faber & Faber Ltd for extracts from *Krapp's Last Tape* in '*Krapp's Last Tape*' *and Other Dramatic Pieces* by Samuel Beckett, © 1957 Samuel Beckett; © 1958, 1959, 1960 Grove Press, Inc.; Grove Press, Inc. and John Calder (Publishers) Ltd for extracts from *The Chairs* in *Four Plays by Eugène Ionesco* by Eugène Ionesco, translated by Donald M. Allen, © 1958 Grove Press, Inc. and *Notes and Counter Notes: Writings on the Theatre* by Eugène Ionesco, translated by Donald Watson, © 1964 Grove Press, Inc.; Grove Press, Inc. and Methuen London for extracts from *Betrayal* by Harold Pinter; Random House, Inc. and Methuen London for extracts from *Life of Galileo* by Bertolt Brecht, translated by Wolfgang Sauerlander and Ralph Manheim, in *Bertolt Brecht: Collected Plays*, V, edited by Ralph Manheim and John Willett.

Part I
A critical framework

1 Theatres and worlds

The theatre motif

One of the more obvious characteristics of modern drama is the sheer diversity of the plays that have earned an important place in the field. Any category that must prominently include Ibsen's *Hedda Gabler*, Strindberg's *The Ghost Sonata*, Chekhov's *The Sea Gull*, Shaw's *Man and Superman*, Pirandello's *Henry IV*, Brecht's *Mother Courage*, Genet's *The Balcony*, Ionesco's *The Bald Soprano* and Beckett's *Waiting for Godot* is indisputably heterogeneous. The question is whether one can fruitfully generalize across such diversity.[1] Is there, we might ask, a way of thinking about modern drama in general that materially assists our understanding and enjoyment of individual plays? An evident danger is that a general framework can become counter-productive if it draws excessive attention to common features among plays that otherwise differ significantly. An impression of substantial similarity is likely to be substituted for the reality of extensive diversity, and this can be seriously misleading. Criticism within such a framework is also incipiently reductive if it focuses attention on features that seem, on balance, more important to the framework than to the individual plays. Yet generalizations in the context of diverse material seem always likely to produce precisely this result.[2]

Though the problem of diversity is peculiarly acute for those interested in modern drama, the study of this field is otherwise similar to the study of any other heterogeneous field. We need some generalizations that will give us an adequate grasp of the types of things we are studying and we need some detailed descriptions of particular instances which exemplify the types. This will then enable us to approach other instances, as audiences, readers, or critics, with some sense of the important things to look for. Such a procedure is not a once-and-for-all event, nor is it a one-way movement (e.g. from type to particular instance). Rather, it is a recurring back-and-forth movement in which we constantly discover more adequate general statements about the field by matching them against more adequate particular statements about individual plays. These more adequate general statements then provide an improved framework for studying particular plays, and the cycle renews itself indefinitely. Such a cycle of discovery seems at best intermittently operative, however, in criticism addressed to modern drama. Though there are many fine studies of the works of individual dramatists and of local movements in the drama, larger generalizations have not always been so persuasively presented nor so enthusiastically received.

The questions posed by this situation are twofold. Is there something not quite right about the ways in which critical activity has been pursued, or is there something about this field that is peculiarly resistant to some traditional features of our critical activity? We have already noted some complementary problems in the two domains. On the one hand, our modes of generalization seem to depend on, but fail to locate, important common ground, and, on the other, the drama seems to display more variety than homogeneity. But the situation is further complicated by long-standing disagreements among drama critics themselves about the appropriate basis for critical work on the drama.

For many years there has been a troublesome disagreement between those who see a play primarily as a literary text to be interpreted, and those who regard it primarily as a theatre script to be performed. Each side has tended to characterize the other's position as limited and limiting. The danger of the 'literary' approach is that it seems to explore the thematic implications of a text as if theme were not in part a product of performance, while the danger of the 'theatrical' approach is that it seems to limit discussion of a play to actual productions of it, productions which may or may not do demonstrable justice to the possibilities of the text. The 'literary' approach can claim generality of implication by rejecting the limiting particularity of actual performances, and the 'theatrical' approach can claim concrete support for the status of a performed interpretation while questioning the viability of the other side's untested conclusions. Like most simplifications, these versions of the two positions are not entirely accurate, but they are not without the support of actual instances. In recent years, however, the bulk of good drama criticism has tried to treat the two approaches as complementary rather than contrasting, and also to take some deliberate steps towards reconciling them.[3]

The need for such reconciliation has become increasingly urgent in the modern era, for one dramatist after another has advocated the renewal of the theatrical environment as an integral part of the process of renewing the drama. Whatever justification might once have been claimed for separating literary and theatrical approaches, it is not easily maintained in the face of so widespread a concern among dramatists of so many kinds for linking reform in the structure of the drama with reform in the structure of the performance environment. We see this persistent concern in Zola's call for a new dramatic talent capable of 'remaking the stage until it is continuous with the auditorium',[4] one who can 'scour the boards, create a world whose elements he would lift from life, from outside our traditions'.[5] We see it in Strindberg's famous preface to *Miss Julie* in which he offers a programme for theatrical reform which concludes with the wry comment that 'while waiting for such a theatre it is as well for us to go on writing so as to stock that repertory of the future'.[6] We see it in Ibsen's complaint that 'the artistic reforms that I might wish to introduce would be impossible in the present theatre . . . if theatrical art in our country is not to perish altogether, we must have an up-to-date playhouse'.[7] We see it in Ghelderode's desire 'to break the conventional frame of the theatre'.[8] We see it in Brecht's comment that 'any theatre that makes a serious attempt to stage one of the new plays risks being radically transformed'.[9] We see it in Artaud's advocating 'a revolving spectacle which, instead of making the stage and the auditorium two closed worlds, without possible communication, spreads its visual and sonorous outbursts over the entire mass of the spectators'.[10] We see its influence, too, in many comments of critics and directors. Paolucci, for example, suggests that central to Pirandello's work is the fact that 'he saw the stage as something to be shaped anew with each new play',[11] and such a view is also shared by Peter Brook who argues that the theatre should 'redefine itself each time it occurs'.[12] There is thus clearly more than a morsel of persisting truth in Lukács's argument (summarized by Bentley) that

> in the great ages, the drama flowed 'naturally' from the existing theatre, while, from Goethe on, the poet-dramatist rejects the theatre, writes plays which are 'too good for it', and then calls for the creation of the kind of theatre which will be good enough for the plays.[13]

Though the specific aims of the dramatists may vary when they advocate the creation of new theatres, their shared concern for linking renewal of the drama with renewal of the theatre is evident enough. The unfortunate result of the process of theatre-following-upon-play would be, however, the thoroughly impractical situation in which a new theatre had to be built for every new play, and every production would be unique. Whatever the artistic desirability of such a situation, the more practical consequence of these calls for reform has been a movement towards increased flexibility in each theatre's use of space. In a flexible performance environment the appropriate *type* of performance arena can quickly be constructed for a specific *type* of play. But to speak of types of arenas and types of plays (rather than of particular arenas and particular plays) is immediately to provide one means of reconciling the seemingly opposed 'literary' and 'theatrical' approaches to interpretation. The choice between an unperformed general interpretation and an ungeneralizable particular production is not one we need to force upon ourselves. The emerging choice is not between a non-performance and an actual performance but between more and less persuasive versions of *possible* performances in possible *types* of theatrical space. The persuasiveness of an interpretation, from whatever source, derives not from its basis in a single production, nor from its ability to transcend production, but from its capacity to locate potential thematic values in the context of potential theatrical values.

In one sense, this seems no more than a truism. Yet, like many another truism, it can offer more subtle and more complex implications than those that most readily catch the eye. The dramatists' concern for linking renewal of the drama with renewal of the theatre not only compels a convergence of 'literary' and 'theatrical' approaches to the drama, but also offers, in that convergence, a not yet fully exploited ground for linking the varied creative activities of the dramatists themselves. The potential power of this basis for linking the otherwise diverse activities of the dramatists has not gone unnoticed. Some evidence of its emerging importance is registered in the recent popularity of attempts to generalize about modern plays, locally or at large, in terms of 'theatre' metaphors. From playwrights interested in reforming theatres as part of the process of reforming plays, such use of the metaphor should come as no surprise. Thus Artaud coined the phrase 'Theatre of Cruelty' to describe his programme for reform of the drama, and Brecht advanced the case for an 'Epic Theatre' consisting largely of his own plays. Drama critics then followed suit. Extensive cases have been made for the existence of a Theatre of Revolt, a Theatre of the Absurd, a Theatre of Protest and Paradox, a Theatre of the Marvellous, a Theatre of Commitment, and a Theatre of War.[14] From time to time, others have suggested such critical categories as the Theatre of Panic, the Theatre of Silence, the Theatre of Communion, the Theatre of Event, and the Theatre of Joy. But if we leave to one side Artaud's and Brecht's categories, most of the others seem rather inappropriate. The metaphor of a 'theatre' sits uneasily upon groups of plays which do not seem necessarily tied to any specific kind of use of performance space. What holds many of these 'Theatre of X' categories together is not some notion of a common performance environment but of common textural, structural and thematic concerns.

This difference is important, for it suggests a not yet fully developed recognition of the potential value of generalizing about plays in terms of their use of theatre space. For Artaud and Brecht, on the other hand, the 'theatre' metaphor is earned by the range of issues linked by this mode of generalization. Their 'theatre' categories are based upon a comprehensive notion of how the local detail of a play (its texture) relates to its overall thematic shape (its structure), to its use of performance space (its theatrical function), and to its role in the social structure outside the theatre (its social function). The critics' 'Theatre of X' categories are only metaphorically about theatres, for they consist primarily of generalizations about the texture and structure of the plays they embrace. Consequently, such critics deal largely with the relationships of various parts of various plays to each other, and only intermittently include modes of performance when assessing larger social function. This, I would suggest, radically undermines such attempts to use 'theatre' metaphors as a persuasive means of generalizing about the diverse field of modern drama.

The word 'theatre', we should also note, does not offer an obviously appropriate basis for metaphors that seek to establish categories in terms of 'common-core' descriptions of local features of plays. A theatre is an arena, a circumscribed domain, and what goes on within it is not fixed and unvarying, but changeable and often surprising. What is fixed or fixable in a theatre (and particularly a modern theatre) is not the structure at its centre, but the lines of its circumference, the edges of the domain, whether marked by a moat, a hillside, a circle of onlookers, a set of seats, or an arrangement of walls. Peter Brook aptly called his book on theatre *The Empty Space*,[15] and if one wishes to develop the word 'theatre' into a metaphor about plays, it will seem most appropriate to do so in terms of the types of ways in which plays fill the empty space by organizing, controlling and rendering meaningful the various portions of that space. The appropriate metaphoric use of the word 'theatre' is thus, as the writings of Artaud and Brecht suggest, a use that links texture, structure and theme to the mode of performance that is characteristic of a particular kind of play in a particular kind of theatrical space.[16]

The 'world' motif

When we look for further examples of Artaud's and Brecht's use of the 'theatre' metaphor, however, its popularity as a motif begins to become subordinate to one that serves a similar, significantly related, but somewhat different function: the motif of a 'world' or 'worlds'. The popularity of this motif is everywhere in evidence, and when directors, playwrights and critics link reform in the drama with reform in the theatre, they resort to this metaphor with remarkable regularity. Zola, we noted, talks of creating a new kind of world on-stage, and Artaud talks of the way in which established theatres make the stage and the auditorium into two closed worlds. Pirandello, elsewhere, talks of art creating in the theatre its own 'little world',[17] Ionesco describes the theatre as a place where the 'two antagonistic worlds' of the real and the imaginary collide,[18] and Adamov claims that 'a stage play ought to be the point of intersection between the visible and invisible worlds'.[19] Further examples can be found almost anywhere one looks. Bentley excludes a potential theme from one of Brecht's plays on the grounds that 'it is not relevant – is not *possible* – to the experience Brecht depicts, the world he creates'.[20] Wellwarth describes Jarry's rebellion against established conventions as a rebellion against all things 'to the point where he had to invent a new "reality" beyond the physical and metaphysical worlds'.[21] Esslin suggests that Genet's *The Balcony* 'represents a world of fantasy about a world of fantasy'.[22] Orenstein argues that 'the true surrealist protagonist must be free to explore both the world of consciousness and that of the dream', and that it is the possible role of women to 'mediate between the two worlds'.[23] These are not isolated examples. The 'world' motif occurs with remarkable regularity both in the plays and in all kinds of discussion of all kinds of modern theatre. In one sense, this should not be surprising. Use of the 'world' motif in the context of theatre issues has a long history,[24] but its prevalence in contemporary discussion of theatre is such that it seems to have achieved a new importance. We will thus want to consider whether there is something about the simultaneous popularity of 'world' and 'theatre' metaphors that will help clarify the importance of both.

Such clarification, for our purposes, must lead in a particular direction. The question that needs to be addressed is whether it is possible to use world and theatre metaphors as a means of grounding a framework, not just for a local kind of theatre, as did Artaud and Brecht, but for modern theatre as a whole. If we are to follow the path Artaud and Brecht have charted, we must be able to locate in terms of world and theatre metaphors an illuminating correlation among textural detail, structure, theme, performance space and social function. Only in that context can critical use of theatre metaphors serve as an appropriate basis for a critical framework. And if world and similar motifs (universe, planet, island, etc.) are to contribute to that controlling framework, they must likewise demonstrate a capacity to link the various components of the theatrical event. For guidance on the appropriate use of world and theatre metaphors in this context we would thus do well to consider the use the playwrights themselves make of them in the plays. If these terms are to justify their emerging importance, there must be something about their viability as spatial metaphors that makes them particularly appropriate to the ways in which modern playwrights conceive, not only of plays and of the theatre, but of the whole structure of social, psychological, spiritual and empirical relations that provide the basis for life as they wish to portray it.

At this point we find ourselves making large demands on a set of local metaphors, but the potential powers of the world motif emerge very quickly when we turn to actual examples. At first glance, the motif can seem popular in the plays but otherwise unremarkable. As we might expect, there are many instances of the use of the word 'world' to designate everything that exists in a domain of universal scope. For example, Cathleen, in Yeats's *The Countess Cathleen* (1892), greets a merchant with the words:

> There is a something in you that I fear;
> A something not of us; were you not born
> In some most distant corner of the world?[25]

The sense of remoteness and distance is one that is registered by the implied universality of the world motif. But it is important to note how we, as audience, are guided by this spatial metaphor. We are invited to stand with Cathleen *inside* her world and contemplate *from within* the notion of its distant and remote horizons. Once we have noted this we are then in a position to recognize the importance of another tendency visible in late-Victorian use of the world motif – a tendency to characterize social or psychological remoteness in terms, not of separation within a single domain, but of separation of one domain from another. There is a particularly instructive clash between these two uses of the 'world' motif in Pinero's *The Second Mrs. Tanqueray* (1893). When Aubrey Tanqueray and Cayley Drummle disagree on the issue of appropriate criteria for judging the Victorian 'fallen woman', we find the world motif used to exemplify, on the one hand, the notion of a homogeneous world with homogeneous values and, on the other hand, a competing notion of pluralistic worlds with pluralistic values:

AUBREY: To you, Cayley, all women who have been roughly treated, and who dare to survive by borrowing a little of our philosophy, are alike. You see in the crowd of the ill-used only one pattern; you can't detect the shades of goodness, intelligence, even nobility there. Well, how should you? The crowd is dimly lighted! And, besides, yours is the way of the world.

DRUMMLE: My dear Aubrey, I *live* in the world.

AUBREY: The name we give our little parish of St. James's!²⁶

Drummle's appeal to 'the' standards of 'the' world is challenged by Aubrey's suggestion that Drummle's horizons of value mistake a part of the world for the whole of the world. And in equating that local world with the parish of St James's, Pinero transforms the world motif as spatial metaphor from one that exemplifies large scope and distant horizons to one that exemplifies limited scope and narrow horizons. The values of St James's parish are brought into implied contrast with values beyond that local domain, and this in the context of a discussion that invokes the old double standard of values applied to male and female sexual conduct. Inconsistent values within the domain are used as a means of introducing the notion of incompatible values between one domain and another, and, in the process, the 'world' motif changes from a measure of largeness to one of limits. The characters are then presented with a choice between locating themselves *inside* or *outside* the circumscribed domain with its circumscribing set of values.

These competing implications of largeness and limits, and of inside and outside, are but first glimpses of a spatial orientation towards pluralistic values that is much in evidence in modern plays of many kinds. The notion of a single world with a single set of values is repeatedly brought into conflict with a concern for pluralistic worlds with pluralistic values. This simple contrast leads in turn to the more complex issues of precedence, privilege and priority among competing domains. Examples, once more, are legion. In Jones's *The Liars* (1897), Sir Christopher Deering, a strong defender of established values, concedes the possibility of other worlds and other values, but cleverly reduces their relevance to the world he lives in. His recognition of the possible viability of other worlds and other values is so grudging that it locates them at best in remote societies in remote parts of the universe. He cleverly juggles with the notions of largeness and limits to make the most of the former and ward off the dangers of the latter.

> SIR CHRISTOPHER: Now! I've nothing to say in the abstract against running away with another man's wife! There may be planets where it is not only the highest ideal morality, but where it has the further advantage of being a practical way of carrying on society. But it has this one fatal defect in our country – it won't work![27]

The narrowness of Sir Christopher's horizons of value is here defended, not in terms of some implicit ideal, but in the pragmatic terms of what will or will not work in a certain place at a certain time. This rather cleverly transforms the limitations of narrow horizons from the negative status of exemplifying provinciality and ignorance to the more positive status of exemplifying an awareness and acceptance of what enables a particular social system to work. Shaw, in his best ironic vein, makes a similar point about Lady Britomart in the opening stage direction of *Major Barbara* (1905):

> *Lady Britomart is a woman of fifty or thereabouts . . . a very typical managing matron of the upper class . . . with plenty of practical ability and worldly experience, limited in the oddest way with domestic and class limitations, conceiving the universe exactly as if it were a large house in Wilton Crescent, though handling her corner of it very effectively on that assumption.*[28]

There is thus a way of using the notion of limit, not as an indication of a major shortcoming, but as a necessary part of understanding what is and is not viable in a particular context. This is a further step in developing the implications of the world motif, for it relates the issue of space to issues of convention and power. And if we look at the notion of semi-enclosed worlds with their own systems of value in Barrie's *The Admirable Crichton* (1902), we see that this is not just a local pluralistic motif in the play, but something fundamental to its overall structure and impact. The action of the play carries the major characters from England, not to a remote planet, but to a remote island in which social values change with the scenery. In the course of these changes the characters try to come to terms with the pluralism of social values and social systems. The characters are dramatized first in one domain and then in another, as the impact of the image of contrasting worlds extends from local texture into larger structure and emerging theme.

LORD LOAM: Can't you see, Crichton, that our divisions into [social] classes are artificial, that if we were to return to Nature, which is the aspiration of my life, all would be equal?[29]

As the play develops, the image of contrasting worlds is extended to cover not only texture, structure and theme, but also the appropriate orientation of the audience towards the action. The audience, like the characters, is guided towards viewing its own habitual social values as fundamentally provisional. The play's division of the action equally between two domains gives each domain equal status and invites the audience to perceive each domain from both inside and outside. Two acts are set in England and two on the island, and the stage direction for the fourth act, the return to England, seeks to capitalize on the characters' journey and the play's duality by reorientating the audience in terms of a new pluralistic perspective. The stage direction describes the final scene, in England, as taking place on '*the other island*',[30] i.e. England contemplated from without.

The scope of implication of the world motif in linking various dimensions of the dramatic event is matched by the range of thematic domains to which it can be applied. In the same play, the cleverly controlled geographical and social pluralism is subsequently extended to embrace the further notion of temporal and social pluralism. Crichton quotes a poem by W. E. Henley which adds to the competing world perspectives of England and the other island the similarly competing perspectives of the present world versus that of the past:

Or ever the knightly years were gone,
With the old world to the grave,
I was a *king* in Babylon,
And you were a Christian slave.[31]

It is but a small step in modern drama from recognition of social pluralism based on geographical and temporal variation to the notion of psychological pluralism in a single space at a single time. For Harry, Lord Monchensey, exploring (like Yeats's Countess Cathleen) his strange feeling of the remoteness of another character (Mary), this sense of psychological pluralism produces a feeling of vulnerability and unease. The dialogue registering the menacing contiguity of incompatible worlds occurs in T. S. Eliot's *The Family Reunion* (1939):

HARRY: What is that? do you feel it?
MARY: What, Harry?
HARRY: That apprehension deeper than all sense,
Deeper than the sense of smell, but like a smell
In that it is indescribable, a sweet and bitter smell
From another world. I know it, I know it!
More potent than ever before, a vapour dissolving
All other worlds, and me into it.[32]

The audience, of course, is drawn into sharing Harry's perspective and participating in this experience of invasion and dissolution. Once we are reminded of the narrowness and vulnerability of the boundaries of his world, we are led to contemplate the fragility of our own.

What we begin to recognize in these examples of the world motif is that it is not just a handy emblem for a pluralistic universe, but that it controls in important ways our approach to the notion of pluralism itself. Thematic concern for pluralistic values in modern literature is not, of course, an unusual thing to note. If that were all the world motif were drawing attention to, we would be labouring an obvious point. What is important and not so obvious is what happens in the drama and in the theatre when issues of pluralism are extensively embodied in images of contrasting worlds. These spatial metaphors influence, in significant ways, the orientation of members of the audience towards the values of the play and towards their own values. An audience can be invited metaphorically to stand deep within a world and experience the vastness of its remote horizons, or to stand just inside the horizon and contemplate its restrictiveness, or to stand just outside the horizon and experience its limitations from a stance of superiority and difference; it can be asked to compare and contrast competing worlds from a position outside both, or it can be asked to share the experience of otherness and unease that accompanies the intrusion of unexpected elements into a world that seems unready to accommodate them. This concern for horizons can also provide the basis for radical disorientation by the portrayal (as in *Waiting for Godot* (1953) and *Rosencrantz and Guildenstern Are Dead* (1966)) of a domain of experience that lacks established horizons and limits, and therefore a recognizable and potentially controllable structure. Furthermore, these issues are not simply local textural issues, or simply dramatic issues: they lend themselves, as we shall see in the next chapter, to complex theatrical embodiment and invite subtle theatrical extension. The theatre, with its given lines of demarcation (world outside theatre v. world inside, world on-stage v. world off-stage) and with its capacity to create new lines of internal demarcation (via sets, props, lighting, etc.), offers a peculiarly appropriate forum for exploring this aspect of the world motif. And it is this potential for linking thematic implications with the structure of plays and the structure of the performance environment that is the most important of all the varied possibilities of the world motif.

The popularity of the world motif can thus be explained in part because it offers a peculiarly appropriate emblem of consistency in the context of domains of diversity, in part because it captures a key element in crises of pluralism by orientating characters and audiences towards horizons and frontiers, and in part because it offers playwrights interested in linking reform in the drama with reform in the theatre a powerful means of exploring pluralistic themes in a pluralistic spatial environment. The variety and complexity of discontinuities among domains, whether geographical, social, spiritual, psychological, epistemological, or whatever, confer upon the frontiers of these domains a similar variety and complexity. Once just an image of a comfortably established enclosure viewed from deep within, the world motif is transformed into an image of threatening limits or vulnerable frontiers viewed from just within or just without the margins of a domain. No longer a simple emblem of stability and persistence with assumed positive values, the world motif can become an image of unwanted constraint or of undesired provisionality and fragility. Variations on these themes recur throughout the period. Proctor, in Storey's *Cromwell* (1973), pondering in wartime the recurrent process of historical change, sadly reflects 'What world was made that wasn't unmade for its good?'[33] Waters, in Griffiths' *Comedians* (1975), views with horror the alien world of a concentration camp, and is even more appalled when everyday elements obtrude in its bizarre ugliness: 'Then I saw it. It was a world like any other. It was the logic of our world . . . extended'.[34] And, in much quoted lines, Jimmy Porter, in Osborne's *Look Back in Anger* (1956), turns from ranting and raving about contemporary society to glance back in part scorn and part nostalgia at the Edwardian world of yesterday:

> JIMMY: I hate to admit it, but I think I can understand how her Daddy must have felt when he came back from India, after all those years away. The old Edwardian brigade do make their brief little world look pretty tempting. All homemade cakes and croquet, bright ideas, bright uniforms. Always the same picture: high summer, the long days in the sun, slim volumes of verse, crisp linen, the smell of starch. What a romantic picture. Phoney too, of course. It must have rained sometimes. Still, even I regret it somehow, phoney or not. If you've no world of your own, it's rather pleasant to regret the passing of someone else's.[35]

The pervasiveness of the world motif in plays, in drama criticism and in drama theory is thus easy enough to establish. In noting its complex relationship to pluralistic values and perspectives we have also located a means of connecting, in modern plays, texture, structure and theme. And, in noting the ways in which the world motif can be used to orientate the audience, we have begun to establish a connection between play, performance and theatre. One more connection has, however, gradually emerged. We have noted that the world motif in the context of pluralistic domains orientates audiences, not towards the centres of domains, but towards their horizons. It was precisely this orientation towards horizons that we discovered earlier to be the key difference between Artaud's and Brecht's use of theatre metaphors and drama critics' use of theatre metaphors. Where critics use 'Theatre of X' categories to locate common ground at the centre of a category, Artaud and Brecht were interested in the ways in which changes in the texture, structure and theme of a play embody changes in the nature of the theatrical event.

Their concern for this larger context provides a justification, we noted, for the use of theatre metaphors that is lacking in the use of those metaphors by theatre critics. Theatres, we recognize, are enclosed areas whose fixity lies at the edges, not at the centre, of the domain. We thus find ourselves in a position to note a convergence between the implications of the world motif and of theatre metaphors. Both invite attention to horizons, not as a way of ignoring what lies within them, but as a key method of guiding attention towards the nature of what lies within and without them. It is also clear that certain common uses of the world motif – the world of the theatre, the world of the stage, the world of the audience – suggest the potential of these interacting terms to establish in the space-sensitive performance arena a series of important horizons that, in a pluralistic world, become images of considerable creative possibility. And the exploitation of those possibilities depends upon the playwrights' capacity to link reform in the drama to reform in the theatre by grounding their exploration of theme in the exploration of the various horizons of theatrical space.

Pluralism and pluralistic domains

The peculiar appropriateness of the world motif for describing the domains of the theatre is, as we have noted, registered in the fact that the two terms have been linked since classical times. Characteristically modern uses of the world motif, however, derive their importance not just from an emerging concern for pluralistic perspectives along with the consequent need to orientate audiences appropriately towards them, but also from the radical nature of modern pluralistic divisions. It is, of course, the radical nature of these divisions that confers special prominence on the boundaries of divided domains, and it is the theatre's unique capacity to give visual embodiment to these bounded domains that gives it such potential power as an instrument for exploring their complex status. But before we consider further the various functions of these divisions of theatrical space, we need to glance at certain non-literary uses of the world motif that register and reinforce its widespread popularity in the modern era.

In a culture like ours in which there is a well-established use of the 'world' motif to designate the relationship between life and death (this world and the next world) and another to designate the relationship between European and American civilizations (the old world and the new world),[36] it is hardly surprising to find the motif much used in our literature. But we may note, in these examples, an ambiguity in our use of the word 'world' that is fundamental to its more complex significance in the field of modern drama. We use the word 'world' as an all-embracing term that includes everything that exists, but we also use it to designate a series of smaller spheres of lesser scope. The word 'world' can designate regions with the most elastic of horizons: the world can be the universe as a whole, the world of human life as distinct from the world of eternal life, the world of earth versus the other worlds of other planets, the ancient world of the past versus the modern world of the present, the animal world versus the human world, the world of music, the world series of American baseball, the world of the individual, or even the several worlds of different aspects of an individual, and of course, the world of the theatre. One can note various examples of these uses in titles like Synge's *Playboy of the Western World* (1907), Osborne's *The World of Paul Slickey* (1959) and Bond's *The Worlds* (1980). But if we look more closely at the implications of the two major uses of the world motif, (1) for a domain of all-embracing scope, (2) for smaller spheres of lesser scope, we can begin to locate a major uncertainty in the relationship of the larger to the lesser notion of a world. On the one hand, we can think of the large world as being made up of a series of related smaller worlds, and on the other hand, we can think of an extensive open-ended domain in which the several worlds that constitute it offer no clear grounds for establishing a single larger whole. When Brecht's Galileo, having removed Earth from the centre of the universe, contemplated the open-ended domain, he described it thus:

> Overnight, the universe has lost its centre and now in the morning it has any number of centres. Now any point in the universe may be taken as a centre. . . . In the constellation of Orion alone there are five hundred fixed stars. Those are the many worlds, the countless other worlds, the stars beyond stars that the man they burned talked about.[37]

We can thus focus on the relationships among smaller worlds in terms of the way in which they contribute to our larger sense of the ultimate unity of *the* world (e.g. microcosm/macrocosm), *or* we can focus on similarities and differences among smaller worlds without attempting to assimilate them to some given larger whole. In the former case our interest is in locating the larger unity that transcends the differences among smaller worlds, but in the latter case our interest is not in the certainty of unity, but in the possibility of continuity – continuity in the context of fundamental difference.

Such continuity is not always easy to establish, however, for differences in the domains of modern pluralistic thought can seem even more radical than those we have so far encountered in modern plays. Indeed these differences can seem so striking that notions of continuity of any kind can be rendered quite problematic. It is in this context that we can approach one use of the 'world' motif that has proved important to modern thought in general and to modern theatre in particular – *the notion of other worlds not simply as partially differing domains, but as potentially incompatible domains.* We can see the influence of this emerging issue in the dilemma with which Strindberg confronts the Daughter of Indra in *A Dream Play* (1901). Strindberg sets up a hierarchy of contrasting worlds through which Indra's Daughter descends to visit Earth. The Daughter descends to Earth at the beginning of the play and ascends from it once more at the end. In between, she mixes with the people of this other world of Earth on the assumption of a basic continuity among the worlds she traverses. But this assumption is steadily undermined in the play, and the Daughter never quite manages to understand the world she visits. As a result she fails in her efforts to help resolve the problems of those she meets. Her final acceptance of the radical incompatibility of her own world and that of Earth is registered in the acknowledgement of defeat with which she concludes her various attempts to 'explain' things to the Poet:

POET: Say a parting word!
DAUGHTER: No, I cannot. Do you think your language can express our thoughts?[38]

When the Daughter poses that question, she draws attention to a dilemma of central importance to modern notions of relationships among worlds, words and people – the notion that what holds a world together is a particular mode of intelligibility, but that the very thing serving thus to unify a world cuts it off from full interaction with any other world. Thus, for an individual, the language that is fundamental to his world simultaneously enables him to operate within it and constrains his participation in any other world. What one system of intelligibility enables to be done and said differs from what another system of intelligibility enables to be done and said. And it is, of course, language that provides the basis for most systems of human intelligibility. The Daughter of Indra thus registers a recognition of the limitation of her strengths – she knows more in the thoughts of her world than she can possibly say in the language of the Poet's world.

To link the world motif in the modern theatre to systems of intelligibility and to language problems is to provide a needed bridge to further important non-literary concerns for the same motif and the same problems. When the Daughter of Indra poses the question, 'Do you think your language can express our thoughts?', she is posing a question of importance not just to Strindberg's play, or to the modern theatre as a whole, but to a central strand in modern intellectual thought that has its roots in eighteenth-century philosophical speculation.[39] As Hirsch puts it:

> It was chiefly Herder in the late eighteenth century who challenged the assumption that the perspective of human nature is essentially the same in all times and places. Herder's contrary view of history has been called 'historicism' by Meinecke, who judges it to be 'one of the greatest revolutions that Western thought has experienced'. Undoubtedly Meinecke is right. And one effect of this revolution was to introduce the metaphor of perspective into the domain of historical description. Not until historians began to assume that men's perspectives are essentially different in different eras did they begin to write monographs on the Romantic *Zeitgeist* or the Medieval Mind. In various degrees of sophistication, such perspectival concepts are now the staple of literary history.[40]

The problems of contrasting systems of intelligibility encountered by the Daughter of Indra differ only in degree and not in kind from the potential problems we have come to acknowledge in dealing with people who lived in other eras, who live in other countries in our own era, or who live in socially distinct domains of a single country. What was for Herder and subsequent historians primarily a matter of perspectival variation on a temporal axis became for linguists, sociologists and anthropologists a matter of perspectival variation on a spatial/linguistic axis. Herder (1744–1803) noted a clear connection between language and national character, but Wilhelm von Humboldt (1767–1835) made this notion more precise and more powerful when he claimed that every language has its own structure which both enables and limits the modes of thinking and interacting that are characteristic of particular communities. And when he seeks to describe those structures, he does so, interestingly enough, by means of an image of a magic circle – an image which registers the same kind of concern for horizons that we have already encountered in this discussion in the context of theatre and world motifs.

> Man lives with his objects chiefly – in fact, since his feeling and acting depends on his perceptions, one may say exclusively – as language presents them to him. By the same process whereby he spins language out of his own being, he ensnares himself in it; and each language draws a magic circle round the people to which it belongs, a circle from which there is no escape save by stepping out of it into another.[41]

This trend of separating, by a metaphor of encirclement, particular complexes of modes of being, modes of intelligibility, and modes of language reached a further point of development in the linguistic-relativity hypothesis advanced by Sapir and Whorf in the 1930s. Stuart Chase helpfully summarizes the strong form of this hypothesis in the following way:

> There is no one metaphysical pool of universal human thought. Speakers of different languages see the Cosmos differently, evaluate it differently, sometimes not by much, sometimes widely. Thinking is relative to the language learned.[42]

And the trend has reached an even more differentiated stage in the recent work of the socio-linguist Basil Bernstein. He challenges the primacy of the notion of the homogeneity of single national languages, and replaces it with the notion that each 'language' consists of a series of sub-languages – codes, as he calls them – and these codes govern the ways in which users interact with the people and objects they confront:

> A number of fashions of speaking, frames of consistency, are possible in any given language and . . . these fashions of speaking, linguistic forms, or codes, are themselves a function of the form social relations take. According to this view, the form of the social relation or, more generally, the social structure

generates distinct linguistic forms or codes and these codes essentially transmit the culture and so constrain behaviour. . . . [This view] shares with Whorf the controlling influence on experience ascribed to 'frames of consistency' involved in fashions of speaking. It differs [from] and perhaps relativizes Whorf by asserting that, *in the context of a common language in the sense of a general code, there will arise distinct linguistic forms, fashions of speaking, which induce in their speakers different ways of relating to objects and persons.* (my emphasis)[43]

The notion of competing community perspectives has thus shifted steadily from the contrast between one era and another, to one nation versus another in the same era, and then to one group versus another in the same linguistic community. Such a line of development leads directly to the kind of comment that we encounter in Jerry's defeatist response to Peter in Albee's *The Zoo Story* (1959): 'of course you don't understand . . . I don't live in your block'.[44] As these groups diminish in size and the potential divisions within the human community multiply, that multiplicity extends finally to the notion that individuals exist isolated and alone in their own little spheres of intelligibility. For Jerry and for others, we either share everything or we share nothing; but some have managed to make a problematic virtue of painful necessity. The literary movement of impressionism could find virtue in Pater's comment that

> The whole scope of observation is dwarfed into the narrow chamber of the individual mind. . . . Every one of those impressions is the impression of the individual in his isolation, each mind keeping as a solitary prisoner its own dream of a world.[45]

But whether we focus on the problems of individual isolation or the virtues of idiosyncratic perception, we can recognize that these trends in historiography, anthropology, linguistics, sociology and literary theory utilize precisely those links between language, knowing, relating and being that encourage the adoption of the world motif in modern drama and its use as an emblem of incompatible domains. It is just this connection between multiple worlds and multiple ways of knowing that is fundamental to the crises of pluralism present in the texture, structure and themes of modern drama. Hoijer makes this equivalence evident when, in seeking to summarize the linguistic work of Sapir, he has recourse to the very motif that is used so much in discussions of modern theatre: 'Peoples speaking different languages may be said to live in different "worlds of reality", in the sense that the languages they speak affect, to a considerable degree, both their sensory perceptions and their habitual modes of thought.'[46]

By this time, of course, we recognize that the term 'language' does not necessarily imply a large community of participants, and that the world motif can be regarded alternately as a register of social divisions (external) or of social connections (internal). We do not, however, in the context of the present work, need to be drawn into arguments over the extent of Hoijer's 'considerable degree', nor over the logical priority of language and social structure, nor over the relationship between a language and its subsets. These issues are rightly debated in their appropriate domains by those conducting research in those areas. It is interesting to note, however, the new importance bestowed upon the world image by these intellectual developments, an importance registered in the appearance, while this work was under way, of a book called *Ways of Worldmaking*, by Nelson Goodman. His topic, his interest in the world image, and his argument for its claim to a central location in post-Kantian thought are all relevant to our interest in modern uses of the world image and its connection with local systems of intelligibility. In his introduction Goodman announces that:

> I think of this book as belonging in that mainstream of modern philosophy that began when Kant exchanged the structure of the world for the structure of the mind, continued when C. I. Lewis exchanged the structure of the mind for the structure of concepts, and that now proceeds to exchange the structure of concepts for the structure of the several symbol systems of the sciences, philosophy, the arts, perception, and everyday discourse. The movement is from unique truth and a world fixed and found to a diversity of right and even conflicting versions or worlds in the making.[47]

We will consider later the larger implications of Goodman's phrase 'versions or worlds', but, for the moment, we need only note that the link between the world motif and competing systems of intelligibility has a clearly traceable history and an evident popularity, not only in modern drama, but in the larger modern intellectual domain. Indeed, Toulmin, in his book on *Human Understanding*, has sought to establish Captain James Cook's arrival at the enchanting island of Tahiti on 13 April 1769 as one of those

> dates in human history [that] acquire a retrospective significance that no one could have recognised at the time. Looking back from a later age, we see in them the point at which some new factor, influence, or idea entered – imperceptibly but irreversibly – into the course of historical development.[48]

The idea was, of course, an emerging recognition of the potential implications of the radical cultural and conceptual diversity displayed in human societies and human worlds: 'Cook's voyage was planned to establish finally the eternal structure of God's Creation; instead, its outcome was to concentrate attention on the variety and apparent inconsistency of men's moralities, cultures, and ideas.'[49] What Cook encountered in his physical exploration of the exotic worlds of the South Sea islands has since been matched in a variety of domains of theoretical exploration. Whatever the virtues of these explorations in their appropriate disciplines, it is their combined impact that is of significance to us. In linking the world motif to problems of historicism and of cultural and conceptual relativity, we have established the potentially radical nature of differences between worlds. These differences are not just of perspective, or value, or custom, but of systems of intelligibility – of the very ground upon which knowledge itself stands.

That this more radical division between domains is important to modern drama is evident in many ways, not the least of which is the recurring focus on language that is so characteristic of the modern theatre – a focus not just on what language enables but *upon what it constrains*. Again and again we are invited to see ourselves not just as the beneficiaries, but also as the victims of our modes of intelligibility, as people not just linked, but also separated by the languages we speak. When the central character in Handke's *Kaspar* (1967) is finally forced to speak, his sadness registers a sense of loss rather than gain: 'Already with my first sentence I was trapped.'[50] When an Orator shows up to deliver, posthumously, the final message of an Old Man in Ionesco's *The Chairs* (1952), he grunts incomprehensibly to an audience quite unable to comprehend the sounds he makes. In Adamov's *The Invasion* (1950), Pierre struggles desperately but unsuccessfully to make sense of literary papers he has inherited from a deceased brother-in-law. Mr Rooney, baffled by his wife's enigmatic remarks in Beckett's *All that Fall* (1957), comments, 'Do you know, Maddy, sometimes one would think you were struggling with a dead language.'[51] And in the same author's *Krapp's Last Tape* (1958), Krapp is unable to understand his former self speaking on a tape recording, partly because he is no longer familiar with the words his earlier self used. Krapp is located at centre stage, surrounded by a circle of light from an overhead lamp,[52] and listening in occasional bafflement and frequent disdain to the linguistic manifestation of a former self. That circle of light is a local emblem of the larger image of constraining worlds that cover all these cases and many more. The encircled image of a man looking, with puzzlement, at a dictionary for clues about a former self offers a powerful picture of language as an enabling and constraining social and psychological device.

The technique of depicting individuals, groups and larger realms as separated by radically differing grounds of understanding is seen in such diverse plays as Strindberg's *The Father* (1887), Pirandello's *Six Characters in Search of an Author* (1921), Brecht's *The Good Woman of Setzuan* (1940), Genet's *The Balcony* (1956) and Pinter's *The Caretaker* (1960). In more rarefied form it occurs in Chekhov's *Uncle Vanya* (1899), *The Three Sisters* (1901) and *The Cherry Orchard* (1904), in Ibsen's *Ghosts* (1881) and *The Wild Duck* (1884), Ghelderode's *The Death of Doctor Faust* (1925), Giraudoux's *The Mad Woman of Chaillot* (1945), Frisch's *The Firebugs* (1959) and many more. We thus find ourselves compelled to grapple with the complex connections among the world motif, use of performance space, systems of intelligibility, and problems with language. To have recognized the potential power of the world motif as a means of linking texture, structure, theme and performance space is not yet to have come to terms with all of the possibilities or with all of the problems it also raises. If it is the case that differences between spheres established by the world motif can be differences not just of perspective, value and custom, but of the epistemological grounds of community knowledge itself, what possible means of access can there be from one sphere, one world, one way of knowing, to another? If theatre metaphors, world motifs and pluralistic concerns repeatedly draw our attention to the horizons of domains, what needs to be recognized about the status of these horizons in the theatre, and how should we address the question of their relative opacity and transparency?

2 Marking and merging horizons

To explore further the peculiar status of the foregrounded horizons of separate domains on the modern stage, we might turn first to that most fundamental of theatre horizons, the one that divides the world of the stage from the world of the audience. If domains in modern pluralistic thought are separated not just by differences of degree but differences of kind, if what distinguishes one world from another is akin to differences between contrasting systems of intelligibility, then what kind of epistemological claim can be made for the world of the stage? Does its unique capacity to give visual embodiment to the multiplication and merging of spatially distinguished domains confer upon it a unique system of intelligibility? Is there, indeed, an implication that the phrase 'the world of the theatre' suggests a distinctive language of the theatre? Such a conclusion would have large and positive implications for the status of the theatre, but it would also raise disturbing questions about the relationship between the language of the theatre and the language of the world outside the theatre. What kinds of mutual opacity and transparency characterize the horizons of these opposing domains? And what can we learn from those transactions about interaction among other radically contrasting domains?

Artaud, as is well known, makes the major claim here, arguing that we have considerably underestimated the visual possibilities of the theatre by regarding them as mere illustrative background to the words of a play. Instead of regarding the theatre environment as an extension of a play's dialogue, we should, he forcefully argues, reverse that order of priority. The theatre, he claims, has its own non-verbal language, and it is a language which can incorporate, but may not finally need, the verbal language of written texts.

> This idea of the supremacy of speech in the theatre is so deeply rooted in us, and the theatre seems to such a degree merely the material reflection of the text,

that everything in the theatre that exceeds this text, that is not kept within its limits and strictly conditioned by it, seems to us purely a matter of *mise en scène*, and quite inferior in comparison with the text.

Presented with this subordination of theatre to speech, one might indeed wonder whether the theatre by any chance possesses its own language, whether it is entirely fanciful to consider it as an independent and autonomous art, of the same rank as music, painting, dance, etc. . . .

One finds in any case that this language, if it exists, is necessarily identified with the *mise en scène* considered:

1. as the visual and plastic materialization of speech,
2. as the language of everything that can be said and signified upon a stage independently of speech, everything that finds its expression in space, or that can be affected or disintegrated by it.

Once we regard this language of the *mise en scène* as the pure theatrical language, we must discover whether it can attain the same internal ends as speech, whether theatrically and from the point of view of the mind it can claim the same intellectual efficacy as the spoken language. One can wonder, in other words, whether it has the power, not to define thoughts but *to cause thinking*, whether it may not entice the mind to take profound and efficacious attitudes toward it from its own point of view.[1]

I quote this passage at some length because it represents an important step in the argument we have been tracing. The notion of the theatre as an autonomous world and the notion of a world as a sphere of intelligibility with its own language (we should not overlook Artaud's concern for that language as expression in *space*) are extended by Artaud to embrace the further important implication that such a world can lay claim to a capacity to embody and articulate original and potentially revelatory thematic material. The very independence and autonomy of the world of the theatre provide the foundation for its capacity to offer an independent way of knowing and, hence, independent knowledge that is not otherwise available.

These are large claims with large implications, but we should note that the notion of the theatre as an independent world with its own language has emerged as a logical consequence of a variety of programmes for dramatic experimentation. If we remind ourselves of Lukács's generalization about the modern theatre, we can now see that it has implications much larger than those that might appear at first glance. Lukács claimed that

> in the great ages, the drama flowed 'naturally' from the existing theatre, while, from Goethe on, the poet-dramatist rejects the theatre, writes plays which are 'too good for it', and then calls for the creation of the kind of theatre which will be good enough for the plays.[2]

The phrase 'good enough for the plays', in the context of Artaud's remarks, now becomes something more than a matter of appropriate background; the theatrical environment is, in these terms, not just a decorative background to structure and theme, but a means of helping to constitute both. In this context, non-verbal elements of the theatre are radically revalued and the spatial and visual dimensions of the theatrical event become of paramount importance. No longer serving only to illustrate what is already verbally manifest, the performance environment invites exploration of its potential for making manifest thematic material that is not manifest in any other way. The theatre no longer needs to disguise its conventionality but to expose its full conventional range as a means of extending its consequent thematic range. These are the important results of conceiving of the world of the theatre as precisely that – a world of its own with a language of its own.

Such a conception of the status of the theatre brings with it an adjustment in our notion of the roles the theatre might play in the worlds beyond it. The theatre achieves an importance far beyond that of merely replicating or illuminating a pre-existing world off-stage: it becomes a potential rival to the world off-stage, an independent ground for original knowledge. The concern of the naturalists that the theatre must minimize its 'theatricality', its conventionality, in order to become as much like the world off-stage as possible is instantly vitiated. The stage in this new context derives its importance not from its ability to reduplicate the world off-stage, but from its ability to replace it and go beyond it.[3] Artaud carries the logic of his argument inexorably forward:

> This leads to the rejection of the usual limitations of man and man's powers, and infinitely extends the frontiers of what is called reality.
> We must believe in a sense of life renewed by the theatre, a sense of life in which man fearlessly makes himself master of what does not yet exist, and brings it into being.[4]

Artaud's enthusiasm for such a positive view of the autonomy of the theatrical world is widely shared. Wilder reminds us that:

> The history of the theatre shows us that in its greatest ages the stage employed the greatest number of conventions. The stage is fundamental pretense and it thrives on the acceptance of that fact and on the multiplication of additional pretenses.[5]

Brecht insists that the theatre 'stop pretending not to be theatre',[6] that it make undisguised and constitutive use of song, dance, orchestra, lights, slides, narrators, placards and so forth. Ionesco argues that every work of art is 'an autonomous creation, an independent universe with its own life and its own laws'.[7]

> I . . . consider art to be more concerned with an independent search for knowledge than with any system of morals, political or not. It is of course a way of knowing that involves the emotions, an exploration that is objective in its subjectivity, testimony rather than teaching, evidence of how the world appears to the artist.
> To renew one's idiom or one's language is to renew one's conception or one's vision of the world. . . . Any new artistic expression enriches us by answering some spiritual need and broadens the frontiers of known reality.[8]

Gradual recognition of the importance of these issues preceded their definitive formulation, and these emerging concerns are manifest in the modern theatre wherever one encounters the linking of experimentation in the drama with experiment in the theatre. The more urgent claims, however, occur later in the period, and a striking example is provided by Handke's insistence upon the importance of the autonomous reality of the stage in his foreword to *Kaspar*. He demands a specific kind of presentation of the performance environment as a means of embodying the structure and theme of his play. When the audience enters, the stage set is open to view, for precise theatrical and dramatic reasons.

> The front curtain is already drawn. The audience does not see the stage as a representation of a room that exists somewhere, but as a representation of a stage. *The stage represents the stage.* On first glance, the objects on the stage look theatrical: not because they imitate other objects, but because the way they are situated with respect to one another does not correspond to their usual arrangement in reality. The objects, although genuine (made of wood, steel, cloth, etc.), are instantly recognizable as props. . . . *Nor should the audience be able to imagine that the props on stage will be part of a play that pretends to take place anywhere except on stage: they should recognize at once that they will witness an event that plays only on stage and not in some other reality.* (my emphases)[9]

This insistence on the fundamental theatricality of the theatre registers the steadily emerging recognition of the notion articulated by Artaud that the theatre does, indeed, have its own language. The functional theatricality of the theatre is as basic to the later Strindberg as to Brecht, as important to Pirandello as to Beckett, as crucial to Ionesco as to Genet. It is strongly in evidence in radically experimental plays, for example in Pirandello's theatrical creation of Madame Pace in *Six Characters in Search of an Author*,[10] in Genet's admonition to the audience at the end of *The Balcony* that they 'must now go home, where everything – you can be quite sure – will be falser than here',[11] and in Stoppard's *Rosencrantz and Guildenstern* where two characters from another play become the central characters in this play. But it is not something restricted to radically innovative plays. It is visible in a recurrent insistence upon the theatrical component of reality which is manifest in such things as fancy dress, role playing and story telling, and which occurs in plays as original or conventional as *Peter Pan, Playboy of the Western World, Saint Joan, The Plough and the Stars, A Man's a Man, The Iceman Cometh, Harlequinade, Death of a Salesman, The Connection, The Maids, The Entertainer, The Caretaker, The Mad Woman of Chaillot, The Bald Soprano,* and *Marat Sade.* We also see the influence of these ideas in critical attempts to establish a genre of metatheatre (attempts which unfortunately take the issue of the theatricality of the theatre out of its modern context and lose track of its specifically modern function by seeking the common ground of a distinct genre or tradition[12]).

We should also take care not to overlook the further manifestation of these ideas in the increasing importance of the director in the modern theatre. If there is indeed a theatre language as well as a drama language, then we need not only an appropriate expert in the latter domain (the dramatist), but also an expert in the former domain (a director). And the growing importance of the expert in the language of the theatre is necessarily accompanied by an interest in allowing him access to the complete range of that language. Hence the significance of the work of people like Gordon Craig and Adolphe Appia who recognized very early the constitutive nature of the theatrical environ-ment and the consequent need for theatre structures flexible enough to enable utilization of the full range of theatre language. Craig argued that if we are to save the theatre, we must first 'destroy' it[13] – destroy, that is, existing rigidified theatre structures that constrained too much and enabled too little. Appia made the point just as strongly: 'The arbitrary conventions of our auditoriums and stages placed face to face still control us. . . . Let us leave our theatres to their dying past and let us construct elementary buildings designed merely to cover the space in which we work.'[14]

This concern for renewal of the theatrical environment is, as we have seen, also dear to the hearts of playwrights interested in reforming the drama. In this context, however, the larger implications of attempts to link reform in the drama with reform in the theatre have clearly emerged. As they have done so, the need for flexibility in the theatrical environment has likewise become apparent. Consequently, we are in a position to understand the importance of the variety that is such a notable feature of the theatre structures that have been created or re-created in the modern era. If the major trend in Victorian theatre design was carried to its logical conclusion in the Bancrofts' picture-frame stage at London's Haymarket Theatre,[15] the major trend in twentieth-century theatre design reached its logical conclusion in the three auditoriums of England's National Theatre. The three auditoriums exemplify three main forms of theatre architecture – the proscenium stage, the open stage and the flexible studio – establishing as fluid and varied a relationship as possible between the building and any drama to be presented there.[16] Peter Brook, we recall, has made the case that the 'theatre today should no longer be confined to a conventional building, but redefine itself each time it occurs'.[17] In doing so, he summarizes a trend that has developed steadily in the modern theatre since the latter part of the nineteenth century. Neither the National Theatre nor any other building can be quite as flexible as Brook would wish, but those three auditoriums register the importance of a persistent concern – that what can be thematically embodied in a play is to some extent constituted by the theatrical environment in which it is performed, by the language of that environment. As Brecht put it: 'Simply to comprehend the new areas of subject matter [we must impose] a new dramatic and theatrical form.'[18]

There thus seems to be a widespread consensus that to some extent at least the theatre has its own language, its own verbal and visual sign systems, its own grounds of knowing, and its own potential to offer knowledge not available elsewhere. It is not difficult to recognize here the romantic heritage of the modern era with its widespread commitment to the epistemological creativity of the poet.[19] But it is important to recognize the larger intellectual movement of which this is only a part. The issues involved are not just literary, but also philosophical and social, with implications fundamental to our conceptions of the worlds of art, the worlds beyond art, and the problematic relationships contracted among them.

When Goodman sought to characterize the implications for life in general and not just for art in particular of certain philosophical developments in post-Kantian thought, he suggested that we try to come to terms with the recognition that 'if worlds are as much made as found, so also knowing is as much remaking as reporting'.[20] There is not, he suggests, a given world of which all smaller worlds are a partial replication, but a continuing series of created and re-created worlds which continually extend what we know and what we can know. This confers upon each of the several worlds in which we participate a certain special significance and irreducible authenticity. Instead of each domain offering a version of some fixed underlying reality, each helps constitute the very knowledge and experience it makes available. The consequent cultivation of subjectivity, individuality and small-group integrity is evident in many areas of modern endeavour. It finds its literary manifestation in the movements of impressionism and expressionism, its anthropological manifestation in the value attributed to uncontaminated primitive societies, its sociological manifestation in the defence of regional idiosyncrasy against urban compromise, and its socio-linguistic manifestation in the privileging of local dialects over national standard languages. But having noted the positive side of these arguments for privileged pluralistic domains, we should now consider the negative side. The values attributed to local domains clearly bring with them problematic consequences. These distinctive domains appear to purchase their integrity at some cost to their accessibility. If, as seems to be the case, the values attributed to these autonomous domains derive from their being radically different from each other, by what means do the values of one domain become available to people based in another?

These large social questions offer no easy answers, but they have their theatrical embodiment in the very means by which Artaud argues for the existence of an independent theatre language. The dilemma to which his claims lead is shared by all the playwrights whose arguments for theatrical autonomy we have just been quoting. It is Artaud, however, who provides the most explicit and most sustained justification for an independent language of the theatre, and it is Artaud who takes the argument to its logical extreme. Artaud believed he had located in the Balinese theatre a most persuasive example of a drama whose themes are constituted by the performance environment, and his enthusiastic description of it brings to the fore the emerging dilemma:

> The themes selected derive, one might say, from the stage itself. They have reached such a point of objective materialization that *one cannot imagine them outside this close perspective, this confined and limited globe of performing space* . . . the Balinese offer us a stupefying realization, suppressing all possibility of recourse to words for the elucidation of the most abstract themes – inventing a language of gesture to be developed in space, *a language without meaning except in the circumstances of the stage.* (my emphases)[21]

Artaud's words capture precisely the emerging dilemma. These themes derive their existence and their significance from the originality of the stage language itself, and the value of that language is exhibited in the recognition that these themes can only be encountered in this way. But the very means of affirming the value of the revelatory autonomy of the theatre instantly undermines it. Artaud's rhetoric of affirmation informs us that these themes not only cannot be embodied outside, but cannot be imagined outside, this confined and limited globe of performance space. If we wish to enjoy their benefits, we must come to the theatre to encounter them. But if they are so exclusively grounded in theatre language, what can we do with them, and how can we subsequently take them away with us? The circle providing the ground of knowledge seems simultaneously to limit its application and its accessibility. Things can perhaps be known via the language of the theatre that cannot be known in the everyday language of the world outside the theatre, but the negative implications seem to undermine the positive. And they do so in terms that the Daughter of Indra would doubtless approve. If the revelations the theatre has to offer are the products of an autonomous domain, another system of intelligibility, another world, must they not remain inaccessible, even opaque, to the audience whose experiential base is outside that domain?[22]

The problematic implications of regarding the theatre as an autonomous world with its own internal system of intelligibility will become more clear if we glance, for a moment, at the way in which the philosopher Bradley formulated for himself the situation that emerges when the issue of epistemological pluralism is taken to its logical extreme.

> My external sensations are no less private to myself than are my thoughts or my feelings. In either case my experience falls within my own circle, a circle closed on the outside; and, with all its elements alike, every sphere is opaque to the others which surround it.[23]

If pluralism is extended to such epistemological relativism, three key features emerge: the boundaries around experiential domains become fixed and rigid, the area within each circle becomes homogeneous, the domains outside the circle become opaque. What we first encountered in Herder's historicist thesis as perspectival variation distinguishing different eras has progressed by this point to the contemplation of incompatible systems of intelligibility that separate groups and individuals within a particular era. As the circles have proliferated, the domains of social exchange have shrunk and the degrees of difference between encircled domains have steadily increased. Inside a circle everything is the same, outside the circle everything is different: we either share everything or we share nothing. As horizons become insurmountable barriers, we all end up trapped in our internally homogeneous and externally opaque spheres, and the problems of pluralism degenerate into the dilemmas of radical epistemological relativism.

The development of this trend has its most obvious theatrical manifestation in the charges of obscurity which are so often addressed to the modern theatre. There undoubtedly are many who find the extremity of modern drama's experimentation with the language of the theatre unclearly motivated and ultimately baffling. But it is not necessary to assume that the problems of pluralism in the modern theatre must recapitulate the problems of epistemological relativism. We would obviously be wrong to believe that experimental playwrights fail to take steps to make their experimentation accessible. Indeed, the very playwrights who most strongly affirm the independence of the world of the theatre often seem most strongly concerned with finding new ways to relate the new theatre to old audiences. It might thus be tempting to resolve the problem of the accessibility of what the experimental theatre has to offer by suggesting that playwrights in general and Artaud in particular simply overstate the case for the independence and autonomy of the language of the theatre. Their arguments, we might conclude, are simply polemical gestures that project a difference in degree between the world of the theatre and the world outside it into a difference of kind. But such a conclusion would not suffice, for it requires us to reinstate the notion of a single world with multiple manifestations to replace the notion, much exemplified on the modern stage and in many domains of modern thought, of multiple worlds with multiple manifestations.

The important distinction here, we should recognize, is not between single and multiple worlds, not between monism and pluralism, but between pluralism and relativism. It is for this reason that Bradley's formulation of epistemological and experiential relativism is useful. In relativist domains, repeated subdivision on the basis of difference proceeds to the point at which each tiny sphere is internally homogeneous and externally opaque. Bradley's formulation is valuable for it helps us to recognize that the internal homogeneity and external opacity of domains are complementary and related concerns. To assert one is to assert the other; but this also implies that to undermine one is to undermine the other. And it is in just this respect that pluralism and relativism are distinct. In a pluralistic world, unlike a relativistic world, what is inside each domain exhibits continuity but not homogeneity, and the barriers that divide domains are radical but not rigid. Playwrights in a pluralistic world are not indulging in polemic when they insist upon the autonomy of domains, and they are not acting inconsistently when they also insist upon a potential continuity between separated domains. Paradoxically enough, it is only the insistence upon the former that can bring about appropriate recognition of the latter.

We will explore later the larger implications of playwrights' attempts to make autonomy and accessibility complementary rather than contrasting concerns. For the moment, we should simply note the range of examples that compels us to conduct that exploration. Ionesco's work is the focus of the most celebrated debate on this issue. In a series of letters to the London *Observer*, Ionesco and the theatre critic Kenneth Tynan debated the social duties of playwrights and the consequent social constraints upon their dramatic experimentation. Ionesco, as we have seen, insists upon the autonomy of the theatre and its independence from the world outside the theatre, but the more he did so in this debate, the more Tynan accused him of writing plays of no consequent social relevance. Ionesco adamantly refused to concede that it was his duty to teach anyone in the off-stage world anything, but also refused to concede that his primary focus of attention on the on-stage world made his plays socially irrelevant. Rejecting the notion of 'teaching', which Ionesco regards as a betrayal of the theatre by subordinating it to pre-existing ideology, Ionesco advocated instead the 'testimony', that a playwright can offer of other kinds of knowledge in other worlds. But we should note at this point that though this testimony is at some remove from, it is not necessarily unrelated to, the everyday world of the audience: 'this work is [a] testimony: having perhaps some basis in reality, but going beyond it, bringing it to life, transfiguring it.'[24] The testimony/teaching distinction is an important one. Teaching, for Ionesco, is a transaction occurring within one world; therefore it offers nothing really new. Testimony, on the other hand, offers new kinds of information that go beyond, but do not abandon, those available in the world off-stage. The insistence upon autonomy is not a substitute for, but a prelude to, re-engagement between the separated worlds. Ionesco's acknowledgement that his created world has 'some basis in reality' is, however, a crucial step back from claims to complete theatrical autonomy. And that concession of a lack of autonomous homogeneity within the domain is accompanied by a series of practical attempts to deal with the potential problem of opacity between domains. Ionesco thus contemplates various possibilities for provoking appropriate interaction between the semi-autonomous world of the theatre and the world of the audience. These take on polemical form in the various endings Ionesco contemplated to *The Bald Soprano*, and more subtle and successful form in the ending of *The Chairs*. In the former case,

> two or three accomplices in the audience start catcalling, kick up a row, shout protests and invade the stage. This brings on the manager of the theatre, followed by the Superintendent of Police and his men, who open fire at the rebellious audience.[25]

In the latter case, rows of chairs appear gradually on-stage and the structure of the stage set increasingly resembles and merges with the structure of the auditorium.[26] In both cases, there are alternating attempts to establish and then break down and thus re-form the boundaries between on-stage and off-stage worlds.

Brecht set himself a similar task for different purposes. He too argues that if we are to learn anything new from the theatre, we must focus our attention on its theatricality and thus on the divisions between on-stage and off-stage worlds. These divisions are not, however, a means of achieving total separation, but of carefully controlling *both* distance and linkage. Brecht's celebrated alienation techniques are designed to force the audience into a recognition of similarity in the context of difference: 'A higher type of interest can be got from making comparisons, from whatever is different, amazing, impossible to take in as a whole.'[27] These differences are not, however, simply barriers; rather, they promote an informative kind of interaction with the dramatic event. Brecht advocates techniques that will make the audience react to his provisional theatrical worlds by recognizing its own world as similarly provisional, a possible, rather than a necessary, structure: 'if we play works dealing with our own time as though they were historical, then perhaps the circumstances under which [the spectator] himself acts will strike him as equally odd; and this is where the critical attitude begins.'[28] Clashing sounds, disorientating lighting, non-empathetic acting, along with intrusive narrators, slides and placards, all contribute to this guidance and control of an audience alternately alienated from and engaged with the action on the stage.

Artaud advocates an even more aggressive stance towards the audience. His basic technique is not one of emphasizing and then merging long-established theatrical horizons, but of creating and transcending new ones. In his 'Theatre of Cruelty', the audience is not to be located on one side of the auditorium with the stage on the other. Instead, 'the spectator is in the centre and the spectacle surrounds him'.[29] The audience is bombarded with light and sound as Artaud creates 'a theatre in which violent physical images crush and hypnotize the sensibility of the spectator seized by the theatre as by a whirlwind of higher forces'.[30] And this arrangement is designed precisely to overcome the incipient dilemma of theatre-as-other-world, in which two mutually opaque spheres of intelligibility confront each other:

> It is in order to attack the spectator's sensibility on all sides that we advocate a revolving spectacle which, instead of making the stage and auditorium two closed worlds, without possible communication, spreads its visual and sonorous outbursts over the entire mass of the spectators.[31]

These strategies for linking on-stage and off-stage worlds are characteristic of the work of the very playwrights who insist on the stage's creative autonomy, and we must ponder the apparent inconsistency they manifest. Is the stage autonomous or not? Oddly enough, these extreme attempts to bridge the gap between spectator and spectacle simultaneously affirm the existence of that gap and the possibility of creative bridging of it. These efforts are the necessary *practical* consequence of theories which insist on the autonomy of theatre language and thus on the difficulty, but not the impossibility, of access to it. The theoretical argument which places auton-omy and accessibility in an either/or relationship gradually gives way to a practical exemplification of the fact that they should rather be regarded as in a both/and relationship. But this is not necessarily the both/and relationship of Hegelian dialectics with its implication of ultimate synthesis; it is much more of a 'first this, and then, to the appropriate degree, that' relationship, *one in which access to otherness rather than assimilation of otherness is at issue.*[32] This is an issue to be explored further in subsequent chapters, but at this point we should note that this both/and relationship is very much in line with our earlier recognition that horizons in the modern theatre are not just a handy exemplification of the divisions attendant upon pluralistic concerns, but also an important means of guiding audiences towards appropriate ways of dealing with them. In this respect, pluralistic domains separated by epistemological incompatibility are analogous to domains separated by contrasting moral, ethical, aesthetic, economic, class or race criteria. As the degree of difference between domains increases, the lines between domains move steadily to-wards barrier status, and as they do so, there is an ever more urgent need to do two complementary things in the theatre: *to find new ways to draw attention to horizons, and to find new ways of showing how they can be transcended.*

We thus encounter in the modern theatre a variety of techniques for marking and merging theatrical horizons. These are the spatial manifesta-tions of the depiction of a pluralistic world which insists upon the autonomy and accessibility of distinctive domains. The most characteristic of these problematic horizons is, as we have noted, that between the stage and the auditorium, and one play after another in the modern period seeks overtly to incorporate that line of demarcation into the theatrical event. In Miller's *After the Fall*, Quentin constantly seeks to justify himself by appealing to a Listener 'who, if he could be seen, would be sitting just beyond the edge of the stage itself'.[33] In Genet's *The Balcony*, the recurring concern for the recipro-cal relationship between fact and fiction is embodied in a projection, by means of mirrors, of the world of the stage into the front rows of the auditorium.[34] In Gelber's *The Connection*, characters repeatedly enter and exit from the auditorium, and the audience, finally unable to distinguish actors from characters from real people, finds itself incriminated in support-ing, by its ticket purchases, the drug habits of characters who (it is told) are real junkies acting these parts for money. In Beckett's *Waiting for Godot*, the repeated attempts to align the experience of the characters with that of the audience involve several episodes in which the characters react with horror at the prospect of moving in the direction of the space occupied by the audience. Pirandello's *Tonight We Improvise* begins in the auditorium with a discussion among some apparent members of the audience about noises on-stage, whether they are or are not part of the show, and whether or not the theatre is on fire. The multiple audiences to plays-within-plays in Weiss's *Marat Sade* merge with the off-stage audience and involve it actively as both spectator and participant in the events enacted on-stage. In Osborne's *The Entertainer* and Griffiths' *Comedians*, the audience in the theatre occupies a space co-extensive with that of audiences in the world of the stage production. [35]

Similar concerns emerge among directors and are visible in such modern theatre movements as Environmental Theatre, Ontological-Hysteric Theatre, the Living Theatre, and the Poor Theatre. These theatrical events focus as much on provoking and controlling audience/stage interaction and audience participation as on the transfer of any pre-formulated information. Examples again are legion, but Styan's description of Grotowski's Poor Theatre will suffice:

> Grotowski sees the players as one ensemble, the audience as another: when the two are integrated, a play has begun. . . . In this way theatre is an encounter: the actor's lines are his point of departure, his performance is human contact, the whole operation is something growing and organic. In an interview Grotowski stated, 'In each of our productions we set up a different relationship between actors and audience. In *Doctor Faustus*, the spectators are the guests; in *The Constant Prince*, they are the onlookers. But I think the essential thing is that the actor must not act for the audience, he must act *vis-à-vis* with the spectators.' . . . Both Stanislavsky and Grotowski have worked within a tradition which separates the worlds of actor and audience; both worked to close the gap between. [36]

In theatre structures, too, the rapid growth in the number of open stages and theatres in-the-round is a further visible sign of the ongoing need to change and redevelop modern modes of audience/stage interaction. [37]

The issues explored in some plays through a radical exploitation of the stage/audience line of demarcation are explored in other plays through other spatial divisions – divisions that mark similarly important lines of conjunction between contrasting domains. The theatre, we have noted, not only has obvious and given lines of demarcation in its very structure, it also has a unique capacity to generate and exploit new ones, and thus embody, in spatial terms, horizons of many kinds. We have already discussed Barrie's use of a remote island in *The Admirable Crichton*. We might also note the split-staging in Pinter's *The Collection* that keeps 'off-stage' action visible, the door that slams shut on so much in Ibsen's *A Doll's House*, the lava-like areas in Miller's *After the Fall* that divide and connect Quentin's ever present but intermittently activated memories, the uniform that Barbara wears in Shaw's *Major Barbara* to distinguish herself spiritually from everyone else, the garbage cans in Beckett's *Endgame*, the wall that provides a 'massive set and prop'[38] in Bond's *Lear*, the behaviourally manifest horizons that separate Lopahin from Varya in Chekhov's *The Cherry Orchard*, and Olga, Masha and Irina from Moscow in *The Three Sisters*, the coastline that divides the sea from the land and the men from the women in Synge's *Riders to the Sea*, and the internalized coastline exhibited in characters' alternating fascination with and rejection of the sea in plays as various as O'Neill's *Anna Christie*, Ibsen's *The Lady from the Sea*, and Beckett's *Embers*. These lines of demarcation separate and connect domains of many kinds for many purposes. In Williams's much-revised *The Two-Character Play*, the divided stage initially distinguishes and subsequently merges the outer play and the play-within-the-play. Felice, the character responsible for scripting the play-within-the-play, is accused by the other character, Clare, of failing to maintain the distinction between the two domains spatially separated on-stage: 'Sometimes you work on a play by inventing situations in life that, that – correspond to those in the play, and you're so skillful at it that even I'm taken in.'[39] And the glass walls marking the borders of Mrs Alving's house in Ibsen's *Ghosts* become, in many ways, a summarizing image of the solid but permeable horizons of the modern theatre. The solid penetrability of the glass wall gradually becomes an emblem of repeatedly asserted but repeatedly undermined divisions between inner and outer, good and bad, past and present, self and other, and so on.

Throughout the modern era we thus encounter manifestations of this trend towards the marking and merging of horizons. The dramatic foregrounding of the line between stage and auditorium is only part of a much larger movement. Whether physical, social, or psychological horizons are at issue, whether the psychological and social horizons are given physical or behavioural embodiment, the issues are related and similarly grounded. And it is important to recognize that this technical device serves to link every level of the theatrical event, whether what is at issue is experimentation with texture, structure, theme, performance space, or generic convention. We might note Coe's comment on the worlds of reality and illusion in Genet's plays:

> it is precisely at the point where the two meet that poetry is created – the point at which dream is simultaneously reality, where the invisible coincides with the visible, where the object is both itself and the revelation of something not-itself.[40]

Valency makes a similar comment about the ways in which Giraudoux links and merges seemingly opposed worlds:

> The chief nexus . . . between the world of matter and the realm of the spirit is the young girl, a form of existence which perfectly combines these antithetical elements and which is, for this reason perhaps, completely absorbing to Giraudoux. It is at this point of junction between the two worlds that he ordinarily sets his stage.[41]

But what is important is not just that Giraudoux sets his stage at this point of juncture, but that the mode of interaction between the two realms registers that alternating opacity and transparency that seems so characteristic of horizons in modern theatre. Valency captures precisely Giraudoux's marking and merging of horizons when he goes on to describe the playwright's home town of Bellac in terms designed to demonstrate its fundamental role as the prime locale of all his plays, no matter what their ostensible location:

> Bellac is a modest concept, as cities go, but it is not simple. For above and in this little world, enfolding it at every point like a spiritual exhalation, one can sense another world, turbulent, beautiful, wild, and dangerous, a world full of irresistible urgencies, in which every rock harbors a mystery and every brook a nymph. Between the visible town and the invisible empire which surrounds and defines it there are infinite points of connection. *The gates through which these worlds communicate are carefully locked, and for eternity, but the keys are under the mat; the doors open at the slightest touch; the signs that say 'Eintritt verboten' also read 'Enter without knocking'*. (my emphasis)[42]

The marking and merging of theatrical horizons within particular plays is accompanied by a similar mingling of opposed realms in the generic structure of plays. As Cohn points out:

> In contemporary drama traditional heroes are re-viewed, and traditional genres are re-formed . . . Dürrenmatt calls his *Visit* a tragic comedy, Beckett calls his English translation of *Waiting for Godot* a tragi-comedy, and Ionesco calls his *Chairs* a tragic farce. By these labels, the playwrights emphasize a modern mixture of moods.[43]

Throughout the modern era, traditional lines of demarcation between kinds of plays are drawn, and to some degree transcended, as are traditional distinctions between plays and other kinds of performance. The modern stage incorporates elements of dance, song, puppet show, film and music hall, and this contrasting and merging of distinct domains registers the search for new conventions and new modes of audience attention to facilitate the embodiment of new themes. When Melchior clambers over the churchyard wall in the final scene of Wedekind's *Spring Awakening*, he leaps from a domain dominated by spring, youthfulness and life, to one dominated by winter, ageing and death. The wall marks spatially an experiential division in his life and a generic division in the play, which switches kinds by introducing, in startling manner, a masked man and a ghost with his head under his arm. This sudden reorientation of the audience at the end of *Spring Awakening* is something that occurs repeatedly in Pirandello's *Six Characters in Search of an Author* – a play that brings out clearly the link between subversion of domains and subversion of the audience. The play posits a series of domains of competing realities and brings them, both on-stage and off-stage, into disturbing confrontation. The play uses contrasting lighting to make an initial distinction between the worlds of the Actors and the Characters: '*the whole left side of the stage where the Actors are is lit by a vivid white light'*, while the domain of the Characters, on '*the other side of the stage . . . is suddenly bathed in fantastic light'*.[44] These two domains are then distinguished from and linked to a third, that of the audience, which is brought visually into conjunction with the others when the Stepdaughter moves out of the Characters' area of illumination to lean '*against the proscenium arch*'.[45] These separate domains are then fused and confused. Actors and Characters compete to play roles, and they enter from and exit through the domain of the audience.

We see in these examples the direct connections between the erecting and dismantling of demarcation lines on-stage, the establishing and revising of generic kinds, and the separating and relating of audience and play. What is explicit in these examples is implicit in others, for the marking and merging of theatrical horizons is a marking and merging of differences and similarities that guide audience participation in the theatrical event. It is only through an insistence on autonomous domains that the theatre can enable its own language to embody novelty of theme; but it is only through an accompanying creation of new means of linking domains that this novelty of theme can be made accessible to the audience and thus functional in the world outside the theatre. Horizons must be marked, and subsequently merged, and appropriate theatrical techniques are needed for both.

3 Reconciling worlds

A recognition of the practical efforts that playwrights make to bridge the very theatrical divisions they have insisted on does not constitute a full clarification of the issues raised by that process nor of its consequences for the larger social function of the modern stage. It is important that we recognize, therefore, when we consider further the process of reconciling distinctive worlds in the theatre, that playwrights register a concern not only for the autonomy of separate domains, but also, oddly enough, for their vulnerability to mutual contamination. Ionesco, we have noted, has argued that every work of art is 'an autonomous creation, an independent universe with its own life and its own laws'.[1] But when discussing the period before he began writing plays, Ionesco recalls that he found the theatre an intrinsically disturbing place. And what disturbed him was the confusion of these supposedly autonomous domains:

> What worried me in the theatre was the presence of characters in flesh and blood on the stage. Their physical presence destroyed the imaginative illusion. It was as though there were two planes of reality, the concrete, physical, impoverished, empty and limited reality of these ordinary human beings living, moving and speaking on the stage, and the reality of imagination, face to face, overlapping, irreconcilable: two antagonistic worlds failing to come together and unite.[2]

The distinction that Ionesco recognizes between the world of the imagination and the everyday world, 'two antagonistic worlds', is somewhat undermined by the disorientating spectacle of seeing real people operating as a means of embodying that other reality of the theatre and the imagination. Pirandello encounters a similar problem: for him, the world of the imagination (of art) is imperfectly rendered by any theatrical manifestation of it, and any theatrical performance is also an imperfect rendition of the world outside the theatre. Three distinct worlds thus mingle with each other in Pirandello's theatre, and each world is in part constituted by, and in part contaminated by, the others.[3]

A similar problem presents itself for Artaud: if the language of the theatre is separate from the language of the everyday world, what is the role of the text in the performance of a play? Artaud vacillates. At times he writes of a 'pure theatrical language which does without words'.[4] At other times he writes of a theatrical language which does not ignore, but exceeds, ordinary language. Such a language is 'active and anarchic, a language in which the customary limits of feelings and words are transcended'.[5] At another point he suggests that, 'It is not a matter of suppressing speech in the theatre but of changing its role.'[6] And when he finally acknowledges the dilemma with which he is confronting himself, he eventually announces that his aim is not to devalue spoken language but to reshape it and revitalize it:

> Far from restricting the possibilities of theatre and language, on the pretext that I will not perform written plays, I extend the language of the stage and multiply its possibilities. I am adding another language to the spoken language, and I am trying to restore to the language of speech its old magic, its essential spellbinding power.[7]

And we have noted that when Handke insisted in his Preface to *Kaspar* on the theatricality of the stage, it was a theatricality that exceeded but included certain elements of the world off-stage:

> On first glance, the objects on the stage look theatrical: not because they imitate other objects, but because the way they are situated with respect to one another does not correspond to their usual arrangement in reality. The objects, although genuine (made of wood, steel, cloth, etc.), are instantly recognizable as props.[8]

For Ionesco, the issue is real people partially embodying that other reality of the stage. For Pirandello, the world of the theatre seems to combine the opposing worlds of imagination and reality. For Artaud, it is everyday language operating as part of, rather than in opposition to, the language of the theatre. For Handke, it is everyday objects participating in and helping constitute the theatrical world that he wishes to oppose to the off-stage world. And a moment's further thought makes it clear that this dilemma is inherent in the very nature and structure of the theatre itself. This supposedly autonomous domain exists by virtue of its including and enclosing an audience from another world that it temporarily enfolds in its own domain. The mutual contamination of the world of the theatre and the world of the audience is not just unavoidable, it is fundamental to the theatre's structure and function.[9]

These complex issues of mutual contamination obviously trouble those who wish to insist on the independence and autonomy of the theatre. But the issue of mutual contamination of domains is more than just a theatrical and theoretical concern; it is also a recurring thematic concern in modern plays. We should not, perhaps, be surprised that a drama that thematizes the spatial horizons of the theatre should also thematize the contamination of one domain by another. But there is much to be learned from the ways in which these issues arise in the modern theatre. We should first note the variety of instances. The economic concerns that link Wilton Crescent with West Ham and Perivale St Andrews in Shaw's *Major Barbara* provide an obvious example, as does the so-called Life Force that decisively controls the behaviour of Jack and Anne in *Man and Superman*. The past contaminates and controls the present in plays as diverse as *Ghosts* and *Long Day's Journey into Night*. Social conventions undermine and control individuality in Chekhov's *The Cherry Orchard*, Giraudoux's *The Mad Woman of Chaillot*, Williams's *Streetcar Named Desire*, Frisch's *The Firebugs* and Ionesco's *Rhinoceros*; and in Sartre's *No Exit*, Garcin sadly concludes that psychologically and emotionally 'Hell is – other people!'[10]

This issue achieves epistemological and not just psychological and sociological force in Genet's *The Balcony*. The play is set in a brothel which consists of a series of studios to which clients come to act out their favourite fantasies. Sexual relationships are framed by studios and roles, as clients and whores play the parts of Bishop, Sinner, Judge, Thief, General, Beggar, Saint and so forth. Each studio is soundproofed to keep it separate from the other little worlds of the brothel and from the world outside. But the soundproofing is never adequate to the task. Screams, cries and sighs from each studio repeatedly contaminate the others, and all are in turn contaminated by sounds from the world outside. We hear cocks crowing, hammers striking anvils, and even machine-guns firing in the rebellion going on in the world outside the brothel: 'everything's padded, but some sounds always manage to filter through.'[11] Initially this contamination seems a small point, but it gradually becomes central to the play when we learn that the world inside the brothel and the world outside not only depend on but help constitute each other. The man acting the role of Bishop feels cheated unless the whore playing the Sinner has committed real sins for him to forgive; the Judge likewise insists that the Thief have committed real crimes; and the sexual relationship between a client and his whore is itself an inextricable mixture of the real and the fake. Furthermore, the pretence enacted in the brothel has real effects – one of the whores recalls the impact her role as the Virgin Mary had on a client: 'I saw the effect I had on my bank-clerk. I saw his state of terror, how he'd break out in a sweat, I heard the rattle in his throat.'[12] And the Madame of the whorehouse claims: 'When it's over, their minds are clear. I can tell from their eyes. Suddenly they understand mathematics. They love their children and their country.'[13] The invasion of the realm of fact by the realm of fancy is also manifest in the ways in which symbolic roles (like Queen, Judge and General) are more important to the real world outside the brothel than are the real people who play those roles ('the Queen is dead . . . Long live the Queen'[14]).

The play thus repeatedly demonstrates the necessary contribution of selective reality to the constitution of persuasive fantasy and the necessary contribution of selective fantasy to the constitution of persuasive reality. And at a key point in the play, the unclear line between reality and fantasy is given concrete embodiment when the action is transferred outside the brothel. The outer wall of the brothel is lined up at the edge of the stage with its balcony located at the horizon between the domains of the stage and audience.

> The scene is the balcony itself, which projects beyond the façade of the brothel. The shutters, which face the audience, are closed. Suddenly, all the shutters open by themselves. The edge of the balcony is at the very edge of the footlights.[15]

This precise location of the balcony at the edge of the stage is an explicit attempt to mark a fantasy/reality horizon which is initially insisted on and then repeatedly undermined. The scene on the balcony, a battle for power in the on-stage real world, is one fought not with armies but with symbols – with some of the very elements that are shared by the otherwise opposing domains. The Queen of the old order confronts the Saint of the new order, and this 'combat of allegories'[16] is decisive. It matters little to the outcome that both roles are played by whores; the roles and their symbolic power are more important than any real occupants of the roles. In a play in which a bullet from the outside world strikes and kills a man in the brothel who is preparing to play the role of a corpse, the line between the real and unreal remains simultaneously uncertain and obvious.

This thematization of the problematic status of well-marked divisions captures the complementary nature of concerns for horizons and concerns for the mutual contamination of domains on either side of those horizons. The issue is one manifest thematically in plays, spatially in theatres, and dramatically in various embodiments of the way in which the real and the fictional are not radically separate in the theatre. The world of the audience and the world of the play are not radically separable, and neither are the world of the play and the world of the theatre. *Each of these opposing worlds in part constitutes and is in part constituted by the others.* The issue comes up repeatedly in the modern theatre in such problematic themes as the relationships between self and other, past and present, social versus psychological, and selflessness versus selfishness. It comes up outside the theatre in relationships between past eras and our own, between one society and another in the current era, between one generation and another, between one dialect and another, and between each person's idiolect and the national language to which it belongs. The continuities among these separable domains are as evident as the discontinuities, so much so that we might well wish to consider whether the pervasive world motif is as appropriate for the characterization of pluralistic domains as it first appeared. If there is such widespread mutual contamination of domains separated by social, psychological and theatrical horizons, is it not then the case that the world motif encourages an excessive concern for difference at the expense of similarity? Are the theatrical and dramatic horizons so regularly insisted on in modern theatre presenting problems that outweigh their benefits? We could focus the question more narrowly by asking ourselves what degree of misunderstanding between characters is needed to mark the difference between two people in the same world failing to understand each other fully and two people in opposing worlds failing to understand each other. That is a puzzling question for it asks us to decide at what point differences of degree in a pluralistic world become differences of kind.

To pose this question is to approach the problem of distinct but related worlds from a new angle. Earlier we were considering how continuity could be established between discontinuous domains; now we are asking how we can substantiate the notion of sufficient discontinuity among related domains to justify use of the world motif. These issues are, of course, complementary, but they develop a puzzling relationship in the context of pluralistic domains. To help resolve the incipient paradox we should look more closely at the notion of pluralism itself. So far, we have adopted the word 'pluralism' without acknowledgement, but it is, of course, a term that was elevated to technical status in the work of the philosopher William James. Himself an enthusiastic user of the world motif, James had his own approach to the problems outlined above. The title of one of his major works, A Pluralistic Universe, nicely captures the terminological ambivalence of the world motif by simultaneously affirming monism and pluralism. As Goodman puts it:

> The issue between monism and pluralism tends to evaporate under analysis. If there is but one world, it embraces a multiplicity of contrasting aspects; if there are many worlds, the collection of them all is one. The one world may be taken as many, or the many worlds taken as one; whether one or many depends on the way of taking.[17]

James thus addresses to himself the question 'What at bottom is meant by calling the universe many or calling it one?'[18] And we must ask ourselves: if monism and pluralism can merge, what 'way of taking' the world motif justifies its pluralistic use in the context of discussion of modern theatre?

James's response to his own question is instructive, for it fits a pattern of argument that we have been steadily developing from one arena to another – the notion that horizons in a pluralistic world take on a particular significance. He suggests that:

> Pragmatically interpreted, pluralism or the doctrine that [the universe] is many means only that the sundry parts of reality *may be externally related* [the emphasis is James's]. Everything you can think of, however vast or inclusive, has on the pluralistic view *a genuinely 'external' environment of some sort* or

amount. Things are 'with' one another in many ways, but nothing includes everything, or dominates over everything . . . If a thing were once disconnected, it could never be connected again, according to monism. The pragmatic difference between the two systems is thus a definite one. It is just thus, that if *a* is once out of sight of *b* or out of touch with it, or, more briefly, 'out' of it at all, then, according to monism, it must always remain so, they can never get together; whereas *pluralism admits that on another occasion they may work together, or in some way be connected again.* (emphases mine)[19]

James, we note, characterizes pluralistic uses of the word 'world' in terms of external relations, and of alternating separation and connection of the distinctive domains. It is precisely this concern for the edges of domains, for the points of contact between alternately separated and related worlds, that has been our evolving concern in discussing the modern theatre. Monistic systems focus attention on the core, the fundamental common ground at the heart of a domain; pluralistic systems focus attention on the edges, on the horizons of domains, where contact with other realms occurs, the arenas in which things initially separate subsequently become connected again. But this very process of alternating separation and connection in the context of mutual contamination has epistemological implications that are central to our understanding of its importance on the modern pluralistic stage.

James considers the practical implications of this alternating separation and connection at greater length in another context. Discussing the several philosophical 'worlds' of abstract reality, collective error, relative or practical reality, ideal relations and the supernatural, James notes that

> The popular mind conceives of all these sub-worlds more or less disconnectedly; and when dealing with one of them, forgets for the time being its relations to the rest. . . . The various worlds . . . appear . . . to most men's minds in no very definitely conceived relation to each other, and our attention, when it turns to one, is apt to drop the others for the time being out of its account.[20]

This seemingly innocuous statement is useful for our purposes, for it takes the issue of autonomy and relatedness out of an either/or logic and relocates it in a temporal before-and-after logic. Separation is *initially but not finally* opposed to connection. What we choose at one moment to treat separately, we can, at another, choose to connect. But we should immediately note that the temporal choice is not one of arbitrary whim, and to recognize this is to take a key step in understanding the significance of the process of separating and reconciling worlds on the modern pluralistic stage. To treat things as fundamentally similar is to treat them selectively on an established ground of comparison. To treat things as initially different from and subsequently similar to each other is to make a move of a significantly different order. To learn more about something in a given domain is to experience continuity in the discovery of novelty, but *to learn more by moving from one domain to another is to cope with the kind of discontinuity that may bring, not only new facts to attention, but also new ways of knowing* upon which facts may be grounded. One kind of knowledge acquisition is cumulative and less philosophically challenging, the other is initially discontinuous and more philosophically reorientating in nature.

> The complete philosopher is he who seeks not only to assign to every given object of his thought its right place in one or other of these sub-worlds, but he also seeks to determine the relation of each sub-world to the others in the total world which *is*.[21]

We should regard with some suspicion the notion of a 'total world which is', as this suggests a given and final horizon of implication, while ours, as critics or philosophers, must always be pragmatic and chosen. But it is important to recognize in this linking of contrasting worlds a correspondence between the activity of the philosopher, the role of the critic, and the engagement of an audience with a play, because the unavoidable implication of the modern theatre's insistence on distinctive grounds of knowing is that participation in what the theatre has to offer involves philosophical work. This is not necessarily, of course, a knowledge of pre-existing philosophical systems, but a recognition of, and a capacity to put at risk, the assumptions that ground our own attitudes and expectations about the nature and value of what occurs in life both on-stage and off. And this capacity necessarily opens us up to the possibility of recognizing and adopting others.

Language differences again provide the most useful example here. Language in general and language conventions and strategies in particular become the focus of attention in the modern theatre in much the same way that other thematic material is explored. We are directed by spatial images to the horizons, to the limits of domains, to the points at which what they include is brought into illuminating contrast with what they exclude. We are thus discouraged from focusing on one at the expense of the other. But when aspects of language are at issue, many are disposed to resort prematurely to the tiresome conclusion that communication problems and language problems exist. As a starting-point for discussion, such an observation may well prove valuable, but as a conclusion it leaves much to be desired, for it reduces plays to reiterations of clichés. Yet such observations are frequently offered as conclusions to discussion and interpretation, with the result that prematurely abandoned description is asked to masquerade as explanation. The first step with a particular play may well be to recognize that communication problems or language problems exist, but the essential second step is to ask what kinds of communication problems and what kinds of language problems exist. This then draws attention to the issue not as a metaphysical and irreducible given (e.g. language is inadequate), but as one involving the recognition that, as Artaud's arguments on the language of the theatre remind us, all languages both enable and limit. We thus encounter particular linguistic problems in the context of a clash between particular domains. Spatial images, suitably deployed, draw attention to the horizons of those domains in such a way as to help us to locate precisely what the linguistic problem is and how and to what extent it might be resolved. The problem then becomes a matter for investigation and analysis, rather than something dictating the conclusion of investigation and analysis. But it is important to see that the epistemological ground upon which discontinuity first appeared has itself to become the focus of attention before new modes of continuity can emerge. What is at issue here is not just the acquisition of new knowledge, but of a new ground for linking knowledge in one domain with knowledge in another.

We have thus moved from the implications of Bradley's formulation of epistemological relativism to the recognition that horizons between domains may become barriers and may not, or, to put it more precisely, they may initially be barriers and subsequently not. And as the barriers shift in status from one moment to the next, so also do the domains they enclose; at one moment they exhibit internal homogeneity and external opacity, and at the next internal heterogeneity and external transparency. And the shifting status of these domains is linked to changes in the stance we take towards them.

The spatial language of the theatre thus has thematic consequences which are exemplified in the nature of the issues we are invited to consider and in the kinds of questions we are invited to ponder when we evaluate social interaction. The key shift in our approach to horizons is from taking the possibility of mutual understanding for granted, and thus focusing our attention on the need to explain and remove isolated misunderstandings, to taking the potential for misunderstanding for granted, and consequently needing to promote and exploit local possibilities for achieved understanding. Many of the key crises of life in this view of the modern theatre involve encounters between domains so different that the metaphor of opposing worlds seems thoroughly appropriate; but these domains are so insistently juxtaposed that some kind of transaction between them becomes essential and unavoidable. Contact across these horizons becomes simultaneously problematic and indispensable as discontinuity and continuity become, not opposing, but related concerns. And because the seemingly impossible becomes pragmatically indispensable, we, as audience, are forced to consider, not just what the realms within horizons enable, nor just what those horizons limit, but what degree of merging and what kind of interaction are possible when horizons of discontinuous domains are brought into compulsory contact. It is at just this point that the unreliable epistemological foundations of human interaction in a pluralistic world become the basis for crises that might seem, at first glance, remote from epistemological concerns.

In this context it is possible to see clearly the dual function of the spatial image of the world motif on the modern stage as it serves to register both the autonomy *and* accessibility of distinctive domains. The attention the world motif directs towards horizons is a necessary part of the process of establishing initial discontinuity and subsequent continuity. Radical divisions between pluralistic domains are not offered as insurmountable barriers to the audience (though they may be for particular characters). On the contrary, the line of contact between contrasting domains is the way into the play, into the various domains it dramatizes, and is not an excuse for focusing on the mutual opacity of domains at the expense of their potential, but problematic, transparency. The marking and merging of theatrical horizons is a means of reshaping our attitude towards what we encounter within a set of horizons when what lies within them is presented in the context of what lies beyond them.

Such revision of audience attitudes by means of a focus on horizons thus links with other modes of reorientation in the modern theatre. The opening remark, 'Merdre',[22] of Jarry's Ubu Roi is as designedly subversive of audience/ stage relationships as is the gunfire Ionesco contemplated for the conclusion of The Bald Soprano. Antoine's use of real meat dripping real blood in his production of Les Bouchers is no less disruptive of audience expectations than is the transformation of audience-members into characters in Stoppard's The Real Inspector Hound. The drums in O'Neill's Emperor Jones undermine conventional audience responses as steadily as do the masked members of the audience in Genet's The Blacks. But the issue of horizon adjustment is not just one of reorientating the audience with a sudden surprise or a persisting threat; rather it is one of controlling audience reorientation to, and participation in, the whole theatrical event, and providing the dramatist and the director with sophisticated means of exerting such control. In the marking and merging of theatrical horizons, and in the context of pluralistic epistemology, the modern theatre has foregrounded and extensively exploited such a complex and necessary means to such complex and compelling ends. But these ends, we should now go on to note, are not limited in their function to the domain of the theatre itself.

To recognize the challenging complexity of the mode of participation required of critic and audience alike is to recognize that some of these emerging characteristics of modern drama have large implications not only for the nature of the theatrical event and for the audience's participation in it, but also for the theatre's social function in the modern world. And this is, of course, very much in line with Artaud's and Brecht's insistence on the interdependence of texture, structure, performance space and social function. The recurring emphasis, in the modern theatre, on the creation of other worlds (whether it takes the form of Strindberg's expressionism, Wilder's theatricality, Pirandello's epistemological gamesmanship, Brecht's alienation techniques, Artaud's non-verbal language, or Ionesco's testimony) is a manifestation of a trend that strikes at the heart of one of our traditional aesthetic assumptions: that art is primarily a mirror of the existing world and that its shape is governed by world-reproducing mimesis. This assumption is closely linked to other assumptions about what functions the theatre can and should perform in the social world. To challenge the former assumption is also to raise questions about the latter.

Though there are well-established arguments against them, mimetic assumptions persist to this day, and influence theoretical inquiry, critical activity and audience expectations. The strongest theatrical manifestation of mimetic priority in the modern period is, of course, the naturalistic drama, and its contemporary competitor was the Victorian well-made play.

> The well-made play was one of almost entire visibility, which is to say it possessed almost no dimension beyond what was literally placed before the audience's eyes and ears . . . its characters moved through dramas whose values were wholly corporeal, or else abstractions for corporeality – myths of love, power, social prowess, etc. – which its audiences uncritically accepted as the reflected truths of their own lives.[23]

This notion of the stage as an objective mirror reflecting the world it confronts off-stage seems to capture the most fundamental of the relationships between on-stage and off-stage worlds. But, as the obvious differences between mimetic forms like naturalistic plays and well-made plays suggest, and as our preceding discussion has indicated, the issue is by no means as simple as it seems.

If the well-made play, for example, offered a mirror that simply confirmed what the audience already knew, the mirror in other plays suggested something more. For Shaw, reproduction on-stage of the world off-stage is not just confirmatory, but revelatory:

> The labourer who has never seen a picture does not know that the scenery round his village is worth looking at. By looking at pictures one learns to appreciate nature. And by looking at plays – if they are reproductions of life as they ought to be – one learns to look intelligently at life.[24]

What Shaw is claiming here, even as he builds on the notion of the world on-stage as a mirror of the world off-stage, is that the mirror is not only reflecting but also selecting. And it immediately becomes problematic whether a mirror that selects is really a mirror at all. Shaw's selective approach to mimesis is not just a contemporary phenomenon, but can also be noted in earlier periods. There are many examples, but one useful one occurs in the introduction Wilson supplies to his edition of Restoration plays – plays which he describes as presenting a 'picture', but a selective picture, of the world off-stage:

> None of these four comedies is a literal copy of the life and manners of the age; the authors selected and refined their materials, presenting a picture of the smart set of the day not as it really was but as it liked to imagine itself.[25]

Selective reproduction of the world off-stage is thus capable of challenging (for Shaw), or of confirming (for Wilson), the working assumptions of the audience about the nature of the world off-stage.

We thus have two opposed notions of what is to be gained from a faithful reproduction of a selection of life: one, the simple entertainment of audience members with examples of their own favoured attitudes, the other, the enlightenment of audience members through a presentation of often over-looked elements of the world off-stage. In neither case is the notion of art as a mirror of reality an adequate description of what is going on on-stage. As Eagleton puts it:

> If we are to speak of a 'selective' mirror with certain blindspots and refractions, then it seems that the metaphor has served its limited usefulness and had better be discarded for something more helpful. What that something is, however, is not obvious. [26]

Indeed, it is not obvious, and for that reason the rejected notion repeatedly reasserts itself. We should look more closely, therefore, at what is being rejected and why it seems so difficult to come up with an alternative. And we should recognize that these are vital questions because a major commitment to mimetic poetics carries with it major assumptions about the nature and function of art itself. Closely intertwined with the notion of mimesis is the notion that artists must commit themselves to *entertaining or instructing in a given world*, and we might well wonder, in the context of other worlds, whether there is a further function to add to the traditional two.

It is as well, when encountering a persistent assumption about the theatre, to take a step back from our own experience and our own culture to get a larger perspective. Indeed, we might well take our cue from the implications of our own basic argument and allow modern forms of theatrical discontinuity to guide us towards new forms of continuity. The modern theatre's insistent use of the world motif as a means of reorientation suggests that we explore the horizons of our cultural world by comparing this world to others. We might then ask ourselves whether the notion of art as a mirror is as dominant elsewhere as it has been in our recent past. The answer is, quite simply, no. As Earl Miner put it recently, 'no account of the nature of literature can be anything other than parochial' if it does not allow for the fact that '[mimesis] is unknown in traditional Asian poetics'. [27] Miner, as we shall see, has in mind here a particular kind of mimesis, but his point is important. Whether we follow Plato and regard mimesis as mimicry, or Aristotle and regard it as imitation of universals, the notion of a mimetic poetics has exercised a more powerful influence on our culture than it has on others. It has developed in combination with an affective element formalized by Horace, who was responsible for establishing the enduring notion that the twin goals of literature are to delight and instruct the audience. [28] Miner's argument quickly makes us aware of the historical contingency of the mimetic–affective tradition in western poetics and makes it clear that there was no inherent inevitability in it.

The contrast Miner indicates between western mimetic–affective poetics and Asian affective–expressive poetics thus provides the kind of other-world perspective needed for us to rethink our assumptions about what the western stage must necessarily be doing.[29] The notion of the on-stage world as a mirror, or even as a selective mirror, is, as many have argued, not a controlling option, but one component of a much more complex system of choices. But when Horace sought to extend mimetic poetics by characterizing its affective element, his contribution to poetics reinforced the mimetic imperative in literature. If the primary purposes of literature are to delight and to instruct (or to instruct by pleasing as it was subsequently formulated), then the requirement of verisimilitude is made much stronger than it might otherwise be. The twin notions of mimesis and affectivism thus reinforce each other, and in doing so, limit each other, because each has possibilities beyond those most readily encountered when the two are linked so closely together.

The important point about the perspective introduced by a glance at Asian poetics is that it forces us to consider the complexities of the options which western audiences tend to take as given. The point is not whether the western stage should or should not reject the concept of mimesis, but that what is being accepted or rejected should be properly understood. For that purpose, and for the purpose of understanding the role of 'other worlds' in the modern theatre, we need to establish a clear recognition of the complexity of the notion of art as imitation. The notion itself is not, we should note, single. It is not, for example, the case that imitation is simply a matter of reduplication of the empirical world. There was, indeed, a lengthy period in western poetics when literature was valued because of the way it imitated not just life, but other literature, and only more recently did mimesis become primarily a matter of copying off-stage reality.

> To the estheticians of mimesis the best writers always were imitators, but for a long time the emphasis was on literary models, especially the most perfect works of the greatest ancient writers. Only very late did this emphasis shift to so-called reality, and the best writers became those who were best at 'copying' whatever 'reality' surrounded them.[30]

Once we realize that the concept of mimesis can extend from literature imitating the real world to literature imitating itself, we can see the potential complexities of the mimetic trend. Characters are modelled on other characters, inside or outside art, scenes are modelled on other scenes, and even the use of a word is necessarily modelled on previous uses of it. Spariosu, introducing a recent study of these issues, takes the point further:

> In The Mirror and the Lamp, M. H. Abrams describes four types of literary theories: mimetic (oriented toward the universe), expressive (oriented toward the artist), pragmatic (oriented toward the reader), and objective (oriented toward the work of art). A close look at this by now standard classification will show that all its four types can in fact be reduced to a 'mimetic' or 'representa-

tional' one. . . . As I have already suggested at the beginning of this discussion, while openly rejecting mimesis (in the sense of imitation), expressive or romantic theories are still secretly controlled by it. The opposition imitation/creation (*mimesis/poïesis*) seems to negate any identity between the two terms, and yet, more often than not, they turn out to be one and the same.[31]

Spariosu's 'one and the same' needs further consideration, but he does go on to show that the expressive theory involves mimesis as the artist provides a selective imitation of himself, the pragmatic theory invokes a mimetic chain of model readers, and objective theories invoke a mimetic chain of other texts. And even if a text did manage to achieve the impossible by becoming uniquely and non-mimetically into being, it could only function in our lives by itself becoming a model for subsequent use. To turn the copy into the model simply reconstitutes the very chain that is thought to be broken.

It is thus difficult, as Spariosu points out, to draw clear lines between creation and imitation – the former must retain links to, and is in part constituted by, the latter. But this problem exhibits a similar structure to one that we encountered earlier in Pirandello, Artaud, Brecht, Ionesco and Handke's claims for the independence of the world of the theatre from the world outside it. The persistent contamination of one domain by another led us to recognize that the real and the fictional, the past and the present, the conventional and the original are not distributed in rigid either/or terms; rather they help constitute each other in ways that neither compromise nor eliminate their distinctive domains. Thus we can see that it is not necessary to assume that the creation of other worlds on-stage involves a complete rejection of mimesis. Though it has been argued that the modern theatre, with its manifest theatricality, is anti-illusory and seeks desperately to break the chain of imitation,[32] it is important that we recognize that the chain is not being broken but repeatedly reconstituted. The key issue is not how modern playwrights eradicate mimesis from the theatre, but how they understand and control its function.

A novelty with no mimetic links of any kind will not, of course, be understandable, even as novelty, for novelty must always be approached in terms of a specific kind of departure from something we already know. In this context, Abrams's four types of literary theory, the mimetic, the expressive, the pragmatic and the objective, do not become all the same because they are all at some level mimetic. Rather, *they draw attention to differing kinds of mimetic tendency and, consequently, differing bases for anti-mimetic originality.* Originality must take some kind of mimesis as its starting-point, but that mimesis is not a means of undermining its status as originality; it is simultaneously the ground upon which originality stands *and* the basis for our access to it. When Ionesco describes *The Bald Soprano* as an anti-play,[33] we begin by recognizing that, in opposing itself to plays, it locates itself in our cognitive environment as related to plays, and our concern is then to work out which aspects of other plays are being rejected and for what purpose. This then leads us to see which aspects of a play are being retained, and what this combination of continuity and discontinuity achieves in forming a new kind of play. That new kind of play then extends the chain of play-possibility that grounds our subsequent assumptions of what plays are. Ionesco's term 'anti-play' is thus used in ways that make its seeming either/or logic of play or anti-play into a logic of similarity and difference that requires interpretive work by us. But the focus on discontinuity achieved by horizons drawn within the world of the play guides the audience's attention towards similarity and difference in ways akin to those achieved by the term anti-play. In both cases, the audience is asked to focus on difference as a means of locating subsequent continuity. To recognize the multi-mimetic basis of conventionality is thus to recognize also the multi-mimetic basis of originality and to revise our understanding of the ways in which the modern theatre's use of other worlds relates to the issue of mimesis. The single either/or choice of mimesis or non-mimesis gives way to a recognition that a series of choices among kinds of mimetic and anti-mimetic trends is at issue. And these complex mimetic questions open up access to other social functions the theatre might serve.

For Ionesco, as we have seen, the insistence upon difference, upon the anti-mimetic, is part of a process whereby changes in the nature of the play link with changes in the nature of the theatrical event, changes in the mode of audience participation, and thus changes in the social function of the drama. This linkage of the local and large is a shared concern of many modern playwrights who seek to link reform in the drama with reform of the performance environment as a means of reforming the theatre's social function. Thus, when Ionesco argues that the theatre is by no means exhausted by the functions of 'instruction and entertainment',[34] he is raising an issue of widespread concern. His subsequent argument that the theatre is not just a mode of instruction and entertainment, but also *a mode of inquiry* is one that many would agree with, but we need to clarify it by adding that in the modern theatre this mode of inquiry is an inquiry of a particular kind. When modern dramatists conduct their inquiry they do so in such a way as to focus attention not just on results, but also on the complex mimetic basis of the inquiry itself. Once we see that mimesis is no given anchor to investigation, but that a particular selection of particular aspects of pre-existing potential models provides the pragmatic basis for all modes of inquiry, we find ourselves involved not just in concern for the conclusions a play offers, but for the very grounds upon which such conclusions might stand. The mimetic and the epistemological are thus intricately intertwined for audience and author alike: 'the creation of a theatrical work is a walk in the forest, an exploration, a conquest, the conquest of unknown realities, unknown sometimes to the author himself when he begins his work.'[35]

The notion that the author himself finds things out by exploring new possibilities of an established genre parallels a concern for discovery on the part of the audience that Ionesco, Pinero, Artaud, Strindberg, Chekhov, Ibsen, Brecht and others have stressed in the modern theatre, the full implications of which will emerge in the next chapter. But we should note that such discovery is also fundamental to the exploratory experimentation of directors. As Grotowski puts it:

> I do not put on a play in order to teach others what I already know. It is after the production is completed and not before that I am wiser. Any method which does not itself reach out into the unknown is a bad method.[36]

This extended notion, that the social function of the drama can be one of inquiry for playwright, director and audience alike, leads us to recognize that though the inquiry is initiated in the theatre, its consequences continue in the worlds beyond it. And these consequences provide the logical completion of the pattern we have been tracing.

To multiply the implications of mimesis is to multiply not only the possible modes of interaction between reality and fiction, but to reconsider the nature of both. If the fictional world is both creative and imitative, if it is creative in its selection of features to be imitated and creative in its modes of modelling on those features, then the whole notion of a 'given' world to be imitated crumbles under our feet. *The mode of imitation not only helps constitute the newly created world, but also helps reconstitute what we took to be the given world.* Trevor Griffiths described his dramatic rendition of a 1911 dockers' strike in Liverpool in just these terms when he claimed 'to enlarge our "usable past" and connect it with a lived present'.[37] For Griffiths, a Marxist playwright, this is a matter of rescuing a suppressed past, but the point holds equally well for those who reuse, revitalize, or reform any aspect of the past as a means of reconstituting the present. What is thus at issue in the multi-mimetic modern theatre is not simply an endless exploration of the other worlds that theatre makes possible, but repeated efforts to establish *the kinds of novelty that enable new kinds of continuity with preceding worlds, both on-stage and off-stage, to emerge, become accessible, and become usable.*

James and Goodman, we recall, have already raised the issue of the problematic status of a single given world, and we can now perceive an important convergence between the implications of multiple mimesis and multiple worlds. If, as James informed us earlier, everything, in a pluralistic world, must have 'a genuinely "external" environment of some sort',[38] this must not only be true of the several realms of reality, but of any larger notion of its existence as a whole. And on the borders of reality are, of course, the worlds we variously contrast with it: the worlds of dreams, of imagination, and of fiction. The connections among these worlds are as important as their differences, and Goodman notes how we may focus on one or the other:

> For the man-in-the-street, most versions [of the world] from science, art, and perception depart in some ways from the familiar serviceable world he has jerry-built from fragments of scientific and artistic tradition and from his own

struggle for survival. This world, indeed, is the one most often taken as real; for reality in a world, like realism in a picture, is largely a matter of habit.[39]

To recognize the multi-mimetic basis of art is also to recognize the multi-mimetic basis of our habitual notions of reality. This is not to make art and reality the same but to reconsider the nature of the oppositions between them, and to see once more that there are similarities as well as differences between opposing domains. And it is here that the link between mimesis and the theatre's social function leads beyond the realm of the theatre itself. We do not have to choose between a mimetic–affective tradition with a goal of pleasing and instructing in a given world and an anti-mimetic modern theatre with a goal of disturbing and subverting by creating other worlds, because the initial contrast is only the starting-point for revising our notion of the nature of mimesis, the nature of given worlds, and the nature of the relationship between reality and fiction. The modern theatre is, as we noted earlier, characteristically epistemological in nature, but it relocates epistemological issues at every pragmatic level of social and individual life. The local implications of this relocation we will subsequently explore in a variety of plays; its larger implications, however, emerge in the impetus it gives us to reconsider the complex relationships between the real worlds we inherit and create, and the fictional worlds we inherit and create. And the more closely we scrutinize the relationships between these two kinds of worlds, the more we will understand Iser's claim that, though 'many people regard "fiction" as the opposite of "reality", it is, in fact, not the opposite, but the complement'.[40]

It is in this context that we can recognize the full epistemological implications of the mode of inquiry the modern theatre offers us, and the entailed consequences for its social function. Iser may well be right in his assertion that we should view fiction and reality as complementary domains, but we must once more bring forward the notion that the multi-mimetic possibilities exploited by the modern theatre indicate that there are many modes of complementarity between stage and auditorium, between the fictional worlds of the theatre and the real worlds that lie beyond it. If those modes of complementarity are stabilized for a while, audiences begin to take for granted, to take as given, conventions of complementarity that are only conventions. Once radical experimentation is to be dealt with, *the audience is challenged not only to learn new things, but to learn how to learn new things in the theatre and thence new things in the world outside the theatre.* The mode of inquiry offered in modern theatre is thus a mode of social inquiry into thematic material, into the nature and mimetic possibilities of the dramatic genre, and into the nature and mimetic possibilities of preceding and succeeding real worlds. The concept of mimesis is transformed from a given ground of knowledge into a multiplying set of grounding devices. An experimental play will not only reconstruct on-stage and off-stage worlds, but reconstitute our notion of the nature and function of appropriate constructing in the theatre and in the worlds beyond it. Such reconstruction of the chain of imitation is thus simultaneously a reconstitution of our notion of the nature of inherited theatrical worlds and of inherited real worlds. It therefore invites audiences not just to receive entertainment and instruction, but to participate in an inquiry that questions both what we know and how we know it – an inquiry that also helps us recognize the complex dependence of our knowledge on our ways of knowing both in the world of the theatre and in the worlds beyond it.[41]

As the modern theatre has moved from a primary concern for a world-reproducing mimesis which reflects or illuminates the off-stage world, to one of selectively replacing the off-stage world, its major social function has also moved. That movement has been steadily away from a nineteenth-century tradition that gave priority to entertaining and instructing audiences, to a modern tradition that gives priority to offering audience members the opportunity to participate in a particular mode of social inquiry. Such participation requires audience members to respond to the challenge of reconsidering their role as audience as a first step in reconsidering the nature of the theatre and the nature of the larger worlds in which they and it participate. This conception of the modern theatre and its social function serves not to separate it completely from the past, but to establish its appropriate alignment with other experimental art forms of other ages. Goodman makes the emerging point explicit in his own survey of the epistemological complexity of a world that consists of worlds in the making:

> The arts must be taken no less seriously than the sciences as modes of discovery, creation, and enlargement of knowledge in the broad sense of advancement of the understanding, and thus . . . the philosophy of art should be conceived as an integral part of metaphysics and epistemology.[42]

To recognize the epistemological social function of art in general, and of modern theatre in particular, is to take the final step in understanding the role of experimentation in the modern theatre and of the worlds it creates. But we should note that this function is not an option which necessarily excludes the two traditional functions of teaching and entertaining. Epistemological inquiry can be imaginatively abstract or socially concrete, playful or painful or both, as the plays of Wilde, Pirandello, Wilder, Stoppard, Gray and others have variously shown. But, as Hodgson puts it: 'Greater understanding of its nature and potential as a means of human inquiry and expression should . . . facilitate the appreciation of [drama's] importance and help to enrich the quality of entertainment we look for.'[43] A mimetic–affective tradition tends to put the mirror, the instructor and the entertainer at the heart of the drama. If we follow through the logic of the argument we have been mounting, we find that what is emerging in the modern theatre is a different notion of its function and a different notion of the relationships between means and ends that facilitate that function. Theatre as a means of human inquiry is not committed to re-creating, in the mimetic sense, any specific aspect of the world off-stage. It selectively imitates and selectively re-creates life as we know it off-stage and embeds its selections in new and diverse contexts available only in the world on-stage. *This creative inquiry is simultaneously an inquiry into the evolving nature of the worlds on-stage and into the evolving nature of the worlds off-stage.* And it is this simultaneity of experimentation with selected features of both realms that enables the theatre to justify and make functional its claim to create other worlds on-stage – other, of course, not in the sense of completely other, but other in the sense of selected and emphasized difference as a prelude to establishing new kinds of continuity.

4 Generalizing about worlds

At this point, it is appropriate to note the range and variety of the work of playwrights whose plays have been linked by these emerging elements of coherence. We are able to discuss the work of Zola, Strindberg, Ibsen, Shaw, Pirandello, Wilder, Brecht, Genet, Chekhov, Ionesco and many more in terms of related concerns. This does not, of course, imply that they are all at a fundamental level the same. It simply means that experimentation in the modern theatre is often grounded in similar concerns for the establishment and transcendence of theatrical horizons. Four related issues govern these concerns: an interest in the pluralistic basis of human activity, a need for a means of embodying separate but not unrelated pluralistic domains, a recognition of the constitutive nature of the theatrical environment in manifesting themes, and a rediscovery of the centrality of space and its boundaries in the language of the theatre. The complexity of spatially embodied pluralistic themes draws attention in a variety of ways to a variety of established and newly created theatrical horizons, the most visible of which is that between on-stage and off-stage worlds. In a period which seems to lack unquestioned bases for knowledge and value, pluralistic enclaves are rescued from the ashes of radical relativism by a constant focus on the recognition of, and potential assimilation of, difference. With the unity of a single world steadily disappearing under our feet, the concern is to retrieve possible modes of continuity that can transcend, but not obliterate, radical discontinuity. And the theatre itself becomes both the ground for establishing and the potential means of transcending horizons of difference. The playwright creates new worlds and copies old ones, and, recognizing his twin roles, seeks to give the audience an appropriate orientation towards both. For one modern playwright after another, the issue of creativity in the drama is linked to creative control of the horizons of the performance environment. But to recognize this shared context of creativity is to return to the task that we originally set out to undertake. Is there, we asked at the outset, a way of thinking about modern drama in general that materially assists our understanding of individual plays? In preceding chapters, the basis for an appropriate general framework has steadily emerged as we have learned not just how playwrights and directors have employed world and theatre motifs, but also how we might use them as instruments in critical understanding. But the benefits these motifs offer as a means of linking the works of a variety of playwrights bring with them problematic implications that require further clarification.

To recognize that constructing other worlds in the modern theatre is but a prelude to establishing new kinds of continuity between those worlds and pre-existing worlds is to remind ourselves of the dangers, not always avoided by playwrights and critics, of giving radical experimentation and originality too exclusive a value in the field. Any experiment of lasting worth is important not just because of its originality, but because it offers new modes of continuity with the history of the genre and with other worlds off-stage.[1] Experimentation occurs in the context of received conventions and can only be appropriately understood in that context. Such experimentation within the genre may promote initial obscurity and apparent remoteness from the world of the audience, but these are preconditions for new modes of contact, new kinds of continuity between the domains of stage and audience. In this process, separation is as important as connection, difference as important as similarity, and discontinuity as important as continuity. And therein lies the problem.

If continuity and discontinuity are both important in relationships between domains on-stage, between the domains of the stage and the audience, and between the domains of the modern stage and earlier stages, how, we might ask, do we set about employing generalizations about the field? If we must persistently pay close attention to both similarity and difference between domains in a play and between the domains of groups of plays, is it not likely that we will be badly served by generalizations that seek to justify themselves upon the basis of locating similarity alone? Repeated attempts to generalize about modern drama have often foundered on precisely this difficulty – the difficulty of locating among diverse plays the kind of common ground that will justify the attention that generalizations direct towards it. Three major problems have repeatedly emerged: the plays are too diverse, the common ground, when it has been located, seems not extensive enough or important enough to justify the establishment of categories, and attempts at generalization have too often remained at the level of texture, structure and theme, instead of moving up to include performance space and larger social function. Our argument so far has suggested that we may resolve some of these problems by changing the level at which we seek to generalize. But it is important to see that, in changing the level at which we generalize, we have not eliminated, but simply redescribed and reorganized the diversity of the field. To recognize the similarity of interest various playwrights display when working with the spatial language of the theatre is not to have encountered sameness nor to have overlooked the variety of uses to which circumscribed domains can be put. To do justice to these similarities *and* to their accompanying differences we need to change not only the level at which we generalize, but also the ways in which we seek to generalize, and this, of course, means we must change the ways in which we seek to come to terms with particular cases. These adjustments, as we will see, involve not only changes in our critical habits, but also changes in our epistemological expectations, and changes in ourselves.

Such are the critical consequences of the principles of coherence we have been tracing in the modern theatre, and, to clarify their implications, we should return for a moment to the efforts critics have made to use 'Theatre of X' categories as a means of establishing generalizations in the field. Critics offering these categories follow procedures that seem well-established in the history of critical practice, and the strengths and weaknesses of those procedures are now our immediate concern. The initial steps taken by each of the critics in setting up their categories seem, at first glance, to be unexceptionable. Each of the 'Theatre of X' books sets off on the promising track of seeking to locate extensive common ground among a variety of plays. Esslin (*The Theatre of the Absurd*) draws attention to a series of recurring details – epistemological problems, language problems, communication problems and a trend towards philosophical nihilism. Wellwarth (*The Theatre of Protest and Paradox*) locates another set – a pattern of protest against the social order, a quiescent cynicism, frequent recourse to the technique of paradox. Orenstein (*The Theatre of the Marvellous*) focuses on discordant juxtaposition, pictorial images and a visionary alchemical quality derived from surrealism. Brustein (*The Theatre of Revolt*) notes a recurrent sense of spiritual disintegration, a series of revolts against God, the bourgeoisie, the audience and the status quo, an aching sense of nostalgia, loneliness and regret, and an increasing formlessness. Each writer then seeks to develop these recurring textural details into a structural and thematic generalization which characterizes a particular kind of theatre. And it is at this point that problems begin to arise.

As long as these generalizations remain at the level of commentary about the recurring texture of many modern plays, they are persuasive and convincing. But when the textural patterns are asked to provide the basis for structural and thematic generalizations, the issue shifts from one of their pervasiveness, which is unquestionable, to their centrality, which is not. One could, for example, note the recurring concern in modern drama for male/female love relationships, and the social, moral, psychological and emotional barriers to the fulfilment of these relationships, and then search for plays that include these elements in their texture, e.g. *Trelawney of the 'Wells'*, *The Father*, *The Master Builder*, *Playboy of the Western World*, *Man and*

Superman, *Six Characters in Search of an Author*, *Mother Courage*, *No Exit*, *Long Day's Journey Into Night*, *The Balcony*, *The Visit*, *After the Fall*, *Saved*, *Happy Days*, *The Lover*, *In Celebration*, *Night and Day*, and so on. But if we were to try to make this recurrent textural detail the basis for a Theatre of Romance, we would deserve the disdain our effort would receive. It is not easy to see precisely what has gone wrong here, until we recognize that pervasive textural detail inappropriately raised to the level of structural generalization is incipiently reductive in its application; furthermore, when raised to the level of a generalization about the theatrical and social function of the plays, it seems not only reductive but arbitrary. A feature that is pervasive at one level of the theatrical event is not necessarily central to another, because other features will also need to be taken into account.

The important point is that not all recurrent textural detail can use its pervasiveness as a justification for claiming its centrality – either to one particular play, or to a whole series of plays. Common ground, is not, *by itself*, a guaranteed basis for illuminating generalization. Though the various 'Theatre of X' books are valuable because they focus our attention on recurring detail, further steps are needed to establish the larger significance of the pervasive local features. At times those steps are convincingly taken, but when they are not, differences remain inadequately accounted for and tend to emerge in disconcerting ways. It is not that differences are ignored, for all these writers take extensive note of them; it is rather that the differences are not always persuasively related to the similarities that particular 'Theatre of X' categories emphasize. When Bentley, for example, comments, in his *Theatre of Commitment*, that Brecht's plays, 'whatever else they may be as well', [2] are in the first instance examples of the Theatre of Commitment, he is registering in that very phrase what is intermittently visible in similar works – the not clearly justified leap from the existence of a recurring feature to a claim for its central role in defining a distinct kind of theatre. Indeed, the problematic status of Bentley's category becomes even more problematic when he goes on to explain that the popularity of Brecht's plays is due, in no small part, to their transcendence of the limits of the very category Bentley wants them to exemplify: 'that Brecht's plays are Theatre of Commitment but other things as well has won him approval of a sort from critics who did not share his commitment.' [3] A point made by Esslin about his Theatre of the Absurd has similar implications. When further explaining the category, some years after writing his book, Esslin argued that the category is

> not all-embracing or exclusive. A play may contain *some* elements that can best be understood in the light of such a label, while other elements in the same play derive from and can best be understood in the light of a different convention. [4]

The emerging problem here is a major one. If several kinds of elements can coexist in the same play, it is not clear what is to be gained by treating such elements as if they exemplified separate 'theatres'. To study a play first as an example of the Theatre of the Absurd, then as an example of the Theatre of Revolt, then as an example of the Theatre of Commitment, and so on, seems an unpromising activity. We might thus be exercising an extensive array of analytical tools, but we would be doing so at some cost to the process of establishing a serviceable synthesis. What we are encountering here, in the midst of otherwise interesting work, is the problematic impact of a characteristic use we make of generalizations. We expect these general categories to guide us to the heart of particular plays, but they subsequently turn out to characterize only a single slice, a cross-section of similarity in an otherwise diverse set of plays. Critics then encounter difficulty, at times, either in deflecting the reader's expectation or in demonstrating how he can move expeditiously from noting a cross-section to understanding any play as a whole. We are thus left to ponder the appropriateness of the reader's expectations and to wonder about the status of generalizations that lack general applicability.

What is equally important, however, is that the process of generalization on the basis of cross-section seems incipiently endless. In a highly diversified domain, the kinds of common ground are so local and so varied that an ever-proliferating set of 'Theatre of X' categories can and does result. For those interested in the whole field of modern drama, it might seem that these categories ultimately promise a complete map of the overall terrain. But no book now exists or seems likely to exist that could link these categories to each other on the basis of some universal grid. There is, it seems, no emerging common ground among these proliferating common grounds. As a consequence, the multiplying categories offer no basis for illuminating contact and display no means of entry into any larger cycle of discovery. Instead of transcending the divisions in the field, these categories create new ones that serve individual plays obliquely and allow the same play to exemplify more than one 'Theatre of X' category. The potential dangers of generalizing about a diverse field are thus at times disturbingly actualized. The common features isolated for attention, though undoubtedly deserving attention, seem, in this context, more important to the frameworks than to the plays, and the dangers of reductive and misleading categorization and criticism begin to appear. But it is also important to note that these dangers are, at times, circumvented, and it is to this process that we must turn.

We should now bring forward the second of the two questions we addressed ourselves at the beginning of this study. Noting the absence of an active cycle of discovery in the field of modern drama criticism, we wondered whether the problem lay in the diversity of the material, which might be peculiarly resistant to generalization, or in the ways in which our critical activity seeks to establish and employ generalizations. We have dealt extensively with the former point, and we are now in a position to take up the latter. There is something about our approach to the notion of generalization that encounters difficulty in dealing with diversity. Whatever our theoretical sophistication on the issue, in practice, and particularly in critical practice, we frequently operate as though generalizations must be justified solely by the common ground they isolate and to which they draw attention. Difference tends to enter discussion in defensive asides or as manifest counter-evidence, rather than as something which emerges because of the work a generalization has successfully done and is continuing to do. Generalization is often regarded as the culminating goal of investigation, not as an instrument of subsequent investigation. As a result, we find ourselves repeatedly confronted with what the jargon of our trade has dubbed the premature generalization. And we might wish to add to that the premature categorization and the premature cessation of analysis. Yet there are other ways of using generalizations, ways that allow similarity and difference to coexist, categorization to become a starting-point for further thought, and generalizations to lead towards, rather than subsume, experience of particularity.

If we are to set up categories on the joint basis of similarity and difference, categories which serve to accommodate diversity rather than disguise it, we need a notion of generalization other than the one we have considered hitherto; one which enables us to gain appropriate access to the diversity of individual domains but does not insist on the emergence of an underlying homogeneity at the expense of manifest diversity. It is only by means of such generalizations that we will be able to do justice to a field in which the prominent world motif reminds us of the prominent roles in a pluralistic world of both similarity and difference. One philosopher concerned with such an approach to the nature of categorization and the nature of generalization is Ludwig Wittgenstein. He argues persuasively that our categories can be based, not upon a structure of common core features, but upon a structure of continuity and discontinuity, or, as Wittgenstein puts it, upon a structure of 'family resemblance':

> Consider for example the proceedings that we call 'games'. I mean board-games, card-games, ball-games, Olympic games, and so on. What is common to them all? – Don't say: 'There *must* be something common, or they would not be called "*games*"' – but *look and see* whether there is anything common to all. – For if you look at them you will not see something that is common to *all*, but similarities, relationships, and a whole series of them at that. To repeat: don't think, but look! – Look for example at board-games, with their multifarious relationships. Now pass to card-games, here you find many correspondences with the first group, but many common features drop out, and others appear. When we pass next to ball-games, much that is common is retained, but much is lost. . . . And we can go through the many, many other groups of games in the same way; can see how similarities crop up and disappear. . . . I can think of no better expression to characterize these similarities than 'family resemblances'; for the various resemblances between members of a family: build, features, colour of eyes, gait, temperament, etc. etc. overlap and criss-cross in the same way. – And I shall say: 'games' form a family. And . . . the kinds of

number form a family in the same way . . . we extend our concept of number as in spinning a thread we twist fibre on fibre. And the strength of the thread does not reside in the fact that some one fibre runs through its whole length, but in the overlapping of many fibres.[5]

Popular notions of Wittgenstein's family resemblance categories have often failed to do them justice, and we should be careful to note the subtlety and complexity of this mode of categorization. It exemplifies a creative linking of continuity and discontinuity that has, at times, been missing in attempts to generalize about the modern theatre. We see clearly that the nature of generalization invoked by family resemblance categories cannot be that of a common-core kind. That approach to generalization precipitates the endless pursuit of smaller and smaller categories as generalization strives to locate homogeneity in heterogeneous but distinctive domains.[6] Wittgenstein's mode of categorization and generalization, on the other hand, readily accommodates both similarity and difference. Furthermore, it contrasts with the other mode not only in structure, but also in function, and this, too, is of major importance. Generalizations, Wittgenstein suggests, might be thought of as measuring rods, and he describes his own favourite generalization – the language game – in precisely those terms:

> The language-games are . . . set up as *objects of comparison* which are meant to throw light on the facts of our language by way not only of similarities, but also of dissimilarities. . . . For we can avoid ineptness or emptiness in our assertions only by presenting the model as what it is, as an object of comparison – as, so to speak, a measuring rod; not as a preconceived idea to which reality *must* correspond.[7]

To think of a category or of a generalization as a measuring rod is to change both the way in which we construct it and the way in which we use it. And to use it as Wittgenstein suggests, as a means of continuing an inquiry, is to locate in the framework with which we study modern drama a feature that is characteristic of the drama itself: a commitment not to conclusions but to improved means of inquiry. Our instinctive demand that generalization be based on unity cuts us off from the recognition that generalizations can also be based on *continuity* and that they can serve functions other than those of establishing rigid grounds for inclusion, exclusion and conclusion. An appropriate response to a 'unity' generalization is 'now I have arrived at the fundamental and concluding general truth of my investigation'. An appropriate response to a 'continuity' generalization is 'now I can renew my ongoing contact with particular cases'. The former privileges similarity at the expense of difference, and the general at the expense of the particular. The latter accommodates both similarity and difference, and places the general in the service of the particular. The former closes off the cycle of discovery, the latter renews it, inviting us to take what we know as a recurring starting-point for knowing more. The 'measuring rod' of the continuity generalization provides, not a summary of all instances, but a useful mode of access to their similarities *and* differences. And it is in their capacity to render appropriate justice to similarity and difference, to general and particular, that the world motif and the theatre motif as critical instruments contribute usefully to discussion of modern theatre. We need, and they allow us to have, appropriate grounds for recognizing and establishing significant continuity both within and among plays that also register significant discontinuity. We group these plays together not because we believe that they constitute, in some sense, a closed set, but because the continuity of their experimentation, appropriately characterized, enables them to shed important light on each other. In this context, it is indeed possible to move expeditiously from noting general characteristics to encountering particular instances in all their manifest individuality.

The world motif is thus valuable as a critical tool in large part because of the pressure it imparts to give discontinuity its due in the pursuit of continuity. Like the theatre metaphor, it can be abused and could consequently mislead us. But if we have grasped its potential critical value when appropriately used, we can also go on to recognize the implicit consequences for the user. By imparting a pressure to give discontinuity its due, it prevents us from reducing novelty to the nearest thing we already know. By demanding recognition of differences as a means of locating continuity, it forces us to contemplate changing our use of generalizations and our approach to particular instances. The consequent emphasis on horizons of difference demands of us an effort of intelligence, and a willingness to learn new things by learning new ways to understand. Our access to individual plays via generalizations about them is thus not achieved by reducing their differences and forcing them to fit modes of understanding we have already mastered; rather, it involves clarifying the differences and the grounds upon which they stand so that we can adjust the grounds upon which we stand. And the major consequence of such a process is that we must be prepared to have constant recourse to a capacity of human beings that is much overlooked – a capacity to learn not just by changing what we know, but by changing what we are.

Hirsch reminds us of just this capacity when he tackles the historicist problem of accounting for our means of access to eras other than our own.

> To say with Herder that men and cultures are often very different from one another is not to deny that a man can understand someone with a perspective very different from his own. Vico's conception, later elaborated by Dilthey, was that men share a common potential to be other than they are.[8]

This capacity to change what we are as a means of participating in domains other than our own is one that may seem, at first glance, unfamiliar. But it is a capacity that we exercise regularly, not only when we study other historical eras, but also when we cope with the everyday variety of experience within our own domains and when we conduct transactions with contemporary domains other than our own. We operate in differing ways when performing professionally, socially, religiously, with colleagues, children, parents, old friends, new acquaintances, doctors, clergymen, and so on, and it is important to recognize that this range of variety is not firmly fixed. The modern world, with its electronic media and sophisticated systems of transportation, is one which confronts us repeatedly with pluralistic perspectives and competing values. We constantly have to cope with the pluralistic realms of contrasting cultures, contrasting religions, contrasting languages, and contrasting social, political and economic systems. We are regularly challenged to move from one way of thinking to another, from one set of values to another, from one mode of interacting to another, from one mode of knowing to another, from one mode of being to another. We may, of course, refuse the challenge, but to the extent that we do participate in this variety we have had and continue to have repeated recourse to a capacity to become other than we have so far been. The other worlds of the modern theatre offer a similar challenge, require an equal effort of the imagination, and promise similar rewards.

The motif of other worlds and the process of alternately separating and linking them thus register the epistemological and experiential challenge encountered when someone accustomed to one world, or one range of worlds, is encouraged to participate in another, less familiar world. But this challenge of the modern theatre is continuous with similar challenges we have encountered and will encounter in our own modern world outside the theatre. Pluralistic worlds may well register at first their extensive differences, they may well bring with them the persistent threat of radical change, and they may well provoke initial responses of bewilderment, alienation and *Angst*, but sustained effort at understanding them can reveal and reinforce our human capacity to grow, to change ourselves, by developing new kinds of understanding and new modes of being on the basis of extrapolation from old ones. And the clear means of access to new worlds created on-stage is their mode of interaction with, their alternating separation from and linking to, other worlds that preceded them. In this pluralistic context of marked and then merged horizons, we therefore need not unity, but continuity generalizations, generalizations that serve as instruments of access to new domains. Such instruments link us but do not bind us to domains we start from; they invoke but do not rigidify the selves we have so far been. As Brecht puts it when describing his version of this process in his own plays:

> We need to develop the historical sense (needed also for the appreciation of new plays) into a real sensual delight. When our theatres perform plays of other periods they like to annihilate distance, fill in the gap, gloss over the differences. But what comes then of *our delight in comparisons, in distance, in dissimilarity – which is at the same time a delight in what is close and proper to ourselves?* (my emphasis)[9]

The philosopher Paul Ricoeur has best summed up the epistemological and experiential dynamics of the multi-mimetic aesthetics that characterize the modern era, and he does so, appropriately enough, in terms of the very world motif that has become so prominent in discussion of the modern theatre:

> The coming to language of the sense and reference of a text is the coming to language of a world . . . the reader understands himself before the text, before the world of a work. To understand oneself before, in front of, a world is the contrary of projecting oneself and one's beliefs and prejudices; it is to let the work and its world enlarge the horizons of my own self-understanding. . . . I would say that interpretation is the process by which the disclosure of new modes of *being* – or, if you prefer Wittgenstein to Heidegger, of new 'forms of life' – gives to the subject a new capacity of knowing himself. If there is somewhere a project and a projection, it is the reference of the work which is the project of a world; the reader is consequently enlarged in his capacity of self projection by receiving a new mode of being from the text itself.[10]

Such a mode of contact between the reader and a novel, or the audience and a play, is one that involves, in varying degrees, epistemological complexity and imaginative effort. It requires effort on the part of an audience not just offered entertainment or instruction, but challenged to think for itself and change as it does so. If, as Goodman asserts, 'reality in a world, like realism in a picture, is largely a matter of habit',[11] such habits offer simultaneously a place to start from and a place to depart from. Appropriate understanding of the new knowledge offered involves extension from previous knowledge, and, thus, extensive previous knowledge – knowledge in particular of the possibilities of a genre which is being extended and transformed by the new demands that a new era is making upon it. Assumptions about the nature of reality are challenged by novelty in the nature of the realism with which the audience is confronted and with which it is asked to come to terms in the theatre. Such challenges can be painful and puzzling, but the appeal of the novelty is that it might provide benefits that justify the costs.[12]

For our current purposes we need a framework that provides appropriate access to the modern theatre and to the modes of inquiry it establishes and conducts. Such a framework, we have noted, must make clear the complementary relationship of similarity and difference in the modern field and the way in which dramatists using spatial metaphors can employ difference as a means of temporary disorientation and as a means towards subsequent reorientation; the audience is led to recognize not only internal changes in the genre, but the ways in which renewal of the world within the drama is accompanied by renewal of the means of contact between drama and audience. Artistic novelty, we have also noted, is not opposed to the past upon which it stands, but provides new modes of access to the past by modelling upon it in new ways. We need, not a framework that extends difference to opacity and similarity to sameness, but a framework that can do justice to difference by demonstrating its function in establishing subsequent and novel similarity.[13] We need a framework that can establish modern plays as a series of related experiments that shed light on one another, rather than as a series of unrelated plays, or unrelated groups of plays, that participate in no larger cycle of discovery. We need to see that generalizations do not serve us best by summarizing or concluding thought, or by neutralizing diversity, but by providing appropriate subsequent access to particular events that are both like and unlike those codified in the generalization. Generalizations in this framework do not capture the fundamental truths about the particular phenomena they cover, they provide bridges across discontinuities while reinforcing the role discontinuities play in helping us recognize new kinds of continuity. Such generalizations capture, not the fundamental common ground of static, fixed categories, but the recurring generative concerns that fuel and guide artistic commitment to experimentation and novelty.

At the beginning of this argument, we noted that the study of the modern stage, while different in some ways from studies of other genres and other periods, is none the less similar in important respects to the study of any other field. We need some generalizations that will give us an adequate sense of the types of things we are studying, and we need some detailed descriptions of particular instances which exemplify the types. This enables us to study other instances with some sense of the kinds of things to look for, and these in turn inform and reform our notion of characteristic types. This cycle of discovery then renews itself indefinitely. With our extensive exploration of the textural, structural, theatrical, social and critical function of the world and theatre motifs, we have set up such a framework. What follows is a series of studies of particular plays that display the creative processes we have outlined above. These studies exemplify the framework in action. Like any such framework it is open to abuse if it is regarded as the repository for the final truths about the field. It offers simply a mode of orientation, a series of measuring rods, a set of places to start from. The moment it begins to be allowed prescriptive rather than descriptive status, it will become reductive and constraining, instead of illuminating and enabling. It points a way forward, rather than positing a necessary destination. Readers thus informed should not leave their study of this framework with a primary reaction of the form 'now I know what modern drama is all about!' Rather, they should be able to say 'now I have a better sense of how to set about interacting with and understanding a modern play by myself, now I know how to go about dealing with the modern theatre on my own.' All members of the audience must have their own engagement with a play, and must bring to it their own capacity to be what our shared culture has so far made possible. But they must also bring with them a readiness to use what our shared humanity has given us all – the capacity to extend our current horizons, to become other than what we have so far been, by participating in worlds other than those we have so far known.

Part II
The plays

5 Pinero:
The Second Mrs. Tanqueray

Clayton Hamilton, an early editor of Arthur Wing Pinero's plays, argued enthusiastically, in 1917, for the importance of the playwright's work to the evolution of modern English drama:

> The existence of that modern drama in the English language to which it is now possible to point with pride was established at a date which is absolutely definite. The modern English drama was ushered into being on the night of May 27th, 1893, when *The Second Mrs. Tanqueray*, by Arthur Wing Pinero, was acted for the first time on the stage of the St. James's Theatre in London. . . . It is now possible to assert with certainty that *The Second Mrs. Tanqueray*, at the time of its original production, was the *only* great play that had been written in the English language for one hundred and sixteen years.[1]

In the light of our earlier discussion of the valorization of novelty, we should be wary of exaggerated claims for the originality of any dramatist, not least one whose work seems, in retrospect, more conventional than original. But there are virtues in beginning a study of modern plays, not with a startlingly novel play like Büchner's *Woyzeck*, Goethe's *Faust*, Strindberg's *To Damascus*, or Pirandello's *Six Characters in Search of an Author*, but with a play which exhibits the full strength of an established tradition while also laying claim to significant originality. From such a play we might derive an important perspective on the relationship between conventionality and originality in plays throughout the modern period. There was not, we may take it, any sudden transformation of the drama from one thing to a completely different thing. There were, instead, a series of changes which, in varying combinations, gave drama of the modern period a different overall character from that of the preceding century. Our concern is not to establish dates of changes, modes of evolution, or patterns of influence, but to locate characteristic mixtures of originality and conventionality that can help provide an illuminating perspective on the drama of the period as a whole. *The Second Mrs. Tanqueray* is particularly valuable for this purpose because it attempts to make constructive use of a potential liability in the dramatic conventions it inherits and exploits; this demonstrates simultaneously the strengths and weaknesses of those inherited conventions, and the ways in which weaknesses, as well as strengths, can be turned to advantage.

The play is even more valuable for our purposes because the conventions it inherits and exploits are the structural conventions of an internationally known dramatic model – the French *pièce bien faite*. The well-made play, established by Eugène Scribe and refined by Victorien Sardou, dominated the nineteenth century, has yet to lose its grip on popular comedy, melodrama and television drama, and regularly resurfaces, in one form or another, in the work of accomplished playwrights in every decade of the twentieth century. As Stanton puts it: 'The well-made play . . . has "paid off" in the theatre. Every successful modern dramatist, beginning with the younger Dumas, has had to reckon with Scribean theatre, whether in principle he favored or denounced it.'[2] A glance at the structural principles of the well-made play, which have been extensively explored elsewhere,[3] provides a useful starting-point for any consideration of conventionality and originality in the modern theatre. Valency provides a helpful summary of the structural and textural blueprint of the well-made play as established by Scribe in the first half of the nineteenth century:

> This blueprint served as the master pattern of dramatic construction, and it acquired in its day the authority of a science. Until the first decades of the twentieth century, the system of Scribe was *'le système du théâtre'*. . . . Scribe employed a five-act structure, with the climax in the fourth act, the denoue-ment in the fifth and a quick curtain. The first act was mainly expository; its tone was gay. Toward its end, the antagonists engaged, and the conflict was initiated. For the next three acts, the action oscillated in an atmosphere of mounting tension. In the fourth act – 'the act of the ball' – the stage was generally filled with people, and there was an outburst – a scandal, a quarrel, a challenge. At this point things usually looked pretty black for the hero. But the last act arranged everything; in the final scene, the cast was assembled, there were reconciliations and an equitable distribution of prizes, and the audience came out of the theatre smiling.[4]

This programme for the structure of the play was matched by a similar pattern for its texture:

> The scenes were composed in somewhat the same manner as the play itself, but in miniature. Each scene had its initial situation, its progression, compli-cation, climax, peripeteia, and conclusion, so that it formed an autonomous whole within the total arrangement. It was, consequently, quite possible to come to the theatre in time for the performance of a favorite scene, and to leave immediately after, having enjoyed a complete, and often sufficient, dramatic experience.[5]

It is not surprising that such intricacies of plotting could be achieved only at the expense of other elements of the drama, and this, as we shall see, provides problems of some importance to our understanding of the experimentation that has been so prevalent in the modern theatre. But we should note that, in one sense, 'Scribe invented nothing. He used the technical methods of all the great writers of comedy.'[6] What Scribe provided was a framework within which established 'technical methods' could be crammed densely together and yet remain under control. Indeed, one of the pleasures provided by such plays is enjoyment of the skill with which the dramatist can add complication to complication and still find a way towards a sudden and speedy resolution.

Stanton describes Scribe as 'the theatrical juggler supreme',[7] and there was much with which to juggle, for along with the well-made play's highly patterned structure came a series of stage contrivances needed to maintain the flow of that structure: 'Scribe considered it essential that the action proceed smoothly and elegantly from the exposition, through the successive stages of complication, climax, peripeteia, and denouement, and to this narrative progression all other considerations were subordinated.'[8] The series of devices employed to maintain the smoothness of the process thus became of major technical importance, and they consisted of such contrivances as intercepted letters, overheard conversations, unexpected encounters, sudden strokes of fortune, secrets which cannot be revealed, lost papers, spectacular conversions, newly discovered heirs, last-minute revelations, radical misunderstandings and improbable coincidences.[9] The smoothly running and complicated plot was thus sustained by the kinds of techniques that required the audience to value the ingenuity of the dramatist at least as much as the consistency of the play's characters and the subtlety of its themes. And therein lies the problem for modern playwrights seeking to adapt the structure of well-made plays to more serious purposes.

As Valency points out, the structural and textural patterns established by Scribe and reinforced by his successors on the French stage provided the basis of the stagecraft of a generation of playwrights. French comedy, often mangled in translation, made its way across Europe and America, as well as to England: 'Scribe, Sardou and to a lesser extent Labiche were constantly translated or adapted into English, imitated by the English playwrights of the 1870s and 1880s, and held up by conservatives to proponents of the New Drama as models of craftsmanship.'[10] Though this craftsmanship provided the benefits of a tried and tested theatrical method, it also brought the liabilities of a plot-dominated drama, a drama which, in spite of its local ingenuities, finally portrays life in terms of a repetitive and predictable pattern of restricted change. How, for example, can one write a play dramatizing a sustained mood, or depicting an unchanging state of affairs, if the play's structure insists on taking the characters through a sequence of exposition, complication, crisis and resolution? How does one write a play about an unresolvable problem if the play's structure insists on a resolution? The well-made play has its own complexity, but it is a complexity of a predictable kind which seems to allow little freedom for the exploration of original ideas or unconventional characters. As a result, the principal point now made against the well-made play is that it 'has become synonymous with trashy playwriting – with the play that amuses but says nothing'.[11]

What we are encountering here is an important horizon of the world of the well-made play. Its internal structure generates certain possibilities and precludes others. But if we have learned anything from our general survey of modern drama, it is that social, psychological, spatial and generic horizons in the modern field provide peculiarly suitable grounds for dramatization of modern thematic concerns. The points at which structures register their limits are also the points at which alternatives can emerge for scrutiny and evaluation. But if we are to understand what those alternatives are, we need to establish, with some precision, the limits that a particular structure is generating and encountering. The term 'well-made play' may have become synonymous with trashy play writing, but the power and persistence of this kind of play suggests that we should not, too hastily, overlook what the play enables when noting what it constrains. There may well be a measure of persisting truth in Dumas's claim that 'the dramatist who knows *man* as Balzac did and the *theatre* as Scribe did will be the greatest of the world's dramatists.'[12]

It is widely agreed that many of 'the most significant dramas of the late nineteenth and early twentieth centuries in France, England, and America were born out of the union of . . . the *pièce bien faite* . . . with serious social or psychological subject matter'.[13] Even Shaw, who dismissed the well-made play as 'Sardoodledum', made extensive use of it, and no one would accuse Shaw of writing plays that amuse but say nothing. Much depends on whether the demands of the well-made plot are given precedence over everything else in the play, or whether ways can be found to give other elements of the play their due in spite of the foregrounded plot. Is it indeed possible to forge a satisfactory alliance between the well-made play structure and 'serious social or psychological subject-matter', or is it, as Taylor argues, quite impossible?

Taylor, reviewing the impact of the well-made play on modern English drama, makes the case strongly that reliance upon a well-made plot is crippling for serious drama as the consequent limits upon thematic range and character complexity are inescapable. 'From Scribe to Somerset Maugham', he argues, the well-made play is dominated by 'lots of plot',[14] and heavily contrived plots depend on similarly contrived characters. A truly unpredictable character would, Taylor concludes, provide the kind of complication that could not be resolved by the well-made scheme, and the whole structure 'would instantly fall apart'.[15] Stanton makes a similar point when he notes that 'the will of the characters in this type of drama is always subordinate to the exigencies of the plot and to the artifices employed by the author.'[16] And Valency goes on to develop the issue in detail:

> Neatness in plotting . . . depends largely on the manipulation of stereotypes. Unless it is assumed that, in general, good people act well and bad people badly, that captains act like captains and tradesmen like tradesmen, it becomes difficult to motivate a story with the sort of precision the well-made play requires. The moment good people begin to act like bad people, they involve the dramatist in questions foreign to the logic of the well-made play. . . . When characterization becomes a matter of depicting the individual rather than describing the archetype, motivation ceases to be a matter of logic, the events of a narrative are no longer predictable, and the emphasis shifts decisively from plot to character.[17]

Valency even goes so far as to suggest that 'when the idea of characterological types is entirely rejected . . . plotting becomes difficult, or even impossible.'[18]

There is evidently a critical consensus here, but we must go beyond a recognition of this inherent limit in the well-made play to ask whether this limit is itself susceptible to dramatic exploitation. Must the confrontation between the demands of this kind of plot and the demands of character be solely destructive of one or the other? Isn't there, perhaps, some way of thematizing the conflict? Taylor, interestingly enough, takes several steps in this direction, but he does so largely in the context of demonstrating the limitations of the English well-made play. He argues that the privileging of plot over character in these plays gives them an incipient theatricality and consequent loss of verisimilitude. Action is motivated not by character will but by theatrical whim, as events proceed in terms of a pattern characteristic of the world of the theatre, but not of the social world of the audience. Life, an audience might well feel, is just not like this. But, Taylor also notes, some aspects of life are indeed like this – relatively fixed values generate relatively fixed patterns of responses to certain kinds of events. And they do so in segments of society that, for a time, establish, at least in public, a fixed and shared notion of the nature of society and of the value of any actions within it. In that country's upper-middle-class drawing-rooms, English dramatists were provided with precisely the setting they needed to exploit the predictable strengths of the well-made play.

> The well-made drawing-room drama was above all a theatrical pattern based on a social pattern; essential to its effect was the imaginative presence of a rigid convention of behaviour against which everything done by anyone (in certain classes, at least) would always be measured and judged. . . . But when that convention is lost or broken . . . the form crumbles too.[19]

Taylor notes the convergence here between strong social and dramatic conventions, but continues to insist upon the fragility of the form. We should certainly recognize that the English well-made play makes thematic use of the all-powerful plot structure of the well-made play by uniting it with the all-powerful value structure of the social stratum it dramatizes. We should also recognize that the plot of the well-made play finds itself at odds with any character who wishes to grow in unpredictable ways, and that the inherited social values of this class of people are regularly at odds with anyone who seeks to deviate from their long-established prescriptions for good social behaviour. But we need not be forced to Taylor's conclusion that such conflict between plot and character is solely destructive if allowed to develop very far.[20]

Another way of approaching this issue is to say that a conflict in the play that exists because of the recent history of the on-stage world is a liability only if that conflict itself cannot be integrated into the thematic concerns of a play exploring selected aspects of the off-stage world. If, on the other hand, a dramatist can integrate the two, then we have, as our earlier chapters suggested, the possibility of a play that foregrounds one horizon of its own structure as a means of foregrounding simultaneously an important horizon in the world of the audience. And when we encounter, as we do in *The Second Mrs. Tanqueray*, a character who describes himself as 'a spectator in life . . . a man at a play . . . [an] old-fashioned playgoer' (p. 35),[21] we might well be alerted to the possibility that such a play is at hand. To what extent, we might ask, does this notion of a limited (old-fashioned) playgoer link audience with characters, structure and theme on the basis of foregrounded limits?

Critical exploration of *The Second Mrs. Tanqueray* has indeed focused on limits in the play, but more often negatively than positively. Such discussion has raised three major issues: whether the play's action is supposed to be demonstrating the limiting power of established social values; whether the decisive limitations are supposed to be those of Paula Tanqueray rather than those of society; and whether the play itself is limited in its inconsistent thematic exploration of both issues. These points are evidently related as the charge of inconsistency is based on the claim that the play first invites us to sympathize with Paula's rebellious character but subsequently with the values of those she rebels against. A further problem for critics is the play's puzzling use of the family friend, Cayley Drummle.[22] His actions appear to be restricted to those of an observer and family counsellor, yet his structural prominence is such that further explanation is required. The play begins with a stage set depicting his absence as a dinner guest and the first topic of discussion is his failure to appear. In the final moments of the play, as in the opening moments, attention is focused on Drummle and his actions: '*He pauses for a moment irresolutely – then he goes to the door, opens it, and stands looking out*' (p. 174). In between, Drummle serves as confidant of Aubrey and Paula, provides a normative social perspective on their actions, but does little, it seems, to justify the attention the play invites us to give him.

The structural prominence of Drummle is not easily explained in terms of either of the two major interpretations of the play. He is not, it seems, responsible for Paula's character or behaviour; she unhesitatingly ignores his advice and at one point likens him to 'a very romantic old lady' (p. 101). And, though he clearly operates as the mouthpiece of established social values, he is not the kind of unforgiving, unswerving, moral judge who might openly denounce Paula and thus serve as the intolerant representative of long-established and inflexible social attitudes. Indeed, the more we ponder Drummle's relationship to the action, the more we become aware that we must take our cue from Drummle's self-description and recognize that his importance in the play derives not just from his relationships with the characters, but also from the relationships he contracts with the audience in the theatre:

DRUMMLE: I'm merely a spectator in life; nothing more than a man at a play, in fact; only, like the old-fashioned playgoer, I love to see certain characters happy and comfortable at the finish. (p. 35)[23]

The questions that then emerge for members of the audience are whether they, like Drummle here, are content to remain benevolently serene, old-fashioned spectators, or whether they, like Drummle at the end of the play, have become aware that *the attitudes of the spectators are not without implications for the lives and fortunes of the participants.* And this, in turn, will have important consequences for the audience's response and attitude to Paula's self-condemnation and suicide.

Those who would wish to remove both Cayley Drummle and the seeming inconsistency of development from the play usually have in mind a version of the play rather different from the one Pinero actually wrote. But their version is certainly one of the play's components – a well-made-play plot in which a character's reprehensible past catches up with her and wrecks her hopes of achieving something of lasting value in the present and future. The Exposition informs us that Paula Ray has for some years disposed of her favours where she chose, rather than where respectable society might have preferred her to dispose them. The Complication arises when she meets an older man, a widower, Aubrey Tanqueray, and the two attempt to build a successful marriage upon rather shaky foundations. They make a partial success of this, in spite of being ostracized by genteel society, but the Crisis arrives *when Paula's past catches up with them.* Hugh Ardale turns up as the suitor to Aubrey's daughter (from his first marriage) Ellean, and it turns out that Hugh, unfortunately, is one of Paula's many lovers from the past. This destroys any hope Paula has of becoming a successful mother for Ellean and a successful wife for Aubrey. The play's Resolution makes it clear that Paula's past cannot be buried, and she takes the only way out and kills herself. There we have a neatly structured plot with Exposition, Complication, Crisis and Resolution following upon each other with the inevitability of a moral judgement on a moral error in a morally homogeneous universe. The only trouble with this version of the play is that it leaves out Cayley Drummle and overlooks the fact that *what catches up most quickly with Paula and Aubrey is not Paula's past in the person of a former lover, but Aubrey's past in the person of his daughter Ellean.*[24]

Both points are of major importance. Drummle functions, in part, to help the audience become conscious and potentially critical of stock responses to the world on-stage, and also, in part, to help the audience become conscious and potentially critical of established values in the world of the play. Both Drummle and Aubrey deal with Paula by offering initially a flexible attitude towards her past and later a much less flexible attitude towards its lingering effects on her. Their initial attitude seems incipiently critical of established social rules, but their subsequent attitude seems to reaffirm them once more. This pattern of events anticipates, and puts in question, a similar pattern that emerges in Paula's evaluation of herself, and in the audience's evaluation of the whole action of the play. To understand the significance of this repeated pattern, we need to trace its emergence with some care, for it seems as much a consequence of Aubrey's past as it is of Paula's.

The play provides some highly visible stage business involving letters to draw attention to the fact that it is Aubrey's respectable past rather than Paula's *risqué* past that first catches up with them. Aubrey is initially portrayed as a strong-minded individual, ready to take risks and defy established conventions if his own sense of rightness is in collision with one based on inherited values. He is ready to risk his friendship with Misquith, Jayne and Drummle, abandon his home in the Albany, reject the judgement of his peers in the 'little parish of St. James's' (p. 32), and challenge unswervingly its conventional wisdom that a good marriage cannot result from a union with a woman with a 'past'. But at the end of the first act, this Aubrey, the individual choosing his own values and his own friends, is confronted by two letters – one from Paula confessing the full details of her past, the other from his daughter Ellean reasserting the claims of his own past. The two letters invite comparison in terms of Aubrey's reaction to them. He immediately burns as no longer relevant the letter dealing with Paula's past – but he stands, transfixed, at the climax of Act One, reading the letter that emerges from his own past. That letter from his daughter Ellean announces her imminent return from a convent to live with him once more. In that moment, Aubrey the flexible individual is forced to come to terms with Aubrey the conventional father, and it is the re-emergence of this role from his past that provides the first major difficulties for Aubrey and his future bride. A lovingly intimate episode with Paula is transformed by the letter from Ellean into a moment of awkwardness, hesitation and uncertainty: '*Paula re-enters, dressed in a handsome cloak. He stares at her as if he hardly realised her presence*' (p. 46). The second act begins, several months later, with Aubrey and Paula married, and Paula jealous of the attention Aubrey gives Ellean in preference to her. Aubrey the embryonic free-thinking individual has been subordinated to, though by no means eclipsed by, Aubrey the conventional moralist.

Aubrey, we should note, goes ahead with his marriage, continues to love

Paula, and at no point wavers in his commitment to their relationship. But the nature of that commitment, we must recognize, has shifted in ways that have disastrous consequences, not just for Aubrey, but for Paula, too, and for the whole action of the play. To overlook its significance is to overlook one of several structural features that undermine the conventional acceptability of the death of the attractive but flawed heroine. In his behaviour we encounter a pattern that is similar to one displayed in both Paula's and Drummle's behaviour. It is this pattern that provides the basis for the play's structure and theme, along with its accompanying exploitation of audience response. This pattern is one of *temporary independence from established values and a subsequent acceptance of them* – a pattern which, interestingly enough, has led many to believe that the play is inconsistently structured, that Paula's behaviour is inconsistently motivated, and that Pinero is daring enough to raise questions about established values but not daring enough to follow up the implications of these questions. The appropriate response to these criticisms is, however, that the play is consistently structured, for the changes that occur in Paula are paralleled by changes in Aubrey and Drummle. The ultimate lack of radical fervour of the characters should not be attributed to Pinero's lack of nerve, but rather be seen as part of a more sophisticated structure than has usually been noted in the play. Our recognition of that structure depends in no small part on our understanding the full significance of Paula and Aubrey's initial rebelliousness and subsequent conventionality, and the consequences of both for the audience's readiness to accept the moral inevitability of Paula's demise.

If we look first at Aubrey's brand of rebelliousness early in the play, we note that he raises two related issues – the right of any individual to stand beyond the reach of inherited generalizations, and the likelihood that inherited generalizations reflect the values of small groups of people who have projected their own values into universal values. The issues arise in the context of a discussion between Aubrey and Cayley Drummle about women who have a 'past'.

AUBREY: To you, Cayley, all women who have been roughly treated, and who dare to survive by borrowing a little of our philosophy, are alike. You see in the crowd of the ill-used only one pattern; you can't detect the shades of goodness, intelligence, even nobility there. Well, how should you? The crowd is dimly lighted! And, besides, yours is the way of the world.

DRUMMLE: My dear Aubrey, I *live* in the world.

AUBREY: The name we give our little parish of St. James's. (p. 32)

To see in the crowd of the ill-used 'only one pattern' is to impose established judgements on a class of people on the basis of only one trait in their characters. Yet, as Aubrey rightly points out, these people may have little in common other than a sexual freedom that exceeds the bounds deemed appropriate by the 'little parish of St. James's'. And to see, as Aubrey does, the 'little parish of St. James's' as *a* world, and not *the* world, is to take the first step towards liberation from inherited values and stock responses by recognizing the incipient limitations of any group's point of view.[25]

These are important issues in a play that repeatedly draws attention to contrasting values and contrasting social spheres in an actively pluralistic society. When Ellean returns from the convent to live with Aubrey, he is so struck by her character and behaviour that he remarks on 'how Ellean comes to me, from another world I always think' (p. 69). When he considers introducing Ellean into high society, it is in terms of 'placing my daughter in the world I've left' (p. 72). When he contemplates with regret the social implications of men's sexual behaviour, he terms it 'the little hellish world which our blackguardism has created' (p. 69). And when Paula and Aubrey move out to the country, Aubrey characterizes the move as from one parish to another, building on the notion of parish as world and way of life: 'I avoid mortification by shifting from one parish to another. I give up Pall Mall for the Surrey hills; leave off varnishing my boots, and double the thickness of the soles' (pp. 32–3). These social divisions are multiplied wherever one looks in the play. Paula, responding to being ostracized by country society, argues: 'I wonder we didn't see that we should have been far happier if we'd gone in for the devil-may-care, *café*-living sort of life in town! After all, *I* have a set, and you might have joined it' (p. 55). The play begins with an all-male dinner from which women are excluded and at which male friendships are celebrated. At that dinner there is open discussion of the changes that marriage brings to a man's social life: 'in nine cases out of ten a man's marriage severs for him more close ties than it forms' (p. 5). And this social severance is matched, in the same conversation, by Aubrey's argument that the past and the present, too, are capable of radical separation:

AUBREY: The lady, my dear Frank, belongs to the next chapter, and in that her name is Mrs. Aubrey Tanqueray.

JAYNE: [*Raising his coffee cup*] Then, in an old-fashioned way, I propose a toast. Aubrey, Frank, I give you 'The Next Chapter!' (p. 7)

What we thus encounter repeatedly in the play are indications of radically separate domains based upon friendships, marriages, class distinctions, parish boundaries, town or country life, past or present chronology, general or local values. But we should also note that though these domains are distinguishable, they are not completely distinct. Marriage, we are told, can taint pre-nuptial friendships ('a worm has begun to eat its way into those hearty, unreserved, pre-nuptial friendships' (p. 5)) and, as we see later in the visits of Ardale and the Orreyeds to the Tanquerays, pre-nuptial friendships can also taint marriages. The key issues raised by the action of the play are thus whether single sets of values can cover pluralistic domains, whether these distinguishable domains can ever be fully distinct, whether partial or total separation of them is for the better or the worse, and whether those with the power to make that choice exercise it responsibly. And these questions return us to Aubrey's behaviour, its parallels to Paula's, its relationship to Drummle's, and its implications for the audience and the play as a whole.

Is there, we must ask ourselves, one Aubrey who is a free-thinker and one who is conventional? And are there two Paulas and two Drummles similarly divided? And if so, is the play radically inconsistent in its structure, promoting individual values early in the play and conservative values at the end? To understand Aubrey's behaviour is to discover the key to the behaviour of the others. We have already noted that it is Aubrey's past, not Paula's, that first catches up with both Aubrey and the second Mrs Tanqueray. And we should now note that Aubrey's rejection of his past, and of the inherited wisdom that governed it, was not as decisive as it seemed at first glance. Even as he rejects the application of those values to his situation with Paula, he rejects them for a carefully defined situation, and not, therefore, for all situations:

> AUBREY: I know what I'm doing, and I do it deliberately, defiantly. I'm alone: I injure no living soul by the step I'm going to take; and so you can't urge the one argument which might restrain me. (p. 33)

As he rejects established values, Aubrey acknowledges a potential factor that might restrain him from doing so. It is because he believes himself to be 'alone', without dependants, that Aubrey feels free to be 'defiant'. Once that circumstance changes and Ellean returns home, Aubrey is no longer alone, no longer defiant, no longer so willing to see the shades of goodness in the ill-used, and no longer able to keep at bay the values which threaten to undermine his relationship with Paula. Aubrey the conventional father is much less willing to oppose inherited values than is Aubrey the widower seeking a second marriage. We see with striking clarity that though Aubrey's rebellious arguments are of large potential consequence, his underlying attitude towards inherited values does not require the complete rejection of reductive generalities and premature judgements. It merely *involves their temporary suspension in the context of a single case.* In short, *he sees those inherited values not as fundamentally wrong, but as simply insufficient to cope with a particular circumstance.*

It is thus the suspended values of Aubrey's past becoming present once more that provides the first major threat to the Tanqueray marriage, and it is a threat with a striking manifestation in the letter from Ellean at the end of the first act of the play. The arrival of Hugh Ardale, the embodiment of Paula's past, in Act Four, is thus not the climactic event without which all would otherwise have been well. His arrival is simply the culmination of a process that was well under way before he arrived.

This point is important to any understanding of the play, not only because it governs how we view what is happening, but also because it changes our notion of the kind of play this is. The arrival of Hugh Ardale can look like the cheap well-made-play coincidence required to keep the plot moving to its assigned destination. But coincidences only seem contrived if one feels that, without them, the course of events would have been very different. Here, it is clear that the destruction of the marriage is already well advanced and that, as a consequence, having Paula and Hugh dissemble would solve nothing.[26] If Hugh's arrival had not precipitated the final disaster, something else would have. Plot does not thus appear to be imposed upon thematic process, but to embody it. And that process is one of the gradual undermining of a marriage by inherited values latent in the marriage, not by inherited values imposed solely from without. It is also important to our understanding of the structural pattern of the play that we recognize latent inherited values not only in Aubrey, but also in Paula, for Paula's rebelliousness is no more firmly grounded than his.

Paula enters the play splendidly dressed, mischievous, gay, and seemingly quite independent of conventional rules of behaviour. She takes great pleasure in calling on Aubrey an hour before midnight, enjoys the consternation it causes him, and is quite unmoved by what people in general and the servants in particular might think of her arrival at so late an hour. This initial manifestation of the joy she takes in her own independence reinforces the image of her unconventionality that has already emerged in the discussion of her by Cayley Drummle and Aubrey. And, as Aubrey has already made clear, she makes no pretence about her past way of life and is thoroughly honest with him about it. One side of Paula, at least, is quite independent of the little world of St James's and all its conventional values. Indeed, when things later begin to go wrong between Aubrey and herself, she blames it upon their recent confinement to the social mores of middle-class life *and* reminds him that there are, or at least were, alternatives. Thence her reference to former friends in the 'devil-may-care, *café*-living sort of life in town!' (p. 55). But Paula immediately goes on to concede that part of the reason they did not join her friends is that she had her heart set on being a married woman. What she does not add here is what she makes explicit elsewhere – that she had in mind not just being a married woman, but being a particular kind of married woman, and therein lies the problem.

Paula's rebellion against conventional values turns out to be just as pragmatic as, and no more fundamental than, Aubrey's. The free-thinking, independent and unconventional side of her nature is accompanied *from the beginning* by an underlying attachment to the very values she so delightedly opposes. When she envisages her future married life with Aubrey, it is not in terms of reconciling her unconventional values with more conventional ones. It is, instead, in terms of a radical switch from one set of values to the other. Like Aubrey, she wants the rules for entry to this society to be suspended so that she can be accepted within it. Or, better still, she would like her past to be completely forgotten so that her place in this society could be quite secure. One of her earliest images of their life together includes dinner parties at which she and Aubrey will be surrounded by 'the nicest set imaginable . . . the sort of men and women that can't be imitated' (p. 40). But this wonderful group of dinner guests is not to be made up of broadminded, flexible thinkers who know of Paula's past and are undaunted by it; it is to be made up of those who do not know of Paula's past and have had no opportunity to make any judgement on it at all: 'Well, although we had been married only such a few years, I seemed to know by the look on their faces that none of our guests had ever heard anything – anything – anything peculiar about the fascinating hostess' (p. 40).

The rebellious Paula of the play's first act carries within her the suspended values that will eventually condemn her. Like Aubrey's, *her initial rebelliousness, though potentially of large social consequence, soon gives way to a situational rebelliousness that seeks not to overthrow inherited values but to establish an exception to them.* Rather than justify what Paula has done with her life, and rather than simply accept what she has done, Aubrey and Paula adopt the strategy of seeking to circumvent or forget it all:

AUBREY: My dearest, you don't understand me. I – I can't bear to hear you always talking about – what's done with. I tell you I'll never remember it; Paula, can't you dismiss it? Try. Darling, if we promise each other to forget, to forget, we're bound to be happy. After all, it's a mechanical matter; the moment a wretched thought enters your head, you quickly think of something bright – it depends on one's will. (p. 43)

To recognize that the values antagonistic to the marriage of Paula and Aubrey are shared by both characters and built into their early planning of their relationship is to recognize that arguments about whether the action depends primarily upon character values or upon social values are quite misplaced. The central characters carry within them from the outset the very social values that later undermine them. Nevertheless, as we have seen in Paula's and Aubrey's early actions and statements, and elsewhere in the dialogue, more than one set of values are indeed present in the play: conventional values which are identified with the 'little parish of St. James's' and unconventional values which are located in other worlds beyond. But what is often misconceived in criticism of the play is the way in which it seeks to give dramatic embodiment to the conflict between values. Those who criticize the play as inconsistent envisage Paula espousing one set of values and everyone else adopting, to various degrees, the other, with the play inviting us to side initially with Paula but finally with everyone else.[27] But the play begins to take on quite a different shape when we recognize that while there may indeed be competing sets of values in the world of the play, those of the worlds outside the 'little parish of St. James's' have no fully committed advocate in the play at all. This is very much in keeping with the notion that neither the well-made play nor the segment of society on-stage could cope with the problem of alternative values. But this limit in the well-made play is, we have argued, one that is susceptible to thematization as a functioning component of the structure of this play, and we need to go on to indicate how such an assumption is supported by a different notion of the way in which the play embodies the clash between competing values.

We should thus turn from the notion of a fundamental clash between Paula's and society's values to a search for some more convincing explanation of the structure of the play. And the nature of that emerging structure becomes more clear when we note that the convergence we have traced between Paula and Aubrey in terms of their values and behaviour has its parallels, too, in those of Cayley Drummle. Drummle, we have noted, has seemed something of an anomaly in the play because (1) he seems not to participate in the play's thematic concerns, and (2) any attempt to justify his presence on the grounds that he provides us with an example of the social group Paula wanted to join, but which rejects her, seems counter-productive. Cayley is the one member of that social set who is ready to accept Paula and forgive her for her past. Instead of reinforcing the notion of a hostile society driving Paula to despair, he repeatedly undermines that notion by embracing her presence and her friendship. But by now we should be alert to the fact that *his flexibility simply recapitulates the pattern set by Aubrey and Paula – he too wishes established values to remain intact, but social rules to be temporarily suspended to admit the Tanquerays to good society.* And in Mrs Cortelyon he introduces another member of genteel society who is ready to do likewise – with the accompanying indication that others (including, no doubt, sympathetic members of the audience) might eventually follow suit.

Cayley Drummle's role in the play is also, in part, one with a specific and easily recognizable history. When Scribe was establishing his blueprint for the well-made play, he regularly utilized one character as the mouthpiece for the moral norm of the play. Whatever else this character did on-stage, he was responsible for establishing the appropriate moral tone and for keeping the audience informed of the right attitude towards whatever events or characters became the focus of attention. Meier is right to suggest that 'Drummle functions as the *raisonneur*, well known from the French drama',[28] – a traditional role which required that the character establish and maintain 'a confidential relation with the audience throughout the course of the play'.[29] Valency describes the development of this traditional character in nineteenth-century drama:

> Scribe's *raisonneurs* were almost always his protagonists. Dumas often followed the practice, as in *Le Demi-monde*, but occasionally his *raisonneur* is a marginal character whose sole function is to comment on the events of the play. At first the presence of such characters could hardly be justified in so thrifty a form of drama, but in time Dumas hit on the ingenious idea of giving this role to the family doctor, whose presence required no explanation, and whose opinions automatically inspired respect. Among the first of these medical *raisonneurs*

was Dr. Remonin in *L'Etrangère*. From him stems that long and illustrious line of stage physicians which includes Ibsen's Dr. Rank, Dr. Relling, and Dr. Stockmann, Chekhov's Dr. Astrov and Dr. Chebutikin, and innumerable other articulate medical men down to Sir Henry Reilly of *The Cocktail Party*.[30]

Drummle, in this play, is obviously no medical man, but he is clearly the embodiment of established common sense and the moral norm of the play. Drummle's status as a voice of authority and as an embodiment of established limits are both of some consequence to the play, not in terms of Drummle's adequacy to those tasks, but in terms of the ways in which his apparent adequacy provokes the audience to adopt attitudes that they and Drummle will have reason to regret.

In a play which, following the well-made-play tradition, seeks to imitate on-stage aspects of the off-stage world of the audience, Drummle's is the viewpoint which the audience is expected to adopt. Drummle is calm, poised, articulate, independent, witty, understanding and forgiving. He is the respected confidant of both Aubrey and Paula, and the person to whom Misquith and Jayne immediately defer when the question of discussing Aubrey's impending marriage arises. Drummle is the character with whom the audience is most likely to identify, and whose views, in spite of Drummle's self-criticism, they are most ready to espouse. His readiness to forgive Paula and invite her into society is calculated to win their approval. What is dramatized on-stage is not Paula's *risqué* past, which the same audience would be expected to condemn, but her repentant present, which, in a charming and beautiful woman, must surely justify forgiveness and sympathy.

Drummle's behaviour on-stage seems, as many have pointed out, more often that of a spectator than that of a participant; as such, he takes on the audience role of observer, but he is a privileged observer, one who is allowed to view things, for our benefit, from close up. Meier notes this tendency in the play's stage directions:

> Apart from two or three directions referring to the gallant manners of the day, the directions read as follows: 'Drummle watches him for a moment', 'looking at Aubrey', 'eyeing Aubrey', 'watching Paula apprehensively', 'looking at Aubrey keenly', 'he goes to the door, opens it, and stands looking out'.[31]

But in her desire to establish the similarity of these stage directions through-out the play, Meier makes little of the contrast in the final stage direction: for the first time, Drummle is looking not in the direction of the main characters, but away from the environment in which their relationship has flourished and foundered. The importance of that environment is that it provides, as we shall see, spatial horizons that embody crucial value horizons in the world of the play. And to come to terms with those horizons we need to note the trap that is laid for Meier, or for any members of the audience who adopt Drummle's perspective as their own: this perspective is radically undermined by the final events of the play. The all-knowing, all-forgiving Cayley

Drummle, the man who claims not to have been surprised for twenty years, turns out at the end to be ignorant of the most important event of the play, astonished by the death of Paula, and quite unable to comprehend what has happened and why. Having chanced upon the scene of disaster, incongruously relaxed, content and singing, he struggles to grasp what is happening around him; the best he can finally manage is to pause '*for a moment irresolutely – then he goes to the door, opens it, and stands looking out*' (p. 174).

If we are to understand the significance of Drummle's final action of gazing out of the door, we need to recognize the role in the play of the room that the door encloses. The very first stage direction in the play seeks to establish a link between physical environments, physical horizons and social values. We are asked to note that Aubrey's chambers in the Albany include '*a richly and tastefully decorated room, elegantly and luxuriously furnished. . . . Everything in the apartment suggests wealth and refinement*' (p. 1). The linking of 'rich' and 'tasteful', and 'wealth' and 'refinement' is an important indication that even the décor of this environment implies specific kinds of values. Aubrey's house in the country, the scene of Aubrey's and Paula's married life, exhibits similar wealth and taste. The morning-room has '*a large recessed window through which is obtained a view of extensive grounds. Everything about the room is charming and graceful*' (p. 48). The implications of these stage directions are made explicit in the dialogue when Paula mockingly refers to 'the refining influence of these intensely respectable surroundings' (p. 88). The value of the refinement they offer is challenged by Paula's earlier rebellious values, her current mixed feelings, and her subsequent enforced suicide. Even as she learns to readopt the values she has temporarily suspended, something in Paula resists the process of adjustment. And that resistance is linked to the contrast between this local world of refinement and worlds that lie beyond it. This contrast is given persistent visual and verbal embodiment in the play. Paula, we note, gazes distractedly out of the window when Drummle pressures her to make up a quarrel with Aubrey (p. 100). And when Drummle first visits the house in the country, she is prompted by his presence to gaze out of the window of this world towards something beyond it, towards her other life and other kinds of encounter in the past with Drummle and his friends:

PAULA: I'm sleek, well-kept, well-fed, never without a bone to gnaw and fresh straw to lie upon. [*Gazing out of the window*] Oh, dear me!
DRUMMLE: H'm! Well, I heartily congratulate you on your kennel. The view from the terrace here is superb.
PAULA: Yes; I can see London.
DRUMMLE: London! Not quite so far, surely?
PAULA: I can. Also the Mediterranean, on a fine day. I wonder what Algiers looks like this morning from the sea! [*Impulsively*] Oh, Cayley, do you remember those jolly times on board Peter Jarman's yacht when we lay off – ? [*Stopping suddenly, seeing Drummle staring at her*] Good gracious! What are we talking about! (p. 66)

The pattern of signals linking the boundaries of the room with the boundaries of a way of life, and with Drummle's role as participating spectator, is quite clear. She gazes out of the window away from this way of life; he gazes at her in terms of this way of life. The same relationship between Drummle's staring and Paula's gazing out of the window is exhibited in the later scene (p. 100). For Drummle, the reference to the house as a 'kennel' is a joking one; for Paula, its implication of limits contains more than a morsel of truth. Her life on Peter Jarman's yacht might well seem ugly and appalling from the public perspective of upper-middle-class society, but its continuing appeal to Paula is evident.

The persistent linking in the play of Drummle's staring, established values, and refined, elegant sets is designed to undermine, ultimately, Drummle's philosophy of benevolent forgiveness, established on-stage social values, and the off-stage values of the 'old-fashioned' playgoer. All are implicated in the process of benevolently suspending values that must, when no longer suspended, condemn the very person their suspension admits, however partially, to good society. The effect upon Paula of this apparently generous attitude of forgiveness is both subtle and savage. She enters the play not at all adversely affected by the unconventional life she has led thus far. Indeed, she enters the stuffy world of the Albany like a breath of fresh air. 'She is a young woman of about twenty-seven: beautiful, fresh, innocent-looking. She is in superb evening dress' (p. 37). Yet, after a few months of marriage to Aubrey, she is afraid to look at her appearance in a mirror; her physical exhaustion, she fears, is a public revelation of her inner flaws. What happens in between is not a sudden shift in her character. Rather, it is the gradually increasing adoption by Paula of the very values she had earlier suspended, rather than rejected. Instead of judging her past by the standards she adopted early in the play, she gradually comes to judge it by the standards of the society she is now seeking to join, and which she has long desired to join. The dilemma is a crucial one and central to the play. The point is not that she becomes a puritanical convert. It is that the only way open for her to join this society is to reassert the suspended rules, to regard herself as a sinner, as one in need of forgiveness. It is but a short step to realize that one who has sinned in this way is not and cannot be like one who has not transgressed. Forgiveness is bestowed on those in need of forgiveness. The more Paula wants acceptance in this society, the more she becomes like the members of this society. And the more she adopts their moral stance, the more she sees herself through their eyes, and the more she believes that their judgement of her erroneous ways is the only one possible. It is thus vital to note that when Paula looks into the mirror that condemns her, the one who offers the mirror, and holds it in front of her, is none other than that persistent spectator, Cayley Drummle (p. 106). Cayley, the old-fashioned playgoer, becomes Cayley, the agent of condemnation, because his sentimentality and forgiveness perpetuate rather than revise the very standards to which Paula's youthful behaviour might pose a challenge.

It is thus important to recognize that it is not just the rebellious rhetoric of the first act that brings into question the conventional acceptability of the death of the flawed heroine, but also the steady exposure of the limitations of the process whereby hero, heroine and *raisonneur* seek to reconcile conventional and less conventional values. To see only the first factor is to see the play as inconsistently structured; to see also the second factor is to recognize the thematization of a structural pattern that is repeatedly recapitulated in the play and which is most strikingly embodied in the judgements of the otherwise unnecessarily prominent *raisonneur*.

The key issue in the play is that, under the increasing influence of Aubrey, Ellean, Cayley Drummle and 'these intensely respectable surroundings' (p. 88), Paula accepts that she needs to be forgiven for her past. As her past is not an accident but a continuing part of her, she must stand constantly in need of forgiveness and hence constantly deserving of condemnation. When she acknowledges the 'wisdom' of Cayley Drummle's mercy and Aubrey's forgiveness, she finds herself in the anomalous position summarized rather humorously by Groucho Marx when he vowed he would never join any club that would have someone like him as a member. A forgiven Paula, in ongoing need of forgiveness, remains like a splinter under the skin of this society, constantly in the process of being expelled no matter how deeply it inserts itself. Forgiveness is not, and cannot translate into, acceptance. But forgiveness and suspended rules are the best that the conventional wisdom, voiced by Cayley Drummle, can offer. And it is important to note how specifically this limitation in Drummle's thinking is set up, and how his limits are equated with the spatial limits and value limits exemplified in the rich and tasteful set.

Advising Aubrey on how to deal with Ellean, Drummle insists that the right approach is not to confine her to this safe little house, but to allow her some freedom in her social movements. Then she will have the knowledge and experience needed to cope when she eventually learns the truth about Paula's past. The exchange is a vital one as it points directly to the play's conclusion and its own eventual inadequacy.

> DRUMMLE: Well, if your daughter lives, she *can't* escape – what you're afraid of. [*Aubrey gives a half-stifled exclamation of pain.*] And when she does hear the story, surely it would be better that she should have some knowledge of the world to help her to understand it.
> AUBREY: To understand!
> DRUMMLE: To understand, to – philosophise.
> AUBREY: To philosophise?
> DRUMMLE: Philosophy is toleration, and it is only one step from toleration to forgiveness. (pp. 71–2)

This forgiveness is explicitly the ultimate benevolence that Drummle's philosophy has to offer, the philosophy of temporarily suspended rules to cover cases where the rules seem inadequate. At the end of the play, Ellean, ironically enough, seems to have learned Drummle's lessons, and discovered the wisdom of his flexibility; she thus condemns herself for having failed to offer Paula this forgiveness. But even as Drummle makes this convert to his views, the action of the play has demonstrated their fundamental inadequacy. Ellean's affirmation of Drummle's philosophy ironically occurs at the moment Drummle begins to recognize its unacceptable consequences:

DRUMMLE: She – she has –!

ELLEAN: Killed – herself? Yes – yes. So everybody will say. But I know – I helped to kill her. If I'd only been merciful! [*She faints upon the ottoman. He pauses for a moment irresolutely – then he goes to the door, opens it, and stands looking out.*] (p. 174)

Drummle's 'irresolute' response to Ellean's cry and to Paula's death takes him and us to the limits of the room as the play aligns the limits of his philosophizing with the limits of an environment that has become the embodiment, for Paula, of society's tastes and values. Ellean is offering a solution that has become part of the problem. Her 'mercy' would be one more suspension of the rules, but only a suspension. For Drummle, 'philosophy is toleration, and it is only one step from toleration to forgiveness'. But where is the step from toleration to acceptance? It is never presented or envisaged by anyone on-stage as a viable option, and Paula immerses herself in this society only by recognizing her unworthiness to enter it. Learning how to internalize the judgements of others, she gradually becomes her own accuser and her own judge. The first time the condemning mirror confronts her, it is held up to her by Cayley Drummle (p. 106); the second time, she picks it up herself (p. 138). And her ultimate fear is that Aubrey, too, may come to see her solely in this distorted way, once her youthful beauty ceases to cause him and Drummle to suspend the rules of St James's society and gaze upon her sentimentally. By this point in the play, Paula has become fully aware that suspended rules are not negated rules, but rules of general application awaiting their moment of contact with any and every particular case.

PAULA: You'll see me then, at last, with other people's eyes; you'll see me just as your daughter does now, as all wholesome folks see women like me. And I shall have no weapon to fight with – not one serviceable little bit of prettiness left me to defend myself with! A worn-out creature – broken up, very likely, some time before I ought to be – my hair bright, my eyes dull, my body too thin or too stout, my cheeks raddled and ruddled – a ghost, a wreck, a caricature, a candle that gutters, call such an end what you like! Oh, Aubrey, what shall I be able to say to you then? And this is the future you talk about! I know it – I know it! (pp. 169–70)

It is at this point that Cayley Drummle, ignorant of the consequences of his philosophy of forgiveness, and unaware of the long-term impact his gaze has had on Paula, enters singing gaily. Paula's final self-condemnation is voiced in terms of how other people see her. Though her version of how she will look when seen through the eyes of others is an extreme one, it is the very process of seeing herself through the eyes of others that has resulted in her current inability to find herself acceptable to herself.[32] She has become the agent of the society that condemns her even as it forgives her, and as such, she becomes first her own accuser, then her own judge and finally her own executioner.

What the play eventually makes clear are the shortcomings of existing methods of reconciling conventional and less conventional values in an actively pluralistic society. Drummle's philosophy of benevolent forgiveness serves only to injure and finally destroy Paula. Fundamental rejection and hostility she could cope with, as she had already coped with them, by rejecting that segment of society that rejected her. What destroys her is a qualified, and seemingly flexible forgiveness that Drummle (and other old-fashioned playgoers in the audience) would regard as the generous embodiment of the right thing to do. But by temporarily suspending rules, rather than reconsidering them, Drummle, like Paula and Aubrey before him, saves short-term happiness at the cost of long-term disaster. The short-term happiness is based upon forgiving what went before, not upon understanding and accepting the significance of Paula's behaviour. With the former attitude in place, the values of the little parish of St James's remain unchallenged, and Paula and Aubrey have to make the necessary long-term adjustments. With the latter attitude adopted, Paula and Aubrey could retain and develop their early unconventional stance, and the parish of St James's would have to do some adjusting to come to terms with the standards and mores of a world outside its own. Suspended rules are not, however, revised rules, and the values not subjected to revision await the moment when they reassert themselves once more. What all three characters overlook is the fact that forgiving, in this situation, is not the same as forgetting, and that forgiving is not to be equated with acceptance. Without that acceptance, established society has not changed, and, as a consequence, Paula has to change – in ways that none of the characters initially anticipates or finally understands. The action takes the characters and the play to an inbuilt limit as a way of guiding the audience to look beyond the barriers that the action of the play runs up against. And those barriers, those value limitations in the world of the play and the world of the audience, are what Drummle is helplessly trying to see beyond when he gazes irresolutely out of the room at the end of the play.

What the play thus finally focuses on is not the single conflict between two sets of values – those of the early Paula and the later Paula – but upon the way in which conflicting social values are mediated and resolved in a world that refuses to concede the possibility of radical alternatives. Though several worlds are contemplated in the play, their mode of interaction is thus finally more important than their similarities and differences. Paula might well join with Aubrey in remarking, as he does, on 'how Ellean comes to me, from another world I always think' (p. 69). The truth of the matter is that Ellean, Aubrey, Paula (and Aubrey's first wife) all come from separate worlds,[33] and the play's ultimate focus is not on the rightness or wrongness of any of these worlds, but on the nature of the social transactions that occur between them. Society seems determinedly uniform in its approach to public values, no matter how pluralistic its ways of life or how various its local modes of behaviour.[34] *The Second Mrs. Tanqueray* provides us with what we are explicitly directed to regard as a cellular society, one with pluralistic divisions, and pluralistic lived values, but with only one set of publicly acknowledged values.

The theatre audience that allies itself with Drummle is thus challenged and undercut by the action of a play that undermines the very perspective the audience is encouraged to adopt. To be on Cayley's side is to be on the side of debilitating homogeneity, whatever the sentimentality and generosity that manifest, at best, a mere pseudo-flexibility. The play lacks, as the well-made play must, a convincing advocate of alternative values; but *the action of the play itself* becomes an advocate of alternative values, an action that outruns, and demonstrates the limitations of, the benevolent perspective of its *raisonneur*. There is indeed a structural clash in this play, but it is not a clash of inconsistent characterization in Paula or anyone else; nor is it a clash of inconsistent moral perspective on the part of the author; rather, it is a functional clash between the action of the play and its benevolent interpreter.[35] We, the audience, are purposely asked to ally ourselves with a perspective which turns out to be inadequate, and our expectations are challenged by that inadequacy as much as are the expectations of the *raisonneur* whose perspective we so readily adopt.

If the audience feels that Paula was more than and other than a sinner, if it feels that the old-fashioned playgoer must be succeeded by one more up to date, then it must fall back upon and re-examine its own belief in the value of applying moral judgements to moral errors as if all sinners existed in a morally homogeneous universe. The solution to the problem is not to suspend temporarily the rules, nor to eradicate the 'double standard' by reining in the men, but to consider whether the 'double standard' has already conceded the necessity of multiple standards which take into account the limitations of, and the pragmatic basis of, all social standards. This is not a first step towards relativism and anarchy, but a recognition that in a pluralistic society homogeneously viewed, judgements may be more readily to hand than justice.[36]

The repudiation by the events of the play of Cayley's philosophy of benevolent forgiveness is a repudiation of an attitude in the off-stage world that the play reflects, encourages, and then radically undermines. The adverse effect of the enacted events upon Drummle's moral and emotional perspective thus justifies his prominent place at the beginning and end of a play which seeks to utilize the limitations of his perspective as a way of exposing the limits of the well-made play and of that segment of the off-stage world represented by the play. Pinero thus successfully thematizes the conflict between plot and character in the well-made play by enabling it to exemplify the limits that established social values place upon sympathetic characters. To gain social acceptance Paula must change, but as the play makes abundantly clear, that change is not a viable one, nor is it necessarily for the better. When Paula claims to have 'outgrown' (p. 102) Mabel Hervey, she has become, in one important sense, narrower as a person, not more flexible. Her education in this new society is not into wider but into narrower views. She, like Drummle in the first act, has lost sight of 'the shades of goodness' (p. 32) that even someone like Mabel might well have in her character; like the others of her new set, Paula inevitably contributes to the decline of Mabel and her husband George. The limitations of the social values of the world of St James's travel with Aubrey and his family wherever they go. They may be able to suspend them temporarily, but there is finally no escaping them, because they are internalized values that limit the very moral perspective they are supposed to enhance. And as Paula, too, has internalized them, she must subsequently adopt and make her own the damning mirror that Drummle (constructively he thinks) so readily hands her. The audience, its sympathies undermined as Drummle's are undermined, gazes with Drummle at and beyond the edge of a stage set that once embodied only wealth and refinement, but now suggests inadequacy, unfairness and injustice. The play has taken us, as it has taken Drummle, from the comfortable centre of an unchallengeable domain, to an uneasy awareness of its spatial, generic and moral horizons.[37]

6 Ibsen:
A Doll's House

Ibsen's *A Doll's House* was written fourteen years before Pinero's *The Second Mrs. Tanqueray*, but the relationship between convention and innovation in its stagecraft is much more complex. For the purpose of establishing an explanatory framework, it is thus more fruitful to deal with Ibsen after Pinero. Both dramatists, we should note, rely extensively upon the well-made play, and both make important use of the margins of dramatized domains. But in Ibsen's case, those margins have more subtle implications, as the famous conclusion of *A Doll's House*, carefully examined, will reveal.

Much has, of course, been written about Nora's slamming shut the door at the end of *A Doll's House*. It seems to summarize in a single action Nora's rejection of her husband, her children, her home and her social position, along with the society that had taught her to need such things. As Meyer puts it:

> The terrible offstage slamming of that front door which brings down the curtain resounded through more apartments than Torvald Helmer's. No play had ever before contributed so momentously to the social debate, or been so widely and furiously discussed among people who were not normally interested in theatrical or even artistic matters. [1]

Lucas, in the same vein, remarks that 'that door slammed by Nora shook Europe.' [2] Contemporary discussion of Nora's dramatic exit was so extensive and so heated that stories circulated about 'certain Scandinavian families [who] even went so far as to add to their cards of invitation to evening parties the request: "Please do not discuss the *Doll's House*"'. [3] But discussion of the play continues now as it continued then, with that slammed door operating as the persistent catalyst for repeated debates between Nora's defenders and detractors. What is surprising, however, is that, though the final action of the play, Nora slamming the last of several doors behind her, is the focus of everyone's attention, the initial action of the play, Nora entering through the same series of doors, seems not to have attracted so much attention or provoked such detailed discussion.

It should not be overlooked that the stage directions for the opening action focus prolonged attention on the very doorway through which Nora will finally exit in disappointment, disillusionment and anger:

> The front door-bell rings in the hall; a moment later, there is the sound of the front door being opened. Nora comes into the room, happily humming to herself. She is dressed in her outdoor things, and is carrying lots of parcels which she then puts down on the table, right. She leaves the door into the hall standing open; a Porter can be seen outside holding a Christmas tree and a basket; he hands them to the Maid who has opened the door for them. (p. 201)[4]

This extended attention to the doorway at the beginning of the play should not be forgotten when we find ourselves staring at it once more at the end, and neither should we forget the momentary tableau of the unadorned Christmas tree framed by the doorway. In case we should be inclined to forget, the play draws attention to that doorway and others repeatedly throughout the action. The moment Nora is alone at the beginning of the play, she steals over to her husband's study door and listens to hear whether he is home (p. 201). When Krogstad comes to call on her, Nora goes across and bolts her husband's door (p. 251). When disaster confronts her, and Nora sadly notes that she has only thirty-one hours to live, she is interrupted by her husband, standing 'in the doorway', asking what has become of his little lark, and she moves towards him and the doorway 'with open arms' (p. 261). When Krogstad leaves after his concluding conversation with Mrs Linde, 'the door out into the hall remains standing open' (p. 266); our attention is focused on it and on the music wafting down from Nora's dancing upstairs. As we watch and listen, the outer door is unlocked, and Torvald 'pushes Nora almost forcibly into the hall', and, dressed in her Italian costume, she lingers reluctantly 'in the doorway' (p. 266). Torvald subsequently locks the front door to keep Nora in when her forgery is revealed (p. 275). Furthermore, the letter which is to betray Nora's secret is conspicuously inserted into and obtrusively remains in the mailbox attached to the same outside door. Conversations or actions are interrupted repeatedly by the doorbell ringing, or someone knocking, and, in a play with several characters and a single set, exits and entrances are legion.

It is also important not to overlook the fact that it is not just at the beginning and ending of the play, but at the beginning and ending of each act, that action and attention are focused on a doorway. We have already noted Nora's entry at the beginning of the first act; at the end of that act, Nora is directing the maid to bar the door to the children; at the beginning of the second act Nora goes to the door, listens, opens it and looks at the empty mailbox; at the end of the second act, as we have seen, she rushes with open arms towards Torvald who is framed in the doorway; at the beginning of the third act, Mrs Linde is in the room, listening '*tensely, for a sound at the front door*' (p. 262); moments later she opens the door to admit Krogstad; and at the end of that act Nora leaves the stage slamming the door. If we had not noticed before, we should certainly note, at some point, the fact that the whole of the play's action takes place in a room which has no fewer than four doors, one of which leads to a fifth and sixth, the outer doors through which Nora makes her entrance and exit at the beginning and end of the play.

These ubiquitous doors, and the persistent focusing of attention and action on them, could, in the work of a lesser playwright, be dismissed as simple mechanics. But in the work of Ibsen, and particularly in a play that ends with a slamming door, such a conclusion would be hasty and premature. What must not be overlooked, once the pattern of entrances and exits is observed, is that Nora's exit at the end of the play is not only an ending of one element of the play's action, it is a continuation of another. And if we see at the end a rebellious Nora launching herself towards individuality and freedom, we might wonder about the implication that she seems to be beginning by following a much-travelled route. To pluck her exit from the context of the play is to see it as a spectacularly singular event; to place it in the context of the play, with its insistent focus on exits and entrances, is to see it as significantly like, as well as unlike, the exits that have preceded hers.

It would, of course, be dangerous to place too much emphasis on a single detail in interpreting a play. But early attention to this persistently fore-grounded detail and to its possible implications serves two purposes: it draws attention to the fact that something rather different is occurring in Ibsen's stage sets and plays from what is the case with Pinero's, and it provides an immediate link between this play and the larger issues we have discussed as characteristic of modern plays in general. The several doors of this set and the repeated exits and entrances draw attention to the importance of the margins of this domain, to what it includes and what it excludes, and what it means for Nora to enter it and leave it. These issues may, in turn, help us to recognize that the play's insistent focus on the margin of the dramatized domain may have major consequences for our notion of the kind of play this is. For what the title of the play directs our attention to is not the heroine of the action, but the arena in which the action is located.

As it stands, the English title of the play suggests that the scene of the action is a house belonging to, or at least most closely associated with, the doll-figure of Nora. From time to time, various scholars have registered dissatisfaction with the English title, and Rolf Fjelde, in his translation of the play, has preferred to render it *A Doll House*. This translation has not yet caught on, but Fjelde's point seems accurate enough: 'Aiming for . . . universality of reference, Ibsen titled his play *Et dukkehjem* – *A Doll House*, without the possessive 's.'[5] Haugen, also discussing the English title, takes the point even further: 'In spite of the English translations, this title does not mean a house for dolls, which in Norwegian is *dukkehus*, or *dukkestue*. Before Ibsen, *et dukkehjem* was a small, cozy, neat home; his play gave it the pejorative meaning.'[6] Haugen's comment serves to remind us that translations are always, to some extent, interpretations, and if our interpretations change, we may well find that possibilities overlooked in early translations become of some importance in later ones. But it should also make us aware that even in the original language, the title of the play which helps to constitute the meaning of the rest of the play has its meaning, in turn, partly constituted by the rest of the play. As Haugen puts it, 'his play gave it the pejorative meaning'.

We should not, therefore, feel we are helplessly in the hands of translators. Meaning accumulates via a variety of mutually defining details and, if we pay careful enough attention, we will be able to locate the major channels through which meaning flows. The play's insistent focus on doorways leads us to a reconsideration of the importance of the heroine, the importance of the house, and the significance of the title. And this, in turn, makes us more sensitive to comments like the one Meyer offers in passing, that we might wish to consider further the fact that 'fifty years ago Gunnar Heiberg (a distinguished director of Ibsen's plays) pointed out how important it is when staging *A Doll's House* that the audience should have the feeling that a *home* is being broken up.'[7]

Heiberg's comment has considerable support in the dialogue as the issue of a happy home is raised repeatedly (e.g. by Torvald (p. 203), by Nora (p. 216), by Mrs Linde (p. 266), by Rank (p. 271)). And when Nora's relationship with Torvald begins to founder, she characterizes their marriage in ways that startle Torvald, but are consistent with the emerging pattern we have located:

> NORA: [Daddy] used to call me his baby doll, and he played with me as I used to play with my dolls. Then I came to live in your house. . . .
> HELMER: What way is that to talk about our marriage? (p. 280)

Nora can speak of it like that, of course, because coming into this house has become for her, and for the play, emblematic of a way of life that in part defines and is in part defined by the domain in which the marriage is conducted.

To recognize this is to recognize a ground for comparison with Pinero's *The Second Mrs. Tanqueray*. That play, too, makes use of the stage set as an emblem of a limiting way of life. But the resemblance does not end there; and if we are to gain an adequate understanding of the originality of Ibsen's play, and of the larger significance of an Ibsen set (a significance which will justify the detailed attention we have begun to give it), then we must first recognize the large element of conventionality upon which that originality stands. And like so many dramatists of that era, Ibsen, wherever else he subsequently goes, starts from the standard dramatic pattern of the day, that of the well-made play.

The relationship between the structure of Ibsen's plays and the structure of the well-made play has been much discussed. It is well known that Ibsen spent ten years, from 1851 to 1862, directing and producing plays in Bergen and Oslo. Prominent among these were well-made plays of the French theatre, and there seems no reason to doubt that for Ibsen, as for every other playwright of the era, the well-made play provided a touchstone for received knowledge of stagecraft.[8] Ibsen, however, manages simultaneously to preserve and reform so many of the major components of the well-made play that confusion often ensues. To some, he continues to seem a very old-fashioned playwright; to others, he seems so radically new that 'he is not just the "father of the modern drama" – he *is* the modern drama, the most representative dramatist of our age.'[9] Such disagreement registers the importance of both conventionality and originality in Ibsen's stagecraft and suggests we consider the possibility that the conventionality is not a matter of unexamined habit but as much a matter of deliberate choice as the originality. Ibsen's stagecraft is so complex, however, and the readiness to criticize it for the seeming simplicity of its well-made components so prevalent, that consensus of interpretation is very difficult to establish. With *A Doll's House*, in particular, the degree of disagreement is considerable and no movement towards consensus is discernible – but a glance at two of its major features will provide a means of approaching the play that will clarify its significance and the function within it of Ibsen's fruitful combination of conventionality and originality.

In many discussions of the play, criticism tends first to focus on Nora and the significance of her actions, but questions raised there seem to lead inexorably towards the more basic question of the kind of play this is. Northam worries about whether it is best regarded as a comedy, a problem play, or a tragedy.[10] Shaw rejects all established classifications in favour of a new one: the discussion play, which revises the well-made-plot structure of Exposition, Complication, Crisis and Resolution into one of Exposition, Complication, Crisis and Discussion.[11] Williams rebuts Shaw's argument by pointing out that the final conversation between Nora and Torvald is more of a confrontation than a negotiation, more of a declaration than a discussion. He suggests, instead, that this clash between representatives of fixed ideas shows that the play remains an abstract drama of intrigue, an impoverished 'thesis' play or 'problem' play, one which provides only a diagrammatic clash between stereotyped characters.[12] Williams thus saves the play from dismissal as a failed discussion play by reinterpreting it as a failed problem play, for no complex human problem, he believes, can be satisfactorily explored by characters who register little internal complexity. Nora's originality is simply that of the anti-type, not of the rounded and complex character.

Williams's criticism of the play thus returns us to the recurring problem of the relationship between character type, plot structure, and play classification. But the way in which he poses the problem is useful, for it takes us back to a problem Ibsen shares with Pinero and, though Williams does not see it as such, forward to a new resolution of it. Ibsen, Williams notes, seems to believe that 'Nora and Torvald and Krogstad and Rank can function *simultaneously* as the stock figures of romantic melodrama and of the problem play.'[13] This, for Williams, is the key indication of Ibsen's inadequate stagecraft in *A Doll's House*: Ibsen, he feels, has failed to choose between two incompatible kinds of character. In terms of our discussion, the issue is one we have already encountered in Pinero's work. The characters' typological limitations seem to set complementary limitations upon their ability to discuss or embody complex thematic concerns. Problems seen through the eyes of such characters can only be reduced to polarized simplicities. But if we accept, as we must, that issues seen through the eyes of Nora and Torvald are simplified and distorted by their character limitations, we might then go on to ask just how much the play depends upon what is seen through their limited and limiting eyes.

What is seen through their eyes is neither very striking nor very original. Furthermore, the events of the play, as perceived by them, look very much like the events of a well-made play. Though they might disagree on some details, the action of the play, seen in their terms, exhibits a pattern that could have been constructed by any one of a number of hack playwrights. The Exposition informs us that a loving, but highly conventional, husband has worked hard to build a happy, but limited, home life around a vivacious, but frivolous, wife. His protectiveness of her is matched by her protectiveness of him, and when his conventionality threatens his health, she risks forgery to save him. The Complication is that she has had to repay the money the forgery gained her, and the villain to whom she owes the money has discovered the forgery just when she was about to complete the payments. The Crisis arrives when the villain begins to blackmail her, and it reaches a climax when he reveals the hidden secret to the husband and seeks to blackmail him too. As a result, both husband and wife discover that the other's loving protectiveness has disappointing limitations, and they quarrel and part. The conventional reconciliation is missing; instead the wife rejects the husband on the grounds that they have never understood each other. Furthermore, she claims to have spent much of her married life playing roles to amuse her husband, instead of being treated by him as an equal individual. But more than one commentator has ventured to suggest that the reconciliation has simply been delayed, and that Nora is likely to reopen, in the near future, the door she so precipitately closes behind her.[14]

But to look at the play in this light is to focus primarily on the major characters, and to ignore the pattern of events that has already led us to focus, as the play's title might suggest, on the significance of the domain, its margins and its repeatedly foregrounded doorways. But if we take our eyes, for a moment, off Torvald and Nora, and if we look to see what they may well not see, we begin to put ourselves in a position to understand the new use that Ibsen was able to make of the conventional trappings of the well-made play. Where Pinero uses the comparatively simple device of confronting the action with a deceptively reliable observer, Ibsen uses a much more complex set of contributing perspectives to enlarge and amplify the perspectives provided by the two major characters. It is already well known that the motifs of the tarantella and the Christmas tree, and the notions of disease, inheritance and disguise are all contributing factors in the play. What is not so well known is precisely how they work, what they mean, and what their contribution is to the play.

Northam is undoubtedly the person we must thank for a landmark discussion of the ways in which non-verbal factors operate in Ibsen's plays. And several of these factors are of particular importance to our discussion. Northam describes for us a set of techniques which contribute to our understanding of Ibsen plays in general and of *A Doll's House* in particular. These include the following: (1) illustrative action, such as Nora's eating macaroons and dancing the tarantella; (2) stage properties, such as the Christmas tree and the change from light to dark at various points in the play; (3) costume; (4) parallel situations shared by main characters and minor characters.[15] It is certainly important for these elements of the play to be made the object of study, but Northam's framework for utilizing them is, at times, rather restricting. On the one hand, he tends to interpret each element individually rather than as part of a network, and, on the other hand, in spite of avowedly different aims, he relies on a terminology ('illustrative' and 'parallel') that treats these elements as if their major function were to reinforce or extend, rather than to revise, the significance of information garnered from other aspects of the play. This approach to the function of visual detail invites the criticism that the visual elements offer mere restatement of matter already embodied in the dialogue.[16] But Ibsen's images are not mere parallels, or illustrations, or equivalent analogies. Rather, they function as *interpretative analogies*, i.e. visual and verbal motifs which suggest a way of interpreting what is said in the dialogue. In effect, they provide new perspectives on, and new clarifications of, the significance of what the characters say. And if this can indeed be shown to be true in *A Doll's House*, we have taken an important step towards providing an answer to the question of how Ibsen can use conventional situations and stereotyped characters, yet still allow the play to transcend the limited and limiting perspectives they initially provide. And such a recognition can help us establish the full significance of the play's insistent focus on the arena of the action and its ubiquitous doorways.

A comparison between the sets of Pinero's and Ibsen's plays provides an instructive perspective. The sets of Pinero's plays are designed primarily to make the on-stage mirror a convincing reflection of that part of the off-stage world it seeks to represent. In *The Second Mrs. Tanqueray*, the set functions as background, as a way of locating the foreground in a specific time and place. The drawing-room furniture is designed to make the audience aware that this is a drawing-room, that the residents have a certain social status, a certain degree of wealth, and a consequent attitude to social and moral values. Here we do indeed have something akin to illustrative background, as the playwright's gloss on the scene in the penultimate sentence makes quite clear: '*Aubrey Tanqueray's Chambers in the Albany – a richly and tastefully decorated room, elegantly and luxuriously furnished. . . . Everything in the apartment suggests wealth and refinement. The fire is burning brightly.*'[17]

It should be noted that there is nothing wrong with using sets in this way; Ibsen does it too. The point is that Ibsen's sets and stage properties frequently do other things as well – an indication that while Pinero often seeks to use the on-stage mirror primarily as a mirror, Ibsen frequently wishes to make complex use of the selectivity of the mirror as a means of illuminating the world it also reflects.[18] And Ibsen achieves this by making some aspects of the background become themselves part of the foreground; they serve not merely to reinforce knowledge made manifest elsewhere in the play, but to provide knowledge that is not necessarily available elsewhere at all.

It is in this respect that elements from the well-made play that serve in such plays as illustrative background can serve simultaneously in Ibsen's plays as mimetic and expressive features. Fjelde, noting his debt to Northam in arriving at this recognition, makes a strong case for

> what it was Ibsen's genius to discover, namely, that the stagecraft of the theater of realism could be transformed into metaphors for the condition of modern man. The bold insight that gave him the stylistic solution to his later plays struck to the very root of the medium: all dramatic art, even the most literally realistic, could ultimately be seen as – to adapt Fergusson's phrase – an idea *in* a theater . . . he taught himself, and a few others, *to see through the outward object*. The implications of this approach are only beginning to be explored in Ibsen criticism. (emphasis mine)[19]

Fjelde's comment links nicely to the notion of the theatre as independent ground of knowing that has been a major concern of this book, and to the notion that the persistent foregrounding of doorways in *A Doll's House* is not a matter of mere stage mechanics. Rather, the realistically mimetic elements of Ibsen's plays serve simultaneously to reflect the world off-stage and to contribute a perspective to it. We both look *at* and '*through* the outward object', through the domain of the action, and as we look through it, Nora, interestingly enough, passes through it, entering by the main door at the beginning, and leaving by it at the end. But to understand precisely what we see as a result of this process, we must recognize that the verbal and visual motifs of the play function not independently of each other, but in terms of mutual interaction and reciprocal definition.

The very first sentence in *A Doll's House* demonstrates this process at work.

Nora, we have noted, makes an extended entrance through the main doorway, and then addresses a seemingly innocuous instruction to the maid: 'Hide the Christmas tree away carefully, Helene. The children mustn't see it till this evening when it's decorated (p. 201). The Christmas tree, we recall, is, at this point, visible in the hallway and framed by the door to the inner room. The tree is there in part because it is Christmas Eve, but it rapidly takes on other values – values that provide immediate indications of why the tree is initially framed in the doorway of Nora's home. For Northam, these are primarily reinforcing values, registering in one visual symbol the notions dramatized in character interaction – family happiness, celebration and security. He also notes that when Nora later feels threatened, she asks for the Christmas tree to be placed in the middle of the room where she can decorate it and at the same time feel reassured of the values it represents. And when Nora later becomes even more insecure, and slightly desperate, the Christmas tree again appears, this time stripped of its finery and with its candles all burnt out (p. 235). Northam then asks us to note the way in which the tree externalizes the shifts in Nora's moods, and the way in which it functions negatively now as 'the symbol of family security'.[20] All of this seems quite convincing and serves to make an immediate distinction between Ibsen's stagecraft and that of Pinero. But what we also need to take into account are the ways in which the Christmas tree contracts relationships with other parts of the play – in particular the way it functions as part of an extensive network of related visual and verbal motifs.

The Christmas tree, we should note, is dressed and then stripped – which links it with the later fancy-dress ball and the costume Nora first dons and later discards. The tree is also to be hidden until it is dressed, so that the children do not see it in its non-dressed form. The 'real' tree for the children is to be the dressed tree, not its unadorned version. And this links the notion of dress and costume to that of deception and masquerade, which in turn links with Nora's deception of Torvald about borrowing money and Dr Rank's disguising for twenty long years his true feelings for Nora. This, in turn, makes us aware that some kinds of deception, like hiding the unadorned Christmas tree, can be for potentially good purposes. The ambivalent value thus attributed to deception later interacts with Nora's lying in general, with her role playing for a variety of purposes, and with Mrs Linde's unhappy solution of honesty as the best policy in improving Nora's and Torvald's relationship. The ambivalent value thus attributed to both deception and honesty then leads to other ambiguous values in the play and makes us wonder why we have a character who is both doctor and patient, why we have a villain who wishes only to be a good man, why we have a bad husband who wishes only to be a good husband, and why we have the tarantella, with its dual implications of potential cure and warning symptom of potentially fatal disease, and how the ambivalent value of spiders and their webs ('come into my parlour said the spider to the fly') might connect with the motif of the doll's house and with the ambivalent values of paradise and prison that Nora alternately attributes to it. And the ambivalent values of this home will, we suspect, at some point enable us to link the unadorned Christmas tree, framed in the doorway at the beginning of the play, with the figure of Nora, no longer in fancy dress, passing through the same doorway at the end of the play.

This is a fascinating network of interrelated verbal and visual images, and the network's seemingly autonomous components are so subtly interwoven that one can start from almost any part and make one's way to all of the others. The pluralistic values and pluralistic perspectives that hover on the edges of the action of Pinero's play thus find complex embodiment in the world of Ibsen's play. Pinero provides us with one initially privileged, and subsequently undermined, on-stage perspective to frame the well-made component of *The Second Mrs. Tanqueray*. Ibsen provides us, throughout the play, with a complex network of perspectives which is made up of a series of interpretative analogies, each of which sheds light on different aspects of the well-made component of *A Doll's House*.

This scattering of interpretative information is matched in the play by Ibsen's distribution of the role of the *raisonneur*. Instead of one single overall voice of authority, we have a series of characters who can make limited claims to the right to educate other characters (and the audience) about local situations. Torvald's experience of the banking world provides him a plat-form for instructing Nora on financial responsibility. Mrs Linde does likewise on the basis of social duty and family responsibility. Krogstad's experience with legal problems gives him a foundation for explaining to Nora (and the audience) the nature of her crime. Dr Rank's experience with illness and society justifies his lecturing Nora about the relationship between moral and physical degeneration. Even the old Nurse can tell Nora something about motherhood, of the way it feels to abandon one's children when necessity provides no other alternative. And a curious pattern is noticeable here: all of this information (with one notable exception) is directed at Nora. Small wonder then, that when Nora's way of life begins to disintegrate, in spite of the help and advice of this assembled band, she angrily rejects any further guidance and becomes her own *raisonneur* in the so-called discussion scene. And small wonder, too, that we, who have watched the action of the play and discovered the limited nature of each of the other characters' perspectives, initially sympathize with Nora's rebellious point of view, but finally begin to wonder whether this point of view, like all the other moralizing perspectives in the play, may also be based on the insecure foundation of premature certainty. And that process of persistently demonstrating the limitations as well as the validity of each character's knowledge and experience brings us back to the central role of the image network in the play. It is a network which, in a well-made world of limited perspectives and limited characters, provides the audience with knowledge and perspectives not fully available to any of the characters. It is in this sense that Ibsen successfully achieves what many felt was impossible: the successful use of conventional plot patterns and limited characters to explore issues more complex than any of the characters can fully understand.

To recognize this important fact is to begin to recognize what *A Doll's House* offers us in that seemingly innocuous opening scene. Nora, we recall, enters, bubbling with happiness, through the door of the house and brings with her a Christmas tree that remains framed in the doorway. *That doorway opens, for her, onto a house and a home that she values initially on the basis of one kind of certainty and rejects finally on the basis of another.* She passes through this domain from one kind of certainty to another, and her entrance and exit are thus both like and unlike those of the other characters, who also carry their dogmatic certainties with them. But, for the audience, the door that opens to reveal Nora also opens to reveal the Christmas tree. And its presence provides an immediate occasion for the raising of issues to do with deception, disguise and double values – issues that become central to the play. The door that opens upon Nora, and upon other characters who live by premature certainties and pragmatic deceptions, opens also for the audience upon the first embodiment of *the image network – a network, as we shall see, that trades, not upon premature certainties and the deceptions designed to sustain them, but upon doubt, doubleness and diversity.*

We thus turn, as we must, to a close look at the complex interaction in the play between its well-made components and the verbal and visual analogies that have twined themselves around the simple narrative action. And we might glance at once at the point of crisis in the well-made component of the play, to consider precisely what the crisis is that emerges from an action not fully understood by any of the characters. We should look with particular care at Nora's description of the basic problem she feels she has encountered in her life, and at the ways in which she describes its genesis and assigns blame for its persistence. And we should ask ourselves whether these are the views of someone who knows *what* it is that has gone wrong, or the views of someone who knows only *that* something has gone wrong.

If we look more carefully at Nora's claims, we find that they are not entirely consistent, and this itself should signal to us that her views stand in need of supplementation. Nora attacks Torvald at the end of the play for: a) having persistently played his masculine hero role, and b) not playing the role when she most wanted him to (by refusing to take the blame for the forgery). Nora then leaves, denying that she believes in miracles but basing much of her justification for leaving on the fact that Torvald hasn't provided one. These inconsistencies should lead us to regard with some suspicion the conclusions that Nora offers about the nature and genesis of her problems. And if we look closely at them, we find them less and less persuasive.

Nora's major accusation is directed against her husband and her father: 'I've been greatly wronged, Torvald. First by my father, and then by you' (p. 280). And she goes on to explain this as follows:

NORA: At home, Daddy used to tell me what he thought, then I thought
the same. And if I thought differently, I kept quiet about it, because
he wouldn't have liked it. He used to call me his baby doll, and he
played with me as I used to play with my dolls. Then I came to live in
your house. . . .

HELMER: What way is that to talk about our marriage?

NORA: [imperturbably] What I mean is: I passed out of Daddy's hands into
yours. You arranged everything to your tastes, and I acquired the
same tastes. Or I pretended to . . . I don't really know . . . I think it
was a bit of both, sometimes one thing and sometimes the other.
When I look back, it seems to me I have been living here like a
beggar, from hand to mouth. I lived by doing tricks for you,
Torvald. But that's the way you wanted it. You and Daddy did me a
great wrong. It's your fault that I've never made anything of my life.
(p. 280)

The argument here is by no means convincing. Nora seeks to blame her father
and her husband not just for the ways in which they wanted her to please
them, but also for the fact that she wanted to please them. This abdication of
responsibility for her own actions, whatever its partial truth, seems less than
the whole truth. If it came to a choice between pleasing them or disagreeing
with them, she preferred to please them, and this was presumably what
pleased *her* most. Furthermore, she is not entirely sure whether her tastes
tended to coincide with theirs or whether she simply pretended that they did.
And by this point in her argument, the implication is that to be guided or
moulded in any way by others is, of necessity, a bad thing, and something to
be blamed entirely upon those doing the moulding. These are large conclusions with large implications. But if we have watched with care the details of
the preceding action, we will be in a position to see that Nora's conclusions
are not the play's conclusions. There is evidence for Nora's position and
evidence against it, and the play invites us to consider the questions of
whether it is necessarily a bad thing to be moulded by others, and whether
Nora's father and husband were the prime moulders in her case.

To take the second question first, it is surely clear that Nora is misrep-
resenting the past as we have come to know it. Her life is not structured solely
by the wishes of either her father or Torvald. She herself makes the
distinction between people one loves and people one would rather be with
(p. 250). And as she is clearly acting upon this notion currently by spending a
lot of time with others, including Dr Rank, to whom this statement is
addressed, and as she has acted upon it in the past, when she was living with
her father, it is evident that there are and have been other major influences
on her life: 'When I was a girl at home, I loved Daddy best, of course. But I
also thought it great fun if I could slip into the maids' room' (p. 250). While
she does recall that one appeal of the servants was that they didn't preach at
her, she also recalls how exciting it was to hear them talk. And the
implication is that she learned from them – as she learned from the midwives

who helped deliver her children – ideas and attitudes somewhat at variance with those she learned from her father and her husband. What is at issue, then, is not just restricted knowledge, but the restricted use she chooses to make of her knowledge. And there the issue of moulding becomes not one of imposed patterns, but one of offered and accepted patterns.

Looked at in this light, the moulding then becomes not just a matter of coercion, but of selective and willing acceptance. And this selective acceptance is most persistently manifest in Nora's propensity for lying. The most obvious lie we are presented with early in the play is her fervent avowal that it would never occur to her to go against her husband's wishes (p. 205), even as she hides in her pocket a bag of the macaroons that he has forbidden her to bring into the house. In a play which deals with the ambivalent value of deception, we should not make too hasty a judgement about the moral implications of Nora's lies, but the point to be made here is simply that she goes along with Torvald's views only as far as it suits her and no further. She is just as ready to lie to Krogstad and to Dr Rank, and it is clear that she feels that a certain amount of deception is useful in dealing with men. Here again, one could ask whether this is the fault of the moulders or the moulded, and it is clear, by now, that the answer is by no means simple. Though the terminology is dated, it is difficult to reject entirely Weigand's contention that: 'Whatever the identity of her father, we have to watch her for only two minutes to know her as a daughter of Eve, adept in an infinity of little arts that make her irresistibly winsome to the masculine eye.'[21]

This perception is important because it forces us to recognize the limitations of Nora's final position, and to look elsewhere in the play for clarification of the issues raised. Nora's position is unpersuasive and could easily be reversed. She argues that her behaviour is the consequence of the attitudes of the men who moulded her. Is it not possible, we might wonder, that we could regard their behaviour as the natural consequence of hers? Nora's prime concern seems to be to please rather than to reach agreement and understanding. And that determination to please seems designed, at least in part, to get her what she wants without the need for agreement and understanding. We then end up with a complementary relationship between men and women in which each sex provides what the other seems to feel it needs, in order to manipulate it for its own purposes. And when the woman in this case not only declines to challenge the needs the men seem to manifest, but reinforces them by extensive pretence, it becomes apparent that her responsibility for the ensuing situation is no less than that of the men. Indeed, one could go one stage further and say that the men behave in these pompous, self-assertive, moralistic ways to compensate for the women's mercurial inconsistencies. It would then be the daughters of Eve who, by their characteristic behaviour, mould the sons of Adam.

The sheer inadequacy of this view of female responsibility in the play should serve to make us at least wary of the adequacy of Nora's counter-claims. But there is clearly some truth in both of these positions. And there is also some truth both in Nora's assertion that she is what she is because of what her father and husband have taught her, and in Weigand's assertion that Nora is what she is because of what she inherits from other women. What is missing is the generalization which covers both of these assertions, and which neither Nora nor Weigand provides for us. The key point is that whether Nora is primarily the daughter of her male relatives or the daughter of her female forebears, she is in either case someone whose way of life follows, in important ways, inherited rather than individual patterns. And it is this implication that is raised by Nora's determination at the end of the play not just to leave Torvald, but to 'learn to stand *alone*' (p. 281) (my emphasis). And if we wish to link the beginning of the play to the ending, we should note that the notion of inherited conventions is an overlooked implication of the Christmas tree framed so eloquently in the doorway of the doll's house at the beginning of the play. The tree is an inherited symbol, and Nora, by wishing to hide it from the children, and dress it for them, deals with it at the outset in inherited ways – ways not learned primarily from father or husband, but from society at large.

This recognition takes our argument forward in three different ways. First, in keeping with the notion of the distributed *raisonneur* in the play, the notion that inherited patterns of behaviour contribute to Nora's basic problem distributes across all of the characters vulnerability to this problem and responsibility for causing it (and presumably for curing it). Second, it provides us with a way of linking the question of responsibility for Nora's moulding with the question of whether this moulding is necessarily a bad thing. Third, it returns our attention to the domain in which the question is raised, and to the role of the image network in posing and answering it. And if we turn to the image network to discover how, in the light of our generalization about inheritance, we should view the process of social moulding, we will discover that what finally is at issue in the play is not, as Nora finally asserts, its avoidability, but its control.

To see how the image network guides us towards a recognition and understanding of the complexities of controlling and creatively adapting inherited views, we must remind ourselves of the notion that we not only see the well-made component of this play, we also see by means of it. And *this applies not only to the stage set and props, but to characters, too.* And we are led to a crucial component of the analogy network by the very sequence that Nora's argument follows when she announces her separation from Torvald. She is leaving, she says, because the one thing she must shake off is the influence of others, and in particular the influence of Torvald.

> NORA: I must take steps to educate myself. You are not the man to help me there. That's something I must do on my own. That's why I'm leaving you.
> HELMER: [*Jumps up*] What did you say?

NORA: If I'm ever to reach any understanding of myself and the things around me, I must learn to stand alone. (p. 281)

This determination to stand alone, be alone, educate oneself alone, sounds more convincing when one translates being alone as not being with Torvald. But when we recognize that the fundamental problem is not Torvald (he is only an instance of it) but inherited modes of behaviour, we must begin to wonder how alone Nora will have to be in order to educate herself anew. Does self-education require seeing no one at all? How then is she to learn anything she doesn't already know? And if being alone simply means being away from people like Torvald, where are the other people she hopes to meet? What she knows is, she claims, largely what she has learned from others and she now wishes to reject them for having taught her. The dilemma is apparent. There is nowhere to go. There is no place to be free from the constraining influence of others. As the repeated opening and closing of doors in the play has persistently revealed, an exit from one social domain is always the prelude to an entrance into another. The doors to the doll's house are not, in this respect, divisions between radically different domains. The process of social moulding is unavoidable. Nora is departing through a doorway that can only direct her back to the problem she wishes to escape. And there is much in the play that might make us wonder whether it would be a good thing to avoid such moulding even if one could. And it is here that the image network becomes central once more.

One of the major ironies of the play is Nora's somewhat inconsistent choice of staying her first night 'alone' with Mrs Linde (p. 281). But more than simple consistency is at issue here. If we have, by this point, learned to use interpretative analogies as ways of helping us see what Nora cannot see in the play, then we have noticed that one of the analogies to Nora's current position is that of Mrs Linde herself. Mrs Linde has already tried and tested the role of the relatively isolated female, and her experience with the world of solitariness has taught her not to follow Nora's current track, but to beat a hasty retreat to the world of shared, not solitary, experience. Describing her life after her escape from responsibility to husband, parents and younger siblings, Mrs Linde informs Nora, early in the play, of the feeling of sadness and uselessness that comes with such freedom.

MRS. LINDE: My poor dear mother doesn't need me any more, she's passed away. Nor the boys either; they're at work now, they can look after themselves.
NORA: What a relief you must find it. . . .
MRS. LINDE: No, Nora! Just unutterably empty. Nobody to live for any more. (p. 211)

The kind of freedom Nora seeks at the end of the play has thus already been tried and found wanting by the very person to whom Nora flees when she leaves Torvald. And if we are inclined to say it may yet be right for Nora, we have found our way to the heart of the dilemma the play seeks to dramatize. There is no guarantee that what is right for Mrs Linde will be right for Nora; nor is there any guarantee that it won't. There is every reason for an individual to assert his or her own claims to knowledge, but no reason to ignore the possibility of learning from others.

Mrs Linde's return to social life and social responsibilities is not to some ideal world that has been cleansed of inherited patterns and mutual moulding. Instead, it is a social world *within which* she is prepared to function, accepting both its moulding effects on her and the moulding effects she might have on others. Indeed, it is vital to note that she regards mutual moulding not, as Nora finally does, as a manifestation of social and individual repression, but as an opportunity for individual and social renewal. She hopes to set up just such a life with Krogstad, the putative villain of the play, with whom she proposes to live on the basis of need and being needed:

MRS. LINDE: now I'm completely alone in the world, and feeling horribly empty and forlorn. There's no pleasure in working only for yourself. Nils, give me somebody and something to work for. (p. 264)

And when Krogstad reminds her of the risk she takes with someone who has a criminal past, she responds quite positively with the belief that she can mould him anew: 'Just now you hinted you thought you might have been a different person with me' (p. 265). But the dialogue forging this new alliance on the basis of mutual moulding takes place, oddly enough (given the fact that neither character lives there) in the doll's house – in the very environment Nora is later to reject because she feels moulding is necessarily a negative constraint.

This emerging link between Krogstad/Mrs Linde and Torvald/Nora is given a direct but subtle manifestation when the conversation between Krogstad and Mrs Linde merges with the music from the dance upstairs at a point at which explicit mention is made of the particular kind of dance being performed:

KROGSTAD: I'm convinced I would.
MRS. LINDE: Couldn't it still happen?
KROGSTAD: Kristine! You know what you are saying, don't you? Yes, you do. I can see you do. Have you really the courage . . . ?
MRS. LINDE: I need someone to mother, and your children need a mother. We two need each other. Nils, I have faith in what, deep down, you are. With you I can face anything.
KROGSTAD: [*Seizing her hands*] Thank you, thank you, Kristine. And I'll soon have everybody looking up to me, or I'll know the reason why. Ah, but I was forgetting. . . .
MRS. LINDE: Hush! The tarantella! You must go!
KROGSTAD: Why? What is it?

MRS. LINDE: You hear that dance upstairs? When it's finished they'll be coming. (p. 265)

The words of Krogstad, deciding to make himself anew, vowing to forge himself a new image in the eyes of Mrs Linde and of others, merges with the activity of Nora upstairs, wearing fancy dress, dancing the tarantella, and trying desperately to find new images and new ways of using images to get herself out of her impending crisis. The comparison is clear, even though its implications are not yet fully apparent, but the episode indicates once more the persistent way in which character interaction leads the audience repeatedly to the image network to locate knowledge and perspectives beyond those recognized by the characters.

Taking our cue from the dialogue, we turn directly to the dance of the tarantella, and to another angle on the complex interaction of images in the play. Mention of the dance comes at precisely the point where we see the possibility of two characters moulding each other for the better – an event which thus coincides in time with a crisis which Nora later claims to have been caused by others moulding her for the worse. Her final demand that she be left fully alone to escape such moulding seems to have been persuasive to many; yet the woman to whom she goes on her first evening alone is the woman who is planning to restructure her lonely life on the basis of a mutual moulding with a marriage partner. The play seems to be taking two conflicting positions, that such moulding is bad, and that such moulding is good. And one of the functions of the tarantella analogy is to make us think about the Nora/Torvald relationship and its connection with the Mrs Linde/Krogstad relationship in ways that only this analogy and the others with which it interacts can suitably provide.

A glance at the dictionary suffices to set us on the route to clarification. The tarantula spider is reputedly poisonous, and anyone bitten by it is likely to contract the disease of tarantism. This is 'a hysterical malady, characterized by an extreme impulse to dance'. And the cure for this malady was held to be – dancing the tarantella. Thus, 'the dancing was sometimes held to be a symptom or consequence of the malady, sometimes practised as a sovereign cure for it.'[22] The symptom of the disease and the cure for the disease are one and the same. This conclusion is startling and paradoxical, but it provides the key to a resolution of competing truths in the play. The tarantella provides us with an analogy which allows Nora's fancy-dress ball, an extreme form of Torvald's moulding (Nora: 'Torvald, couldn't you give me some advice and tell me what you think I ought to go as, and how I should arrange my costume?' (p. 232)), to be seen as part of the same process of moulding that is to be instituted between Mrs Linde and Krogstad – yet still allow the former to retain its negative implications and the latter to claim more positive ones. The audience, guided by the image network, can begin to see what Nora is unable to see – that mutual moulding, like the dancing, can be for the good of the participants or for ill. And it is this generalization, not Nora's emotional demand that moulding cease altogether, that is offered by the analogy network as the key to the clarification of the issues Nora raises.

We have now taken two steps towards an understanding that escapes both Nora and Torvald. First of all, the basic problem is not that Torvald and her father have invidiously moulded Nora, but that everyone learns by, and must take responsibility for, selectively adopting and testing out inherited attitudes and inherited roles. And because these are inherited, there is no escaping them without escaping people altogether, including oneself. The notion that Nora advances of being alone to become 'an individual' person is in fact only a programme for becoming a non-person. The second step is that, though this inescapable mutual moulding is certainly dangerous – there is always the possibility of successfully fulfilling an inherited role but failing to fulfil oneself – the moulding can nevertheless be constructive: it can provide access to new ways of being when those currently offered are inadequate. The fundamental issue is not, as Nora believes, one of moulding or not moulding, but one of controlling the moulding (as Krogstad and Mrs Linde plan to do) for constructive and self-fulfilling purposes. And with that generalization we can begin to understand why Ibsen offered so much resistance to the notion that he had written a play about women's rights. As he pointed out in his celebrated speech to the Norwegian League for Women's Rights in 1898,

> I thank you for the toast, but must disclaim the honor of having consciously worked for the women's rights movement. I am not even quite clear as to just what this women's rights movement really is. To me it has seemed a problem of mankind in general.[23]

The problem of inherited moulding is not a woman's problem only, but a human problem. And it is a problem with which every character in the play has had to grapple.

Nora herself almost recognizes this when she notes that she has contributed to the transmission of inherited patterns of behaviour as much as she has been the victim of them. And her description of this process makes the analogy of the doll's house, as our earlier discussion of the play's title suggested, spread far beyond the notion of Nora as the only doll in the play, and far beyond the notion that the Helmer household is the only doll's house in the society in which it is placed.

> NORA: You've always been so kind to me. But our house has never been anything but a play-room. I have been your doll wife, just as at home I was Daddy's doll child. And the children in turn have been my dolls. I thought it was fun when you came and played with me, just as they thought it was fun when I went and played with them. That's been our marriage, Torvald. (pp. 280–1)

Nora, horrified at the results of these pleasurable activities, overlooks what the informed audience will not now overlook – that the fun and games, like the tarantella dance and the notion of moulding, can be both symptom and cure for the disease of limitation caused by inherited behaviour patterns. But Nora's determination to see these things now as solely evil is to miss as much as she missed earlier when she saw them as solely good. There are things to be lost as well as things to be gained by leaving the doll's house – a point prepared for at the outset when Nora enters happily at the beginning through the door she leaves unhappily by at the end. And what her comments also make clear is that the evil and the good which such games might cause are distributed across generations, across the society in general, and across the sexes in particular. Two of the chidren she now treats as dolls are boys (Ivar and Bob) and it is obviously important to note that Torvald and her father and Krogstad and Rank were all someone's doll children somewhere at some time. The putative villains are all prospective victims too.

The importance of this point is made clear when Nora mentions the Christmas presents she has bought for her children: 'Look, some new clothes for Ivar . . . and a little sword. There's a horse and a trumpet for Bob. And a doll and a doll's cot for Emmy' (p. 203). While it is the daughter who gets the doll, the presents bought for the sons are no less emblematic of inherited patterns of behaviour. And we perceive the long-term dangers of such influences on male behaviour in the bombastic moral posturing of both Torvald and Dr Rank as they don their inherited masks and act out their inherited roles. The doll's house embraces them as much as it embraces Nora, and the behaviour of all three becomes emblematic of inadequate roles and inherited views. The doll's house is full of doll people, and the image of a doll's house suggests the limited stature, limited knowledge and limited perspectives of everyone in it – including the one who speaks most forcefully against it. One of the many ironies of the play is that Nora's formulation for pointing out the dangers of inherited behaviour patterns is itself inherited – from her father who 'used to call me his baby doll' (p. 280).

Such ironies serve to make clear the difficulty of ever escaping inherited roles and inherited values, and the reason Ibsen could so readily utilize stereotyped and limited characters in this play. These characters are not, as Williams suggested, antithetical to any sophisticated exploration of the play's complex themes – rather they are, in their typologically limited roles, illuminating examples of people suffering from and struggling with and against the disease of inherited behaviour and inherited values. And the play's undermining of Nora's rebellion against such patterns is a subtle but striking manifestation of the way in which symptom can masquerade as cure. The attitudes she expresses in the concluding discussion are no less symptomatic of disease than those expressed earlier. And the distribution of the role of *raisonneur*, which provides a variety of similar instances, demonstrates the extensiveness and persistence of misplaced solutions for misunderstood problems. But it is now important to recognize how carefully Ibsen sets up the role of the traditional *raisonneur* in the play so that its strengths and weaknesses and, by extension, those of the other major characters, can be better understood.

As family friend and confidant of both Nora and Torvald, Dr Rank is the most obvious candidate in the play for the role of the privileged *raisonneur*. [24] He follows the tradition instituted by Scribe and narrowed by Dumas to the medical family friend who provides an independent and knowledgeable perspective on family affairs. [25] By using Rank not just as a constituent of the plot, but also as a component of the image network, however, Ibsen is able to foreground one aspect of the traditional *raisonneur*'s role and exploit it to shed further light on the relationship, in the play, between possible solutions and potential problems. Rank, not untypically, claims to speak for the best interests of 'society' (p. 219), and his high moral tone generates windy abstractions and unyielding moral judgements (Krogstad, he declares, is 'rotten to the core' (p. 218)). But the doctor in this play is himself sick and unable to cure his own disease – a disease that is important to the play in its genesis, symptoms and putative processes of treatment and cure.

Rank, as both doctor and patient of his own physical disease, is suffering from an inherited physical malady of a diseased spine, and it is also clear that he is suffering from an inherited psychological illness of rigid and narrow views. But it is the interaction between the two illnesses that clarifies their contribution to the image network. In his role as doctor, Rank takes what inherited wisdom establishes as the most basic step in curing any disease – studying the symptoms to arrive at certainty about their nature. And it is in terms of the notion of certainty that Rank as doctor and patient contributes to the larger patterns of the play.

In his final meeting with Nora and Torvald, Rank reports on the results of his medical investigation:

> NORA: And may I congratulate you on the result?
> RANK: You may indeed.
> NORA: So it was good?
> RANK: The best possible, for both doctor and patient – certainty.
> NORA: [*quickly and searchingly*] Certainty?
> RANK: Absolute certainty. (p. 271)

The word 'certainty' is repeated three times, the final time as 'absolute certainty' about the nature, extent and inevitable result of the disease. But instead of being potentially beneficial, this certainty, based upon what inherited medical wisdom has to offer, provides only the recognition that nothing beneficial in the way of a cure for Dr Rank's physical disease is available. Actions deriving from inherited values generate Rank's disease, and actions based solely upon inherited wisdom provide the conclusion that there is no cure for it. Within the well-made component of the play, that is all the characters know. But we who have encountered the dangers of premature certainty and inherited wisdom elsewhere in the play can recognize at once the mingling of cause, symptom and cure that have become characteristic of a play in which the doctor is terminally ill. Rank's psychological illness, like his physical illness, derives from his father's certainties and continues with his own. The play's reiteration of 'certainty' as the doctor/patient's most basic value is a crucial link in the image chain that repeatedly undermines the certainties of one character after another.

Rank's presence in the play is thus a vital one because he functions not only as a character within the well-made component of the play, but also as an analogy in the play's image network. We both look at him and through him; we both see him and see by means of him. We recognize that Torvald is like him in adhering to inherited certainties and that Krogstad is unlike him when, under the moulding influence of Mrs Linde, he invests in the possibility that established truths are not the only possible truths. And we see that Nora is, in important ways, like and unlike him, too. Nora has no inherited physical illness to cope with but she does have an inherited psychological illness, and she is as much is need of a cure as is Rank. The need for an accurate understanding of what ails her, of what has gone wrong with her life, is just as much a prerequisite for the cure of her illness as it would be for any physical ailment. What is right about Nora's final position is that she recognizes precisely that. What is wrong with it is that, at the end of the play, as at the beginning, Nora allows partial understanding to masquerade as certainty. She leaves to find knowledge, understanding and certainty about herself and her illness. But the play has already undermined the value of a pursuit of certainty that bases itself upon an assumption of certainty. The 'discussion' which degenerates into declamation reveals the implicit continuity of behaviour when a type-character seeks freedom by becoming simply an anti-type, and thus as much defined by opposing the past as she had earlier been by conforming to it. With Nora, as with Rank, we both see her and see by means of her. And what we see is an example of that premature certainty which is the ready measure of the stock character – someone who has not learned how to doubt constructively and thus has not learned how to grow.[26]

This recognition helps us avoid some of the misleading emphases that have emerged in critical approaches to the play. The concern for Nora at the expense of the other characters has not been helpful. The similarities and contrasts between her life and those of the other characters are fundamental to the play – a point reinforced by the distribution of the role of the *raisonneur* in the play. All have areas of expertise, all have points of view, all suffer and benefit from inherited roles and inherited values. The cure for this social disease is not withdrawal from the transmitter of the disease – society – but appropriate understanding of society and of the provisional, rather than unquestioning, use that must be made of its inherited wisdom. This play is not to be reduced to the cliché that Ibsen (like many other playwrights) is letting us know that there is an inevitable conflict between individuals and society, or between the present and the past. Rather, he is dramatizing and clarifying specific aspects of the subtle processes by which socially inherited views impose themselves upon individuals, even as some individuals set out to reject or transcend them. It is the difficulty of escaping the influence of inherited views, and the insidiousness of the ways in which they make themselves felt, that Ibsen seeks to portray – in particular the ways in which inherited views can masquerade as individual views, and the ways in which the symptoms of inherited disease and the treatment of inherited disease become so similar that the one can easily be confused with the other.

The image network, however, enables us to envisage, not a solution to the problem, but a means of controlling it for constructive social and individual purposes. It enables us to see doubt where characters see only certainty, to recognize possibilities for constructive change where characters can see only conformity or chaos. Nora's diagnosis of her problem is to be admired for its daring and originality, but to be criticized for its inconsistency, its premature certainties, and its consequent limited recognition of what might be learned from Mrs Linde and others, i.e. from part of the very society she rejects when she sets off to learn on her own. For Torvald and Rank, social masquerade seems largely evil because they see little of their own use of it. For Nora, social masquerade has been a deliberate habit; now it is rejected because she regards it as capable only of serving the unsatisfactory ends it has already served for her. For Mrs Linde and Krogstad, investment in masquerade is the first step towards making a partial truth about Krogstad (his goodness) into the major functioning truth – a process that ironically parallels, even as it reverses, the very process by which he once came to be regarded as a criminal and nothing else.

The play provides us with three groups of characters, but it does not ask us to find all of the truth and rightness in any one of these positions. All of the characters remain dolls – limited by inherited experience and by the ways in which personal experience has affected their estimate of inherited experience. The malady of the limited perspective afflicts them all. It is for this reason that the play title draws attention to a common domain, and not just a single character's domain. Those who have elevated Nora's perspective at the end of the play have overlooked much of what the other characters are doing and saying, and much of what Nora herself does and says, both early in the play when she is certain she is in paradise and late in the play when she is certain she is in prison. As the play moves from Nora's entrance into the doll's house to Nora's exit from it, she moves from one kind of premature certainty to another. The doll's house, as a variety of details demonstrates, participates in the image network as one more double-valued component. The games, deceptions and masquerades that occur there can be used for good or for ill. Nora is right at the beginning when she sees the good things in the doll's house, and right at the end when she sees the bad. She is wrong at the beginning when she sees only the good things, and wrong at the end when she sees only the bad. But the audience, both seeing Nora and seeing by means of her, can perceive her experience, via the image network, as one in which disease and cure mix and mingle. It is, the play recognizes, in the nature of society to reinforce rather than undermine the commonplaces that bind it together, but it is, as Mrs Linde and Krogstad demonstrate, only in and through society that such commonplaces can be partially transcended. But if there is no quick or radical solution available to the characters in the on-stage world, that very fact, suitably dramatized, can illuminate the same problem in a similar society in the world off-stage. And Ibsen's network of visual and verbal analogies makes it possible for the world off-stage to look for diagnoses and treatments that go largely undiscovered by those in the world on-stage.

The play, in one sense, does no more than send us looking, but it does offer guidance as to the usefulness of differing kinds of looking. Were it to provide a definitive solution to the problems it raises, it would, of course, fall foul of the very difficulties it sets out to dramatize. Its certainties would become the inherited beliefs of the next generation, the commonplaces and received ideas of a new generation of Helmers and Ranks. Social problems, as this play dramatizes them, are not susceptible to fixed solutions nor treatable by new sets of fixed ideas. Indeed, such solutions and ideas are as likely to become manifestations of the problems as they are to become cures for them. But the play is not advocating as a solution Nora's rejection of what society has to offer.[27] The play thus includes a well-made component that displays inherited truths and characters constrained by them, and an image network that gives the audience, but not the major characters, awarenesses that help control and transcend them. The structure of the play is neither one of simple narrative progression (Exposition, Complication, Crisis, Resolution) nor one of progressing revelation (Exposition, Complication, Crisis, Discussion). It makes use of elements of tragedy, comedy, problem play, discussion play and well-made play, but it is not circumscribed by any of these categories. It is, instead, a play that forges an original synthesis from inherited elements and new components. The fundamental structural interaction between an inherited well-made-play plot, on the one hand, and a novel network of interpretative analogies, on the other, embodies the very theme the play seeks to dramatize.[28] The individual, like the playwright, must seek the same creative linkage between conventional and original ideas, between inherited and idiosyncratic goals.

By sharing with us the task of further exploring the issues raised in the play, Ibsen is consistent with the larger implications of his image network. What frames and qualifies the well-made component of this play is not the single image of the unreliable *raisonneur* that we encountered in *The Second Mrs. Tanqueray* along with a challenge to the audience to come up with alternative wisdom, but a complex set of mutually defining images that require complex interpretative work by the audience. Instead of being invited to 'see' the action through the eyes of a particular character, we are invited to see more than any of the characters sees, by looking at and through the image network. The play thus extends the ways of knowing characteristic of nineteenth-century theatre and thereby adjusts both the kind of information to be gained from a play and the appropriate kind of audience participation in it.

The imagistic component of the play thus has epistemological consequences, for it enables the play to challenge not only our received ideas, but also our notion of the role of received and new ideas in our lives. Such changes have important implications for the social function of the theatre. With Ibsen's work, we take a large step towards understanding an evolving conception of modern drama, one in which the drama serves, not as a repository of received and summarizable truths, nor as a dispenser of social slogans or social programmes, but as an incitement to exploration and inquiry. This inquiry explores new possibilities in the generic nature of the on-stage world, as a means of shedding new light on the nature of an off-stage world which it not only selectively reflects, but also aggressively confronts, challenges and illuminates.

7 Strindberg:
A Dream Play

To think of the drama more as a mode of inquiry than as a means of instruction is to take an apparently small but vital step. One can learn from inquiry as one can learn from instruction, but there is an important difference in the status of the results and, as a consequence, in the means of pursuing those results. The drama of inquiry concedes in advance the provisional nature of its discoveries and the problematic status of its methods. It is the drama of the pluralistic universe, in which fundamental and unchanging values give way to possible and pragmatic values. Ibsen's dramatization of the dangers of inherited certainties cannot conclude with a new set, for they would, in turn, be undermined by their status as inherited certainties in any subsequent use of them. The drama of inquiry and exploration does not exclude the possibility of pragmatically grounded stopping-points, but it does exclude the possibility of ultimate stopping-points. Thus, when Strindberg, in his highly experimental *A Dream Play*, confronts characters and audience with an ultimate question like 'the riddle of the world' (p. 78),[1] he quickly brings up against their limits the very freedoms that his new dramatic structure offers him.

Strindberg's determinedly innovative work naturally invites us to focus critical attention on the new opportunities that his experimentation offered him in the course of his long career, one 'in which he tried almost every theatrical style known to the modern theatre'.[2] But we must not overlook the fact that the constantly renewed urge towards further experimentation derives, in part, from the speed with which Strindberg discovered not just the possibilities, but also the liabilities of each new dramatic form. Strindberg's achievement in writing plays that continue to interest us is thus a consequence of his ability to put to good use the limitations as well as the new possibilities he encountered in his new dramatic and theatrical structures. And in A Dream Play, Strindberg's raising of an ultimate question in an avowedly idiosyncratic context is not simply a matter of a logical error in the world of the play, but a matter of embodying in the world of the play a dilemma that can also be traced in the modern history of the theatre and in the social world of the audience.

To say that the dilemma can be 'traced' in the world of the audience is to acknowledge that a play which asks us to do some creative thinking in order to understand it also asks us to do some creative thinking if we are to link its characters, actions and situations to those we encounter in the world off-stage. The well-made play's selective duplication of an aspect of the world off-stage did much of our thinking for us. It invoked a set of conventional values in conventional situations and measured everything on-stage and off-stage by them. This single set of values was challenged, as we saw, by Pinero's play, and radically undermined by Ibsen's, but it supplied a basic orientation to the action of both plays. Only so much, however, can be done with a creative utilization of the limitations of well-made conventions. And when dramatists seek radically to depart from the well-made format, they have to relinquish a solid footing in established theatrical and social traditions. For audiences watching the Pinero and the Ibsen plays, well-made conventions provide, if not a traditional conclusion, at least a familiar point of departure. For audiences watching Strindberg's play, the way in is as problematic as the way out, and the mode of interaction between the world of the play and the world of the audience is as much a matter for inquiry as is the nature of the play itself.

We have noted, however, the importance of margins, horizons and barriers, in the modern theatre, and we should not be surprised to find them as important in this play as in the others we have discussed. Nor should we be surprised to find that, in this radically experimental play, the edges of dramatized domains function, as our opening chapters suggested, as a means of providing the audience with an appropriate orientation to the action. But of the two major horizons of this play – the locked door and the painted wings – the former, not the latter, has been the major focus of attention for critics, as for characters. In theatre worlds based on homogeneous and readily accessible knowledge, it is a prudent activity for the audience to seek to share what the characters know or discover; in theatre worlds based upon pluralistic and not easily accessible knowledge, an audience that settles for knowing what the characters know is in danger of missing much of importance to a play. The characters and the action of A Dream Play may well focus at several points on the fascinating door with the clover-leaf hole in it, but those characters and that action are constantly framed for the audience by an unchanging border of oddly decorated wings. And if we are to derive more from the play than the characters do, we must seek to understand the function of that persistent stage border: 'The side wings which remain throughout the play *are stylized wall paintings, at the same time rooms, architecture, and landscapes'* (p. 22).

Instead of blending with any of the settings they frame, these wings seem to be a constant reminder of other possible locations. We could thus begin to think of them as emblems of variety hinting at the limitation of whatever lies within them. But an unchanging emblem of variety seems itself somewhat limited and even self-contradictory. We thus find ourselves forced to do some thinking about the possible function of the wings as an emblem of circum-scribed variety, what that range of variety might be, what it includes, and what it excludes. And these are, of course, precisely the things that the play's Prologue and prefatory note invite us to ponder, not just for the world of the play, but for its very nature as a play.

We may take the first issue first as it leads inexorably towards the second. And we can begin to consider what the painted wings include and exclude by looking closely at the Prologue, the play's opening scene. This is the only scene that is not framed by the painted wings, and it is located, we find, not on Earth, but somewhere above it:

> *Prologue. Cloud formations resembling castles and citadels in ruins on crumbling slate hills form the backdrop. The constellations Leo, Virgo, and Libra can be seen, and among them is the planet Jupiter shining brightly. Indra's Daughter is standing on the uppermost cloud.* (pp. 19–20)

We hear the Voice of Indra warning his Daughter not to stray too near Earth, the 'dark and heavy world' (p. 20). The Daughter has, he tells us, 'left the second world and gone into the third' (p. 20) and, as we watch, she continues to sink towards this other world of Earth. We hear, as the Daughter floats down towards it, that Earth is an unhappy planet, one with a dusty atmosphere and some beauty, but one which also bears the scars of some ancient cosmic accident:

INDRA'S DAUGHTER:	I see . . . it's beautiful . . . with green forests, blue waters, white mountains, and yellow fields. . . .
INDRA'S VOICE:	Yes, it's beautiful as everything Brahma created . . . but it was still more beautiful in the dawn of time; then something happened, a breakdown in its orbit, perhaps something else, a rebellion accompanied by crimes that had to be suppressed. (p. 21)

This Prologue is an interesting phenomenon, and it clearly functions as part of an explanatory frame for the action of the play, a means of orientating the audience towards the subsequent action.[3] This is, of course, an important component of a play so experimental in nature that it could quite easily lose its audience in a welter of disorientating confusion. In terms of the patterns we have been establishing in modern plays, it is not difficult to see that the Prologue is offering us a certain interpretative perspective; it is guiding the audience towards a position just beyond the horizon of the Earth. Instead of beginning the action within the world of Earth, the play begins outside the domain it is largely to portray. And it is in order to remind us that the play's action is occurring in an 'earthbound' (p. 70) domain that the play begins just outside that domain and frames its subsequent action with the unchanging wings of the set. The two domains, as so often in modern theatre, are distinct, but not wholly different, and what is important is the orientation of the audience towards the margins of these juxtaposed domains.

The Second Mrs. Tanqueray invites us into the world of the Tanquerays and leads us steadily towards its limiting horizons. *A Doll's House*, with its persistent focus on doors and doorways, guides us beyond the doll's house by means of an image network that lets the audience discover more than the characters know. Both plays invite us inside a domain and then guide us towards its horizons. *A Dream Play*, however, situates us from the beginning outside the margins of the domain it will predominantly dramatize. We begin with, rather than discover in the course of the action, the need for and the possibility of other worlds. And this perspective, this knowledge, however small, of the world beyond Earth, links the audience with the only character who shares this double perspective, the play's most puzzling character, the Daughter of Indra.

Many have noted and sought to explain the precise significance of the privileged relationship the Daughter contracts with the audience.[4] There is obviously a sense in which those in the audience might more readily align themselves with the other characters, those who, like themselves, live within the 'earthbound' frame. We will consider later the ways in which Strindberg's use of type-characters initially inhibits such an alignment, and continue, for a moment, to weigh the role of the Daughter. To anyone familiar with the nineteenth-century theatre and its tradition of establishing one character as a *raisonneur*, the role of the Daughter is at once familiar and unusual. The Daughter is the privileged character, the one whose views assume, for the audience, an authority not granted to those of other characters. But instead of the *raisonneur* being (like Drummle or Rank) at home in the society of the play, she is a stranger to it, someone whose authority is based less on a knowledge of this world, than on an assumed capacity to acquire it. We thus have in this drama of inquiry, a *raisonneur* who functions less as the voice of established wisdom, and more as the voice of enlightened investigation. But a major irony emerges in this context: though the Daughter enters the Earth-world on a mission of inquiry, she is immediately treated, because of her transcendent perspective, as if she were already an authority on this world and others. The inquirer comes to be regarded as a sage; the audience's guide becomes, not just the potential discoverer of earthly knowledge, but the potential source of transcendent knowledge. Built into the character of the Daughter is a radical dilemma that inhabits the whole structure of the play: is it seeking to reveal, via the Daughter, overlooked earthly truths, or is it seeking to establish new transcendent ones?

The issue is fundamental not just to this play, but to the whole notion of dream plays and expressionist plays. We have noted earlier that the world of the stage can seek to duplicate, to illuminate, or to replace the world off-stage; in doing so, it can establish its social function as one of reflecting established knowledge, revealing hidden but pre-existing knowledge, or creating new knowledge. These options are not, of course, mutually exclusive in any single play; but a recognition of the basic orientation of the play towards one or another goal is important to any attempt by the audience to come to terms with what it offers. But establishing this orientation in any consistent manner seems to have been peculiarly difficult for Strindberg. When we note the ambivalent status of the Daughter as investigator of existing truths or source of transcendent truths, we encounter an ambivalence that registers a tendency we have already noted – Strindberg's capacity to take a new form very rapidly to its limits, to the point at which it threatens to change its basic orientation and become another kind of play. But what is particularly important is the way in which the pattern of Strindberg's experimentation with different kinds of plays throughout his dramatic career can be regarded as exemplifying a larger pattern in modern theatre itself.

Benston makes the salient point that:

> If we trace the evolution of Strindberg's theatrical form, we have a perfect model of the contemporary dramatist's rejection of realism and return to stylized theater. His career offers a typical pattern: naturalism, symbolic naturalism, and, finally, the completely artificial structure of the poetic dream play. His work mirrors the kind of modern sensibility that has been the main impetus of theatrical experiments in our century.[5]

If we follow Benston, for the moment, and allow realism and naturalism an equivalent place in this trichotomy, we can readily note that Strindberg's corpus follows roughly the sequence we have already followed in moving from *The Second Mrs. Tanqueray*, through *A Doll's House*, to *A Dream Play*. The orientation of the drama shifts from selectively duplicating the off-stage world, to illuminating it via symbolic naturalism, and then to replacing it with an expressionist, and deliberately theatrical, drama. But two clarifications of these trends are needed. First, the three options are not mutually exclusive; they register differences of focus and not just differences of contrasting components. Second, the sequence does not end, as it does for Strindberg, with expressionism, dream plays, or highly stylized plays. After these orientations had been taken to an extreme by many turn-of-the-century dramatists, the territory thus acquired became the basis for extensive subsequent experimentation by dramatists who sought a variety of blends of the newly established (one might well say re-established) options. The sequence to which Benston draws attention is certainly visible in Strindberg's career and in the early development of the modern theatre, but, as a schema, it is incomplete. If we pursue it further, we will locate patterns of importance not only to the modern theatre, but to the nature and structure of Strindberg's puzzling *A Dream Play*.

To note a sequence in the development of creative options in some of the work of Strindberg and in some aspects of the modern theatre is to note, not a necessary sequence, but an important relationship between apparently opposed choices. A play exhibits not realism *or* theatricality, but differing and related kinds of realism *and* theatricality. A play is not naturalistic *or* symbolic, but orientates itself towards one or the other poles of off-stage representation and on-stage expressionism, and it can readily balance both in what Benston calls 'symbolic naturalism'. We thus bewilder ourselves unnecessarily when we struggle to find distinctive definitions for different kinds of drama on the basis of their realism or theatricality.[6] As a slogan of reform, a term like naturalism or expressionism is often characterized in theory as opposing and rejecting some of the things it must include in practice if it is to operate in literature at all. There thus tend to be inconsistencies between polemical theories and actual practice, and between polemical and more sophisticated versions of the same theory. What is at issue in any play, however, is the nature of the reality to be depicted and the kind of relationship between on-stage and off-stage worlds that best might serve to put plays and playgoers in touch with it. Strindberg, early in his career, characterized his plays as naturalistic, but by the end of his career he was writing plays which many would call expressionistic. It might thus appear that Strindberg, in the course of his career, had radically changed his aims as a playwright. But we should note that the advantages and disadvantages of expressionist drama are linked to those of naturalist and symbolist drama, and follow logically upon the rejection of the structural format of the well-made play. Furthermore, the logical linking of these various tensions have direct implications for the nature of *A Dream Play*.

The naturalist movement in drama, with Zola as its major spokesman,[7] set out to transcend the spurious realism and reductive theatricality of the well-made play, which characteristically displayed a formulaic structure, narrowness of social concern, limited exploration of character, and conventional themes. Everyone is familiar with naturalism's concern for 'real fires in the grates, and real champagne in the glasses, real food, authentic costume',[8] and so forth. But there are, as we have noted, internal inconsistencies in the movement. Esslin points out that 'the naturalists called for a fresh start in *complete* freedom',[9] and he is able to quote Zola in support of this position: 'There must be no more schools, no more formula, no more literary panjandrums of any kind. There is just life itself, an immense field where everybody can explore and create to his heart's content.'[10] Yet Esslin, without fully recognizing the problem it causes, is soon pointing out Zola's interest in a naturalist tradition that both precedes and succeeds his own work, and also Zola's attempts to characterize Homer as a naturalist and to seek to emulate his achievements.[11] Far from being a basis for rejecting all conventions and ratifying all freedoms at all times for all artists, naturalism became for Zola a movement in search of its own conventional and established form. In his search for 'the naturalistic formula',[12] Zola reveals that he is interested less in exploring all of reality than in ratifying his belief that its most important elements are the forces of heredity and environment.

There is thus, in naturalism, a clash between its demand for complete freedom and its demand for the recognition and acceptance of certain kinds of constraint, both in the larger world and in the theatre. These constraints upon freedom harden inevitably into conventions which, in their turn, become as theatrical as those they were designed to replace. This inconsistency between the basic aims of naturalism reinforces another – that between naturalism's preferred means and some of its avowed ends. Zola clearly believed that the goal of revealing the forces of heredity and environment was best served by exact reproduction of the environment: a precise focus on the visible is regarded as the best means of revealing the not so readily visible forces of nature.

> Most of all we would need to intensify the illusion in reconstructing the environments, less for their picturesque quality than for dramatic utility. *The environment must determine the character.* When a set is planned so as to give the lively impression of a description by Balzac; when, as the curtain rises, one catches the first glimpse of the characters, their personalities and behaviour, if only to see the actual locale in which they move, *the importance of exact reproduction in the decor* will be appreciated. (my emphasis)[13]

But what is an obvious complementarity, for Zola, is less so for Strindberg. His naturalism exploits the ambivalence in the movement between its opposition to all inherited conventions and its advocating new ones, between its urge to reveal hidden realities and its belief that visible realities ('exact reproduction in the decor') are the necessary means.

For *Miss Julie*, a play explicitly characterized as naturalistic, Strindberg wrote a Preface advocating the use of real pots, pans, shelves, doors, etc.[14] But when he described the set for the play, the naturalistic trappings gave way to more complex techniques:

> As regards the scenery, I have borrowed from impressionist painting its asymmetry and its economy; thus, I think, strengthening the illusion. For the fact that one does not see the whole room and all the furniture leaves scope for conjecture – that is to say *imagination is roused and complements what is seen.* (my emphasis)[15]

There could be no clearer indication of Strindberg's recognition of the potential shortcomings of naturalistic conventions than this explicit recognition of the role of imagination in complementing what is seen. Where Zola advocates 'exact reproduction in the decor', Strindberg, here and elsewhere, rejects any reduction of this principle to simple photographic realism and proposes instead 'the true naturalism . . . *which rejoices in seeing what cannot be seen everyday*' (my emphasis).[16]

What we thus encounter in Esslin's arguments, in Zola's theorizing, and in Strindberg's practice is a fundamental tension in the naturalist movement between reproducing the visible world off-stage and revealing its hidden truths. When the count's boots in *Miss Julie* appear persistently on-stage, what matters about them is not whether they are real or fake boots, but whether Jean assigns one kind of value or another to them. They function for him as reminders of his inborn subservience to the aristocracy, and whether they are made of leather or not makes no major difference to this dramatic function. It is not their leatherness but their ownership that gives them their value. For Jean, as for the audience, 'the imagination is roused and complements what is seen'. Ironically enough, where the leatherness of the boots can make a difference is in its capacity to help the imagination to go beyond what is seen. It may well be the case that a highly polished pair of leather boots will make Jean's assignment of symbolic value to them seem more persuasive than might be the case with a pair made of, say, painted cardboard. *But then the issue is no longer a matter of realistic décor offering an alternative to theatrical reality, but of its being one of several possible modes of theatrical reality.* Theatricality is not, as early naturalists assumed, simply a matter of difference between on-stage conventions and everyday realities. Selective but repeated use of everyday realities on-stage bestows upon them their own theatricality – that is, they become typical of the on-stage world. In that situation they become theatrical no matter what their degree of approximation to the off-stage world.

Naturalism thus provided Strindberg not with a new ending-point, but with a new starting-point for writing plays, and as he explored and extended naturalism's notion of reality both on-stage and off, he quickly discovered and exploited the tensions inherent in it. His naturalism situates itself at the heart of the naturalist dilemma, focusing on realistic phenomena as a means of revealing 'what cannot be seen every day'. What Strindberg quickly realized is that naturalism, as a reflection of the off-stage world which aims to reveal hidden aspects of the world off-stage, is, from the outset, incipiently symbolic naturalism.[17] And as the notion of hidden truths to be revealed moves on beyond those of heredity and environment, new modes of revealing them must also be adopted. Interest in hidden realities leads inevitably towards realities hidden not just in material or physiological domains, but also in psychological domains. The sequence of Strindberg's experimentation, and, as Benston points out, that of much modern theatre, runs from naturalism, through symbolic naturalism, to expressionism – from materially manifest knowledge, to materially revealed knowledge, to non-materially revealed knowledge. The path from naturalism to expressionism is continuous and compelling, but, as we have noted, it does not end there.

If the basic tension in naturalism is between reflecting and revealing knowledge, the basic tension in expressionism is between revealing and creating knowledge. To arrive at Benston's stopping-point is to make only an interim pause, for it marks the beginning of a return to the territory recently left behind. Recognition of this lends an interesting circularity to the process Benston regards as linear – a circularity that has large implications for the structure of *A Dream Play*. A brief glance at Sokel's valuable survey of the subsequent history of expressionism will thus help clarify the structure of the play. The expressionist movement encouraged the artist to reject mimetic demands and naturalistic conventions in favour of a freedom to exhibit on-stage a world registering the individual, idiosyncratic perspectives of the artist, rather than public and conventional ones. Sokel traces this basic feature of the expressionist movement back to Kant's *Critique of Pure Reason* which 'unmasks the world as the product of our mind and declares the supernatural unknowable. With these two blows Kant shatters the foundation for art as mimesis and art as revelation.'[18] But what Kant's work undermined was a particular kind of mimesis and a particular kind of revelation. As Sokel goes on to point out, the emerging alternatives are foreshadowed in Kant's *Critique of Judgement*:

> Like Lessing and Herder, Kant expects genius to legislate its own laws. . . . The artist's self-chosen purpose and his freely imposed form for expressing his particular purpose are his only concerns. The work of art is a universe of its own. . . . Both art as mimesis and art as revelation had been subservient to other realities, physical or spiritual, means to an end; for Kant art became an end in itself.[19]

In its idiosyncratically constructed worlds of dreams and hallucinations, expressionism took these views to their logical extreme and developed another kind of mimesis along with the possibility of another kind of revelation:

> The Expressionist dramatist, like the dreamer, concentrates entirely on the purpose of expressing an inner world and refuses to let conformity to external reality divert him from this purpose. . . . The scenery of the Expressionist stage changes with the psychic forces whirling about in it. . . . Landscapes *reflect* the emotional situation of the characters . . . the entire stage becomes a universe of mind, and the individual scenes are not replicas of three-dimensional physical reality, but *visualized stages of thought*. (my emphases)[20]

We discussed in earlier chapters the dangers for art in weaving endlessly its own autonomous worlds. Sokel notes this impending danger for expressionism in particular and for modernism in general:

> In the pure abstraction of the modernist, as in the formless shriek of the naive Expressionist, lies the same basic indifference to the world in its twofold aspect as model and audience. As the naive Expressionist is unconcerned about his offenses to public taste and morals, the true modernist is equally callous as to whether or not the public can understand him.[21]

What is important, for our purposes, is the path expressionism as a movement then follows as it seeks to come to terms with this dilemma. Having first rejected the pre-existing world in order to gain artistic freedom, expressionism soon finds itself compelled to return to it in order to attain artistic function. But the return is not entirely a capitulation, for it is based on the notion of a new art and a new social world. Sokel is again persuasive on this point:

> Violent self-expression or absolute art are only two possibilities open to the creative mind isolated from its environment. The third possibility is one of hope. *The creative mind can seek to create the public for itself by educating the surrounding world.* (my emphasis)[22]

The expressionist movement was thus no more homogeneous than was the naturalist movement, but major trends are visible in both. And what is significant is the complementary nature of those trends in the two apparently opposed movements. The naturalist movement began by privileging realistic décor as a means of opposing well-made theatricality and as a means of embodying overlooked truths. To pursue its search for overlooked truths it soon had to transcend spurious realism and readopt appropriate theatrical techniques. The expressionist movement began by privileging theatrical décor as a means of opposing naturalist realism and a means of discovering new truths. To make new truths something more than solipsistic raving it soon had to transcend spurious theatricality and readopt appropriate mimetic modes. The world-rejecting expressionist movement gave rise to a world-regenerating expressionism, or, as Sokel calls it, a Messianic Expressionism. 'Messianic Expressionism transferred the visionary quality of Expressionism to the social and political sphere. The *visualization* of subconscious or existential states became the *vision* of social renewal.'[23] A new kind of revelation and a new kind of mimesis thus emerge, but in the context of an unresolved conflict between them.

The tension in naturalism between replicating surfaces of the world and revealing underlying forces in the world is thus recapitulated in a tension in expressionism between transcending the world and rediscovering it. Benston, we noted earlier, pointed out the sequence that takes naturalism through symbolic naturalism to expressionism. Sokel has pointed out the sequence that takes expressionism back towards symbolic naturalism once more.[24] The artistic urges to reflect the world, to reveal the world, and to replace the world exhibit not a sequence of opposed choices, but a set of related concerns. The rejection of the well-made play reactivates tensions between freedom and constraint, individual and community, realism and theatricality, that had all reached a stable equilibrium in the well-made play. Once that equilibrium is disturbed, dramatists find themselves repeatedly embroiled in the battle to reassert control without becoming the victims of a new and privileged mode of adjustment. Exploration of the world off-stage thus involves repeated exploration of the world on-stage; what a set of conventions enables is to be weighed against what it restricts; movement towards any of the opposed poles quickly brings about a demand for compensatory adjustment in the other directions. The drama of inquiry consequently involves not just a search for knowledge, nor just a search for adequate stage conventions, but the pursuit of an adequate epistemology.

Strindberg's naturalism and Strindberg's expressionism thus become part of a continuing search for appropriate adjustment and appropriate balance between opposing but related conventions.[25] And this search is much exemplified in *A Dream Play*, for Strindberg uses the complex character of the Daughter of Indra to thematize, and thus integrate into the play, not only the tensions inherent in expressionist conventions, but also those inherent in competing conventions, as the play explores both the relatedness and the distinctiveness of major theatrical ways of knowing. We can thus return with a larger perspective to the character of the Daughter and to her conflicting functions. We have already noted that when we, as audience, first find ourselves viewing our Earth-world through the eyes of a privileged stranger to it, we alternate between an expectation that she will discover hidden truths about our world and an expectation that she might offer transcendent truths about her world and others. This conflict between discovery and transcendence lies precisely at the heart of expressionist drama, but it turns out to be only the first of several such conflicts that are thematized in a play that explores not only the powers and limitations of expressionism, but also, as we shall see, those of naturalism, discussion plays and symbol networks.

In spite of Strindberg's suggestion that there is only 'an insignificant basis of reality' (p. 19) to his dream play, this base turns out, on close inspection, to contain much that would delight the committed naturalist. The play includes instances of, or references to, shawls, telephones, fishing-nets, swords, tables, rocking-chairs, books, underclothing, flowers, candles, trees, theatres, operas and many other aspects of everyday off-stage reality. The characters have equivalent occupations: there is a glazier, a locksmith, a maid, a doorkeeper, a billsticker, a policeman, a lawyer, an officer, a schoolmaster, a couple of coal heavers and even a poet. Relationships between people are similarly conventional – there are fathers, mothers, husbands, wives, daughters, sons, brothers, sisters, lovers, coquettes and so on, in a world that seems in many respects very much like the off-stage world with which every audience is familiar. Zola's recommendation for 'exact reproduction in the decor'[26] is not slavishly followed, but the desire to reproduce much of the off-stage world is eminently visible, even, ironically enough, in Strindberg's prefatory announcement that he seeks, in this play, 'to *imitate* the disconnected but apparently logical form of a dream' (my emphasis) (p. 19). Much of the strangeness of the play is not the strangeness of the unfamiliar, but the strangeness of the familiar encountered in the context of novel stage conventions. This recognition is fundamental to our understanding of *A Dream Play*. If we focus primarily on its novelty we will overlook the important function of its conventionality; if we see it exclusively as an expressionist drama, we will fail to take into account its naturalistic and other elements and their significance for the major transitions the Daughter goes through when she leaves her world for ours. She becomes, as many have noted, 'earthbound', when she stays for a while in this new domain; but what has not been so carefully noted is the process by which she becomes earthbound, the shift in function that her character subsequently undergoes, and the way in which that switch enables her to embody not just the tension at the heart of expressionist drama, but also the tensions at the heart of other kinds of drama.

Our general survey of post well-made-play dramatic issues must thus be borne in mind as we try to make sense of the changing role of the Daughter, the puzzling structure of the play, the strange sequence of its episodes, and its complex mixture of theatrical conventions. The play begins, we should note, by giving visual embodiment to its various tensions. In the first two scenes we encounter a series of contrasting movements. Initially, we see the Daughter of Indra descending from the clouds to Earth. Her *downward movement towards* this other world gives way to the first Earth scene in which are depicted Earth elements reaching *upward* and *away from* this Earthworld.

> The backdrop represents a mass of gigantic white, pink, scarlet, sulphur yellow, and violet hollyhocks in bloom; over their tops can be seen the gilded roof of a castle with a flower bud resembling a crown uppermost. Along the bottom of the castle walls, heaps of straw covering cleaned-out stable litter. (p. 22)

What we encounter instantly is a wealth of naturalistic detail and a wealth of expressionist implication. The Daughter's descent leads us into this scene, and the first words of the dialogue confirm its significance: the castle, like the flowers, is growing upward, reaching away from Earth. We thus consider the Daughter's descent to Earth and the castle's and flowers' attempts to rise up from Earth as opposing but related movements. This pattern of movements is completed by the entry of Indra's Daughter, now the Glazier's daughter, as she enters with him, moving, horizontally of course, across a stage framed for the first time by the painted wings. The Daughter *descends* to begin her inquiry, encounters a world seeking to *ascend*, but begins and continues to conduct her inquiry *moving horizontally*. These contrasting movements are the first embodiments in the play of the contrasting perspectives provided by the juxtaposed margins of the separate domains: a character can be living above and seeking to descend; living below and seeking to ascend; or simply living in the world below with or without a view to learning about what happens on this fundamental plane of human existence. These contrasting perspectives also suggest competing possibilities for the role of the Daughter. Is her function ultimately to synthesize or merely to exercise the available options? Is she capable of reconciling the upward, downward, and horizontal movements of the play?

To answer appropriately these key questions, we must not overlook an important indication of the play's thematic structure. It has been pointed out, from time to time, that *A Dream Play* was initially published with numerals that suggest it is divided into three major parts.[27] These divisions occur just after and just before the two Fingal's Cave scenes, and their function has yet to be persuasively explained.[28] What is clearly needed is some means of linking the play's basic structure to its privileged character. And that link can readily be established if we note a convergence among four elements of the drama: the progress of the Daughter's investigation, the accompanying changes in her role, the consequent shifts in her epistemological orientation, and the contrasting tensions in the various theatrical conventions Strindberg employs.

The Daughter, we have noted, begins as a distanced observer basing her inquiry into the Earth-world upon the privileged perspective and transcendent knowledge of a being from another world. This is, however, only her initial role in the play. To pursue her inquiry further, she switches from the role of distanced observer to that of participating observer and when that, too, proves inadequate, she moves on, with her newly acquired knowledge, to become a ruminating, better informed observer reflecting on and discussing at length the world she has observed and participated in. But the fundamental irony of the play is that the closer she gets to the world she is observing, the more she loses touch with her capacity to know more than other mortals know. She begins with a transcendent perspective and an ignorance about Earth; she ends with some knowledge of Earth but without any ability to provide it with Earthly enlightenment or other-worldly surprise. But what is also of importance is that the three divisions of the play chart her progress from one role to another. These key changes, from distanced observer, to participating observer, to reflecting observer[29] do not register a steady progress from ignorance to knowledge; rather, they exhibit a pattern of inquiry in which the changing means of discovery set changing limits on the inquirer's capacity to discover. And as she moves from role to role, the Daughter explores and tests out the strengths and weaknesses of modes of inquiry that are characteristic of, first, expressionist drama, second, naturalist drama, and third, the symbol-based discussion play.

The drama of inquiry, in Strindberg's hands, thus repeatedly moves towards a variety of epistemological limits and, as a consequence, becomes not only the means of inquiry, but also the subject of inquiry. Or, to put it another way, the play becomes an instance of what needs to be inquired into, even as it serves as a mode of more general inquiry. Though it begins by dramatizing the Daughter's inquiry into life in general on Earth, the play focuses finally on the epistemological complexities of all modes of inquiry, including those generated by its own peculiar mixture of theatrical conventions. In the hands of a less able dramatist than Strindberg, such concerns could become abstract indeed, but Strindberg manages to give concrete theatrical embodiment to the strengths and weaknesses of a variety of dramatic conventions as they tackle, individually and jointly, 'the riddle of the world' (p. 78) with which he confronts them.[30]

To trace this evolving pattern and establish its larger consequences, we should thus look at each of the play's sections in turn. The first section, we recall, dramatizes the tension between the Daughter's transcendent perspective and her Earthly investigation. One scene after another focuses on the disappointing nature of her putatively transcendent knowledge, on her misplaced convictions and premature certainties, and on the persistently opposing evidence provided by human life on Earth. Indeed, the puzzling sequence of these scenes becomes much less puzzling when we note how each succeeding scene derives from a topic or opinion introduced by the Daughter in the preceding one. As the play's structure has seemed obscure to many, it is worth tracing its narrative line in some detail.

In the first Earth scene, the Daughter reacts with delight (p. 23) at the prospect of the castle and the flowers reaching upward towards the light, towards the world from which she has arrived and upon which she bases her values and beliefs. The Glazier, however, offers her a less positive response to this process. Rather than reaching towards something, it seems that Earthly phenomena are stretching away from an environment they find unpleasant: an activity that produces not self-transcendence but self-destruction. He says, 'They don't thrive in dirt; they hurry as fast as they can up into the light to bloom and die!' (p. 23). The Daughter does not readily abandon her other-world belief in the value of reaching towards the light and transfers it unqualified to the next scene and the Officer who is a prisoner in the castle. Convinced that she knows how to guide Earth people, the Daughter sets out to free the prisoner, to help him 'to seek freedom in light' (p. 24). That freedom was not achieved by the flowers, in spite of their movement towards the light, and the Glazier's equation of 'to bloom and die' is an equation very much in the mind of the Officer. He does not know whether he wants to be set free or not, because experience has taught him that 'every joy in life has to be paid for doubly in sorrow' (p. 24).

The play then offers us another kind of movement to contrast with those we have already encountered – the Officer is not moving steadily downward, nor steadily upward, nor steadily on a horizontal plane, but rocking back and forth in a rocking-chair in a movement that takes him nowhere. The oscillating motion of the Officer, movement without progress, action involving repetition, not change, provides a visual embodiment of his state of mind, of his experience of life on Earth, and of the basic problem the Daughter confronts in trying to understand why people on Earth lament so much. She persists, however, in seeking to remedy what she has not yet understood, and urges the Officer 'to seek freedom in light'. But as she does so, the lights go up on the other half of the set, and the light motif once more provides the transition from this scene to the next: '*Voices can now be heard behind the screen, which is immediately drawn aside. The Officer and the Daughter look in that direction, then stop, their gestures and expressions frozen*' (p. 24).

This scene, with the Officer and the Daughter frozen as observers, provides a visual emblem of the major tensions in the first part of the play. We have an observer from the world of Earth and an observer from the world beyond Earth surveying a scene which tests out the claims each voiced in the preceding scene. The Officer registered his fear of the light and the social world it illuminates by remarking that 'every joy in life has to be paid for doubly in sorrow' (p. 24). The Daughter voiced her other-world conviction of the value of living in the light by announcing that that is where freedom lies. The scene that they observe validates his point and undermines hers. A Father and Mother remark upon the sadness of their lives, the evenhandedness of injustice, the sorrows attendant upon all joys, the pain that comes with love, the harm that springs from doing good.

> MOTHER: This life! When you do something nice, there's always someone to whom it's ugly. . . . If you do something good for someone, you hurt someone else. Ugh, this life!
> [*She trims the candle so that it goes out. The stage becomes dark.*] (p. 27)

The scene validates the Officer's rather than the Daughter's opinion of seeking freedom in the light, and the Daughter, for the first time, begins to shift from an optimistic transcendent perspective to a pessimistic Earthly one. 'Human beings', she fears, 'are to be pitied!' (p. 27).

The Daughter is not yet ready, however, to abandon her belief that her transcendent perspective may yet offer saving guidance. 'Yes', she concedes, 'life is hard, but love conquers all. Come and see!' (p. 27). The scene shifts to the outside of a theatre, where the Officer is transformed into a lover rejoicing in the love he has for the actress, Miss Victoria. But the Daughter's belief in love conquering all is quickly undermined by the Doorkeeper whose sweetheart has abandoned her, by the sadness of the dancers who love dancing but are judged to have insufficient talent, and by the persistent refusal, for seven long years, of Miss Victoria to meet the Officer, her endlessly waiting lover.

Once again, however, the Daughter seeks to rescue some of her undermined assumptions, this time by arguing that the Officer, in spite of his unrewarded waiting, nevertheless gains happiness by the perspective that his love casts on the world.

> DAUGHTER: Who is Miss Victoria?
> DOORKEEPER: The woman he loves.
> DAUGHTER: Right! He doesn't care what she is to us and others. She *is* only what she is for *him*. . . .
> [*It grows dark suddenly.*] (p. 30)

The sudden darkness is a prelude to the entrance of the Officer, older and shabbier, still without his love, and clearly losing more than he gains by his belief in Miss Victoria's love. Time speeds up on-stage as a series of flashes of light illuminates the darkened stage and registers the passing of days and years. The Officer has grown older, his hair is grey, his clothes are ragged, his bouquet has lost its petals, and he has lost his hope. He talks to the Billsticker who earlier registered joy at obtaining the fishing-net he had always sought, and now finds that he too is disappointed because the fishing-net turned out to be 'not *just* the way I'd wanted it' (p. 32). The Officer's rejoinder radically undermines the Daughter's announced belief in the value of comforting illusions:

> OFFICER [*emphasizing*]:   Not just the way I'd wanted it. . . . That's marve-
> lously put! Nothing is the way I'd wanted it . . .
> because the idea is greater than the act – superior to
> the object.
> [*Walks about striking the rose bouquet on the walls so that
> the last leaves and petals fall.*] (p. 32)

The play's adjustment of traditional conventions for portraying the passing of time allows it to dramatize the disastrous long-term effects of the Daughter's repeatedly short-sighted advice. Her determination to free him, her confidence in the value of love, and her ratification of the value of illusions all lead to a life of misery. The Officer may gain temporary enjoyment from beliefs that are unsupported by external facts, but, in the long run, his life is squandered by his refusal to come to terms with what is really happening around him. This refusal offers only short-term benefits for himself and none for others. The lessons that emerge for the Officer in these scenes are not lost on the Daughter. Her misplaced convictions about this world have been undermined as steadily as have been his illusions about Miss Victoria and his commitment to the notion that love conquers all. Love, it seems, conquers not all, but common sense; what the Daughter needs to do is to learn some 'common' knowledge before offering any more premature judgements.

The Daughter thus recognizes, at the end of the play's first section, the need to switch from telling to listening, from stating to questioning, from guiding to learning. The opening section of the play has dramatized the tension between the capacity of the Daughter (and expressionism) to offer illuminating transcendent truths and their capacity to reveal hidden earthly truths. The privileged stranger, not yet having proved helpful on either count, has voiced convictions that seem largely unoriginal and conducted an investigation that has proved largely unsatisfactory. But the dissatisfaction is hers, as well as ours, and, to learn more about the Earth-world, the Daughter dons the Doorkeeper's shawl and asks everyone in trouble to come and pour out their hearts to her. The first section of the play then ends in Fingal's Cave, to which the Daughter has withdrawn with a lawyer, an expert on the world's troubles, one whose life is devoted to hearing and seeking to resolve disputes. The Daughter's transcendent perspective, it seems, has failed her; her stance as privileged observer has turned out to be inadequately privileged. Observation has taught her that her other-worldly assumptions and certainties are largely wrong, but it has not taught her why they are wrong. The Daughter recognizes, as the play recognizes, that the framework of inquiry is inadequate. In the second part of the play, the Daughter switches from transcendent observation to participating observation. To learn about human beings, she must live like one.

This next step in the Daughter's investigation seems reasonable enough, but it changes both her function in the play and her capacity to use other-world belief for earthly investigation. As she abandons her inherited assumptions, the certainty and authority of her earlier transcendent perspective give way to the doubts and dilemmas characteristic of human perspectives. The more she participates in this world of Earth, the better she knows its dilemmas, but the less convinced she is that she will be able to explain or resolve them. To the Poet's queries she responds: 'Your questions are so hard to answer because . . . there are so many unknowns' (p. 50). This, the ironic result of an inquirer becoming a participant, is not the result the Daughter initially envisages. When she decides to participate directly in life on Earth, she thinks of herself as a privileged participant, one fully able to recognize and resolve the problems life presents. But her role as privileged participant in the second section of the play is undermined as steadily as was her role of privileged observer in the first.

Having sought to learn about life by listening to people's complaints, the Daughter chooses as her marriage partner someone equally knowledgeable, the Lawyer, who spends his professional life listening to people's problems. Thence follows the notion that typical human problems can be avoided by those widely experienced in hearing about them. The Daughter and the Lawyer ground their relationship upon knowing what not to do wrong:

DAUGHTER: Human beings are to be pitied!
LAWYER: You do understand that?
DAUGHTER: Yes, but in God's name let's avoid the rocks now that we know them so well!
LAWYER: Let's. Why we're humane and enlightened people; we can forgive and overlook! (p. 44)

But this kind of knowledge seems no more helpful in the Daughter/Lawyer relationship than self-deception and ignorance was to the Officer/Miss Victoria relationship. The mutual pain they inflict upon each other quickly recapitulates the problems they have heard others describe and watched others endure. The suffering of the Officer, and of the Mother and Father, are recapitulated in the suffering of the Daughter and the Lawyer. Their incompatible likes and dislikes place in complementary relationship joy for one and misery for the other. Making allowances and offering forgiveness are ways of masking unhappiness, not removing it. Poverty and dirt eliminate beauty, the joys of parenthood are undermined by the strain of child-rearing, the positive commitment to each other is replaced by a duty towards the children which ties them all to a mutual misery.

The recapitulation, in this marriage, of the unhappiness of others is succeeded by a recapitulation in the personal life of the Lawyer of a mode of escape that he confronts repeatedly in his professional life – the Daughter, like many of his clients, runs off with a lover. In spite of having heard her husband lament the rash of separations between husbands and wives, and the misery they cause, the Daughter, undermines her belief that knowledge is the means of avoiding traditional error by eloping with a lover – who turns out to be, ironically enough, the Officer of the earlier scenes. She rediscovers with him the false promise that drives the flowers to blossom and die: a lover, like a spouse, promises a life in Fairhaven, but ends up in Foulstrand. The people she encounters in both places reinforce the repeatedly drawn conclusion that human beings are to be pitied, that the search for happiness leads to the discovery of unhappiness, that every joy must be paid for in sorrow. The play begins to become repetitive, the Daughter, in her participatory role, seems only to follow the paths others have followed, to discover only the dilemmas they have discovered. The role of participant offers human experience but not, it seems, knowledge of its basis or of how to transcend it. The second section of the play ends with the Daughter hiding her face in sorrow, sadly reflecting that even the most beautiful parts of Earth confirm that 'this is not paradise' (p. 66), and withdrawing once more 'into the wilderness to find myself again' (p. 62).

If the first section of the play manifests the basic tension of expressionism between revealing hidden and creating new knowledge, the second section of the play dramatizes the basic tension of naturalism between reflecting established knowledge and revealing hidden knowledge. The Daughter, in the first part of the play, learns the problematic nature of a stance as privileged observer; in the second part of the play she encounters the problematic status of the privileged participant. In the first part of the play, the more the Daughter observes, the less privileged she feels; in the second part of the play, the more she participates, the less privileged she becomes. The limitations of a transcendent perspective are revealed in the first part of the play, the limitations of a participant's perspective are revealed in the second part. But the Daughter's discovery of the limitations of the participant's perspective simply recapitulates those that other characters have encountered before her. The painted wings, that have framed the play and the Daughter's activities since the first Earth-scene, begin to reveal their cumulative significance. And it is in the context of the naturalist dilemma and its continuity with the expressionist dilemma that their function is most clearly revealed.

The play, we have noted, is becoming repetitive. The scenes and situations seem only to recapitulate each other. The Daughter, who held out the promise of transcendent wisdom, is steadily subsiding into a repeated refrain: 'Human beings are to be pitied.'[31] The characters, we noted at the outset, are largely type-characters, individuals caught up in the repetition of roles that precede them and will succeed them. And it is in terms of this use of type-characters that we can grasp what is at issue in these repetitions in the play. We have noted that Strindberg's expressionism was not discontinuous with his naturalism, that his naturalism was always selective, and that this play exhibits yet another blend of expressionist and naturalistic conventions. In his avowedly naturalist period, Strindberg rejected the notion of the type-character, the character who had ceased to grow, and sought to dramatize characters growing 'realistically' in the context of their heredity and environment.[32] In *A Dream Play*, he has returned to the use of type-characters.[33] We might conclude prematurely that Strindberg has abandoned his naturalist interests, but further thought will reveal that he has, once again, put them to new uses. If characters in naturalist drama had their individuality and their potential for growth constrained by their heredity and environment, characters in this play are no different. What has changed is the conception of heredity and environment that is brought to bear upon the characters. Here, the circle of influence includes the whole of Earth in a single embrace. The influence is planetary, and thus fundamental to all earthly life, rather than regional, and thus specific to local groups, families, or classes. The point is only reinforced by its extension to include plant life and the emblematic life of something usually inert like the Growing Castle. With the general planetary influence of heredity and environment operating (rather than more local influences), we encounter the recognition that *what is capable of change in human development is overwhelmed by what is fixed and unchanging*. The single set frame, that image of circumscribed variety, exemplifies in its constant presence the predominance of fixity over diversity in the lives and locales that we see either illustrated on it or framed by it.[34] The outer horizon of the play becomes the single most important dimension of life within the domain it defines.

To recognize the function of the painted wings is to recognize also the function of character, time and space in the play. This drama of inquiry is an inquiry into the whole of human society; concern is for the whole race, not for the idiosyncratic fate of selected individuals or groups. The play acknowledges the variety of fates of different individuals, but it is in terms of a larger perspective of circumscribed variety, a point enacted in the play and reinforced in the emblems of interiors, architecture and landscape on the unchanging wings of the stage. The play's focus is on what is typical, rather than what is idiosyncratic, about its characters. There is something, it seems, about the nature of all human beings that is far more debilitating, and far more important, than anything they might idiosyncratically bring upon themselves. And this recognition of the nature of characterization in the play helps us understand the play's novel use of space and time. The action moves rapidly from one place to another because local environments lose their traditional importance when the fundamental problem is one affecting Earth as a whole. *The* location of the play is Earth, and to make that spatially clear, the play begins among the clouds and stars.

The audience thus encounters from the outset a planetary rather than parochial perspective. To move from place to place on Earth is to move only in a circle. And if one moves in a circle, neither direction nor current location are of major consequence. The suspension of inherited conventions for dealing with space and their replacement with new ones are thus emblematic of the conditions the play seeks to dramatize. The same is also true for the play's handling of time. What goes with our normal notions of sequential time is a sense of potential and purposive change. And along with that goes the logical chain of cause and effect that gives individual action and individual responsibility their importance in both on-stage and off-stage worlds. But what is dramatized here is the fundamentally unchanging and seemingly unchangeable state of humankind. Local changes remain circumscribed by a larger pattern which itself remains unchanged. Time as sequence, as an index of potential progress, is replaced by time as flux, oscillation and repetition, underpinning and exhibiting an Earthly variety that lacks, in the last analysis, significant variation.

The action of the play, however, by taking us beyond the world of Earth and offering us a transcendent guide to life on Earth, has implicitly held out the possibility that the cause/consequence foundation of human thinking and human action could be reinstituted if the relationship between the world of Earth and the worlds beyond it could be fully understood. The possibility that such a reconstituted relationship might provide an answer to 'the riddle of the world' (p. 78) is the drive behind the Daughter's quest; it generates her interest in human beings and the interest of human beings in her. And it is this mutuality of interest that has so far sustained a play that has provided, by the end of its second section, two attempts to bridge the juxtaposed worlds and two failures. The play has, however, a third section to offer in which, as before, the role of the Daughter changes, as does the basic orientation of the action. The Daughter switches from her initial role as privileged observer, through her subsequent role as privileged participant, to a role as privileged discussant of the world of Earth. The play switches from its initial expressionist orientation, through its subsequent naturalist orientation, to its next orientation as a discussion play. The final section of the play is dominated by lengthy conversations between the Poet, as the representative of Earth, and the Daughter, as representative of another world. Through their joint deliberations, perhaps, the putative links between Earth and the worlds beyond it might finally be established.

But if the first two sections of the play portray the tensions in expressionism and naturalism, the third reveals the fundamental dilemma of a discussion play: will it reiterate in discussion what has already been embodied in the action (in which case the discussion is redundant), or will it develop in discussion what has not been developed in the action (in which case the action will be judged inadequate to the task of manifesting its own significance)? But this play, like *A Doll's House*, not only has a concluding discussion, it also has an image network, and both that network and the discussion focus finally upon the inner horizon of the play, the door with the clover-leaf hole in it.

The images and motifs which provided Ibsen with a series of interpretative analogies in *A Doll's House* seem, at first glance, just as prevalent in *A Dream Play*. The Growing Castle, the monkshood flower with poison in its roots and beauty at its head, the rocking-chair, the painted wings, the shawl, the inverting mirror, and a series of other revelatory devices have two major functions in the play. They illustrate information already explicit in the dialogue *and* they hint at a way of understanding that transcends what is explicit in the dialogue. There is thus, in the image network, a tension between revealing knowledge and creating knowledge that is at the heart of the play as a whole. The play encourages, in a variety of ways, our expectation that transcendent knowledge might be provided: by its title and its unconventional structure – both of which suggest that new ways of knowing may be at issue here, by offering a character with a transcendent perspective, and by having the Daughter affirm the importance of the dreamer/poet's creative way of knowing: 'farewell, child of man, you the dreamer, you the poet who best understands living' (p. 85). But this imagistic way of knowing, this reaching for an earth-based means of transcending the knowledge of 'earth-bound' mortals, leads discussion inexorably to the play's inner horizon and most prominent image – the ubiquitous door with the clover-leaf hole in it. As the Daughter puts it: 'there's a suspicion that the solution to the puzzle of the world is kept in there' (p. 75).

The explanatory promise of the play's images thus leads steadily, as do the play's action and discussion, to that door and to what lies behind it. Yet when the door is opened, 'there's nothing there' (p. 79). The concluding discussion between the Daughter and the Poet is thus a discussion of life on Earth in the context of what the Daughter has observed of it, what she has experienced of it, what the Poet knows of it, and what the puzzling image network has revealed of it. We look, as we looked in *A Doll's House*, for a revelatory synthesis of the knowledge derived from its various components. Here we look to see how the play's expressionist elements, its naturalistic elements, its symbolic elements and its discussion elements might promote a revelatory synthesis. What we learn, however, is what the Daughter's changing roles suggest: that the play's pluralistic use of conventions and its pluralistic approach to the acquisition of knowledge are not preludes to transcendent synthesis, but manifestations of the irreducibly pluralistic nature of our knowledge. The discussion scene does not resolve the dilemmas of the

action, it simply provides them with their most general form. The culmination of the discussion thus deserves quoting at length:

POET: Instead of asking questions, won't you explain the riddle?
DAUGHTER: Yes. But to what point? You'll not believe me.
POET: I'll believe you, for I know who you are!
DAUGHTER: Well, then, I will tell you. In the morning of time before the sun
              shone, Brahma, the primordial divine force, let Maja, mother of
              the world, seduce him in order to increase and multiply. This,
              the union of the divine and the earthly, was heaven's fall from
              grace. The world, life, and human beings are therefore only
              phantoms, appearances, visions. . . .
POET: My vision!
DAUGHTER: A true vision! . . . But, to free themselves from the earthly,
              Brahma's descendants seek self-denial and suffering. . . . There
              you have suffering as the savior. . . . But this longing for
              suffering is in conflict with the instinct to enjoy or love. . . . Do
              you yet understand what love is with its greatest pleasure in the
              greatest suffering, the most pleasant in the most bitter? Do you
              understand what woman is? Woman, through whom sin and
              death entered into life?
POET: I understand. . . . And the end? . . .
DAUGHTER: What you feel. . . . The struggle between the pain of joy and the
              joy of suffering . . . the penitent's anguish and the voluptuary's
              pleasures. . . .
POET: A struggle, then?
DAUGHTER: Struggle between opposites generates power, just as fire and
              water produce steam. . . .
POET: But peace? And rest?
DAUGHTER: Sh-h! *You may not ask any more, and I may not answer!* (my
              emphasis)
              (pp. 82–3)

The 'discussion' is cut off before the Poet is satisfied and long before an
explanation is reached that would resolve the riddle of the world or satisfy any
of those whose sufferings we have seen portrayed on-stage. The Daughter's
'explanation' is a pseudo-explanation: it simply redescribes the riddle rather
than resolves it. It tells the Poet, as the Daughter concedes, little more than
he already knows. Furthermore, Williams is surely right when he suggests
that 'When Indra's Daughter prepares to go back to the heavens, and asks:
"Have I not learned the anguish of all being, learned what it is to be a mortal
man?" one is bound to answer "No."'[35] And we must ask ourselves, as we
asked with A Doll's House, is this unsatisfactory discussion a flaw in the play or
part of a larger scheme of dramatization?

The play seems to offer us, and then undermine, a variety of controlling
perspectives. There is the notion that the play reproduces the logic of a dream
– it clearly does not. The prefatory note claims that the play has a logic based

upon the mind of a specific dreamer – but that dreamer never appears in the play, and the question of the structure of his logic is thus the same question as the structure of the play. Any announcement of his controlling presence is just an indication that the play has a unified structure, not an added indication of what that structure is.[36] The Daughter is then offered to us as a source of understanding beyond that of the rest of the world on-stage, but her seemingly privileged perspective is undermined equally by her inability to understand what she sees, her inability to explain what she has seen, her unwillingness to answer key questions, and her final readiness to abandon the world she is unable to satisfy or change. The sequence of revelatory images reveals the same truths over and over again, and largely reiterates what is already present in the dialogue. The promise of the images adding up to something more seems to be undermined when the culminating image, the door to the truth about life, reveals only 'nothing'. And it seems that Strindberg's investment in the freedom offered by the notion of a dream play provides him with nothing more than enough rope with which to hang himself. But Strindberg himself was quite insistent that the play did offer answers to the questions it raises, and it may well be that much of our scholarship has been looking too closely at the questions the characters raise, and not closely enough at the questions the play raises.

To take this tack is to return to the issue first explored in the opening chapter – to look at the ways in which the modern drama of inquiry regards the exploration of the genre as a simultaneous means of exploring the world off-stage. And in a play which features prominently a Poet, it seems more than likely that this process is in operation here too. Furthermore, if we look at what Strindberg's famous diary entry says of the play, we find it directs us to the very issue that the images of the play seem to lead us towards: the nothing behind the door with the clover-leaf hole in it = 'the explanation of my dream play, and of the meaning of Indra's daughter, the secret of the Door-Nothingness'.[37] This suggests that the images of *A Dream Play*, the 'poetic' element of exploration in the inherited drama, has consequences that are not eliminated by their leading us towards the nothing behind the door. To consider this issue further, we must return to the notion that the play is, in important ways, an instance of its own themes. We should note, therefore, the ambiguous status that poetry, in its most general sense, achieves in this play.

The Poet in *A Dream Play* is, significantly enough, a retired poet. He once wrote poetry, but no more. He persists, however, like many modern dramatists, in situating himself between opposing worlds. He continues to walk the earth to which he is tied, and to gaze at the heavens to which he is drawn, but he is no longer able or willing to distil this conflict into poetry. The reasons for this are important. Two perspectives on the nature of poetry are offered us, one by the Daughter and one by the Poet himself. The Daughter lists a series of events in which she has participated on Earth, and the Poet comments:

POET:	I put it into poetry once. . . .
DAUGHTER:	Then you know what poetry is. . . .
POET:	Then I know what dreaming is. . . . What is poetry?
DAUGHTER:	Not reality, but more than reality . . . not dreaming, but waking dreams. . . .
POET:	And the children of man think we poets only play . . . invent and make up! (p. 69)

The Poet offers the notion that poetry is only escape from reality, while the Daughter suggests that it reaches towards a higher reality. Both notions are well-known attitudes towards both poetry and dreams, and the Poet's linking of the two registers what we are now looking towards – the way in which the play turns its own status into an instance of its basic themes. A dream play that discusses the status of dreams and of poetry is offering directions we should examine with care. And, when we do look at the play in this light, a variety of details begins to fall into place.

The inner horizon of the play, the horizon that is the focus of so much character attention, is a door. It is not, however, just any door, but a door of a theatre. The people who congregate around it when the first attempt is made to open it are theatre people in theatre costumes. The people who congregate around them represent an audience from the off-stage world. Theatre people and ordinary people focus on the inner horizon of a play that is itself framed by an outer horizon of painted wings. The hint that revelatory knowledge might lie behind the door is enough to bring established authority on to the scene to forbid its opening. But when it is opened, this theatrically based knowledge turns out to be incomprehensible. It looks like 'nothing' to the gathered throng, and when the Dean of Medicine points this out, the Daughter agrees, but suggests to him that 'you didn't understand that nothing' (p. 79). This naturally leads us to expect that she *does* understand it, and will explain it to us. But it is here that the play's most fundamental and self-reflexive irony operates. In the discussion section of the play, as in the two earlier sections, the Daughter claims privileged status and privileged access to knowledge, but, as in the two preceding sections, what privilege she has seems to provide neither her nor us with any visible benefits. And the full significance of this point now becomes apparent. It is not that her privileged status is completely fraudulent, but that what privilege she has is not ours to share. It provides her with an idiosyncratic perspective *and* it separates her from the very people for whom she might like to garner knowledge. The implicit irony of the first two sections becomes explicit in the concluding discussion with the Poet. What becomes the final topic of concern is not what revelatory knowledge might be, but whether, whatever it might be, it could also be accessible.

The initial refusal of the authorities to allow the door to be opened is only one indication of the implications of, and difficulty of access to, revelatory knowledge. For us to know something vitally new, established ways of knowing and established ways of living would first have to be transcended.

And there are barriers in our history and in our present world to such transcendent change. The Policeman initially sees nothing behind the door because he forbids anyone to look behind it. The Dean of Medicine sees nothing behind the door because, even when it is opened, he does not know how to see behind it. But the crucial point is that the Poet, lauded by the Daughter for his higher intelligence and his greater capacity to see, cannot understand it either. Furthermore, he cannot even understand or share the Daughter's suffering, because she cannot embody transcendent knowledge in words intelligible to him. This point serves only to remind him of the reason for his retirement as a Poet – the difficulty he encountered in trying to embody, in the language-signs of the Earth-world, thoughts forever reaching towards another world. The dilemma of the Poet becomes the dilemma of the play, and it is also the ultimate dilemma of the Daughter. What finally restrains the Daughter and prevents her from offering revelatory knowledge to the Poet is the lack of sharable means of embodying idiosyncratic or transcendent knowledge.

> POET: Tell me your sorrows!
> DAUGHTER: Poet, could you tell me yours so there wouldn't be an extra word, could your words for once really express your thoughts?
> POET: No, you're right. I seemed like someone deaf and dumb to myself, and when the crowd listened with admiration to my song, I thought it only words . . . that's why, you see, I always blushed with shame when they praised me.
> DAUGHTER: So you want me to? Look me in the eye!
> POET: I can't bear your look. . . .
> DAUGHTER: *How could you bear my words if I were to speak my language?* (my emphasis) (p. 83)

The 'nothing' behind the door that the play's image network focuses on is at one with the nothing that the Daughter offers the Poet in the discussion scene.

> POET: Give me a parting word!
> DAUGHTER: No, I can't! Do you think your words could express our thoughts? (p. 84)

That 'nothing' is not an indication that there is no possibility of anything existing behind that door, but an indication that we have not yet located any means of going beyond the limit it so forcefully symbolizes. The play's inner horizon finally merges in function with its outer horizon. The Earth-world and its inhabitants are irredeemably 'earthbound', as is the very play exhibiting that fundamental fact.

A *Dream Play* invests in and makes extensive use of a wide variety of knowledge-grounding conventions. It includes elements of expressionism, naturalism, symbolism and discussion, taking each to the limiting-point at which it begins to be transformed into something else, but that something else soon reaches a limit too. The play's painted wings take on their culminating significance not only as emblems of the circumscribed variety of the off-stage world, but also as emblems of the circumscribed variety of the on-stage world. The conventional and epistemological variety of the drama, exemplified in its naturalist, expressionist, symbolist and discussion elements, remains 'earthbound' too, manifesting, as does the rest of human life, a variety that promises, but cannot sustain, significant variation. Novelty is possible both on-stage and off-stage, as is variety, and even change; but all three remain finally circumscribed.

The play situates the audience as spectator of rather than participant in the world on-stage. It asks us to see the play through the eyes of an outsider, a privileged observer, and to note the Earth-world's outer horizon, even as the characters turn towards its inner horizon. This outer and inner frame makes the play itself achieve metaphoric status, not just in its parts, but as a framed whole. Fjelde noted the way in which Ibsen's images function as something we both look at and look by means of: we 'see *through* the outward object'.[38] In Strindberg's A Dream Play, the play itself becomes the imagistic object we are both to see and see by means of. We begin by seeking to see and understand the play in terms of our world, our inherited assumptions, but we end by seeing our world in terms that the play provides. The play finally offers no new transcendent facts, but it does provide a disturbing series of perspectives on our world that may persuade us to rethink our notions of the relative priority of established features of our daily experience.

To look 'through', or by means of, this play, is to contemplate our world as one in which constraints circumscribe our freedoms, pain undermines joy, time erodes all happiness, and repetition finally predominates over apparent variety. A play that deliberately exaggerates and distorts our everyday experience tries to provide us with a more comprehensive perspective. Our world, seen through the perspective of the play, can offer us, in the short term, change, growth and progress, but all turn out, in the long run, to be manifestations of an intriguing variety that promises, but cannot ultimately deliver, significant variation. The variety that we experience in the short term encourages us to inquire further, to pursue further variation in the hope of finding ultimate explanations and ultimate control. But the characters on-stage sustain that hope only because they ignore what the audience cannot ignore, an outer horizon to the experience of this world that steadily resists the possibility that it, or a dream, or a poem, or a play, or anything else might offer a conclusive answer to an ultimate question like 'the riddle of the world'.

And with that word 'ultimate' we return to the beginning of our argument and to the recognition that the drama of inquiry is, as the Daughter's journey has suggested, an exploration of a pluralistic domain in which knowledge itself is irreducibly pluralistic. The urge to transcend its irksome pluralism and reach towards ultimate answers gives rise to novelty, experimentation and persistent inquiry. The play itself both dramatizes and becomes an instance of the urge towards ultimate transcendence and the inevitability of its ultimate failure. At the end of the play, the on-stage characters, like the off-stage audience, adopt their recurrent stance of persistent inquiry; at the same time, the burning castle and the flower bud on its roof recapitulate our recognition that transcendent inquiry consists of reaching towards what we cannot grasp, and that in so doing, we, like the flower, 'bloom and die' (p. 23).

> *The backdrop is lighted by the burning castle and shows a wall of human faces, asking, sorrowing, despairing. . . . When the castle burns, the flower bud on the roof bursts into a gigantic chrysanthemum.* (p. 86)

The play, like the Daughter, the castle and the flower, reaches upward towards something it cannot grasp, attempting to establish between different worlds bridges that cannot easily be built. It is a play that countenances pluralism as an index of variety, but not as a means of increasing the significance of that variety. The painted wings enclose a world in which the desire for monistic transcendence repeatedly confronts a circumscribed pluralism that consequently borders on unenlightening relativism. The play's experimentation with genre and exploration of theme merge in generating one and the same conclusion. As the Poet and the Daughter wait for the opening of the door that hides the answer to the riddle of life, they make explicit the fundamental basis of the play: the concern that local revelation dissolves always into global recapitulation, no matter how varied the means of revelation, no matter how promising the variety it so intriguingly and troublingly embodies:

POET:	I seem to have lived through this before. . . .
DAUGHTER:	I, too.
POET:	Perhaps I dreamt it?
DAUGHTER:	Or composed it, perhaps?
POET:	Or composed it.
DAUGHTER:	Then you know what poetry is.
POET:	Then I know what dreaming is.
DAUGHTER:	It seems to me we've stood elsewhere saying these words before.
POET:	Then you can soon determine what reality is!
DAUGHTER:	Or dreaming!
POET:	Or poetry! (pp. 75–6)

8 Brecht: Life of Galileo

Two scenes (the tenth and the last) are often omitted when the *Life of Galileo*[1] is performed. The one dramatizes the reaction of the working people of Italy to Galileo's innovative ideas; the other portrays Andrea, Galileo's pupil, smuggling Galileo's most recent book, the *Discorsi*, across the Italian border. To omit complete scenes in the performance of any major work is to take a dangerous step, and the danger seems even more pressing when the text has been as thoroughly and repeatedly revised as Brecht's *Life of Galileo*. Such extensive revision is no guarantee of final success, but it suggests that we look very carefully before we conclude that any part of the text is irrelevant to the play. What often needs changing is not the text, but the criteria of relevance we apply to it. And in terms of the framework we have been developing, one notable criterion, the prominence of horizons, suggests that the final scene may have an importance overlooked by those willing to cut it from the play. The introductory stage direction sets the scene as follows: '*1637. Galileo's book* Discorsi *crosses the Italian border*' (p. 96).

It seems odd, at first glance, to conclude a play about Galileo with a scene in which he does not appear; but it is less odd, as we have seen, to conclude a modern play with attention focused on the horizon of a domain. The trouble is that the horizon of this play's final scene is a social horizon, that of the Italian people, and not, as the play's title and much of its action would suggest, the individual horizon of Galileo's life. This puzzle leads us immediately to another. Why is the play called the *Life of Galileo* and not just 'Galileo'? The title seems to direct us to stand at some distance from Galileo as a person and to see his 'life' as a unit, as a coherent autonomous sequence. We might thus expect the play to begin with his birth and conclude with his death. Yet the play begins with Galileo middle-aged, and ends with him still alive and no longer the direct focus of our attention. Furthermore, the final horizon of the play, the Italian border, is depicted being crossed, if not by Galileo, at least by his work and his pupil. These issues have important consequences for the audience's orientation towards the action, but, in a Brecht play, they also have a further significance. Brecht rightly recognized that implicit in any concern for the audience's perspective on the action is a concern for its mode of participation, and from that recognition much else follows.

The Second Mrs. Tanqueray, we noted, invites us into the social world of the Tanquerays and leads us steadily towards its limiting horizons. *A Doll's House* focuses on and guides us beyond the doorways of the doll's house by means of an image network that allows the audience to discover more about the situation than the characters know. Both plays invite us inside a domain and then guide us towards its horizons. *A Dream Play*, however, situates us from the beginning outside the margins of the domain it predominantly dramatizes. The play's painted wings provide a constant visual frame to the Earth-domain and remind us of an unyielding limit placed upon variety within that domain. But if the first two plays invite us inside a central domain and the third locates us outside one, the *Life of Galileo* refuses to establish a central domain at all; instead, it invites the audience to participate in the process of deciding what is to be regarded as the major domain of the play. Is it Galileo's life as a scientist (as much of the action would suggest), his life as a whole (as the title would suggest), the domain of Italian society (as suggested by Galileo's travels and encounters, and by the final scene's focus on the Italian border), or is it some larger realm (as Andrea's crossing of the border at the end would suggest)? There is much in the play to indicate that our inquiry can be pursued further, for one of the play's recurring images, and the basis for its disturbing plurality, is an interplanetary perspective of multiplicity and motion:

> GALILEO: Overnight, the universe has lost its center and now in the morning it has any number of centers. Now any point in the universe may be taken as a center. . . . In the constellation of Orion alone there are five hundred fixed stars. Those are the many worlds, the countless other worlds, the stars beyond stars that the man they burned talked about. (pp. 6, 21)

These ever-expanding borders provide, in the texture of the play, information that guides us towards an understanding of its episodic structure and of the new kind of audience role the new structure requires. The play acknowledges the importance of Galileo's cosmic insights[2] by abandoning the notion of a single, privileged, earthly domain with an obvious centre and fixed horizons. It takes up, instead, in social and individual spheres, the notion of provisional domains, their realms of implication, and their modes of interaction. The abandonment of a fixed centre eliminates, with a single stroke, the fixed and limiting horizon that Strindberg placed around the world of

Earth. Analogies drawn between movements in society and movements among the stars reinstate change where A Dream Play offered only circumscribed variety. The life of Galileo becomes, not just the story of an individual, but an emblem of an individual domain which participates in local social domains, which participate, in their turn, in a Christian domain, which participates, in its turn, in a national domain, which participates in a human domain, which participates in a planetary domain, which participates in a galactic domain, and so on. The play's basic concern is not an accurate historical rendition of the life of Galileo, but an episodic exploration of the possibilities open to an individual of participating in and contributing to movement and change in the larger domains that surround him. And that exploration of the role of the individual in larger domains implicates the audience in the process of assigning interpretative and ethical priority to any domain.

The life of Galileo is not, thus, a given centre of the worlds in which Galileo participates. It is a selected centre, one chosen by the author and privileged by the play; the basis of that privilege is not that this is the only possible centre for viewing movement in the depicted domains, but that it is a valuable centre to posit for the pragmatic aims of the play. It offers a useful place to stand, an informative vantage point, an illuminating perspective. In a play which questions the certainty of all centres and the permanence of all limits, the choice of a pragmatic centre is one that must be pragmatically justified by what it enables the audience, by comparison and contrast, to see. What we are thus to look at closely is not just what Galileo sees, but also what other people see of the relationships among dramatized domains – domains that extend from the individual through the social to the cosmic.

To put the issue like this is to return to our discussion of domains of implication as they persistently reassert themselves in the modern theatre. The Life of Galileo seeks to establish links that run from the creativity of the individual to the continuity of the cosmos. The more extreme forms of well-made plays, naturalistic plays and expressionist plays found such inclusiveness impossible to sustain. Indeed, the tendency of each to privilege particular domains of experience was achieved at some cost to others, and gave rise, as we saw in the preceding chapters, to compensatory attempts to revive the neglected domains. However, as Sokel points out in discussing expressionism, this oscillation can generate not ultimate synthesis, but persistent fragmentation.[3] We must thus try to understand how Brecht forged relationships between elements that often remained antithetical to others.[4] He established the anti-mimetic as a means of approaching, not avoiding, the external world; he made interest in the individual a means of access to, rather than an alternative to, the social; he adopted transcendental perspectives, not in preference to earthly perspectives, but as a supplement to them; and he adapted differences between on-stage and off-stage worlds into a means, not only of establishing mutual autonomy, but also of establishing mutual interdependence. The key issue is the context Brecht offers for reconciling the individual and the social, the created and the given, the aesthetic and the ethical, the play and the audience. And that context, for better or worse, interweaves in complex ways the role assigned to the audience in Brecht's notion of an Epic Theatre,[5] and the role assigned to the individual in Brecht's notion of a Marxist society.

At first glance, Brecht's interest in Marxism and his interest in theatre might seem to be on a collision course. Popular notions of Marxism suggest that Brecht must, perforce, be an ideological fanatic intent on imposing his beliefs on the audience; popular notions of Brecht's Epic Theatre suggest that Brecht must be committed, via his alienation techniques, to allowing the audience to make up its own mind about everything. Alternately accused of having only one thing on his mind[6] and of having nothing very clear on his mind,[7] Brecht thus seems susceptible to being viewed as an ideological fanatic or as a radical sceptic. These positions are more easily reconciled when we recognize that Marxism, like most other movements, is not reducible to a single coherent doctrine with fixed beliefs and fixed goals, and that doubt as a constructive instrument of social change is more central to Brecht's Marxism and to his major plays than are certainty, credulity or inherited dogma.

A few lines in a Brecht poem are informative in this respect:

> You who are a leader of men, do not forget
> That you are that because you doubted other leaders.
> So allow the led
> Their right to doubt.[8]

This focus on doubt, with its implicit welcome to change of any kind, is quite consistent with one major strand of Marxist thought, but it is a strand often neglected by those who equate Marxist thinking with vulgar Marxist certainties about capitalism and communism. The two poles of the Marxist movement exist, however, in uneasy equilibrium. As Gray puts it, the 'Heraclitan welcome to the changing world . . . is paradoxically as much a part of Marxism as its eschatological vision of a classless society'.[9] Brecht does not set out to resolve this paradox, but the prime focus of the major plays is on exploring the forces of persistence and change, rather than on prophesying the ultimate results of their conflict.

In this respect, Brecht's thinking is, as many have recently pointed out, linked with that of Karl Korsch.[10] White notes that Brecht developed his Marxism in Korsch's discussion groups and consequently '*sees Marxism . . . more as a method than as dogma*: a tool for interpreting the movement of history and criticising bourgeois society, not a unified world-image or complete system, still less a statement of Utopian historical ideas to be realised' (my emphasis).[11] This focus on a society's ideological superstructure and its contradictions sets Brecht apart from Marxists whose major concern is the economic substructure. That the two are closely related is fundamental to all branches of Marxist thought, but 'Brecht tends to provide a critique of parts of the superstructure of bourgeois ideology – family, science, charity, religion – more than he looks at the economic substructure'.[12] The major plays thus draw attention to clashes in social structures that need to be resolved, rather than to the nature of social structures that might replace them, or to the economic substructures that would be needed to sustain them. Brecht offers no clear answers and no ultimate trans-domain perspective in his major plays, but focuses instead on local transactions among a variety of domains.[13]

The role of the audience in coming to terms with Brecht's plays is thus somewhat different from the role assigned it in the plays we have discussed so far. But it is not so much a radical shift from the attempts by Pinero, Ibsen and Strindberg to control the audience's orientation to the action as it is a logical extension of them. Once the public certainties of Pinero's world have given way to the pluralistic perspectives of other dramatists, the capacity of any single play to offer definitive answers to the questions it raises is consequently diminished. A drama focusing on pluralistic worlds must increasingly share with the audience the responsibility for deciding the rights of the characters to prizes and punishments. In this respect, a major trend in the modern theatre merges with a trend in Marxist thinking as interpreted by Korsch and Brecht. For them, Marxism is not a repository of established dogma, but a technique of shared inquiry that promotes individual intervention in not fully understood social processes. Individuals in society at large or in the theatre in particular have a very different role when asked to participate in an inquiry than when asked to assent to pre-existing values. And to promote the kind of inquiry Brecht has in mind, he needs not only to suggest a change of audience role, but to provoke it and guide it by experimenting with the structures of the drama, the performance arena and the theatre itself. Indeed, the changes proved so extensive that Brecht spent most of his creative life seeking to work them out. And one point that emerges from the Korsch/ Brecht version of Marxism is fundamental to our understanding of the mode of inquiry that became so characteristic of Brecht's Epic Theatre.

For Korsch and Brecht, the dialectical progress of human society is no longer a Hegelian dialectic leading inevitably towards a pre-conceived social and spiritual synthesis, but a mode of social interaction that leads us to examine the need for, and possibility of, intervention in domains neither fully understood nor in their final form. This revision in the nature of dialectical social progress is important, not just for what it reveals of Korsch and Brecht's views, but for the implications it has for the status of any political or aesthetic theory. And the central implication is the provisional status this shift imposes, not only on social domains, but on the very means by which we examine them, whether in terms of theatre productions or of political theory.

Thus, Tatlow, noting 'the characteristic withholding of conclusions in

Brecht's theatre',[14] argues that we need to reconsider what we mean by dialectics if we are to deal appropriately with the term in Brecht's work. But preceding attempts to distinguish 'positive dialectics' from 'negative dialectics', in order to characterize Korsch and Brecht's similarity to and difference from Hegel, are, he argues, less than adequate. Rather, he suggests, we might adopt the term 'critical dialectics' as most appropriate to capture both the positive and negative aspects of Brecht's exploration of social contradictions.[15] Brecht does not, he notes, dramatize or promise 'the cessation of contradiction'; his 'critical dialectics does not supply models for emulation, presupposing closed totalities, but stimulation for intervention. In his view, dialectics enabled interventionary thought.'[16] Kellner builds upon the same point:

> For Korsch, the Marxian dialectic is a *critical dialectic* that aims at the critique and transformation of the existing bourgeois order. The Marxian dialectic sees reality as a process of continual change and is interested in those contradictions and antagonisms that make radical transformation possible.[17]

The key point here is not the term we use to characterize the new dialectics, but the *recognition that changes in the data under investigation promote changes in the means of their investigation*. The dialectical instrument of investigation – the concept of dialectics itself – moves from the single possibility envisaged by Hegel to the emergence of the further possibilities of negative and critical dialectics. These changes are necessary evidence of the historical flexibility of a method for examining historical change, but they exemplify a vital point. In the Korsch/Brecht view of Marxism, nothing, not the social structure, nor the individual psyche, nor the concepts and instruments of investigation, is permanently fixed, and this must perforce include the theatre and the audience's relationship to it. Müller rightly points out that 'the proper use of [Korsch's] scholarly endeavors demands a dialectic view of dialectics';[18] but what, we might ask, is an equivalent attitude towards the theatre as an instrument of inquiry?

When Brecht sets out to criticize preceding modes of theatre, it is very much in terms of their limited and limiting impact on their audiences. Brecht rightly perceived that established play structures and conventional theatre structures tended to precipitate a constant reiteration of inherited views, and it was thus essential to change those structures if the theatre were to do anything new:

> The theatre itself resists any alteration of its function, and so it seems desirable that the spectator should read plays whose aim is not merely to be performed in the theatre but to change it: out of mistrust of the theatre. Today we see the theatre being given absolute priority over the actual plays . . . the theatre can stage anything: it theatres it all down.[19]

This concern for a theatre which 'theatres it all down' is, of course, in accord with Brecht's larger recognition that any inherited structure, institution, or ideology has an unfailing capacity to take new things and transform them so as to make them compatible with everything that preceded them. When Stanton sought to make a similar point about play structure, notably well-made-play structure, he was recognizing the same problem without identifying it quite accurately. He pointed out that the phrase 'well-made play' had become 'synonymous with trashy playwriting – with the play that amuses but says nothing'.[20] The problem is not, however, that the strong structural form makes the well-made play say nothing, but that it is likely to make it say similar things again and again. The play's unchanging larger structure tends to impose conformity upon incipiently idiosyncratic character and theme. Brecht, thus concerned with changing the role of the audience in the theatre, finds himself not only involved in changing play structures, but also in changing performance techniques and theatre structures. Local revisions in the theatrical event will not suffice to establish the appropriate audience role of inquiry into situations depicted in plays, for those revisions might themselves rigidify and consequently inhibit, rather than promote, inquiry.

Brecht's famed table of contrasts (see below), depicting differences between his theatre and established theatre, is thus a comprehensive one. It grapples with every level of the theatrical event from local detail to larger social function, and the scope of that revision is as important as any individual part of it.

Brecht's table of contrasts[21]

Dramatic Theatre	*Epic Theatre*
plot	narrative
implicates the spectator in a stage situation	turns the spectator into an observer, but
wears down his capacity for action	arouses his capacity for action
provides him with sensations	forces him to take decisions
experience	picture of the world
the spectator is involved in something	he is made to face something
suggestion	argument
instinctive feelings are preserved	brought to the point of recognition
the spectator is in the thick of it, shares the experience	the spectator stands outside, studies
the human being is taken for granted	the human being is the object of the inquiry
he is unalterable	he is alterable and able to alter
eyes on the finish	eyes on the course
one scene makes another	each scene for itself
growth	montage

linear development	in curves
evolutionary determinism	jumps
man as a fixed point	man as a process
thought determines being	social being determines thought
feeling	reason

Even as Brecht draws attention to the scope of these differences, he is at pains to make clear one major limitation upon them. He insists on the historicity of his own innovations by reminding us that they are connected to the very past they depart from. This table shows 'changes of emphasis as between the dramatic and epic theatre' – a point registered even more strongly in an accompanying footnote that anticipates possible misunderstanding: 'This table does not show absolute antitheses but mere shifts of accent.'[22] As a historical phenomenon, Brecht's theatre could not suddenly arise as a theatre radically opposed to and disconnected from all that had gone before. But these 'mere shifts of accent' nevertheless amount to a radical revision of the whole theatrical event – the nature of the theatre and of the décor, the role of the actors, and the role of the audience.

The comprehensiveness of Brecht's concern for the Epic Theatre is not, we should note, an indication that he had some persisting set of underlying beliefs, for his ideas evolved over a long period of time. Furthermore, we should not confuse the comprehensiveness of his concern with any incipient desire for overall unity in the theatre or in society. There is, however, a continuity to his developing ideas and to the domains in which he applies them. The mode of inquiry he addresses to the theatre is itself an example of the mode of inquiry he applies, and seeks to induce others to apply, to society at large. And we must look carefully at its nature, for there is a commitment to change in Brecht's political and theatre views that must be at odds not only with inherited theories and structures, but with any new ones that might replace them.

We should therefore note with interest that, characteristically, Brecht's first impulse is to establish, and insist on the autonomy of, several domains, but only as a means of bestowing upon these domains, via the audience, a new kind of interdependence:

> Once the content becomes, technically speaking, an independent component, to which text, music and setting 'adopt attitudes'; once illusion is sacrificed to free discussion, and once the spectator, instead of being enabled to have an experience, is forced as it were to cast his vote; then a change has been launched which goes far beyond formal matters and begins for the first time to affect the theatre's social function.[23]

The relative autonomy of different aspects of the theatrical event is thus no mere rhetorical device. It is methodologically essential if anything new is to be worked into the theatre and if anything new is to be achieved by the theatre. Both factors depend, for Brecht, on the theatre's capacity to confer a new role upon the audience by promoting its interaction with these separate but relatable domains, and it is to be an interaction of a quite specific kind.

Brecht's insistence upon a 'separation of the different elements'[24] in the play and in the theatre is an insistence that invites the spectator to participate in the process of recombining them, in effect, 'to cast his vote' on the issues the play raises. But it is to be his vote, his as an individual, not as the playwright's proxy. And it is here that we encounter Brecht's most radical revision of the audience's role in the theatre. The audience is not just to be offered a fixed set of options to choose between; it is to be led towards a recognition of a mode of inquiry that enables it to construct its own choices. Brecht is thus assigning himself a goal which is incipiently at odds with his claim that a theatre tends to 'theatre it all down'. If this is true of preceding theatre structures, will it not also be true of any, including Brecht's, that replace them? Brecht's solution is a clever one. The playwright must of course offer a structured play, the theatre must offer a structured mode of perform-ance, and the society must always manifest a structured mode of organization; but the audience is to retain a degree of freedom by being offered a perspective that is not restricted to any single one of them.

A comparison with Strindberg's A Dream Play will suffice to establish the important point here. At the beginning of the play, Strindberg seeks to free his audience from the limitations of inherited perspectives by offering us the benefits of a transcendent perspective upon the Earth. By locating its (and our) perspective outside the domain it largely dramatizes, the play suggests the possibility of escape from the limits of any single earthly perspective and of control over the chaos of pluralistic earthly perspectives. But this kind of escape and this kind of control give rise to problems of their own. We are located above and beyond our world and see it from afar, with a perspective that uncertainly mingles transcendent subjectivity with a putative objectiv-ity, but which turns out finally to be just another subjectivity. The adequacy of the Daughter's perspective is steadily brought into question, but in spite of her attempts to change it, it remains a predominantly external perspective, one also imposed upon the audience by the play, and one from which change on the planet seems less decisive than the limits to that change. But for Brecht, the key issue is not whether the audience's perspective is transcend-ent or earthly, but whether or not it is single. The audience is to be offered not one perspective, but several, so that it can contemplate not only the differing stances the play offers towards society, the theatre, the play, and any component of it, but also the possibility of conceiving of new ones. The plays offer not only examples of problems and of possible solutions, but also examples of how to think about problem contemplation and solution construction. Instead of a convergent theatrical event trapping the theatre, the play and the audience in a single perspective, the Epic theatrical event provides a divergent perspective which offers the audience a degree of freedom to put things together for itself.

In one sense, of course, this commitment to a divergent theatrical event itself exemplifies and induces a particular ideology of provisionality and change. The audience is offered a degree of guidance as well as a degree of freedom. There can be no fully objective perspective, no ahistorical knowledge, no 'innocent eye'. But if we agree, as we surely must, that an 'innocent eye' is always an ignorant eye (ignorant of its own presuppositions), it does not necessarily follow that all eyes confessing their lack of innocence are equally knowledgeable of the nature of their bias. And here, Brecht seeks not to eliminate bias that cannot be eliminated, but to control it by revealing it. Again and again he insists that 'we and our forebears have a different relationship to what is being shown',[25] a difference exemplified in Brecht's requirement *that we constantly be shown that we are being shown something* ('he who is showing should himself be shown').[26] This change is crucial in its effect on audience participation in the theatrical event. On the one hand, it confers upon the plays and their parts a degree of distance and autonomy that enables the spectator to judge, and not just assimilate, what they have to offer. And, on the other hand, it enables the spectator to observe and consider, and not just accept as given and inevitable, the kinds of connection any play establishes among its various competing parts.

> As we cannot invite the audience to fling itself into the story as if it were a river and let itself be carried vaguely hither and thither, the individual episodes have to be knotted together in such a way that the knots are easily noticed. The episodes must not succeed one another indistinguishably but must give us a chance to interpose our judgement. . . . The parts of the story have to be carefully set off one against another by giving each its own structure as a play within the play.[27]

This repeated invitation to the audience to judge the contribution of the parts and of the whole is a repeated manifestation of Brecht's desire to construct a new mode of inquiry in a new kind of theatre – a theatre that does not 'theatre it all down'. Such a theatre offers not an institutionally grounded unity, but a functional discontinuity in which juxtaposed domains interact and conflict, and invite audience intervention.

It is fascinating to perceive the consistency with which Brecht insists upon autonomy, distance and considered linkage at every level of his analysis of the drama, the theatrical event, and social and historical events. And it is in that comprehensiveness that we begin to perceive a key feature in Brecht's attempt to develop a widely applicable mode of inquiry. Thus, 'the music must strongly resist the smooth incorporation which is generally expected of it and turns it into an unthinking slavery. Music does not "accompany" except in the form of comment.'[28] The stage designer, with a range of props, costumes, signs, screens, projectors, lights and décors at his disposal, and with the imperative of sustaining an illusion of pre-existing reality removed from his shoulders, can likewise use his range of instruments to comment, criticize and otherwise convey information 'of which the persons on the stage [are] sometimes unaware'.[29] Any of the non-verbal components of the drama can adopt 'an attitude . . . towards the incidents shown'.[30] Each part of the play can challenge other parts, the play can challenge the theatre, the theatrical event can challenge the audience, and the end-result might well be a challenge to society. But whatever level the audience is invited to focus on, the process of alienation, of enforced distance and invited judgement, persists, in a way that proves central to Brecht's whole mode of social inquiry.

The mode of inquiry that the audience is thus asked to participate in requires it to develop new kinds of participatory skills, one of which bears a close relationship to a recurring concern of modern dramatists – the focusing of attention on borders of domains. And in Brecht's case, this focus on borders takes on a particular epistemological and social function. When, for example, he discusses his use of projected or displayed titles in the Epic Theatre, Brecht defends it in a characteristic way – he immediately relates this local detail to larger domains and to processes involved in linking those domains. And that recurring concern for external linkage exemplifies a key point in Brecht's mode of inquiry and in the role offered us as audience – that to understand any domain appropriately, we have to be capable not only of participating in it, and not only of standing back from it, but of stepping beyond 'the confines of the subject' displayed to its larger implications and more distant relationships.

> The orthodox playwright's objection to the titles is that the dramatist ought to say everything that has to be said in the action, that the text must express everything within its own confines. The corresponding attitude for the spectator is that he should not think about a subject, but within the confines of the subject. But this way of subordinating everything to a single idea, this passion for propelling the spectator along a single track where he can look neither right nor left, up nor down, is something that the new school of playwriting must reject.[31]

What Brecht wishes to do to the audience is not to propel it along 'a single track', but to develop in it the capacity and the inclination to do precisely what he does in his own method of inquiry – to step back from the domain in question, locate its borders, and examine its relationships to, and perceive it from the perspective of, other contiguous domains. The audience is asked to weigh differing perspectives, to choose among them, and, if necessary, to invent new ones. Brecht called the ability he wishes the audience to exercise 'complex seeing'[32] – the capacity to recognize, invent and apply competing perspectives to issues arising within any domain by turning quickly to the edges of the domain and to the relationships it contracts there with contiguous domains. Brecht's more general mode of inquiry, made explicit in his defence of the use of displayed titles, thus merges with his interest in historicizing reality, which is designed to serve a similar purpose: '*Historicizing* involves judging a particular social system from another social system's point of view.'[33] In every case, the playwright aims to give the audience the distance and the capacity to see things anew by focusing on the borders that separate and link domains.

Brecht's theories thus give the whole issue of mimesis in the theatre a subtle twist. In order to provoke the audience to see beyond the confines of the play, the stage and the theatre, the play must avoid any illusion of familiar reality or it will undermine its own attempt to provoke thought by means of a distanced perspective. Reality-reproducing mimesis thus goes the same way as empathy.[34] Both, for Brecht, invite the audience into a familiar world and lose it there. The contrast with the naturalistic impulse and its persistence in Strindberg's expressionism is quite clear. Strindberg, wishing to ward off accusations of theatricality and irrelevance to the off-stage world, held on to the notion that his *A Dream Play* was 'imitating' a dream and could thus continue to claim a mimetic link to the off-stage world. *Brecht, however, reverses the argument by claiming that relevance to the off-stage world is grounded in difference as much as in similarity, for it is only because the theatre is a distinct and different domain that it can provide anything that the world outside the theatre cannot provide.* Far from wishing to mask these differences, Brecht wishes to draw careful attention to them: the theatre must 'stop pretending not to be theatre'.[35]

The need for autonomy in the various domains of the theatre (light, music, costume, voice, props, set, etc.), so that each can make an independent contribution to the process of 'complex seeing', thus aligns itself neatly with the need for non-naturalistic phenomena to intrude into naturalistic settings and dispel incipient theatrical illusion and emerging empathy. If the role of the theatre is to promote understanding of, and intervention in, the processes of society, it cannot, in Brecht's terms, pretend to be simply a reproduction of that society. Only by alienating itself from the world outside the theatre can it promote intervention in that world. It achieves its social function not just by selectively reproducing, but by selectively replacing the world off-stage – replacing it with a world that allows and enables distanced consideration of social processes divorced from their familiar contexts. The aim is not one of remoteness from the everyday off-stage world, but one of remoteness from the illusion of reproducing that world – a remoteness that, paradoxically enough, is fundamental to its subsequent relevance to that world.

The logic of Brecht's mode of inquiry thus carries itself inexorably forward. The play that is internally divided into semi-autonomous parts also 'divides its audience'[36] into semi-autonomous parts debating the issues raised by the play; the play also divides itself from the audience by insisting upon the autonomy of the domain of the theatre and its difference from the world outside the theatre; and thematically it displays a social world itself consti-tuted by interacting but divided domains.[37] In this consistent manner, Brecht's mode of inquiry simultaneously separates and recombines domains as local as the lighting in the theatre and as large as crises in the cosmos. And this breadth and comprehensiveness of concern is achieved without a single trans-historical context or a single transcendent perspective. The mode of inquiry, the direction of discovery, is not just from the outside looking in, but also, as Galileo's telescope would suggest, from the inside looking out at other domains, and thereafter looking back, with new knowledge, at one's own. The audience that learns to 'think for itself' is one trained in the technique of 'complex seeing', one that instinctively locates itself beyond 'the confines of the subject' and views it in the context of others. We thus locate in Brecht's mode of inquiry an interest in borders that is characteristic of the continuity of the modern theatre.[38] But for Brecht this mode of inquiry must also constantly exhibit itself as a mode of inquiry. Though Brecht at certain moments in his life, theories and plays lapsed into vulgar Marxist propaganda, that was not his enduring stance as Marxist, playwright or drama theorist. He was more interested in helping people to find out for themselves than in finding out for them.

Brecht's Marxist and Epic mode of inquiry can thus promote discovery without offering transcendent knowledge or calling upon anyone to move beyond the reach of his or her own historical moment. That moment is, of course, where we start from, but not necessarily where we end up, for time moves as we move. Brecht seeks freedom, for himself and for us, from unnecessary constraint, but he recognizes that this seeking is itself always historically contingent. It starts somewhere that is given, that is inherited, and goes on from there. The movement from one domain to another is always a movement that raises its anchor somewhere, whether it be in the domain of the theatre, the domain of science, the domain of a single society, or the domain of a single life – such as the life of Galileo. And with that recognition we turn to the play and to the circumscribed domains it offers as the necessary constraint upon, and the necessary condition for, any pursuit of freedom and change.

Brecht's *Life of Galileo* is based upon an examination of the relationships among three major domains: that of the planets and the stars, that of Catholic society in Italy, and that of an individual life – the life of Galileo Galilei. Each of these domains exhibits certain kinds of fixity and certain tendencies towards change, and the differing rates of motion in these three spheres provide competing perspectives to the play and govern its major thematic conflicts. Whenever one character passes judgement on issues or on other characters, it is in terms of a particular range of implication that is derived from one or more of the competing domains. Scientific knowledge, for example, is viewed alternately as a matter of locating fundamental truths of the physical universe, as a means of improving the material or spiritual welfare of social groups, or as an instrument for satisfying Galileo's appetites for fame and fortune. The value of such knowledge shifts with the shift in perspective; it also shifts from one speaker to another, and from one time to another in the life of a single speaker. And these ever-shifting perspectives offer a critical background to a central character who, repeatedly dropping a stone to the earth, seems committed to the notion of stabilizing truth on the basis of a single, privileged perspective. The action of the play undermines his early convictions and warns us to be wary of the equally forthright judgement he offers of himself towards the end of the play. Galileo's pupil, Andrea, refuses 'to believe that [his] devastating analysis can be the last word' (p. 95), and, as the structure of the play demonstrates, last words are not necessarily any more conclusive than other words. The audience, left without the dominant perspective of any single character, is thus forced, appropriately enough, to set about constructing its own 'last word', its own perspective, from the action of the play as a whole.

The play sets out to interweave its three major domains by giving us a sequence of scenes which are introduced in terms of, and grounded in, the three different domains. Each scene is located for us in terms of planetary time (the calendar year), social location (Padua, Florence, etc.), and a particular stage in Galileo's life. Thus, the opening song informs us:

> In the year sixteen hundred and nine
> Science' light began to shine.
> At Padua city, in a modest house
> Galileo Galilei set out to prove
> The sun is still, the earth is on the move. (p. 3)

We note also that the immediate use of the metaphor in 'science' light began to shine' links one social domain (that of science) to the planetary domain, and to the individual domain of one particular scientist. We are thus prompted to look not only for differences but also for similarities between these domains. The three domains provide the structural and thematic parameters of an on-stage world that we encounter in a series of episodic fragments. These episodes occur during a temporal span that covers twenty-eight years – the major creative period of Galileo's scientific life, a small span in the 2000-year history of Catholic-dominated Italy, and an infinitesimal span in the 10 to 18 billion-year history of the universe.

The central clash in the play seems, at first glance, to be that between two social institutions – science and the Catholic Church – over the status of empirical knowledge. Galileo, as the spokesman for science, seeks to give it the privileged status of unqualified and unqualifiable value. The cardinals, as the spokesmen for the Church, seek to give the Church the same status and to bestow upon scientific knowledge the role of an instrument in society's pursuit of such higher values as faith, hope and charity. The resulting clash is then variously seen as a clash between reason and belief, or between new truths and old errors, or between doubt and faith. The play thus seems to invite the audience to make judgements at a high level of generality on the basis of rather limited and somewhat inconsistent evidence. But this inter-pretation of the play locates the action primarily in two large, but none the less local, social domains, with science seeking support for its views in the larger planetary domain, and the Church doing likewise in more abstract heavenly domains. In neither case do the interests of the power groups relate very closely to the scenes that are so often cut from the play.

If we shift our attention, however, from the social institutions to their spokesmen, the play immediately becomes more complex, and the issues much less sharply drawn. On the one hand, the issues threaten to degenerate into a clash between one kind of self-serving belief and another, and on the other hand, they begin to register a radical disagreement about the possibility, desirability and appropriate speed of social change. But what is more important is that the similarities between the positions of Galileo and of the cardinals become as important as their differences. As they do so, the process of 'complex seeing' is initiated in the play, and issues no longer clear-cut become the responsibility of an audience involved in the choices from a more distant perspective. The similarities and differences between Galileo and the cardinals thus become a major issue of audience concern.

Galileo, initially obsessed by a notion of truth for its own sake, seems opposed to the cardinals when he rejects discussion of the social and spiritual consequences of his discoveries. He claims that he is not a theologian, but a mathematician (p. 23), and thus suggests the possibility of a radical division between these domains. It turns out that he is not, however, without his own social interests: early in the play, he seems to conceive of society as an aggregate of proto-scientists, people who regard doubt and discovery as the unchallengeable agents of joyous social progress.

> Every day something new is being discovered. Even men a hundred years old let youngsters shout in their ears to tell them about the latest discoveries. . . . where faith had ruled for a thousand years, doubt has now set in. . . . The heavens, we know now, are empty. And that has given rise to joyous laughter. . . . The people of our cities are always eager for novelty, they will be glad to hear that in our new astronomy the earth moves too. It has always been taught that the stars are pinned to a crystal vault, which prevents them from falling down. Now we've mustered the courage to let them float free, with nothing to hold them; they're in full sail, just as our ships are in full sail. (p. 5)

The Catholic Church is not, of course, inclined to greet with joyous acceptance such novel truths emerging from doubt and discovery, not least because it has a very different notion of society and of what is good for it. The play seems thus to set its two most visible protagonists in radically opposing camps over the value to society of novelty and discovery. As the Cardinal Inquisitor puts it: 'The gentlemen of the Holy Office are worried that a prelate or even a cardinal might get lost in such enormous spaces. The Almighty might even lose sight of the pope himself' (p. 54).

The fear of 'getting lost' while searching is predominant in the minds of the spiritual and secular leaders of Italy, and they thus prefer inherited truth over novel truth. The fear of being trapped in error and thus prevented from searching is predominant in the minds of those, like Galileo, who prefer newly proved truth over inherited and inadequate truth. These conflicting attitudes towards truth register conflicting estimates of its social consequences, estimates exemplified in the conflicting values conferred upon centres and boundaries that are a major preoccupation of the play. The model of the Ptolemaic system, which attracts attention in the play's first scene, is conceived by the Church as a harmonious structure conferring privileged value on its centre; but it is viewed by Galileo and Andrea as an enclosing set of spheres whose edges mark the boundaries of a human prison (p. 4). The same competing perspectives confer conflicting value on the alternative Copernican system, which removes earth from the centre of the universe. For Galileo, this implies an exhilarating freedom, but for an old cardinal at the Vatican, it offers only a radical reduction in the stature of human beings: 'I hear this Mr. Galilei has moved man from the center of the universe to somewhere on the edge. Obviously he's an enemy of mankind. And ought to be treated as such' (p. 45).

At first glance, these opposing attitudes towards the status of doubt, discovery and empirical facts can seem to be readily resolvable in favour of Galileo. But on this issue, as on others we will encounter, Galileo and the cardinals are not as radically different as they initially appear. The cardinals, we might feel, are simply defending their interests and their power in this case. Galileo claims that he is interested in the general social good while the pope is interested in keeping the Earth at the centre of the universe – 'because he wants the See of St. Peter to be in the center of the world!' (p. 57). The play soon undermines this selfless/selfish dichotomy by demonstrating that Galileo's interest in discovery is also self-serving, and that his understanding of people and of the general good is at times no more or less persuasive than that of the pope and the cardinals. Galileo's selfless vision of a new society, we soon see, is a prelude to a confession of self-concern: 'I'm forty-six years old and I've accomplished nothing that satisfies *me*' (my emphasis) (p. 14). There are also several references in the play to his self-indulgence as a scientist for whom thinking bouts bear some resemblance to drinking bouts. Furthermore, the cardinals' position, while certainly registering their own self-interest, is not without genuine concern for their flock – as the agonized defence by the Little Monk indicates (pp. 56–8). These mixed motives on both sides of the argument are of fundamental importance to a play that insists upon 'complex seeing' and upon avoidance of the polarized simplicities that we encounter in a well-made play (a fixed value system, a closed mind and a conception of the leading character as hero or villain).

It should not be overlooked, however, that both Galileo himself, and many critics of the play, have nevertheless tended to approach Galileo in terms of the hero/villain dichotomy. And we must recognize that there is much in this play of a rather traditional kind. Indeed, part of the narrative line of this play could easily be assimilated into the standard narrative plot of a well-made play. The Exposition informs us that Galileo is an underpaid scientist in Venice who wants only to obtain more time for his research. The Complication is that to get more time he must move to Florence where the financial rewards are better but the social restraints upon permissible truth are much greater. The Crisis comes when Galileo offers proof that the Copernican hypothesis about planetary movement is valid, while the Ptolemaic hypothesis, which accords with Church doctrine, is wrong. The Resolution has Galileo recanting under threat of torture and excommunication and ending his days imprisoned by those he sought to oppose. At the end he endorses, at least in part, the position of those who would subordinate the pursuit of scientific fact to higher social purposes.

There is noticeable common ground between this component of the play and the well-made-play component of *The Second Mrs. Tanqueray*. We have the same rebelliousness, confrontation, conversion and self-condemnation. And for those whose criticism of the play goes little further than establishing a narrative progression, this conversion and self-condemnation can appear to be the major point of the play. It has been argued that

> Galileo becomes a criminal because by his cowardice he has established the tradition of the scientist's subservience to the state – the tradition that, according to Brecht, reached its culmination in the production of the atomic bomb, which science put at the disposal of ordinary, nonscientific men, to serve their power politics.[39]

To take such a view of the play would be to risk reducing it to the very kind of play Brecht, throughout his career, was trying not to write. Such an interpretation would invoke the very homogeneity of perspective and value that the play has repeatedly sought to subvert. If scientists are faced with only two possible modes of behaviour – those of acknowledging or refusing to acknowledge the superior value of non-scientific facts – then we would appear to have a simplistic play in which scientists must choose to be either criminals or heroes, and audiences have only one simple decision to make.

There is no denying the fact that the play offers one perspective not unlike the one suggested above. And there is no denying the fact that Brecht limits severely in this play the range of Epic devices established elsewhere in his dramatic theories and practice. The conventionally strong narrative line is consequently upgraded, but not, we should note, to the point where it becomes the single perspective of the play. The strong narrative movement towards a resolution assigning Galileo the status of hero or villain is given its strength because the play seeks to establish it as a tempting but inadequate approach to social analysis.[40] It is as important to the play to establish how tempting it is, as to establish how inadequate it is. For the larger action of the play demonstrates not that Galileo belongs in the category of criminal (rather than hero), but that the very process of setting up two such mutually exclusive categories is itself an error. The appeal of the error is established by the strong narrative line and by the restriction upon Epic critique addressed to it, and by the fact that the central character himself, Galileo, is prone to make it. But these attempts to give one component of the play its due do not justify any failure on our part to locate it in the context of other components of the play that expose its inadequacy as well as its power.

The simple polarities initially assigned to science and the Church are not, we note, finally so simple. The spokesmen for their positions reveal not just their differences, but also their similarities, not only the internal consistency of their views, but also their internal inconsistencies. And once we begin to focus on these complexities, the simplicities of the strong narrative line are steadily undermined. As the play progresses, the practicality of the beliefs of Galileo, this ostensibly practical man, are repeatedly called in question by the conflicting values that surround him. The domains with which he repeatedly interacts simply refuse to accommodate themselves to his simplistic ethical choices. And it is in the process of establishing the sheer scope of these conflicting and finally unresolved perspectives that the play takes on, what is for Brecht, a predominantly Epic, rather than Aristotelian, structure.[41] Far from resolving conflicts, far from reducing them to a single simplistic conflict, the play sets out to clarify them and give them their appropriate degree of generality. This process of clarification thus proceeds by first depicting the most obvious contrasts between opposing positions, and then undermining and revising their status. In terms which we established earlier as characteristic of modern drama, domains are first radically contrasted and then subsequently, to the appropriate degree, compared, linked and fused.

The initial polarization between a science based upon doubt and a Church based upon faith is thus steadily undermined as the play progresses. Galileo's scientific doubt and the cardinals' religious faith are both shown to have their limits. In Galileo's case, Sagredo is quick to point out that this dedicated scientist is not always ready to give doubt priority over desired belief. When he hears of Galileo's decision to take the risk of moving to Church-dominated Florence to continue his studies, Sagredo scathingly remarks: 'You may be very skeptical in your science, but you're as gullible as a child about anything that looks like a help in pursuing it. You may not believe in Aristotle, but you believe in the grand duke of Florence' (p. 27). And as Mrs Sarti puts it later, when Galileo anticipates the death of the pope: 'Fifty times that man weighs his pieces of ice, but when something happens that suits his purposes he believes it blindly!' (p. 67).

The readiness of Galileo to invest in the as yet unproved registers the limitation of his commitment to doubt at all costs, and reminds us that his commitment to the not fully proved value of scientific facts is, in its own way, as much an act of faith as that of a religious person to his chosen religion. And in the Church's case, the readiness of the cardinals to consider and test out

Galileo's ideas registers the limitation of their commitment to faith at all costs. The Church astronomer, Clavius, upholds Galileo's observations of the satellites of Jupiter (p. 46), and the new pope refuses to set the Church in opposition to the multiplication tables and to the scientific facts proved by them (p. 78).

The cardinals are, thus, by no means blind believers and Galileo by no means an inveterate doubter. But there are limits to Galileo's credulity as well as to his scepticism, and limits to the Church's willingness to doubt as well as to its commitment to inherited belief. In displaying the similarities, as well as the differences, between Galileo and the cardinals, the play has, however, begun to make complex and more puzzling their seemingly simple clash on the basis of rigidly opposing views. The domain of science and the domain of the Church are not rigidly distinct, but related in ways that invite audiences to think, and think hard.

The comparative judgements that the play constantly invites the audience to make are thus designed to preclude the very kinds of rigid judgements that Galileo makes, initially of others and finally of himself. The play displays the possibility of such judgements and also their inadequacy. Galileo's response to Andrea's condemnation of his unheroic behaviour in front of the Inquisition has thus an importance well beyond that which is customarily attributed to it. When Andrea laments the unhappy condition of a land that has no heroes, Galileo responds: 'unhappy the land that needs a hero' (p. 85). This response is important for two reasons: it shows that Galileo has learned something during the play, and it invites the audience to build upon what he has learned by weighing the role and importance of heroes in its approach to the social world of the play and to the social world outside the theatre. A hero, to be a hero, requires a fixed or fixable set of values to measure and establish his stature. Heroes may well exist in the well-made play of homogeneous values, but the absence of such homogeneity is precisely what this play in particular and Epic Theatre in general exemplify both thematically and structurally. Galileo's comment directs his on-stage audience and the audience in the auditorium to recognize the danger of depending upon any one person to remedy a situation by establishing a dominant perspective on their behalf. That is not the function of an individual in the play or in society, nor is it the function of the playwright to provide such a perspective. We must thus return to our recognition of the complexity of the relationship between Galileo and the cardinals, recognizing that we must improve our understanding not only of their disagreement, but also of the role of that disagreement in the play as a whole.

Wherever one encounters a division in the play, e.g. between new truth and inherited truth, or between self-interest and social interest, or between doubt and faith, or between reason and belief, one can always find both Galileo and the cardinals inconsistently straddling the issues and failing to restrict themselves to one side or the other. The clash between Galileo and the cardinals cannot thus resolve their competing claims, because those claims are neither single nor consistent. We may thus find ourselves wondering whether we should turn elsewhere for information as to how we should resolve their conflicts, or whether we may have yet to discover what the central conflicts of the play really are. There is reason to believe that both issues deserve our further attention, for Galileo's disagreement with the cardinals turns out, on closer inspection, to be just one of many disagreements in which he is involved throughout the play. In the course of the action, Galileo disagrees radically with almost everyone he encounters, and even, finally, with himself. We may well wish to consider whether this suggests that the battle between Galileo and the cardinals is not the play's only concern, but is symptomatic of a larger issue whose sphere of implication goes beyond the domains of science and the Church to include much more of Italian society and many more of its members. Such a view might well bestow new importance on the scenes so often cut from the play – scenes that extend our understanding of the nature of Italian society and of the play.

If we note that the various confrontations between Galileo and the cardinals display a recurring conflict between the need for empirical facts and needs that transcend empirical facts, we will discover that we have located in their confrontations a dilemma that is shared not just by Galileo and the cardinals, but by most of the other individuals we encounter in the play. And it is just this recognition that enables us to understand what Dickson describes as 'Brecht's unexpectedly generous treatment of the Church'.[42] If Galileo is no hero, the Church is no villain. Their shared dilemma is fundamental to Galileo's behaviour in front of the Inquisition, as he weighs his interest in empirical facts against his other personal concerns. It also underlies the pope's decision to place him there when he weighs the truths of the star charts against the spiritual needs of his flock and his own responsibilities to that flock. But we miss a great deal in the play if we fail to see how widespread this dilemma is in its action, as one character after another encounters some difficulty in reconciling the need for empirical facts with needs that oppose or transcend those facts.

A conflict of this kind governs Andrea's changing evaluation of Galileo throughout the play. As a child, Andrea enjoys Galileo's attention and the power his 'facts' give him to show off to his mother. In later life, he condemns Galileo, not for failing to discover facts, but for failing to become a sacrificial symbol of intellectual freedom. Later again, he admires Galileo more for his cunning than for his principles, more for his results than for his symbolic status. A similar conflict between the need for empirical facts and other kinds of need is visible in the behaviour of town and university officials in Venice, who reward Galileo's discoveries only when they further immediate economic interests. A similar point is evident in the behaviour of university officials in Florence who have a greater faith in logical disputation than in empirical observation, and consequently reject Galileo's telescope without looking through it. And similar conflicts between values recur throughout the play. Ludovico first accepts and then rejects Virginia as a bride, not primarily on the basis of her personal characteristics, but on the social standing of her father. Virginia, egged on by Mrs Sarti, turns to 'a real astronomer' (p. 61) (i.e. an astrologer), when her own immediate future is at issue, and this attitude links them both to the superstitious Italian officials who try to chase the plague away by using loud noises, and to the Little Monk who agonizes over whether to serve the poor by means of comforting lies or disturbing scientific truths. And the conflict in Galileo's life between a need for facts and other important needs emerges not only in his battles with the cardinals, but also in his having to weigh his desire for the happiness of his daughter against his desire for further scientific facts.

Galileo and the cardinals, we must therefore see, are not waging war for possession of this society's otherwise impassive soul – they are recapitulating in their behaviour the very conflicts encountered on a daily basis and in more localized spheres by all the other characters in the play. What is thus occurring in the play is not a single conflict between putative heroes, nor an isolated battle between two power groups in society, but the concentration of our attention, by means of one large conflict, on a dilemma that permeates the whole society. And what is finally at issue in the play is not which side of the conflict we come down on, but the way in which we come to understand the subtlety and complexity of the dilemma it portrays. For implicit in that understanding will be a recognition of how that dilemma, and others like it, change and are changed by the society that struggles to cope with them. And in noting these changes, we will see how social elements conflict, converge and become reconciled.

Galileo's battle with the cardinals is thus symptomatic of a larger issue whose domain is social, and the responsibility for which lies not just with scientists and clerics, but with every member of the society that has to deal with it. Once we realize that, we are on our way to looking more closely at the variety of perspectives the play offers, and not just at those of Galileo and the cardinals. If the play had only those perspectives to offer, and only the naïve versions of them, it would confuse more issues than it clarified. The play, by turning attention away, at its close, from Galileo to the Italian border, reminds us of the several ways in which it has embodied structurally what it exemplifies thematically – that the very notions of an ultimately privileged individual and an ultimately privileged domain of conflict suggest a tempting but misleading basis for understanding social continuity and social change. The conflict between Galileo and the cardinals is symptomatic of a larger and more complex social conflict, which the audience, not the play, is responsible for resolving.

When Galileo argues that 'Truth prevails only when we make it prevail. The triumph of reason can only be the triumph of reasoning men' (p. 58), he unwittingly invites wider social participation (and ultimately our participation) not only in whether truth will or will not prevail, but also in deliberations over the kind of truth that will prevail. Galileo, at this point in the play, believes that truth is simply a matter of reasoning men establishing timeless and perspectiveless empirical facts. By the end of the play, and in the course of the play, he learns, and we learn, the limitations of that view. And his mode of learning and changing is as important to the play as any conclusion he reaches.

Reasoning men, it turns out, must weigh more evidence than that Galileo is inclined to weigh when arriving at definitive truths. And Galileo learns, in his recurring disagreements with almost everyone else, the importance of casting wide the net that gathers in significant knowledge. Comments of value and importance to the basic thematic issues of the play are thus as likely to come from the partial truths of the minor characters as from the partial truths of the major characters. When Mrs Sarti emphasizes the importance of paying the milkman, she focuses on responsibilities that Galileo is prone to overlook; when little Andrea reminds Galileo that examples can be made to prove anything (p. 8), he draws attention to the incipiently distorting selectivity of all demonstrations of empirical fact; when the industrialist Vanni offers Galileo assistance, he makes us aware of economic and political facts which Galileo is prone to dismiss; when the people of Italy caricature Galileo in their carnival, their behaviour registers social factors which Galileo has not anticipated; and when Galileo contemplates demonstrating to the clergy where they are wrong, he overlooks important human facts that his assistant Sagredo is quick to point out to him: 'Do you think the pope will hear your truth when you tell him he's wrong? No, he'll hear only one thing, that you've said he's wrong' (p. 27). Truth is thus not a single thing in this play, and it must come to terms not just with empirical facts, but also with the facts of emotional, spiritual, psychological, social and economic life. Nor is truth definitively based in any single individual or institution, and its pluralistic nature demands its dispersion throughout the community for which it exists as truth.

The play thus promotes 'complex seeing' by providing important perspectives on the limitations of Galileo and the cardinals via the minor characters. In a play exploring wide-ranging social responsibilities, the Epic device of alienation is grounded as much in the conflict between the different characters as in the conflict between the characters and other elements of the drama. Galileo's own daughter rejects his commitment to empirical facts by consulting an astrologer; the Little Monk of the Vatican rejects the cardinals' commitment to authorized truth by committing himself to science. But a play exploring social issues must also move, in characteristic Epic fashion, beyond the merely social domain, beyond 'the confines of the subject', if it is to give us an appropriately extended perspective. The social must be placed in the context of other realms with which it, too, must come to terms.

We thus discover, in the repeated references to the cosmos, the basic Epic function of the three major domains of the play. The individual domain and the cosmic domain frame the social domain and help testify to its worth. The local textural irony of extravagant claims about the cosmic domain and its relationship to the social, spiritual and psychological domains consequently serves some complex functions in the play. When the Monk at the Collegium Romanum argues: 'I ask you: What is better, to get a lunar eclipse three days behind schedule or to miss out on eternal salvation altogether?' (p. 44), we are meant to laugh – but not just to laugh, for the folly of faith resisting reasoned facts is no more narrow than the belief that reasoned facts will furnish individuals with all that faith might otherwise provide. When the Very Old Cardinal wobbles around the room and assails Galileo for degrading the earth that is his home, we are again meant to laugh, but not only to laugh:

THE VERY OLD CARDINAL: I'm not some nondescript being on some little star that briefly circles around somewhere. I walk with assurance on a firm earth, it stands still, it is the center of the universe, I am in the center, and the Creator's eye rests on me, on me alone. Around me, fixed to eight crystal spheres, revolve the fixed stars and the mighty sun, which was created to illumine my surroundings. And myself as well, in order that God may see me. Hence obviously and irrefutably, everything depends on me, man, the supreme work of God, the creature in the center, the image of God, imperishable and . . . [*He collapses*]. (pp. 45–6)

The collapse of the cardinal invites us to laugh at his pride and folly, but that laughter, while undermining his views, cannot eradicate them. His cosmic imagery establishes an exhilarating connection between the individual, the social and the universal which is not to be given up readily, no matter what empirical evidence calls it in doubt, no matter how foolish the wobbling figure voicing the words. Empirical facts must come to terms at some point with human needs and human expectations which are not empirically based and not without value as a consequence of that lack. When Galileo focuses solely on the domain of empirical facts, he fails to see 'beyond the confines of the subject'. When his clashes with others on this issue begin to re-educate him, they also re-educate us, and we must note carefully how he changes.

It is a recognition of this process of interaction and change, and of its implications, that we must take with us from the play, rather than any single and superficial judgement of Galileo's status as criminal or hero. And if we look back at Galileo's final lengthy statement on the status of science, we will find within it things that not only announce, but also clarify, the implications of what Galileo has learned about science and its social responsibilities. In particular, we will find something of great importance to the play as a whole – *that the views Galileo expresses in his final long speech consist of a radically new*

*mixture of his own beliefs of the past and the beliefs of several who have challenged
and opposed him.* What we have here is, in fact, a key example of a process of
change – a process exemplified in Galileo's life as it interacts with a variety of
competing domains.

From Vanni's worries about the limitations the Church imposes upon
industry and trade (p. 75), Galileo takes his example of wool merchants
having 'to worry about the obstacles that may be put in the way of the wool
trade itself' (p. 93) – an analogy he uses to call for courage among scientists
who are similarly constrained. From the Little Monk (p. 56) he takes a
concern for the misery of the poor (p. 93) – a concern for their economic and
spiritual welfare that extends his earlier concern for their ignorance. From
Mrs Sarti (p. 7) he takes his concern for the Roman housewife's struggle for
an adequate milk supply (p. 94). From the Inquisitor via his daughter
Virginia (pp. 54 and 60), he takes his concern for scientists getting lost in the
great spaces of the universe, and their consequent danger of straying from the
authentic concerns of the mass of humanity (p. 94). And from the Very Old
Cardinal's horrified response to Galileo's realignment of the earth and other
heavenly bodies (pp. 45–6), he develops the notion that the response to
some scientific discoveries might well be 'a universal outcry of horror' (p. 94).
Indeed, the more closely one looks at this speech, the more one finds
evidence of partial fusion between the ideas with which Galileo began and
the ideas that he has had to confront which challenge his own. The synthesis
is by no means a stable and convincing one. It represents one more stage in
Galileo's growth and one more point of provisional stability in the life of one
who changes as he ages.

Such a fragile synthesis is entirely in keeping with those set up by Galileo
earlier in the play and by other characters who are also struggling to change,
grow and understand (e.g. Andrea, Mrs Sarti, Ludovico and almost every
character in the play, in particular, the old cardinal who, confronted with
Clavius's confirmation of Galileo's views, tries to come to terms socially with
the man he had earlier condemned (p. 48)). The most striking example,
however, of another character struggling to establish his own synthesis of
facts, needs and responsibilities occurs in Scene Twelve, which is devoted to
the dressing of the new pope: the 'scientist in the chair of St. Peter' (p. 65).[43]
His initial words are 'No! No! No!' (p. 78) to any attempt to coerce Galileo,
but as the scene progresses and his vestments gradually cloak his figure, the
weight of his responsibility to those committed to inherited belief bears down
upon him and upon his sense of responsibility to the world of provable facts.
His final words: 'At the very most the instruments may be shown to him'
(p. 81) are an attempt to find a middle way between allowing Galileo freedom
of speech and torturing him into silence. That the middle way is not a
satisfactory one is evident to him as well as to us; that some sort of
accommodation must be made between empirical facts and spiritual needs is
likewise evident. And the Church's dilemma is also Galileo's dilemma and

our dilemma as we watch social accommodations being made and remember our own.

If the Church's primary commitment to faith and the scientist's primary commitment to doubt both involve unpalatable costs as well as unquestioned gains, where, we must ask, is the social perspective that would satisfy those who would seek to make the most of what both science and the Church have to offer? By the end of the play, Galileo has certainly changed his position on this issue. The events of his own life have made him come to terms with the complexities of social change and not just the need for establishing empirical facts. His early position that 'as scientists we have no business asking what the truth may lead to' (p. 35) is replaced by one wider in scope, but just as shaky in its foundations:

> GALILEO: To my mind, *the only purpose of science is to lighten the toil of human existence.* If scientists, browbeaten by selfish rulers, confine themselves to the accumulation of knowledge for the sake of knowledge, science will be crippled and your new machines will only mean new hardships. Given time, you may well discover everything there is to discover, but your progress will be a progression away from humanity. The gulf between you and humanity may one day be so wide that the response to your exultation about some new achievement will be a universal outcry of horror. . . . If I had held out, scientists might have developed something like the physicians' Hippocratic oath, the vow *to use their knowledge only for the good of mankind.* (my emphases) (p. 94)

It is not difficult to see why those who focus on the narrative sequence of the play regard this as the definitive statement of the play. Nor is it difficult to see why some regard this statement as Brecht's rejection of both an activity and an implied set of values that give rise to devices such as the atomic bomb.[44] But once again, this is to read the play as one based primarily upon a well-made plot moving towards a well-made conclusion. Such a reading ignores the not fully justified self-condemnation which Galileo makes in the same speech, and the constant conflict of perspectives which provides the foundation of the play. Andrea's rejection of Galileo's self-condemnation is to be taken into consideration, as is our own recollection of all we have seen in the play that undermines Galileo's closing position as radically as the one with which he opened the play. But the key point in this speech is that if we are to accept Galileo's view that science must devote itself entirely to lightening the toil of human existence, how do we decide *scientifically* what does and what does not ease human existence? There is no empirical testing that would validate competing claims that particular research is or is not 'for the good of mankind'. And it is precisely here that the play, with its constantly competing horizons of value, makes its most fundamental and most ironic point. To resolve competing claims about the social value of scientific truth, we would need some enduring source of authoritative value –

a source that would alarmingly resemble, though not necessarily replicate precisely, the very source of value that Galileo has so strenuously opposed, that of the Catholic Church.[45] To govern science in the way he finally proposes, we would need a system of inherited value and inherited belief – a system very much like the one that forced Galileo to recant. For what is fundamentally at issue here is the role of an agent of social continuity and the role of an agent of social change. Neither can be allowed ultimate supremacy but both are needed. Science, as an agent of change, challenges all inherited belief that cannot be supported by empirical tests, and inherited belief is inherently opposed to any new challenge that could undermine it. We cannot have a merging of the incompatible – all that we can have in-stead is the interaction, competition and accommodation of the necessarily opposed.

The key point in the pope's compromise is that it is like Galileo's final position, like Galileo's opening position, and like the various positions adopted at different times by different characters. It offers an uneasy and temporary compromise between competing forces. Neither the individual characters, nor the social institutions, nor the play itself can offer a final reconciliation of the conflicts between varying kinds of fact and varying kinds of need. The play selects and focuses on specific domains, not because they offer the key to such reconciliation, but because they reveal, display and clarify the conflicting factors which each audience, each society and each era must weigh and provisionally resolve for itself. The pragmatic need for provisional resolution must always be both pragmatic and provisional. Galileo, science, or the Church, or some other institution or individual might wish to argue for the final priority of one kind of truth or one kind of resolution of competing truths. But a society armed with a telescope, a drama, and an appropriately informed imagination will always see the value of that world in the context of other worlds with which it must come to terms. The complex Copernican image of continuity and change in the cosmos is simultaneously, in the play, a challenge to Galileo's scientific investigation of laws of physical motion and a challenge to the play's investigation of laws of social motion. In both cases continuity and change must be taken into account. The Epic framing of the social domain between individual and planetary domains thus serves steadily to display to us the complex context of social motion – motion compelled and constrained by individual interests that run from local appetites to cosmic expectations.

When Galileo argued that the stars, like the ships sailing new seas, 'float free, with nothing to hold them' (p. 5), he was wrong about the stars, the ships, the social analogy he wished to draw, and the role of the individual in society. Just as the stars' freedom is a constrained freedom based upon interacting physical forces, so also the freedom of ships is constrained by wind, tide and land, the freedom of social groups is constrained by old needs as well as by new truths, and the freedom of the individual, as Galileo's own life exemplifies, is constrained by other individuals and by human needs that are every bit as potent as professional objectives. Galileo might well wish to argue that: 'Since things are thus and so, they will not remain thus and so. Because, my friend, everything is in motion' (p. 4). But in doing so, he reveals, among other things, his own readiness to believe what he wants to believe. Everything may well be in motion, but it is not unconstrained motion, and some things that are thus and so will remain thus and so whether Galileo desires it or no. And the final issue is not Galileo's desires, but ours, in deciding how we will balance the forces of continuity and the forces of change.

What the play thus sets out to clarify, in setting up its three major domains, is the nature of motion and constraint in the planetary, social and individual spheres, and the similarities and differences among them that enhance our understanding of continuity and change in social relationships and in individual growth. And what is of major importance is the differing rates of change in the several spheres the play examines. We have already seen, in Galileo's growth, the process of competition and accommodation that characterizes the progress of his individual beliefs when confronted by the beliefs of others and by the empirical facts he is able to establish. And we have in the image of Jupiter's satellites, the earth's moon, and the sun's planets, an image of the constrained motion and mutual interaction of planetary bodies. It is the nature of the constraint, as well as of the motion, that the later Galileo is at pains to understand. In his final great work, he is studying not the vagaries of free movement, but the 'laws of motion' – motion, that is, in the context of the constraints that give it its meaning and significance for us. When Galileo recants in front of the Inquisition, the scene concludes with attention focused not on Galileo, but on a reading from his subsequent work – a reading in which Galileo's interest in a single falling stone is replaced by a recognition that falling is itself a complex process, constrained in different ways for different bodies.

> Is it not obvious that a horse falling from a height of three of four ells will break its legs, whereas a dog would not suffer any damage, nor would a cat from a height of eight or nine ells, or a cricket from a tower, or an ant even if it were to fall from the moon? (p. 85)

At the beginning of the next scene (p. 86), we discover Galileo, now physically constrained by the Church and restricted to a villa near Florence, running a small wooden ball down a curved rail – interested no longer just in the fact of falling, but in the constraints that affect the speed and direction of motion.

Galileo's interest in constrained physical motion recapitulates Brecht's in constrained social motion. Linking his Epic Theatre to what he calls 'the new social scientific method known as dialectical materialism', Brecht argues that:

In order to unearth society's laws of motion this method treats social situations as processes, and it traces out all their inconsistencies. It regards nothing as existing except in so far as it changes, in other words is in disharmony with itself. This also goes for those human feelings, opinions and attitudes through which at any time the form of men's life together finds its expression.[46]

This concern for 'society's laws of motion' provides an important perspective on the nature of this and other major plays by Brecht. It proscribes the positing of future Utopias and helps explain Brecht's refusal to offer definitive solutions in the major plays. What matters most is not the positing of final destinations for the audience to reach, but the understanding and control with which it travels. The pleasure this theatre of inquiry offers is not the pleasure of unchallengeable knowledge or diverting emotion, but the 'pleasure of exploration'.[47] And the object of that exploration is the human being in his social context of constrained motion;[48] such an individual is grounded in a social, not just an individual, domain, one with a history, a degree of familiarity, but by no means an unchallengeable inevitability. 'The concern of the epic theatre is . . . eminently practical. Human behaviour is shown as alterable; man himself as dependent on certain political and economic factors and at the same time as capable of altering them.'[49]

This 'all important alterability of our surroundings'[50] is extended in the *Life of Galileo* to acknowledge constraints other than those of politics and economics, but the basic principle of the theatre persists: to offer a new kind of play and new kind of theatre, a new kind of role for its audience, and a new kind of role for members of society in general, that of taking 'pleasure in understanding things so that we can interfere'[51] and thus adjust the balance between continuity and change. But that pleasure depends upon our first having learned how to inquire so that we might understand. As Brecht put it in another context: 'mastery consists in having learned how to learn'.[52]

When the play ends with Galileo no longer the centre of attention, the play embodies structurally what it suggests thematically – that the significance and influence of his life and his work are now in the hands of those beyond the borders of his life, his society and the play. To cut the final scene from a performance is thus to overlook a point central to its structure, themes and function: that it is the responsibility of members of the audience (and of society at large) to construct and control social truths by interacting with the theatrical event and with each other. As Andrea crosses the border of Italy, his exit offers an indictment of a society that could not cope with the knowledge Galileo supplied; it also offers an invitation to other societies beyond Italy to do better. Andrea carries Galileo's lessons on the laws of physical motion across the borders of Italy; the play projects the lessons of Galileo's life across the borders of the stage. Both actions pass on to members of other societies the responsibility not for deciding whether Galileo or the Church was right, but for deciding how they themselves wish to reconcile science's interests with larger human concerns. As Galileo learns from interaction, as he extends his awareness of freedom and constraint in society, and as he comes to recognize the conflicting relationships between our need for facts and our other needs, we learn with him; and we learn not simplistic answers, but complex questions, and how to frame them for ourselves.

Galileo's telescope offers knowledge by compressing space and letting us see beyond the ordinary confines of our physical vision; the play functions by telescoping time and letting us see beyond the ordinary confines of our historical moment; both acts of compression offer challenges to our under-standing and our values by taking us, in fundamental Brechtian manner, beyond the confines of the domains which habitually ground them. The initial differences and subsequent modes of correspondence that we discern when we contemplate conflicts between science and the Church, between Galileo and the cardinals, and between Galileo and the other characters, become emblematic of the process by which we interact, via the play, with a society and individuals at first remote from us, but subsequently disturbingly like us. The play offers the interaction of three major domains so that we can learn to look beyond the confines of our domain, as a prelude to looking back critically upon our own. Issues in the play, initially simply posed, become, on closer observation, more complex and more clearly understood, but, in the compromises achieved by all the characters, they retain a degree of persisting contradiction. As the simple fixities of the Ptolemaic universe give way to the complex freedoms and constraints of the Copernican universe, the audience and the playwright are both implicated in the endless historical process of inquiring further. The final words of the play are Andrea's: 'We've hardly begun' (p. 98) – a point about society, about the audience's interaction with the play, and about the role of Galileo's life in contributing to change in both domains. Andrea recapitulates and extends some of the concerns of Galileo, as Galileo before him recapitulates and extends the views of Copernicus and others, and as we, now located on the edge, rather than at the centre of the universe (p. 45), are invited to recapitulate and extend the views of them all in seeking appropriate links between the creativity of the individual and the continuity of the cosmos.

Brecht thus seeks to close the gap that opened for the expressionists between individual creativity and social continuity by working towards a collective historical creativity. Declining to take his stand on the shaky ground of subjectivity or the equally uninviting ground of empirical objectiv-ity, Brecht seeks his pragmatic ground in the social and the sharable. His fundamental interest, like Galileo's final interest, is not restricted to empiri-cal truth of the planetary domain nor to psychological truth of the individual domain, but focuses instead on social truth, its genesis, persistence and transformation. If there is an objectivity to be located in this world, it is the objectivity of community acceptance, not the objectivity of empirical validation. It thus neither precludes change nor assumes it, but seeks to guide others to ask whether change is necessary, for what reason, with what aims in view. 'Truth', as Galileo reminds us, 'is the child of time, not of authority' (p. 35), and 'the aim of science is not to open the door to everlasting wisdom, but to set a limit to everlasting error' (p. 64). The aim of Brecht's drama is the same, and it thus takes us repeatedly 'beyond the confines of the subject', drawing persistent attention to the limits and boundaries that enable and constrain us in all our activities and beliefs – as individuals, as members of an audience, and as members of society.

> Oh, early morning of beginning!
> Oh, breath of wind that
> Comes from new-found shores! (p. 6)

9 Ionesco:
The Chairs

The published version of Ionesco's *The Chairs* begins with a detailed diagram of the stage set. A semi-circular arena, gradually filled with rows of chairs, confronts an audience which also finds itself observing, in the arena's curved rear wall, two large windows and no fewer than ten doors. The very existence of the diagram reinforces our recognition of the growing importance to playwrights in the modern era of exploiting a play's domain of performance, not just its texture and structure, as a means of embodying theme. Ionesco's desire to control audience participation in the theatrical event thus seems a logical extension of concerns we have encountered earlier in the work of Pinero, Ibsen, Strindberg and Brecht. Indeed, the title of the play, and the proliferation on stage of chairs in neatly aligned rows, make the role of the audience seem even more important than in earlier plays, for the world of the stage in *The Chairs* begins to look more and more like the world of the auditorium. This partial duplication, on-stage, of the auditorium off-stage quickly renders problematic the boundary between the two domains; and the large number of windows and doors in the curved rear wall of the stage set soon makes us wonder about the status of that line of demarcation, that strangely permeable boundary between the dramatized world on-stage and the undramatized domains beyond it. Ionesco's interest in controlling audience participation and his evident interest in the boundaries of the on-stage world register an incipient continuity between his work and that of Brecht.

But even as we begin to note elements of this play that suggest a logical extension of Brecht's work, we find ourselves encountering, in Ionesco's writing on the theatre, a heated rejection of all that Brecht and his plays stand for. And the basis for that rejection is, interestingly enough, a disagreement over the appropriate relationship between the world of the stage and the world of the auditorium. Ionesco's major objection is that Brecht's theatre is gratuitously didactic and ideological in nature:

> The more I see of Brecht's plays, the more I have the impression that time, *and* his own time, escape him; Brechtian man is shorn of one dimension, the writer's sense of period is actually falsified by his ideology, which narrows his field of vision. [1]

This concern is extended and clarified when Ionesco, with Brecht's work obviously on his mind, denounces all didactic theatre as 'the tool of a political creed, of some ideology of which it is the duplicate – a useless and "conformist" repetition'. [2] The phrase 'conformist repetition' is important, because Ionesco identifies art (and particularly his own art) with novelty and originality, and finds neither in the work of Brecht. As a result, he repeatedly denounces Brechtian theatre.

In the light of our study in the preceding chapter of Brecht's commitment to experiment and exploration, Ionesco's criticism of Brecht's work is hard to substantiate. Brecht's major work is not governed by explicit ideological dogma, and it does not give repetition priority over novelty. Ionesco's polemical stance leads him, it seems, to misrepresent his examples, and he conceded in an interview that his knowledge of Brecht's work was actually rather slight. [3] This is in keeping with the generally polemical nature of Ionesco's writings on the theatre. His views are not always consistent and not always accurate, but in trying to characterize his dramatic work, we would do well to focus, as he does, on what exactly it is that he opposes in ideological theatre. This will lead us to explore not just the differences between Brecht's and Ionesco's work, but also their similarities. Ionesco's anti-ideology argument, which he has presented many times in many versions, runs as follows:

> A work of art cannot have the same function as an ideology, for if it did it would be an ideology, it would no longer be a work of art, that is to say an autonomous creation, *an independent universe* with its own life and its own laws. I mean that a play, for example, finds its own way, *explores itself and must use its own methods to make discovery of certain realities*, certain fundamental evidence that reveals itself in the process of creative thinking – for this is what writing is – evidence of an intimate nature (which does not prevent it from joining with the intimate evidence of others, so that in this way solitude ends or may end by identifying itself with the community), intimate evidence that is unexpected at the start and surprising for the author himself, often above all for the author himself. Perhaps this means that *imagination is revelation*, that it is charged with multiple meanings which a narrow and everyday 'realism' or a limiting ideology can no longer reveal: indeed, when a work of art is compelled simply to illustrate ideology, it is no longer a creative process, action and surprise; it is known in advance. (my emphases) [4]

The parallels between these beliefs and those voiced and enacted by Brecht are immediately obvious, and to begin to note them is to begin the process of making finer distinctions than Ionesco has so far offered us. Ionesco wants the theatre to be an independent universe; Brecht, for similar reasons, seeks to draw attention to the differences rather than just the similarities between on-stage and off-stage worlds. Ionesco wishes to ground new ways of knowing and new knowledge in the autonomous world of the theatre; so does Brecht. Ionesco regards the theatre as primarily philosophical in nature; and so does Brecht.[5] Ionesco wishes to escape the confines of everyday realism to avoid perpetuating the process of endless reduplication of what already exists; Brecht seeks to make us estranged from habitual awareness and habitual modes of thought for similar reasons. And in terms of the argument of this book, a major similarity between the work of Brecht and the work of Ionesco is that they have both moved away from a drama that seeks primarily to reproduce and/or illuminate the off-stage world, to a drama that sets out first and foremost to replace the off-stage world, and thence, by comparison and contrast, illuminate it. Brecht's concern that 'the theatre . . . stop pretending not to be theatre'[6] is paralleled by Ionesco's comment: 'It was not for me to conceal the devices of the theatre, but rather make them still more evident.'[7] Furthermore, in Ionesco's remark that the on-stage world 'explores itself' as its means of extending knowledge, we discover an explicit recognition of a process that we have traced through all of the plays we have so far considered.

From the outset, it has been a goal of this book to bridge the gaps that modern criticism has so often encountered when considering differing kinds of modern theatre. So far, it has been possible to trace a continuity of concern from the well-made play, through naturalistic and expressionistic theatre, to the Epic Theatre, and thus to discuss their differences in the context of their similarities. Different but related plays then serve to shed light on each other. In this chapter we begin to see links also between Brecht's Epic Theatre and the so-called Theatre of the Absurd, of which Ionesco's work is thought to be a prime example. I will examine in a later chapter the status of a Theatre of the Absurd, but at this point we need only note that Epic Theatre and Absurd Theatre are generally regarded as radically opposed. It remains the case, however, here as elsewhere, that a precise understanding of differences between kinds of plays emerges more persuasively and more usefully in the context, where appropriate, of acknowledged similarity. Though recognition of similarities is certainly appropriate here, Ionesco is largely unwilling to acknowledge them. His opposition to ideological commitments is so strong, and his dislike of Brecht's work so vehement, that he frequently misrepresents the nature not only of Brecht's work, but also of his own. A lengthy argument between Ionesco and the critic Kenneth Tynan has thus become justly celebrated for pushing Ionesco's arguments one stage further. The famous 'London Controversy'[8] between Ionesco and Tynan enjoyed, as the Ionesco/Brecht argument did not, two active participants. There was thus the opportunity for repeated attack and counter-attack, with an enforced qualification and clarification of positions that initially seemed radically opposed.

A potential problem in Ionesco's anti-ideology arguments was quickly pointed out by Tynan. Anyone who insists on the novelty of his own work and on the autonomous nature of the worlds he creates is in grave danger of creating plays of interest to, and understandable by, himself alone.

> The position toward which M. Ionesco is moving is that which regards art as if it were something different from and independent of everything else in the world; as if it not only did not but *should* not correspond to anything outside the mind of the artist. . . . To adapt Johnson, I am not yet so lost in drama criticism as to forget that plays are the daughters of earth, and that things are the sons of heaven. But M. Ionesco is in danger of forgetting; of locking himself up in that hall of mirrors which in philosophy is known as solipsism.[9]

This is, of course, not quite fair to Ionesco, but it clarifies the problem he confronts in his determinedly anti-ideological stance: in avoiding committing his plays to any specific programme for social change, he at times finds himself refusing to concede that his plays have any social function at all. At one point, for example, he wrote an article in *L'Express* entitled 'Mes pièces ne prétendent pas sauver le monde'.[10] And during his lengthy debate with Tynan, Ionesco begged him not to advocate any programme designed to improve the lot of mankind:

> I beg of you, Mr. Tynan, do not attempt, by means of art or any other means, to improve the lot of mankind. Please do not do it. We have had enough of civil wars already, enough of blood and tears and trials that are a mockery, enough of 'righteous' executioners and 'ignoble' martyrs, of disappointed hopes and penal servitude. Do not improve the lot of mankind, if you really wish it well.[11]

Critics who read such comments may then be tempted to interpret Ionesco's refusal either to endorse or to change what already exists as a refusal to make any contact whatever with what already exists, be it language or society. Such contact suggests repetition, and repetition suggests ideology – and Ionesco is determinedly non-ideological.

It is exactly this kind of progression in Ionesco's writings on the theatre that prompted Tynan's accusations of solipsism, and his attack forces Ionesco to tread a thin polemical line. In earlier opposing the possibility of being regarded as an ideological writer, Ionesco insisted on the autonomy and novelty of his on-stage world. But no writer is likely to accept the charge of solipsism, and in defending himself against it, Ionesco has to find an argument that allows him to claim social relevance without conceding that he has a programme for social relevance and is thus, in spite of his denials, ideologically committed. Seemingly backed into a corner by Tynan's reduction of the argument to two choices – solipsism or ideology – Ionesco offers a third choice which seeks to concede the limitations of neither. But this attempt to make more subtle and sophisticated the distinction he wishes to establish turns him inescapably back towards the overlooked similarities between his work and Brecht's, and to the definitive contrast he had sought to establish between novelty and repetition:

> I am not the first to point out the divergency that exists, in art as well as 'political' life, between ideology and reality. I therefore consider art to be more concerned with an independent search for knowledge than with any system of morals, political or not. It is of course *a way of knowing* that involves the emotions, an exploration that is objective in its subjectivity, *testimony rather than teaching*, evidence of how the world appears to the artist.
>
> *To renew one's idiom or one's language is to renew one's conception or one's vision of the world.* A revolution is a change of mentality. *Any new artistic expression enriches us* by answering some spiritual need and *broadens the frontiers of known reality.* (my emphases)[12]

Like Brecht before him, Ionesco finds himself on 'the frontiers of known reality', seeking to get beyond what already exists. But by here locating himself *within* these frontiers rather than beyond them, Ionesco is offering a continuity between new and old that had been denied in his attempt to establish a radical contrast between novelty and repetition. Ionesco thus rejects both solipsism and ideology in favour of 'testimony' – testimony as to what might be rather than 'teaching' as to what is or must be. Such testimony, for Ionesco, is not solipsistic – it addresses an audience and sets out to 'enrich' that audience by ministering to its spiritual and epistemological needs. This may indeed be characterized as commitment, but it is not, for Ionesco, an ideological commitment to pre-existing belief. It is commitment to possibility rather than to necessity, to experimentation rather than to conclusion, to discovery of truth rather than to pre-existing truth. Ionesco's radical division between art and ideology is thus maintained by clarification of the relationship between novelty and repetition. The either/or of art and ideology does not collapse into a both/and, but (like the either/or of novelty and repetition) is refined into an order of priority. Consequently, Ionesco can argue that an opposition to ideological commitment does not necessarily lead to solipsistic plays or to plays bereft of ideas. As he puts it elsewhere: 'A work of art is not devoid of ideas. *Since it is life or the expression of life, ideas emanate from it: the work of art does not emanate from an ideology*' (my emphasis).[13] And, in a rejoinder to Tynan, he claims that: 'Ideology is not the source of art. A work of art is the source and the raw material of ideologies to come.'[14]

Tynan went on to attack as self-congratulatory Ionesco's view that 'art is the source and the raw material of ideologies to come', but the issues themselves, apart from those to do with Ionesco's views on language and its functions,[15] received no further clarification. The debate had, however, served to clarify the nature of Ionesco's work and of the distinction he envisaged between it and Brecht's work. Those who regard Ionesco's work as ideologically committed fail to see that there can be commitment to something other than pre-existing belief; those who regard his work as 'rooted in the French tradition of "l'art pour l'art"[16] fail to see that experimental art can provide models for life and is not restricted merely to rejecting or replicating those that life already provides. Ionesco has supplied a series of anti-ideology arguments and anti-solipsism arguments; to focus on either one at the expense of the other is to miss the pathway he seeks to establish between the two.[17] Ionesco, like Brecht, is opposed to both extremes, but the two playwrights are not opposed to them to the same degree or in the same ways. And to get that distinction right is to gain illuminating access to the worlds Ionesco creates on his puzzling and varied stage.

Ionesco's notion that art is the source and raw material of ideologies to come is not inconsistent with some of Brecht's claims for the theatre, but there is a key difference between the two playwrights on the source and raw material of art. For Brecht, in his major work, that raw material is social and historical rather than individual and created. For Ionesco the reverse is true. For Brecht, the play is structured as a series of episodes, the sequence of which the audience is free to reconsider. For Ionesco, the play is an organic event which depends on its specific structure for its function. For Brecht, the audience and the play interact in an episodic manner of part-by-part interchange in which neither the ending nor any other part is a necessarily privileged component. For Ionesco, the audience interacts with the play as a whole, but is frequently offered access to the whole via one privileged part; as a result, the dramatic action often leads towards a point of retrospective synoptic revelation.

Thus, where Ionesco and Brecht significantly differ is in the ways in which they conceive of interaction between on-stage and off-stage worlds. But it is not the difference Ionesco imagined it to be, nor is it a simple case of radical contrast. Both writers adopt the notion of the relative autonomy of on-stage and off-stage worlds, both seek to draw attention to that autonomy by insisting upon the theatricality of the theatre, and both locate the social function of the theatre in the new grounds of knowing and consequent novelty of knowledge that the world on-stage provides to those living in the world off-stage. But when they set out to discuss the connection between on-stage and off-stage worlds, so that the constructed world of the artist can interact with the inherited world of society, Brecht stresses and sets out to utilize a process of equal and reciprocal interaction between on-stage and off-stage worlds, while Ionesco gives persistent priority to the influence of the world of the stage upon the world off-stage. And these differences emerge most clearly in the contrast between Brecht's concern for dramatizing historically typical social situations and Ionesco's concern for dramatizing idiosyncratically typifying social situations.

It is in their contrasting fears of what the theatre has or might become, that we see the forces that drive Ionesco and Brecht in different directions, in spite of their extensive theoretical common ground. They are both *for* a series of related reforms in the theatre, but they are *against* two very different possibilities – Brecht firmly opposes the excessive subjectivity of the expressionists and Ionesco, just as firmly, opposes the narrow social concerns of ideological dramatists. As a result, character and incident in Ionesco's theatre seem much more radically distinct from character and incident in the off-stage world than is the case with Brecht's theatre. Ionesco, whose main fear is repetition and perpetuation of what already exists, focuses on novelty at the considerable expense of continuity with the off-stage world. He is less interested in the mutual and repeated interaction of on-stage and off-stage worlds than in the *occasional, sudden and striking effect of the on-stage world on the off-stage*. Brecht's efforts at promoting social change involve the extensive embodiment on-stage of large general movements in society, within which individual voices have their place, and which, in time, cause change in off-stage worlds. Ionesco's efforts at promoting social change involve not large social pictures, but *local and exaggerated* embodiments of social interaction. Ionesco is in search, not of the already established typical, but of the newly typifying; he seeks to locate the key local factor in social behaviour, not the varied manifestations of it, nor the intricacies of the ways in which it insinuates itself into our lives. His plays focus on one or two such manifestations, exaggerate them to enormous proportions, and thus aim to undermine much of what we assume and believe about ourselves, by knocking away one of the key supports in our systems of understanding.

Ionesco is thus at pains to point out the scope of impact of the ostensibly local, rather than general, situations his plays dramatize. He recognizes the problem of the dubious representativeness of characters whose exaggerated behaviour seems idiosyncratic to an extreme, and also the uncertain social relevance of plays that focus on such idiosyncratic individuals. But Ionesco reiterates many times his answer to these problems, *claiming that the particular takes priority over the universal for only in the particular can we encounter the universal*.[18] For Ionesco, authentic individuality and authentic society must transcend existing social machinery because it is that machinery that separates us from our true selves and thus from each other.[19] It is this concern for individuals outside their inherited social roles that prompts Ionesco to write plays that seem so remote from the reproduction of common social behaviour. And it is a consequent interest in idiosyncratic local events that exemplifies his reaching towards, and providing testimony for, other possibilities in other worlds.

This persistent preference for the particular and the idiosyncratic over the general and commonplace is of a piece with Ionesco's distaste for ideology, conformism and repetition. The ideological basis of social living is, for Ionesco, a dangerous ground of constraining commonplaces. When he sets out to dramatize worlds somewhat removed from the ones we are used to, it is because he wishes to evade those constraints and to provide testimony of the possibility of other ways of knowing, being and relating. But such a process raises epistemological problems that require both an initial estrangement of the audience from the action and a subsequent re-engagement of the world of the audience with the world of the play. This is a process we have encountered elsewhere in the modern theatre, but its manifestation here is as complex as any we have encountered so far.

Ionesco himself has made several attempts to characterize this dramatic process, none fully satisfactory to himself or to us. His arguments on this topic are no more conclusive than his arguments about Brecht's work, but, again, they provide a useful point of departure. Describing *The Bald Soprano* and *The Lesson*, Ionesco offered the following guidelines for appropriate performance:

> The aim is to release dramatic tension without the help of any proper plot or any special subject. But it still leads, in the end, to the revelation of something monstrous: this is essential, moreover, for in the last resort drama is a revelation of monstrosity or of some monstrous formless state of being or of monstrous forms that we carry within ourselves. The task is to arrive at this exaltation or these revelations without a theme or subject that justifies or motivates, for his would be ideological and so false and hypocritical.
>
> The progression of a purposeless passion, a rising crescendo that is all the more natural, dramatic and exciting because it is not hampered by content, and by that I mean any *apparent* content or subject which conceals the *genuine* subject from us: the particular meaning of a dramatic plot hides its essential significance.[20]

This is not, of course, a clearly defined argument, but we should note at once the stress on moments of revelation as the key to the structure of the plays. Ionesco, however, does something of further significance in this remark and elsewhere – *he weaves texture, structure, mode of performance and theme together as one reciprocally defining whole.* And the importance of his play's achieving a particular kind of theatrical function is underlined in his remarks that textural topics of discussion are not directly indicative of theme, that structure is very much committed to promoting a certain kind of performance, and that the thematic significance of a play emerges not directly from textural topics or from structural patterns, but from their momentary synthesis in an emblematic environment in the performance of the play. 'Imagination', as Ionesco has commented elsewhere, 'is revelation',[21] and in Ionesco's theatre, revelation is a momentary insight derived from and based upon extended contemplation of the local, the idiosyncratic and the exaggerated.

Commenting twenty years later on the longer statement quoted above, Schechner continues to dwell upon its elusive significance: 'In 1970 these assertions may seem passé, but they are not. We must locate Ionesco's dramaturgy properly. . . . He raises for us the questions of play structure, and questions put powerfully twenty years ago have not been resolved.'[22]

And they have not been resolved. In part, because of Ionesco's conflicting (and at times confusing) statements about them, in part, because of Ionesco's concern for novelty of theme and structure, but primarily because the key to understanding theme and structure has been sought without a necessary recognition of the specific relationship the playwright envisages between on-stage and off-stage worlds. There are those who have approached that relationship in the context of ideological commitment, those who have approached it in terms of a misleading notion of a Theatre of the Absurd,[23] and those who have avoided resolving a complex issue by settling for the notion that Ionesco is concerned with art only for the sake of art. But the seemingly bizarre, idiosyncratic and episodic nature of Ionesco's plots provides the basis for a dramatic structure with a rather different theatrical function involving a rather different relationship between on-stage and off-stage worlds.

The pattern exemplified in these plots is not the steady cause and effect progression of the well-made or the naturalistic play, and it is not the thesis/anti-thesis progression of the debate or epic play – rather it is the steady progression of seemingly random details towards moments of temporary fusion: 'The theatre is a kind of succession of states and situations moving towards an increasing densification.'[24] It is this progression towards the momentary insight, the sudden recognition, the *Gestalt* moment of retrospective synthesis, that is the functional aim, the performance goal, of plays whose texture registers localized detail and whose structure seems, superficially at least, fragmented and non-developmental. It is just this achievement of the momentary insight that exemplifies in performance the recurring thematic concern of locating the general and the newly typifying in the local and the idiosyncratic. Far from being an 'illustration of something already postulated', Ionesco's theatre conducts, he argues, 'an exploration', and it is because of this process of exploration that one arrives at 'the revelation of a truth which is most often unbearable, but which can also be luminous and comforting'.[25] The plays are designed to produce moments of revelation, revelation that is not necessarily shared by the characters or explicit in the topics they discuss. But the topics discussed and the verbal and the non-verbal action that constitute texture and structure are contributions to and contributing causes of the revelations that are designed to occur – revelations that require the initial separation and subsequent reconciliation of the domains of the stage and the auditorium.

Ionesco, as much as any playwright we have considered so far, is thus committed to the creation on-stage of worlds other than our own; but the appropriate re-connection between on-stage and off-stage worlds must at some point be established, if only by something equivalent to an electric spark leaping across a gap between two worlds, providing a moment of illumination:

> Every work is a unique thing, a complete world, a cosmos. A work is important only in so far as it's unique. And since it is unique, it is hard to understand. When you confront a new work, through its world, you must every time be able to discover *the* world.[26]

Such a moment of illumination is a moment of renewed contact between initially contrasting on-stage and off-stage worlds. To note that Ionesco conceives of this relationship as one between distinct worlds is to note the continuity between his approach to pluralistic reality and that discussed in the early chapters of this book. The moment of renewed contact is a moment of revelatory insight that is possible only because of the differences between on-stage and off-stage worlds that enable and promote discovery. The moment of illumination is a moment of such discovery, a moment that takes both audience and author beyond what they already know towards the possibility of new recognition and new understanding. The novelty of testimony offered by the play enables us to see our world anew by seeing it 'through [the play's] world'. This emergent novelty is novel for the play-wright, too, and hence, in Ionesco's terms, non-ideological, as it did not pre-exist the play: 'by creating a world, by inventing it, the creator discovers it for himself.'[27] And from the point of view of the creator of such an autonomous world, 'A writer is not a teacher but an inventor.'[28]

To approach Ionesco's plays, one must thus work from and towards these key moments of discovery, these moments when a revelatory spark of understanding leaps across the gap between autonomous on-stage and off-stage worlds and illuminates both in a glow of renewed contact. The novelty of the discovery prompted by the play is certainly manifest in its structure and themes, but both are embodied in, and understandable only in terms of, this novel mode of performance, these revealing moments of illumination, that the plays are designed to achieve in the theatre. To understand this synthesis of texture, structure, theme and theatrical function we must return to a specific play and to 'the frontiers of known reality' it focuses on, as we explore for ourselves the ways in which this relationship between on-stage and off-stage worlds is exhibited and exploited.

The Chairs, with its theatrical stage set and problematic boundaries, is a confusing play, replete with locally bizarre detail. An old man and woman, living isolated on an island, are visited one evening by an Orator and a large number of invisible people. The action of the play moves towards the delivery by the Orator of the Old Man's posthumous message to the invisible audience. The putative climax of the play dissolves into a scene of thwarted expectations as the Orator (a deaf mute) struggles helplessly to deliver the so-called message to an invisible audience. Things are not, it seems, as we have been led to believe, and these negated expectations have come to seem central to the play. But critical commentary has struggled less than success-fully with the notions of negation and absence in *The Chairs*. It is, of course, too easy to dismiss the play as a failure because certain things we normally expect are missing and/or because certain things the play seems deliberately to lead us to expect also turn out to be missing. But it is no more helpful to take the other tack and try to establish absence as part of some metaphysical schema that Ionesco is trying to establish.[29] Such suggestions are the regular consequence of attempts to explore absence largely as a textural and thematic concern instead of considering the structural and functional contributions that absence also makes. If, on the other hand, we seek to integrate the thematic notion of negation with structural and functional modes of negation, we find that the play is making use of a fairly common semiotic option and putting it to novel, but not metaphysical, use.

Von Humboldt, many years ago, pointed out the paradoxical quality of semiotic systems: they simplify a complex universe by imposing a set of interrelated categories upon it, but once in place, the very categories that enable us to establish order also limit us to the ordering possibilities implicit within them. Other kinds of order, other ways of knowing, are necessarily screened out by the adoption of any one mode of ordering.

> Man lives with his objects chiefly – in fact, since his feeling and acting depends on his perceptions, one may say exclusively – as language presents them to him. By the same process whereby he spins language out of his own being, he ensnares himself in it; and each language draws a magic circle round the people to which it belongs, a circle from which there is no escape save by stepping out of it into another.[30]

It is not difficult to see here the connection between Von Humboldt's concern for the restricting effects of linguistic conventions and Ionesco's concern for the limiting effects of both social and theatrical conventions. But what is not made clear in this quotation is the way in which any semiotic system can extend its own boundaries. Using a set of contrasting prefixes, we can reach linguistically beyond the category limits of our vocabulary, e.g. by employing such prefixes as un, non, super, extra, and so on. Language enables us to project beyond the world already classified in our vocabulary with such compounds as *extra*-terrestrial, *un*-earthly, *super*-natural, and also (for our purposes, important examples) *non*-linguistic and *un*-known. With these words we have ways of linguistically classifying that which our language has not yet characterized *except in contrast to something else already classified by the language*. The negative is thus not an invitation to move beyond classification, but to extend classification by means of comparison and contrast with a specified norm. To say that a strange animal is not an elephant is not the same as saying that it is not a mouse. Leaving irony to one side, we can assume that that which is not an elephant will nevertheless be more like an elephant (in the respects that the speaker regards as important) than it will be like a mouse. The obviousness of this point should be kept in mind when we consider negations that seem more abstract and less precise. Classification by contrast with something else previously classified by the language is a perfectly normal linguistic strategy that requires no metaphysical leaps of faith for understanding.

When Ionesco therefore tells us that he wishes 'to express absence' in *The Chairs*,[31] he is not asking us to participate in a metaphysic of absence. Rather, he wishes to draw attention to specific gaps in our social living that are to be understood by comparison with our expectations that specific kinds of things be present in specific kinds of situations. When the old people speak, he notes:

> They must never be allowed to forget 'the presence of this absence,' which should be their constant point of reference, which they must constantly cultivate and sustain. Without it you could never suggest the unreal (*for this can only be created by continual contrast with what is visible*). . . . What is needed is plenty of gesture, almost pantomime, light, sound, moving objects, doors that open and close and open again, in order to create this emptiness, so that it grows and devours everything: *absence can only be created in opposition to things present.* (my emphases)[32]

What we thus encounter is a carefully created work in which specific kinds of theatrical absence emerge from a particular complex of dramatic presence. We must set out to understand the nature of cleverly created worlds on-stage both by noting their boundaries and by comparing and contrasting what lies within them with specifically invoked aspects of worlds that lie beyond them.

We should note at the outset that the play makes use of a curtain as a means of registering the separateness of two worlds, a separateness that is initially to be insisted on and then gradually transcended. And we should not overlook this change of function of the stage curtain in a modern theatre that focuses so extensively on the problematic relationship between on-stage and off-stage worlds. Where once it was a 'given' and supposedly neutral part of the theatre's existence, it has now become an option to be used for particular purposes – purposes, in this play, hinted at in the closing stage direction, which informs us that the final curtain '*falls very slowly*' (p. 160).[33] And the reason for that slowness is to be sought in the gradual evolution throughout the play of a peculiar relationship between an audience gathering on-stage and the audience gathered in the auditorium – a relationship based very carefully on the play's complex use of presence and absence, similarity and difference.

As we have noted, the curtain rises to reveal a semi-circular room with symmetrically arranged doors, and two empty chairs downstage. The vague impression immediately created of an on-stage auditorium (with few chairs) confronting an off-stage auditorium (with many chairs) is, of course, gradually strengthened by the steady increase in the number of chairs on-stage as the play progresses. But we are now in a position to explore the more complex relationships between the two domains. This is by no means a play in which the on-stage world seeks simply to reduplicate the off-stage world. Rather, there occurs on-stage a series of bizarre events which exemplify Ionesco's wish to portray a 'succession of states and situations moving toward an increasing densification'. Such 'densification' of the bizarre offers a connection between stage and auditorium that depends upon their comparison and contrast and not just upon the reduplication of one in the other. There is something about the off-stage world as auditorium and the on-stage world as auditorium which will help us to understand something new about both, and we must follow the play carefully to get the analogy right.

At the beginning of the play, the two old people squabble over the closing of a window in the dimly lit, sparsely furnished, semi-circular room. Two empty chairs are located downstage, and when the squabbling couple moves towards the chairs we expect them to sit down and continue their fractious discussion. But the hints we have already been given (strange location, green light) not to engage in premature classification of the action become more than mere hints when, instead of sitting on a chair of his own, 'the Old Man seats himself quite naturally on the lap of the Old Woman' (p. 113). In the opening seconds of the play we have confronted two empty chairs, and regarded them as empty chairs. Now we confront one occupied chair and one empty chair, and we are on our way towards a consideration of the status of the empty chair compared to the one that is occupied. The unusualness that occupying chairs has already taken on (Old Man sitting on lap of Old Woman) is the first step in a required reconsideration of the opposing notion of an empty chair. The emptiness of the unoccupied chair is no longer just absence, but the absence of the particular and odd kind of occupation of the other chair – an as yet embryonic notion, which will lead towards the audience's consideration of soon-to-enter invisible people occupying chairs, and towards a reconsideration of what it is to occupy their own chairs.

At this point, however, attention is primarily focused on the chair occupied by the Old Woman with the Old Man seated on her lap. To understand their world we have to come to terms with both the normality and the oddity of their behaviour. They converse like a long-married couple who seem to have made the best of a shared life that has not been all that they might have wished. They dwell on the past as a means of re-experiencing the pleasures of shared memories, but also as a means of avoiding the narrowness of their current lives. And the pleasures of recalling their joint past are interrupted intermittently by expressions of the Old Woman's disappoint-ment that the Old Man has not lived up to her expectations.

> OLD WOMAN: Ah! Yes, you've certainly a fine intellect. You are very gifted,
> my darling. You could have been head president, head king, or
> even head doctor, or head general, if you had wanted to, if only
> you'd had a little ambition in life. (p. 114)

The diversity and extravagance of these claims indicate that the Old Woman is more interested in status in general than in the Old Man's specific talents – a point made even more obvious when she greets his trivial pronouncements as a thinker, mimic and story-teller with similarly extravagant praise and accompanies it with equivalently extravagant regrets that such talents have not been fully utilized. And it is the extravagance that is the key to our understanding of what is going on here, for it is an extravagance of expectation and judgement that is quite out of keeping with the Old Man's remarks, his behaviour and his place on her lap. Furthermore, it is quite out of keeping with the sophistication of the topics discussed in their joint conversation.

As this conversation continues, we begin to see that what we have here is a set of strategies of conversation (reminiscing, story-telling, congratulating, disagreeing) that seem quite typical of an old and fractious couple, *but their strategies of conversation are often inconsistent with the topics of conversation and with the non-verbal behaviour that accompanies the conversation.* The conversation strategies set up expectations about conversation topics and non-verbal behaviour that simply are not met. Here we note that something is missing, but we quickly see that it is not just an absence, but a comparative absence that our attention is drawn to. The Old Woman's disappointed expectations and the Old Man's misery at having wasted his talents are both manifest in conversation strategies, but the disappointment and sense of waste are not matched by any conversation topics or activities that exemplify the wasted abilities. Instead, the conversation topics are a collage of clichés and trivial phrases that register childish self-pity (on the part of the Old Man) and maternal soothing (on the part of the Old Woman). The play is carefully setting up certain kinds of absence by providing us with conversation strategies usually linked to topics of a level of seriousness and sophistication that are here peculiarly absent.

What thus emerges in the opening moments of the play is a major discrepancy between aspirations and abilities on the part of the old couple. And it is in the context of this discrepancy that we view the Old Man's increasing emotional distress and the Old Woman's alternation between irritated regret over his wasted life and soothing optimism over his as yet uncharted future. What we must note in this context is that this alternation is not just a result of her changing moods, it is also a result of her reaction to the Old Man's distress. Her hopes for his future success register simultaneously her desire that the status she seeks for them both may yet be achieved and her resort to the only strategy she can think of to rescue the Old Man from the distress that her expressions of disappointment repeatedly engender in him. These hopes are only partially based on honest expectations and, early in the play, seem primarily to be based upon the need to comfort the Old Man for his failures. What she offers to soothe his injured feelings is a fiction of his still possible success. And it is in these attempts by the Old Woman to make a necessary fiction believable and concrete that we begin to discover a parallel between the existence of the play in the theatre (a fictional event moving towards 'increasing densification') and the existence of the on-stage fiction about the Old Man's future achievements (a compensating fiction that likewise moves towards 'increasing densification'). This parallel is an important part of Ionesco's attempts to renew the link between his other world and the off-stage world – to set up the situation in which the on-stage world, in spite of its increasingly bizarre characteristics, might yet prove not remote and irrelevant but familiar and revelatory. And that goal is to be achieved by a moment of fusion among the textural, structural and performance aspects of the play. The evolution of the on-stage fiction must thus be traced with some care.

The progression of 'increasing densification' in the on-stage use of fiction begins early and develops steadily. The Old Man, seated on the Old Woman's lap at the beginning of the play, complains that he is 'very bored' (p. 114). The Old Woman caresses the Old Man '*as one caresses a child*' (p. 114), and seeks to soothe him: 'Let's amuse ourselves by making believe, the way you did the other evening' (p. 114). The Old Man retorts that it is her turn, not his, to make believe, and gets more and more irritated when she suggests that he first do some mimicry and then recite her favourite story – 'Then at last we arrived':

OLD MAN: Again? . . . I'm sick of it . . . 'Then at last we arrived'? That
               again . . . you always ask for the same thing! . . . 'Then at last
               we arrived' . . . But it's monotonous . . . For all of the
               seventy-five years that we've been married, every single even-
               ing, absolutely every blessed evening, you've made me tell the
               same story, you've made me imitate the same people, the same
               months . . . always the same . . . let's talk about something
               else . . .
OLD WOMAN: My darling, I'm not tired of it . . . it's your life, it fascinates me.
               (p. 115)

The Old Man does indeed go on to tell the story, and he also performs the mimicry as she requests. Neither attempt indicates that the Old Man has a talent for either activity. But what we must focus on is the Old Woman's tactics for distracting the Old Man from his boredom, and her attempts to soothe the distress engendered in him by her reminders of his failures. And the key issue here is *her limited range of tactics and her repeated use of the same ones over and over again.* For it is in this very context that the plans for the Old Man to deliver a great message at some point in the future emerge, develop and intensify.

We note the characteristic exaggeration of Ionesco's plays when the Old Man begins to weep at a further reminder of what he might have been (p. 117). He then begins to moan and groan about his failures, his helpless-ness, and his childlike sense of exposure and loss:

OLD MAN: [*sobbing, his mouth wide open like a baby*] I'm an orphan . . .
               dworfan.
OLD WOMAN: [*trying to console him by cajoling him*] My orphan, my darling,
               you're breaking my heart, my orphan. (p. 118)

But the Old Man continues to sob, and her efforts '*to console him*' continue.

She tries sympathetic noises, rocking him on her knee, singing him a lullaby, and finally, having calmed him down, she introduces the comforting topic of his future message to the world. It is vital that we see this topic as *the last of the sequence of soothing strategies* that the Old Woman adopts to comfort the Old Man at times of deep distress. And it is equally vital that we note its place in a set of strategies that have clearly become habitual for them both. The game of 'the message', their behaviour suggests, is one they have played before in their mother and child roles, and its regular effect, it seems, is to restore them both to their woman/man roles once more. The Old Woman, we should note, both introduces the topic and gives the Old Man his behaviour cues:

> OLD WOMAN: [*he is almost calm*] Now, come on, calm down, don't get so upset . . . you have great qualities, my little general . . . dry your tears; the guests are sure to come this evening and they mustn't see you this way . . . all is not lost, all is not spoiled, you'll tell them everything, you will explain, you have a message . . . you always say you are going to deliver it . . . you must live, you have to struggle for your message. . . .
>
> OLD MAN: I have a message, that's God's truth, I struggle, a mission, I have something to say, a message to communicate to humanity, to mankind. (pp. 118–19)

Within seconds the Old Man's tears have ceased, and we can quickly perceive the confidence he draws from the self-image this game gives him. No longer so helpless, '*he gets off the Old Woman's lap and walks with short, agitated steps*' (p. 119), remarking on his own singularity and value to the world. He has been consoled and revived by a goal which is embedded in the fiction of this game, but a fiction which, in its 'real' effects, is already beginning to blur the traditional line between two opposed terms.

When the Old Man sits down once more, it is no longer on the lap of the Old Woman, but upon his own chair, as he begins to manifest a new and more secure personality. But his acquisition of a new personality serves to make us wonder just how real this new person is who bases his actions and his self-esteem upon a fiction. When the Old Woman reminds him once more of what he could and should have achieved in life, he no longer dissolves into tears, but sits on his own chair in silence, as she sits on hers in silence, as they both take on the momentary image of spectators in an auditorium awaiting a performance. Like those in the theatre audience sitting in their chairs in silence, they seem to await the performance of an event in front of them, but unlike (it seems) those in the theatre audience, they are to be participants in, as well as spectators of, the performance that is to follow:

> OLD WOMAN: You could have been head admiral, head cabinet-maker, head orchestra conductor. [*Long silence. They remain immobile for a time, completely rigid on their chairs.*] (pp. 119–20)

When they speak once more, it is to begin the acting out of the fiction of the message. The formerly empty chair is now occupied by an old man investing in a re-creation, a motivated fictionalization, of self. And the impending question is, should he succeed, will he or someone else be occupying the chair? And if that someone else is a fictional creation, is the chair empty or filled? What kind of presence and what kind of absence will thus have emerged on-stage? And how then do we distinguish the real from the unreal in a pluralistic world in which fiction has a capacity to contribute to, and not just contrast with, the 'real'?

These are, of course, the very questions one must be asking if the link that Ionesco seeks to establish between the on-stage (fictional) and the off-stage (real) worlds is to become operative in the theatre. The re-negotiation of the relationship between opposing realities is an important part of the structural, thematic and functional bases of a play which seeks alternately to emphasize and to eradicate the border between stage and auditorium. But as it does so, the other border of the play, that curved wall with many doors, plays its own important part in the negotiation of reality on-stage. Beyond that curved wall, and entering in growing numbers through its doors, is another group of characters – the startlingly invisible guests. Initially, the very visibility of the Old Man and Old Woman suffices to make their reality seem more closely related to ours than that of the invisible guests. But as the action progresses, the play begins to provide us with a gradual revaluation of the relative reality status of the visible and invisible people. The invisible people are compared to and contrasted with the visible people whose visibility alone is enough to make the audience take them initially as the more fundamentally real. But as the behaviour of the visible people becomes increasingly bizarre, the (indirectly presented) behaviour of the invisible people seems more convincingly 'normal'. The result is a gradual enhancement of the authenticity and social normality of the invisible people, as the visible people's peculiar behaviour makes them seem more and more remote from social normality.

This creation of the felt reality of the invisible people in contrast with the visible reality of the old couple provides us with one of the key examples in the play of the creation of other kinds of people and other kinds of worlds by means of unexpected negation of selected attributes. But we must note that both kinds of on-stage character offer, in their different ways, modes of self-contemplation for the audience off-stage. The role of the visible people in the structure of the on-stage fiction is emblematic of the audience's role in the theatre where visible people sit and watch the on-stage proceedings. The Old Man and Woman progress through the roles of spectators of that fiction, participants in that fiction, and finally pawns of the very fiction they helped to create. The play requires that the audience move through the same progression towards a moment when, like the old couple, they find themselves jolted into seeing their world and themselves through the perspective of the fictional world created on-stage, instead of just seeing the fictional world through the perspective they brought with them into the theatre. And as they do so, they too will find startling indications of the priority of the invisible people.

It is the pursuit of this momentary goal that requires the play to increase steadily the 'densification' of the world of invisible people. That world seems initially opposed to the representatives of the normative, it gradually challenges them, and finally transcends and transforms both the representatives of the normative and the nature of the normative. The old couple's initial aspects of normality (visibility and conversation strategies) are there to draw the audience into a relationship of partial identification with the Old Man and Old Woman, so that the gradual undermining of their normality is participated in and shared by the audience. The gradual 'densification' of the old couple's on-stage fiction is thus directed simultaneously at the old couple's and the audience's moorings in controlled and controlling reality. And it is in this manner that the play begins to achieve the union that Ionesco seeks between the play's texture, structure and performance in exemplifying theme.

The issue of who is controlling the on-stage fiction emerges almost imperceptibly in the play, and progresses slowly but insistently until the audience finds, as the Old Man and Old Woman find, that this on-stage fiction has earned an ontological status independent of any visible person's on-stage control. And the initial indication that the old couple's control of this fiction is not all-embracing comes when we note the failure of one of their clearly habitual moves in playing the 'message' game. As we have seen, the game is one of several strategies the Old Woman employs for soothing the Old Man after he has been reduced to tears by her recurring impatience over his lowly status and wasted talents. The Old Man is comforted by the new status the game offers him, and the two engage in a lengthy discussion of arrangements for the delivery of his message. An orator is said to be contracted, and guests of all kinds invited (though the bizarre classification of guests is one more example of conversation strategies being undermined by conversation topics). The discussion of arrangements progresses to the point at which the Old Man announces with enthusiasm that 'the meeting will take place in a few minutes' (p. 121). At that point the old people are feeling much more secure and happy – the aim of the game has been achieved and the old couple move into what we must regard as their standard routine for aborting the 'arranged' meeting. But the Old Man's routine reluctance to abort is already bordering on a commitment to the fiction in preference to their normal reality:

> OLD WOMAN: It's true then, they're going to come, this evening? You won't feel like crying any more, the intellectuals and the proprietors will take the place of papas and mammas? [*Silence*] Couldn't you put off this meeting? It won't be too tiring for us? [*More violent agitation. For several moments the Old Man has been turning around the Old Woman with the short, hesitant steps of an*

> *old man or of a child. He takes a step or two towards one of the doors, then returns and walks around her again.*]
>
> OLD MAN: You really think this might tire us?
> OLD WOMAN: You have a slight cold.
> OLD MAN: How can I call it off?
> OLD WOMAN: Invite them for another evening. You could telephone. (p. 122)

The Old Man's hesitation prolongs what we must regard up to now as a routine part of their 'message' game. But the hesitation marks an emerging commitment to the reality of the game, and that commitment is surprisingly reinforced by the first manifestation of the potentially independent reality of the game. Suddenly *'we hear the sound of a boat gliding through the water'* (p. 122), a boat which is bearing the first of the invited guests. But the audience in the theatre is as yet uncertain how independent this manifestation is (could the old couple be using sound-effects as part of the game?). Seconds later, there is another such manifestation: *'We hear the doorbell ring'* (p. 122). The old people rush to a recessed door, just beyond the audience's view, and we then get a third manifestation – the sound of the old couple opening a door and greeting a guest. At that point, just as the audience anticipates the final proof of an entering guest, it is offered instead a pantomime in which *'the Old Man and Old Woman re-enter together, leaving space between them for their guest. She is invisible. The Old Man and Old Woman advance, downstage, facing the audience and speaking to the invisible Lady, who walks between them'* (p. 123). The initial comparative absence of conversation topics which would appropriately match conversation strategies gives way to the comparative absence of one of the participants in a new kind of conversation – one which now offers the persuasive presence of convincing conversation strategies *and* convincing conversation topics. The change is important for it registers the immediate influence of the reality of the guests on the reality of their hosts.

The audience, however, must seek to cope anew with the partial absence of an otherwise carefully circumscribed presence. As it does so, the personality of the invisible guest emerges with 'increasing densification' for we see and hear the old couple reacting both to her and to the advances the next guest, the Colonel, makes toward her:

> OLD MAN: Take care, Colonel, this Lady's husband may arrive at any moment. . . . [*Some embarrassing things take place, invisibly.* . . .]
> OLD WOMAN: [*to the invisible Lady*] But my dear, don't let it happen! . . . He's going too far! It's embarrassing. [*She seizes the invisible sleeve of the Colonel*] Listen to him! My darling, why don't you stop him! (pp. 128–9).

The reality of the invisible guests is thus initially posited and steadily sustained by the behaviour of visible characters who seem unprepared for the behaviour of their guests, unwilling to ask them to leave, and, most important of all, unable to control the process of supplantation that seems now under way. The two chairs that were originally empty and facing the theatre auditorium are now 'filled' by characters exhibiting a different set of unexpected characteristics from those exhibited by the old couple previously occupying the same chairs. The invisible Colonel and Lady now sit in the two original chairs while the Old Man and the Old Woman stand behind two new chairs they have brought in, one on either side of the invisible newcomers (pp. 124, 127, 128).

The process of supplantation, once under way, progresses steadily and then chaotically as newly arrived guests fill the chairs as fast as the old couple can drag them into the room. And the initial visual effect of the old couple being driven apart by their invisible guests is steadily extended as the Old Man and Old Woman are driven to opposite sides of the room by the rapidly growing crowd of invisible guests seated on the equally rapidly growing number of chairs. The growing domination of the new reality of the invisible guests over the reality of the visible couple is registered not only in the way that the accumulation of chairs drives them apart, but also by the way in which the old people's activities, their personalities, and finally their very mode of exist-ence is changed by the impact of the gathering throng:

> The doorbell rings louder and louder and we hear the noises of boats striking the quay very close by, and more and more frequently. The Old Man flounders among the chairs; he has scarcely enough time to go from one door to another, so rapidly do the ringings of the doorbell succeed each other. . . . We hear waves, boats, the continuous ringing of the doorbell. The movement culmi-nates in intensity at this point. The doors are now opening and shutting all together ceaselessly. (p. 141)

The commotion gradually subsides thereafter and '*we have the impression that the stage is packed with people*' (p. 142). But as the guests have arrived, we have noted the impact that the 'increasing densification' of the reality of the invisible people has had on the old couple. The Old Man's flirtatious behaviour with an invisible guest named La Belle has been exceeded by the Old Woman's bizarre attempt to seduce the photo-engraver:

OLD WOMAN: [*to the photo-engraver, simpering grotesquely; . . . she shows her thick red stockings, raises her many petticoats, shows an underskirt full of holes, exposes her old breast; then, her hands on her hips, throws her head back, makes little erotic cries, projects her pelvis, her legs spread apart; she laughs like an old prostitute; this business, entirely different from her manner heretofore as well as from that she will have subsequently, and which must reveal the hidden personality of the Old Woman, ceases abruptly.*] So you think I'm too old for that, do you? (p. 132)

Later, the Old Woman, confronted by the presence of a crowd, switches to the role of programme seller and hawker of eskimo pies, caramels and fruit drops (pp. 142–3), and the Old Man, confronted by the Emperor, is reduced to barking like a faithful dog (p. 148).

The result of these personality changes is to register ever more strongly the visible 'real' effects of the invisible and 'unreal' guests. With the old couple supplanted in their chairs, reduced to stage-hands by their own fiction, driven apart by the gathering throng, and led into personality and role changes by the presence of their guests, we have a series of examples of the play's ability to create and sustain a mode of invisible reality by comparing it to, contrasting it with and registering its impact on, a visible reality which it initially influences and subsequently supplants. Furthermore, we have noted, in the sound of doorbells, doors, boats and trumpets, manifestations of the reality of the invisible guests that seem increasingly to be independent of, and not controlled by, the reality of the visible couple – a point given further emphasis by the steady increase of light on the stage as the number of invisible guests increases: 'The light grows stronger. It should grow stronger and stronger as the invisible guests continue to arrive' (p. 132). This 'increasing densification' of the reality of the invisible guests reaches its climax in the unexpected arrival of the Emperor, which produces fanfares, doors opening without the old couple's help, and a sudden burst of even stronger light:

> [Suddenly we hear noises in the wings, fanfares.]
>
> OLD WOMAN: What's going on?
>
> [The noises increase, then the main door opens wide, with a great crash; through the open door we see nothing but a very powerful light which floods onto the stage through the main door and the windows, which at the entrance of the emperor are brightly lighted.] (p. 147)

By this time, the audience has noted the gradual physical separation of the Old Man and Old Woman and the growing psychological separations registered by their sudden personality changes. It has also noted that the steadily increasing authenticity of the ever more numerous invisible people has gradually allowed them to dominate the on-stage world. They have flowed in ever-increasing numbers through the many doors of the curved rear wall and have gradually made this domain their own. At the same time, a striking development has occurred in the relationship between the on-stage invisible audience and the off-stage visible audience. As the stage direction indicates: 'The chairs, turned towards the dais, with their backs to the audience, form regular rows, each one longer as in a theatre' (my emphasis) (p. 139).

Driven apart by the newly densified reality they helped bring into being, the Old Man and Old Woman have reached 'their final positions. Each is near a window. The Old Man to the left, . . . the Old Woman on the right' (p. 144). The reality of the old couple is now subordinate to the reality of the invisible crowd. And the invisible crowd is now seated 'as in a theatre', in rows of chairs which face the same way as the chairs in the auditorium, so that the auditorium and the stage have taken on the unusual shape of continuous space. But what is not yet clear is whether the continuity that is given an emblematic manifestation here is a continuity in which the on-stage world or the off-stage world has established its priority. On-stage, it is clear that the reality of the invisible guests has overcome the reality of the visible characters – the next step in the 'increasing densification' of the invisible on-stage reality is to get it across the footlights.

The play's dramatization of pluralistic worlds and their relationships begins with three worlds separated from each other by a curtain (at the front of the stage) and a permeable wall with many doors (at the back). Part of what the play subsequently displays is the 'increasing densification' of a backstage fictional world of invisible people which gradually supplants the on-stage real world of the old couple. The backstage fictional world gradually flows through the rear wall and takes over the on-stage real world in such a way as to make the latter resemble a theatre auditorium, much like the one that exists off-stage. By this point in the play, the on-stage world of the invisible people has achieved supremacy over the on-stage world of visible people and is approaching parity with the off-stage world of visible people. And it is here that the relationship in the play between texture, structure, mode of performance and theme becomes of crucial importance. In a play in which the way of knowing is the primary manifestation of what is to be known about the novelty of the play, the audience's efforts to understand the newness of the play must provide a key to the understanding they are to reach. The creation, perpetuation and gradual predominance of the fictional component of the on-stage world is a process that has been based upon and embodied in a series of comparative absences – absences, which in their on-stage effects, have achieved a more authentic presence than the on-stage 'real' world has been able to provide. Now, it must be recognized, the same process is already under way in the relationship between the on-stage world of invisible people and the off-stage world of visible people. The approaching parity between the two worlds is strengthened by the role that is forced upon the members of the audience as the action of the play continues and its function in the theatre becomes clear. When the Orator enters, the members of the audience take on the same role as the members of the on-stage invisible audience – but they take it on because the on-stage invisible people have already done so. The off-stage audience is becoming an extension of the on-stage audience, taking its cue for behaviour, and its focus of attention, from that of the on-stage audience; it is even clear that the off-stage audience is now consigned to what are traditionally the worst seats in any auditorium – those most distant from the enacted event. And when the Orator responds on-stage to the invisible rather than to the visible characters, it becomes evident that the visible audience is being steadily downgraded in favour of the invisible audience.

But the Orator has further significance, for he himself is unexpectedly visible. His entrance confirms the independence of the newly created on-stage world from the world of the old couple. They are more than a little astonished at this visible manifestation of the independent existence of the hitherto largely invisible world:

> [He goes along the wall to the right, gliding, softly, to upstage center, in front of the main door, without turning his head to right or left; he passes close by the Old Woman without appearing to notice her, not even when the Old Woman touches his arm in order to assure herself that he exists. It is at this moment that the Old Woman says: 'Here he is!']

OLD MAN: Here he is!

OLD WOMAN: [following the Orator with her eyes and continuing to stare at him] It's really he, he exists. In flesh and blood. (p. 154)

The Orator's visibility, his readiness to ignore the old people, and the surprise the old couple display at his arrival are all manifestations of an independence that has been the culmination of the on-stage fictional world's 'increasing densification'. But there is still another refinement to the play's complex exemplification of its thematic concerns.

The Orator, the man come to deliver a message, is not yet clearly located in any of the three worlds (off-stage, on-stage fictional, on-stage 'real') that have so far been recognized in the theatre. He comes, it seems, to deliver a message. But it is someone else's message. And it is to be delivered by an Orator who looks like a 'typical painter or poet of the nineteenth century; he wears a large black felt hat with a wide brim, loosely tied bow tie, artist's blouse, mustache and goatee, very histrionic in manner, conceited' (p. 154). What we have here is a figure of an old-fashioned author/artist come to deliver a message to an audience – exactly the kind of artist figure and artistic function that Ionesco's stagecraft is designed to transcend.[34] For Ionesco, such a figure has nothing new to say and therefore nothing of consequence to art to say. As we have seen, Ionesco equates art and novelty, and rejects the notion of an ideological art which reiterates pre-existing beliefs. And what Ionesco is setting up here is yet another kind of controlled absence: the absence of an expected contribution from the Orator, from the playwright, and from the major characters – explicit thematic summary of the play's concerns. The new world solidifying on-stage cannot summarize its own significance; the Orator, seen as dispenser of other people's truths, must promise more than he can ever deliver; the Orator seen as artist will create expectations he cannot meet; the play seen as social statement must offer the absence of explicit summary instead of its anticipated presence. For the whole point of the action of this play is to demonstrate the necessary absence of some kinds of expected presence in order to challenge audience expectations and reorientate the audience towards another kind of awareness.

We are thus cued from the Orator's first appearance to beware of looking to him for a summation of information we might otherwise have failed to derive from the play: '*just as the invisible people must be as real as possible, the Orator must appear unreal*' (p. 154). But the old couple overlook this cue and treat him as though he were the final solution to their problems. After a lengthy farewell speech, they abandon their own responsibilities, entrust the delivery of their message to the Orator, and commit a melodramatic joint suicide by throwing themselves out of the windows into the sea. The Orator and the invisible people, now fully independent of the world of the old couple, face each other in silence. But with the death of the old couple, the bright light that heralded the 'increasing densification' of the new on-stage world has suddenly diminished: '*The light coming through the main door and the windows has disappeared; there remains only a weak light as at the beginning of the play*' (p. 159). In some sense, the new on-stage world, having replaced the old on-stage world, has also begun to resemble, as the Orator's visibility suggests, the very world it has gradually supplanted. And the significance of that resemblance becomes apparent when its members cease grappling individually with other existing worlds and settle instead for interacting on the basis of received truths from pre-existing worlds. The former situation is one of growth, change, progress and improvement of existence; the latter, one of stability, stagnation and diminishment of existence. Yet members of the on-stage audience seem riveted to their chairs, attentive to the voice from the past, and anxiously awaiting an explicit justification for having shown up to form an audience in this place on this evening.

What this audience encounters on the dais is, of course, exactly the same problem that the theatre audience confronted on-stage at the beginning of the play – a speaker whose communicative strategies (calling for attention, giving a lecture, illustrating meaning) are not matched by topics of sufficient clarity and consequence to justify the communicative stance taken. His aspirations are as much out of kilter with his abilities as were those of the Old Man and the Old Woman at the beginning of the play. And with a shock of recognition, the off-stage audience now finds itself sharing not only the physical distribution of the on-stage invisible audience but also its unwarranted psychological expectations of a revelatory thematic statement – unless it has by now abandoned the kinds of expectation which Ionesco is determined to thwart, and which can only result in a feeling that something indispensable is missing.

The Orator greets the on-stage audience with '*the signs of a deafmute*' making '*desperate efforts to make himself understood*' (p. 159). The coughs and groans and futile gestures that he produces are no more successful in summarizing and sharing a message than are the scrambled words he scribbles on a blackboard. And we see in his false expectations and disappointed reactions yet another example of a confrontation with unexpected absence. But these expectations and reactions provide the final link in the chain that the play has been creating through its complex use of the performance environment. The Orator's expectations and reactions, though directed at one audience, also implicate another, as the lines of chairs stretch unbroken from the dais to the back of the auditorium.

> *Again, the Orator turns around to face the crowd; he smiles, questions, with an air of hoping that he's been understood, of having said something; he indicates to the empty chairs what he's just written. He remains immobile for a few seconds, rather satisfied and a little solemn; but then,* faced with the absence of the hoped for reaction, *little by little his smile disappears, his face darkens . . . [and he exits] gliding like a ghost.* (my emphasis) (p. 160)

The Orator's disappointment and frustration are aimed directly at the invisible audience on-stage, but they are felt equally by the visible audience in the auditorium which is lined up behind the invisible audience and is just as baffled by the Orator's performance. The line between the invisible audience with its responses and expectations (as registered in the Orator's behaviour) and the visible audience with its responses and expectations has now become almost non-existent. And the final moments of the play seek to undermine it further as the play's function in the theatre becomes the final embodiment of its structure and theme. The play moves from repeatedly confounding the audience and its expectations to reconstituting audience response in an unexpected moment of illumination and renewal of contact.

The stage, after the exit of the Orator, is now without visible characters of any kind, but the curtain does not fall. '*The stage remains empty with only the chairs, the dais, the floor covered with streamers and confetti. The main door is wide open onto darkness*' (p. 160). The light on-stage, like the light in the auditorium, is dim. The open door suggests the breaching of the boundary between what lies on-stage and what lies beyond it to the rear of the stage. The dim light, the chairs, the absence of a speaking character and the uncertainty of audience response, all suggest the dissolution of the boundary between stage and auditorium. The play, having largely eradicated the boundaries it initially foregrounded, seems to have ended. There is silence for a few moments in the theatre and no movement – a situation that leaves the audience in participatory limbo, not knowing what to anticipate, not knowing whether the play is continuing or has ended. At this point, with the audience in the auditorium nervous and uncertain, '*We hear for the first time the human noises of the invisible crowd; there are bursts of laughter, murmurs, shh's, ironical coughs; weak at the beginning, these noises grow louder, then, again, progressively they become weaker*' (p. 160).

The noises of the on-stage audience anticipate and blend with the very noises that the off-stage members of the audience make as they realize (uncertainly) that the performance is over. The ripple of murmurs, shh's and ironical coughs spreads along the on-stage rows of chairs and then across the footlights into the theatre auditorium. The 'increasing densification' of the on-stage fictional world of invisible people has enabled it to flow across the rear border of the stage and supplant the original on-stage real world, and it now flows over the front border of the stage into an auditorium which replicates its behaviour, though, so far, not its appearance. But the audience in the auditorium, having gazed for some time at an on-stage auditorium full of invisible, and thus partially abstract, people, must experience a moment of uncertainty as the house lights go up in the auditorium – uncertainty about whether those sitting to the right and left and making noises like the on-stage audience might turn out to be likewise invisible, or in some other way only partially present and therefore also partially absent. And the audience members most attentive to what has been enacted on-stage will also look at the chairs they themselves are occupying and wonder if they too are in some way or other partially absent. It is to prolong this moment of uncertainty and add weight to the questions arising in the audience's mind that the curtain falls, not with the abruptness of a terminated action, but with the slowness appropriate to a moment of doubt that is to be sustained and not ended by the close of the play: '*The curtain falls very slowly*' (p. 160).

This ending is the moment towards which the whole action of the play moves. It is a moment carefully prepared for and fully insisted upon. The final stage direction focuses on the noises of the invisible crowd on-stage and reminds us that '*All this should last long enough for the audience – the real and visible audience – to leave with this ending firmly impressed on its mind*' (p. 160). And the curtain, which '*falls very slowly*', is no longer separating two distinct worlds, but signalling the end of the performance, without seeking to end the contact between the dramatized world and the world of the auditorium. The moment of uncertainty experienced by the audience is the beginning of a recognition of the play's retrospective significance. It is a moment the play works towards and the audience goes on from. When the first director of the play asked Ionesco to reconsider its puzzling end, Ionesco drew attention to the importance to the play of an ending in which

> the chairs, the scenery, the void, would inexplicably come to life . . . upsetting logic and raising fresh doubts. The lighting should grow pale and yellowish again, for it matches the action, and now the jamboree is over. This is anyway the ending I had in mind when I wrote the play, it was written *for* this ending, an ending I had envisaged before I started.[35]

We should note that this is not an ending which offers the comfort of thematic summary, but an ending which seeks to exemplify the folly of going to the theatre in search of concluding messages – messages which, the moment they are uttered, must switch the play from 'offering testimony' as a basis for further thought towards offering 'teaching', which would (for Ionesco) be a means of stopping thought. The latter strategy would reduce the play to ideological statement and failed art. The former strategy is the one Ionesco favours – it sets out to disturb the foundations of our thinking so that we might think again about the play, think anew about ourselves, and think once more for ourselves. And what the play's 'testimony' offers us is the retrospective significance of the controlled absences that the play has exemplified in its varied manifestations of social living.

In which ways are we, indeed, more 'absent' and less 'present' in our social lives than we might be? To what extent are our own conversation topics commensurate with our conversation strategies? How much of our conversation behaviour consists of habits which simplify interaction, instead of promoting exploration of issues that would justify interaction in the first place? Is it not the case that much of our verbal social behaviour covers up rather than narrows the gaps between individuals? How much of our imaginative behaviour (investing in self-enhancing fictions, visiting theatres) is an abuse of the imagination – using it for escape and avoidance instead of for exploration and understanding? To what extent have we become supplanted as individuals by roles grounded in our own and other people's fictions? And how much do we tend to look to established voices for comforting questions and engaging answers (particularly in the theatre) instead of looking inside for our own questions? And in a pluralistic world, how much do we seek to avoid diversity instead of looking beyond ourselves and towards novelty as a source of better questions than inherited social and theatrical conventions can provide? What may well be eliminated by our habitual social behaviour are the values that only novelty can bring us, values that our inherited expectations and codes of behaviour make us overlook.

The Chairs thus dramatizes and invites us to explore further the potential power of neglected aspects of reality, not just to make the thematic point that these neglected aspects will necessarily prove revelatory, but to embody the thematic concerns of a play seeking to become an instance of its own theme – it offers testimony that contact with new modes of reality is possible, understandable and potentially revelatory. And this testimony is of a world other than our own which, by a process of comparison and contrast, illuminates our own world. Such illumination raises important questions and offers testimony as to possible answers. For Ionesco, 'Ideology is not the source of art. A work of art is the source and the raw material of ideologies to come.'[36] The work of art provides the testimony of the need for new possibilities of being and relating. It is for the audience to take that testimony and remake itself and its world in terms of the testimony the work of art offers: 'To renew one's idiom or one's language is to renew one's conception or one's vision of the world . . . . Any new artistic expression enriches us by answering some spiritual need and broadens the frontiers of known reality.'[37]

10 Beckett: *Krapp's Last Tape*

The stage set for *Krapp's Last Tape* is divided throughout into two distinct domains, one light and the other dark. A single light above a central table serves to establish this division and to focus our attention and Krapp's on what it separates and what it relates: '*Table and immediately adjacent area in strong white light. Rest of stage in darkness*' (p. 10).[1] The importance of this line of demarcation is registered in the repeated visual and verbal action that draws attention to it. Before a word is spoken, Krapp '*begins pacing to and fro at edge of stage, in the light, i.e. not more than four or five paces either way, meditatively eating a banana*' (p. 11). These excursions from one boundary of the light domain to the other not only register Krapp's awareness of and concern for the distinctive nature of this domain, but also help to focus interpretative attention on Krapp's subsequent forays into the area of darkness, forays that require the crossing of the boundary and upon which Krapp himself bestows interpretative comment:

> The new light above my table is a great improvement. With all this darkness round me I feel less alone. [*Pause*] In a way. [*Pause*] I love to get up and move about in it, then back here to . . . [*hesitates*] . . . me. [*Pause*] Krapp. (pp. 14–15)

The 'new light' is not so new, however, for these remarks occur on a tape recording now more than thirty years old. And before we give undue attention to this attempt by Krapp to explain the significance of the light/dark division, we do well to bear in mind that the older Krapp's reactions to his tape recordings repeatedly reveal that he does not always agree with or even respect the ideas, attitudes and values of his earlier days.

A light/dark division invites, as Knowlson points out, all sorts of stock associations:

> Traditionally, of course, light and darkness have often been associated with –
> when they have not actually symbolized – those old polarities in life, the
> after-life and man himself: good and evil, heaven and hell, the spirit and the
> flesh, understanding and confusion, hope and despair.[2]

Deciding which of those polarities applies in the case of this play has proved
somewhat difficult,[3] but the invitation that the light/dark division offers to
approach the play in terms of radical oppositions has led many to focus in
similar terms on the divisions in Krapp's life. The earlier selves manifest on
the tape recordings are thus regarded as not only differing, but quite distinct –
separated by time and the changes time has wrought. Hayman, comparing
the old to the middle-aged Krapp, argues that there are 'two Krapps' in the
play, and not just one.[4] He is supported by Oberg who extends the distinction
further: 'Krapp now is not Krapp past nor Krapp future',[5] by Robinson, who
extends it further still: 'There are three Krapps in the play itself though
many more are locked away on their spools in the drawer',[6] and by
Esslin who projects these multiplying differences into their most radical
form: the several selves of Krapp are, he argues, 'utterly strange' from one
another.[7]

Oddly enough, however, it is possible to find extensive critical commentary that reverses this tendency to give discontinuity in Krapp's life priority
over its continuity. Dukore believes that 'old Krapp is himself essentially the
same as middle-aged Krapp (whose taped voice he hears), who is essentially
the same as young Krapp (unheard by the audience but discussed by
middle-aged Krapp).'[8] Cohn largely agrees: '[the] juxtaposition of Krapp's
two voices implies an ironic comment on the insignificance of the passing of
time. Separated by thirty years, the voices utter the same phrases, are prey to
the same hope and despair.'[9] Hayman inadvertently manages to summarize
this critical disagreement by arguing on the one hand that the play dramatizes
'a complete discontinuity between past, present, and future selves' and on the
other that the tapes offer an image of the mind 'endlessly repeating itself with
the same memories, hopes, anxieties, preoccupations'.[10] Such critical disagreement suggests that there is considerable evidence for both positions.
Krapp's life does indeed display both continuities and discontinuities; there
are manifestations of both persistence and change in various elements of his
existence. And, as we shall see, the problem of dealing with the competing
claims of unity and diversity is not only a critical concern, it is a major
concern for Krapp himself in a play that takes the problems of pluralism from
the individual, social and moral domains in which we have so far encountered
them and extends them further into the domain of the self. The dilemmas
of other worlds that have provided the focus for our study of the modern
stage emerge here as the dilemmas of the several worlds of the pluralistic
individual.

To locate the issue in this context is to recall our earlier discussion of
similarity and difference and of the problems of charting our course in a field

characterized as much by diversity as by continuity. These are also important issues for Krapp who finds himself perplexed by problems of continuity and change in his life and by the difficulty of locating coherence among them. It is no coincidence, of course, that issues fundamental to our understanding of modern drama as a field should also turn out to be major thematic concerns in particular plays. As we noted at the outset, and as the argument of this book has repeatedly revealed, one of the characteristic features of this otherwise diverse field is the tendency of dramatists to conduct an exploration of the genre and of the world on-stage as a means of exploring and understanding dilemmas in the lives of characters both on-stage and off. This frequently involves use of lines of demarcation that divide the theatrical event into distinct domains, and challenge the audience to locate appropriate connections between them. In *Krapp's Last Tape* the problems of the character and the problems of the audience merge in the shared pursuit of continuity in the context of manifest discontinuity.

The peculiar difficulty presented by *Krapp's Last Tape* is that the thread of significant continuity seems to elude Krapp's grasp as much as ours. And when Esslin argues that Krapp's several selves seem 'utterly strange' from one another, he offers a way of approaching this play and others that has earned widespread popularity. If the problem of locating coherence and continuity daunts not only Krapp but us as well, that may be, Esslin would argue, the point. When Esslin located this play, and Beckett's work in general, in the category of the Theatre of the Absurd, he did so because much of the play stresses the multiplicity of the self, the difficulties involved in establishing stable values and stable truths, and the apparent hopelessness of a life lived under such adverse and bewildering conditions. There may thus be no significant thread of continuity in the life of a character in a play of the Absurd. But instead of resolving the problem of relating discontinuity and continuity in Krapp's life, such an interpretation explains the former by ignoring the latter. Questions may thus need to be raised about whether the category of Absurd Theatre has necessarily provided the most appropriate context for interpreting *Krapp's Last Tape*, and this, in turn, raises questions about whether this context is also appropriate for the many other plays to which it has been applied.

In each of our earlier chapters on individual plays, a particular play has been related to established social, generic and critical contexts in such a way that plays and contexts mutually illuminate each other. This is very much in line with the argument of part one, in which it is suggested that generalizations function best in this field when used as measuring rods, as instruments of investigation that are refined and, where necessary, changed in the process of application. It should thus be borne in mind that what we are dealing with in every case is an emergent interpretative context, and not simply an inherited historical context. The two contexts are not, of course, mutually exclusive, but it is important that we recognize the complex status of the contexts invoked. Literary movements that provide such contexts, like naturalism and expressionism, for example, are frequently pluralistic in nature. They are the products of work done by theorists, creative writers, literary critics and others, and it is not always the case that literary movements and their related interpretative contexts are seen similarly by all those concerned with establishing, extending, exploiting and understanding them. Every attempt to invoke an interpretative context is consequently an exploration of the context as well as of the play, and is not just a matter of a mechanical application of the former to the latter. But it also follows that every attempt to invoke a context is a test of that context; what is finally decisive is whether or not we feel that the interpretative guidelines it provides facilitate our access to a particular play or group of plays.

It is thus important, when we encounter a category like the Theatre of the Absurd, that we recognize that it could, in fact, exist and be applied in several different ways. Furthermore, when we seek to link a play like *Krapp's Last Tape* to a category like that of Absurd Theatre, we should not overlook the possibility that something might be learned not only from the established features of the category, but also from the very modes of categorization that such experimental plays both invite and frequently resist. It is often through those tensions between critical generalizations and diverse data that we can clarify confusions shared by critics, audiences and characters alike. We should thus note with care the various possible foundations of a Theatre of the Absurd. It could, for example, characterize a school of creative writers who work out together a programme for theatrical reform and write according to its principles. It could designate a set of related works that manifest important common features, even though no concerted programme is in operation. It could also be a heuristic category, one designed to provide an illuminating framework for the comparison and contrast of works which differ in many ways from each other but which can be significantly related by the framework. The category could thus exist as a historically grounded movement or school, as an empirically observable common ground of the plays, or as a heuristic device. Our attention as critics would thus be guided in three possible ways by the category as we seek to develop an appropriate context for interpretation and evaluation. In the first case we would focus on the *announcements of the writers* themselves and consider to what extent their practice matched their theory; in the second case we would focus on the importance of a set of *common features of the plays*; and in the third case we would focus on *a critical task of the spectator/reader* which is facilitated by the heuristic device. These three kinds of generalizations are not, of course, mutually exclusive, but they are distinguishable and often distinct.[11]

Once we have noted these important distinctions, we can then begin to recognize a major reason for the controversy[12] that has characterized critical discussion of Absurd Theatre: Esslin, it seems, did not make it clear in his original book which kind of category the Theatre of the Absurd is supposed to be.[13] No decision to make the category of one kind rather than another necessarily excludes the use of other types of evidence, but a decision firmly announced and firmly adhered to would have clarified relationships among the various types of evidence – which kind is controlling and indispensable, which is confirmatory but not crucial. In its absence, the tensions within the category have caused problems for both author and reader, and controversy has ensued.[14]

The welter of criticism *The Theatre of the Absurd* attracted seems certainly to have helped decide the issue retrospectively. In the preface to the revised edition of 1969 Esslin argues that the category is simply 'a working hypothesis' which seeks to make the plays 'accessible to discussion'.[15] In his introduction to an anthology of *Absurd Drama*, he notes that 'a label of this kind . . . is an aid to understanding, valid only in so far as it helps to gain insight into a work of art. It is not a binding classification.'[16] And in an essay entitled 'The Theatre of the Absurd reconsidered', Esslin complains that

> what I intended as a generic concept, a working hypothesis for the understanding of a large number of extremely varied and elusive phenomena, has assumed for many people, including some drama critics, a reality as concrete and specific as a branded product of the detergent industry.[17]

It is thus the heuristic claim to which Esslin, in his later writing, finally resorts, but it is not at all clear that the heuristic claim was primary when the book was written. Generalizations subsequently characterized as heuristic have not appeared so to the many readers who have regarded them as either genetic or empirical in function.[18] The heuristic claim seems to come to prominence late, both as a response to tensions in the category and, unfortunately, as a further contribution to them. But, for our purposes, it is important to note that what is emerging here is a conflict between alternative ways of using generalizations that is fundamental not only to literary categorization, but also to Krapp's persistent efforts to locate the basic patterns of his varied experiences.

The key issue here is not just that genetic, empirical and heuristic generalizations call upon differing types of evidence, but that the change from one kind of generalization to another brings with it changes in the relationships between generalization and evidence and between a generalization and its user. Genetic, empirical and heuristic generalizations offer significantly different possibilities for dealing with the diversity of 'extremely varied' phenomena, and to fail to keep them distinct, or to try to change one into another, is to contribute to the very problems that generalizations are aimed at resolving. Before tracing these problems in Krapp's attempts to deal with the multiplicity of his sense of self, we should briefly note their major manifestations in Esslin's attempts to deal with the multiplicity of the plays he wishes to locate in the Theatre of the Absurd. In both cases the relationship between generalization and diversity causes major difficulties – difficulties which, in Esslin's case, recurringly take the form of an uncertain mingling of two major kinds of generalization.

A symptomatic confusion of heuristic and empirical generalizations becomes apparent when Esslin, even as he seeks to give his argument a heuristic basis, feels compelled to support his heuristic claim with an unnecessarily narrow empirical claim. He argues that he wishes to make the fundamental structures of the various plays 'accessible to discussion by tracing the features they have in common'.[19] What is overlooked in this and similar formulations is the fact that though an empirical generalization depends upon the establishment of a set of common features, a heuristic generalization does not. An empirical generalization is based upon the assumption that what is common is what is important – it is the defining core, the organizing centre of each particular case. The function of an empirical generalization is to locate the uniformity that underlies variety, and it thus serves to give similarity priority over difference. A heuristic generalization, on the other hand, functions as a means of providing access to diversity, and does not reduce it to, or make it depend on, a set of common features. A heuristic generalization is validated not by establishing a set of common features, but by guiding attention towards important features, common or otherwise. It will certainly draw attention to a string of characteristic features that indicate continuity, but it will not seek to establish either an exhaustive list or an indispensable set. In Wittgenstein's terms 'this *and similar things*'[20] belong in a category exemplified by selected instances but not limited to them or to the features they have so far exhibited. The similarities may be of many kinds and none necessarily runs through a whole set of instances.

What is also of importance here, both to Esslin's categorizing activity and (as we shall see) to Krapp's in *Krapp's Last Tape*, is the different function the two kinds of generalization attain in investigative activity. The empirical generalization is often the goal of contact with a set of particular cases (as, for example, in the empirical sciences' basic research[21]), but the heuristic generalization, though it results, in part, from contact with a set of particular cases, remains a starting-point for subsequent further access to the individual cases themselves. The empirical generalization focuses primarily on the data and takes the reader's interest in establishing significant common ground as given. The heuristic generalization bases its value on a task to be subsequently undertaken; it offers not the conclusion of investigation, but the means of continuing it. The empirical generalization thus offers a structural model as the basis for locating its replication, while the heuristic generalization offers a structural model as the basis for studying its extrapolation. In the former case, it is the rediscovery of the basic pattern that is at issue; in the latter, it is both the initial pattern and its evolving changes. We can thus distinguish an empirical generalization from a heuristic generalization along the lines used earlier to distinguish a unity generalization from a continuity generalization. The latter offers access to similarities and differences as both potentially important, for it contracts complex relationships not only with valued data, but with a valuer who wishes to go on to make discoveries and judgements for himself.

The conflation of heuristic and empirical generalizations might have less important consequences if the data generalized about were all very similar. But if the plays of the Absurd are, as Esslin acknowledges, 'extremely varied', the reduction of heuristic generalizations to empirical generalizations (i.e. those locating central common ground) quickly becomes confusing. Differences may be acknowledged, but they cannot easily be accommodated, for instead of relating similarity and difference, the 'common ground' argument simply separates one from the other.

> When I wrote my book I had been struck by the fact that the work of dramatists writing quite independently of one another in different countries had *certain fundamental features in common.* . . . A concept like the Theatre of the Absurd *concentrates on certain important elements in individual works* containing a multitude of other elements that make them, in other respects, quite different from one another. *It is a basic mistake to assume that all the works that somehow come under this label are the same, or even very similar.* (my emphases)[22]

There is no better statement of Esslin's basic dilemma as he tries simultaneously to defend his category on the basis of important common ground and to acknowledge that the plays in the category are not necessarily very similar. The phrase 'fundamental features in common' provides the justification for the claim that a Theatre of the Absurd exists, but the same phrase sorts oddly with the accompanying concession that many of the plays are not even very similar.[23] The clinging to fundamental common features as a basis for heuristic generalization registers a commitment to generalizations as statements of basic truths that now concluded investigation has revealed, and this commitment is quite at odds with a heuristic approach to generalizations as instruments that serve their purpose by linking similarity to difference, by guiding us beyond what they pragmatically reveal.

If we move on, at this point, to *Krapp's Last Tape*, we take with us a recognition of what must be avoided as prematurely limiting both the scope and function of generalization. The confusion of empirical with heuristic generalizations in the context of diverse data will make diversity inaccessible, coherence unreliable, and change incomprehensible. We thus find ourselves posed with the following question: what kinds of abstraction from varied features will serve to bring us to grips with things that exhibit continuity with each other, but not necessarily a specific common ground? This pursuit of continuity in the context of diversity is very much Krapp's problem, too, for he finds himself similarly perplexed by the combination of continuity and change in his life and by the attendant problems of locating stable general values in the context of recurring changes. And the changes he has to deal with occur, we should note, not only in the worlds around him, but also in the worlds within himself. The action of the play thus focuses on the continuities and discontinuities in Krapp's life, and on his attempts to forge a viable synthesis of elements of persisting value.

For many years Krapp has celebrated his birthday by tape-recording a summary of the most important events of his life in the preceding year. Armed with a few scribbled notes, he sits alone in his room and elaborates upon the events he has thought worth preserving. The aim each year is, he reminds himself, to separate 'the grain from the husks' (p. 14). Krapp, now in his late sixties, listens to Krapp in his late thirties explaining this distinction to himself:

> The grain, now what I wonder do I mean by that, I mean . . . [hesitates] . . . I suppose I mean those things worth having when all the dust has – when all my dust has settled. I close my eyes and try and imagine them. [Pause. Krapp closes his eyes briefly.] (p. 15)

As the older Krapp repeats the action of the younger Krapp in closing his eyes, we note an implied agreement as to the nature of the task. And the closed eyes make an immediate connection between stocking the tape recorder and manipulating the relationship between light and darkness in Krapp's world. Darkness can help, it seems, and we will return to that point later. For the moment, we should note that the stored information is to function for others, and not just for Krapp. It is to be information worth preserving after his own dust has settled. And there is an evident connection to be made here with Krapp's public ambitions as a writer. Krapp in his thirties speaks of Krapp in his twenties contemplating 'Shadows of the opus . . . magnum' (p. 17). The hope to write a great book goes back as far as the tapes we hear of, and the ambition to put information from the tapes into the public domain for the benefit of others suggests that the planned great work is one contemplated way of making public use of the grain, once it is definitively separated from the husks. A rueful comment on the results of this project is made when Krapp, in his sixties, ponders the notion that only seventeen copies have been sold 'of which eleven at trade price to free circulating libraries beyond the seas' (p. 25).

Whether this is an imagined or an actual record of sales is never clarified, but it does not need to be. The decades of effort to separate 'the grain from the husks' has foundered along the way, and Krapp is no more likely to view with favour a written record of the definitive grain than he does the spoken record which the tape recorder provides him. Krapp's current responses to his earlier tape recording reveal that he has since forgotten and is quite unable to recall things that he once believed central to his life, that he no longer finds value in episodes and ideas that once seemed crucial, and that events that seemed at one time to have one kind of importance seem in retrospect to have another. The project of locating the definitive grain and generalizing about it for the benefit of others has been undermined by repeated changes in the person who conducts the selecting, evaluating and recording of the data. It is impossible to separate the grain definitively from the husks when the data are various and the criteria for distinguishing between the two are not stable.

It is not difficult, in this context, to understand why so many have moved from this recognition to the conclusion that Krapp's life, like the stage set on which it is portrayed, is divided into radically distinct domains. As Krapp changes, he does indeed, in some important sense, become someone else. But this acknowledgement must immediately be matched by another – in a similarly important sense, Krapp remains the same person. This paradox is only confusing as long as we remain governed by a misconception that we use the phrase 'the same person' as a unity rather than as a continuity generaliz-ation about Krapp's several manifestations. Krapp is clearly not the same in the former sense, but he is in the latter, and it is our task to locate, as Krapp struggles to locate, the modes of coherence that give significance to his continuity. Krapp (like many literary commentators) remains baffled by the problem of generalizing across a diversity that lacks a significant common core.[24] But the visual images of the play, in particular the light/dark division and the tape recorder, provide information that helps the audience to see what Krapp only dimly sees.

The first thing we should note is that the activities Krapp engages in as he prepares for recording, records and plays back tapes on the tape recorder serve to undermine whatever oppositions we might wish to impose upon the light/dark division of the stage. His early movements, for example, challenge from the outset any attempt to approach the light/dark areas in terms of mind versus body, understanding versus confusion, hope versus despair, good versus evil, spirit versus senses, or whatever other contrasts of a similar kind we might be tempted to apply. Krapp's psychological and physical selves are not only contrasted by his activities but also connected by them. At the beginning of the play, Krapp eats a banana *'meditatively'* (p. 11) and strictly within the area illuminated by the overhead lamp. This act of physical consumption in the light is matched by the storing of things for both physical *and* psychological consumption in the dark. Krapp goes off into the darkness to drink (physical), but while there he retrieves *'an old ledger'* (psychological) (p. 12). A few minutes later, unable to understand the word 'viduity' on a tape, he *'goes backstage into darkness, comes back with an enormous dictionary'* (p. 18).

This mingling of physical and psychological elements subsequently de-velops into a process of interaction between the two domains, and this, in turn, draws attention to a more subtle use the play is making of its areas of light and dark. That use is suggested first rather humorously and then with increasing seriousness. After several moments of idleness and a brief period of total immobility, Krapp is propelled into the darkness by *'an idea'* – an idea, to be sure, about fortifying himself with a drink, but the drink does indeed fortify him to return to the light and confront the task of making this year's tape recording.

> *Finally he has an idea, puts banana in his waistcoat pocket, the end emerging, and goes with all the speed he can muster backstage into darkness. Ten seconds. Loud pop of cork. Fifteen seconds. He comes back into light carrying an old ledger and sits down at table. He lays ledger on table, wipes his mouth, wipes his hands on the front of his waistcoat, brings them smartly together and rubs them.* (pp. 11–12)

An 'idea' takes Krapp off into the darkness, and the drink propels him back into the light. Krapp's physical and psychological selves are distinguishable but related, and the later action of the play stresses their relatedness as much as the light/dark division suggests their potential distinguishability. The opening movement of the play, Krapp *'pacing to and fro at edge of stage, in the light'* (p. 11) gives way to the dominant movement of the play, Krapp *moving back and forth between the area of darkness and the area of light.* In the process of this transition, we observe a pattern we have encountered in various ways in other plays: the initial drawing of an on-stage boundary and the subsequent and partial transcendence of it.

To note that the rigid polarities do not hold is not to eliminate them or render them irrelevant. The distinction between Krapp's physical and psychological selves, like the distinction between his previous and present selves, is a distinction to be pondered in the context of similarity and difference, continuity and discontinuity, separateness and relatedness. The divisions may not be definitive, but establishing appropriate relationships among distinguishable elements is the task we are set by the verbal and visual texture of this play. [25] And a careful scrutiny of Krapp's movements back and forth in the light and dark, and of the stage image created by the lamp above the table, reminds us of something we have so far overlooked in discussing the light and dark domains. Krapp's room is not divided into two halves by the light from his overhead lamp. If it were, we could well agree that the route most interpreters have taken is the right one: questions about how these two sides of Krapp's world are opposed would seem more important than questions about how they are related, and questions about their relatedness might well be governed by the problem of reconciling opposites. But if we note, as we must, that the stage image is not one of two opposed halves of the stage, but one of a circle of light surrounded by an area of darkness, we will be more likely, from the outset, to consider relationships as well as differences. Furthermore, the pattern of light at the centre and dark on the perimeter invites consideration of similarly constituted images in the play – images which appear with some frequency and some variation both on the tape recordings and elsewhere in the play.

Once we consider light/dark images in terms of encirclement and not just division, a variety of details begins to interact on this basis. The image of separating the grain from the husks by which Krapp characterizes his lifetime project is one in which the important part is at the centre and the less important part on the periphery. Krapp has his moment of revelation about the importance of the light/dark division in his life when he is in his thirties, on a jetty, on a stormy night with waves crashing against 'great granite rocks the foam flying up in the light of the lighthouse and the wind-gauge spinning like a propellor' (p. 21). The 'light of the lighthouse' standing firm against the stormy night is an image of a central light surrounded by darkness. The first of the several lovers Krapp mentions on the tapes is, as many critical articles have pointed out, a woman whose name is linked with white (Bianca) and whose address (Kedar Street) is linked with dark.[26] And when Krapp performs the important task of his life, his annual recording to separate the grain from the husks, he does so in the central area of light surrounded by darkness. As images from the past and present repeatedly recapitulate the pattern of 'a central area of light surrounded by darkness', the image of important things at the centre and peripheral things on the perimeter is steadily reinforced. The stage business with the banana at the beginning thus links with the play's more serious concerns. The task of separating grain from husk is given humorous, but pointed, enactment in Krapp's peeling the banana while meditatively pacing back and forth in the light.

The image pattern is a strong one, and it invites consideration in terms of the unifying goal that governs Krapp's current activity in the light. The task is to isolate the grain, to find 'those things worth having when all the dust has – when all *my* dust has settled. I close my eyes and try and imagine them. [*Pause. Krapp closes his eyes briefly.*]' (p. 15). At the core of things, at the centre of the light, on the tape recorder or on the table, are the events unified by their status as the grain of Krapp's life. Here their common features will be apparent, their common value visible, their common implications manifest, not just for Krapp, but for others. What Krapp seeks is what empirical generalizations offer – the conclusion of an investigation by locating the valued common core of the data.

As we have seen, however, the planned task is never concluded because diversity intrudes repeatedly upon the search for coherence. Ironically, the tape recorder which was to be the instrument for establishing and preserving important coherence in Krapp's life turns out to be a constant reminder of the significant discontinuity of his life – a life that seems to lack any consistent criteria for establishing common ground. The task is never concluded because the common features never emerge. This is Krapp's problem, it is also a critical problem, and it is now the audience's problem: it takes us back to the image patterns to see whether we can learn more from them than Krapp has learned.

Until this point, the encirclement of darkness by light seems only to reinforce recognitions derived from other aspects of the play. But this reinforcement is one designed to precipitate recognition of a contrast that is also crucial to the play – a contrast that suggests a rather different estimate of the relationship of light and dark, one that points the way beyond Krapp's problems. We thus need to look more closely at the episode with the banana, at the episode of revelation on the jetty, and at the episode that succeeds the jetty scene on the tape – the moment in a punt with a woman. This moment fascinates the older Krapp who repeatedly plays and replays his recorded recollection of it.

As Krapp prepares to make the current year's tape, he paces, as we have noted, back and forth in the light with a banana in his hand. He peels off the banana skin, drops it to the ground, and begins walking to and fro until he finally 'treads on skin, slips, nearly falls, recovers himself, stoops and peers at skin and finally pushes it, still stooping, with his foot over the edge of stage' (p. 11). (In more recent productions, Beckett has had Krapp throw the skin into the wings.[27]) This is humorous enough, as we have noted, but it offers an important hint about grain and husks, and about the related light/dark division in the play. We see Krapp here not only separating the 'grain' from the 'husk' of the banana, but also finding that the husk can still trip him up, still play a role in his life other than the one he anticipated when he consigned it to the category of husk and threw it away. This holds true, we have already noted, for information on the tapes: Krapp assigns one kind of value to such information only to discover, or to become dimly aware, that it may have another. But this evolving pattern has a further implication: it also holds true for Krapp's assignment of relative value to the light/dark division in his room. There is much in the play to suggest that though Krapp has understood that the division is important, he has not clearly understood why. And that not-yet-understood issue is one of the things that draws his attention and ours repeatedly to the recording of the episode with the woman in the punt.

As we have noted, Krapp's early movements are back and forth from one edge of the light domain to another. His subsequent movements, and the dominant movements of the play, are back and forth between the light domain and the dark. On the tape recording that fascinates him so much, the one marked 'box three, spool five' (p. 13), there is a lengthy description of the moment of revelation when he made a major discovery about the importance of light and dark domains in his life. That discovery he now greets with impatience and disdain, but its focus on light and dark invites us to note other moments on the tape, particularly the moment with the woman in the punt, that also display a concern for light and dark. They do so in ways that attract Krapp's attention but fail to trigger appropriate understanding. The elaborate visual detail of the play, however, offers the audience access to knowledge which, like that stored on the tape recorder, is not restricted to what is currently Krapp's.

As Krapp searches the tape for episodes that will help him begin this year's tape, he comes across the following:

Spiritually a year of profound gloom and indigence until that memorable night in March, at the end of the jetty, in the howling wind, never to be forgotten, when suddenly I saw the whole thing. The vision, at last. This I fancy is what I have chiefly to record this evening, against the day when my work will be done and perhaps no place left in my memory, warm or cold, for the miracle that . . . [*hesitates*] . . . for the fire that set it alight. What I suddenly saw then was this, that the belief I had been going on all my life, namely – [*Krapp switches off impatiently, winds tape forward, switches on again.*] – great granite rocks the foam flying up in the light of the lighthouse and the wind-gauge spinning like a propellor, clear to me at last that the dark I have always struggled to keep under is in reality my most – [*Krapp curses, switches off, winds tape forward, switches on again.*] – unshatterable association until my dissolution of storm and night with the light of the understanding and the fire – [*Krapp curses louder, switches off, winds tape forward, switches on again.*] – my face in her breasts and my hand on her. We lay there without moving. But under us all moved, and moved us, gently, up and down, and from side to side. [*Pause*] (pp. 20–1)

The moment of revelation, of 'the vision, at last' is rejected by the older Krapp along with its image of 'the light of the understanding' as a central lighthouse surrounded by encircling dark. That moment is passed over for another, as Krapp plays and replays the passage dealing with the unnamed woman in the punt. Krapp rejects the moment of insight into the nature of the light/dark contrast, but we note in the stage image constantly before us that he retains the division in his room even in the absence of a persuasive explanation for it. And that division, as we shall see, is both recapitulated in and revised by the reminiscence about the moment with the woman in the punt, the moment that so inexplicably obsesses him.

The moment that fascinates Krapp has also fascinated audiences and critics, but it has proved very difficult to locate the features that give it such importance. In the context of the play, however, it has undeniable power, and that power is used, among other things, to supply a direct challenge to the image of central light surrounded by darkness – an image that governs Krapp's room and much of his thinking about his life and about how best to establish and preserve its importance.

She lay stretched out on the floorboards with her hands under her head and her eyes closed. . . . I said again I thought it was hopeless and no good going on, and she agreed, without opening her eyes. [*Pause*] I asked her to look at me and after a few moments – [*pause*] – after a few moments she did, but the eyes just slits, because of the glare. I bent over her to get them in the shadow and they opened. [*Pause. Low.*] Let me in. [*Pause*] We drifted in among the flags and stuck. The way they went down, sighing, before the stem! [*Pause*] I lay down across her with my face in her breasts and my hand on her. We lay there without moving. But under us all moved, and moved us, gently, up and down, and from side to side. (pp. 22–3)

Once we have noted that the black/white image in Krapp's room is one of encirclement rather than separation, it is difficult to overlook here the reversal of the pattern of encirclement that dominates his room. There, Krapp has installed a central light and surrounded it with darkness. Here, in the episode in the punt, Krapp rescues a moment of central darkness from the surrounding light as he leans over the girl to shade her eyes from the surrounding glare: 'I bent over her to get them in the shadow and they opened.' The two characters' subsequent physical and spiritual communion is a moment with darkness at the centre and light on the periphery. And once we have noted the image reversal in this key moment in Krapp's life, we quickly recognize that it is not the only moment in the play that reverses the pattern of darkness encircling light, nor is it the only moment that draws attention to a woman's eyes. The two issues we discover are related, and related in ways that enable each to clarify the significance of the other.

Images reversing the light/dark pattern of encirclement recur at important moments in Krapp's life, moments of no clearly definable kind. On the day of his mother's death, Krapp describes himself on a bench by a weir playing with a dog. As his mother dies in a nearby house, the surrounding daylight is excluded by the drawing down of a blind (shade). This image of central darkness and surrounding light is recapitulated in the little black ball Krapp clenches in his hand and then tosses to a white dog.

> I was there when – [*Krapp switches off, broods, switches on again.*] – the blind went down, one of those dirty brown roller affairs, throwing a ball for a little white dog, as chance would have it. I happened to look up and there it was. All over and done with, at last. I sat on for a few moments with the ball in my hand and the dog yelping and pawing at me. [*Pause*] Moments. Her moments, my moments. [*Pause*] The dog's moments. [*Pause*] In the end I held it out to him and he took it in his mouth, gently, gently. A small, old, black, hard, solid rubber ball. [*Pause*] I shall feel it, in my hand, until my dying day. [*Pause*] I might have kept it. [*Pause*] But I gave it to the dog. [*Pause*] (pp. 19–20)

The three images of light encircling dark – daylight/blind, hand/black ball, white dog/black ball – are preceded by a fourth: that of a nursemaid wheeling a perambulator along the banks of the canal: ('One dark young beauty I recollect particularly, all white and starch, incomparable bosom' (p. 19)). But what fascinates Krapp most about this woman and about others who have affected his life is not so much their shape but their eyes. And this fascination, too, has its implications for the priority and centrality of light and dark in his life.

The most startling moments in the play are those in which Krapp, a vaguely comic, sceptical old man, makes positive comments of any kind. But one topic, more than any other, is likely to elicit such comments – the eyes of the women he has loved. The dangers of triteness in the play are obvious in this respect, and it is important to note that the potential sentimentality is avoided because the eyes function, not as vague tokens of romance, but as parts of this pattern of light/dark images that is central to the play. Krapp in his thirties, having listened to the tape of Krapp recalling Bianca in his twenties, comments: 'Well out of that, Jesus yes! Hopeless business. [*Pause*] Not much about her, apart from a tribute to her eyes. Very warm. I suddenly saw them again. [*Pause*] Incomparable!' (p. 16). The word 'incomparable' is unexpectedly affirmative on a tape in which Krapp in his thirties is largely rejecting the views and attitudes of Krapp in his twenties. But the older and younger Krapps evidently share this admiration for Bianca's eyes. And Krapp in his thirties goes on to pay similar tribute to the eyes of the dark nurse he encountered by the canal: 'The face she had! The eyes! Like . . . [*hesitates*] . . . chrysolite! [*Pause*]' (p. 19). The two tributes to women's eyes offer obvious links to the episode of communion with the woman in the punt, which likewise involved a moment of mutual gazing – a moment that continues to intrigue the older Krapp. Characteristically, he begins by condemning his younger self, but the criticism stops short at the thought of the woman's eyes:

> Just been listening to that stupid bastard I took myself for thirty years ago, hard to believe I was ever as bad as that. Thank God that's all done with anyway. [*Pause*] The eyes she had! [*Broods, realizes he is recording silence, switches off, broods.*] (p. 24)

If we have followed this pattern carefully, we will have noted that the black ball encircled by the white dog, the dark room surrounded by the light of day, and the closed eyes surrounded by sunshine are all ways of cueing us into what happens when the girl's eyes open in the shade. What they reveal is a pattern that recapitulates in the shape of the eye the image of an area of darkness (the pupil) surrounded by an area of white (the eyeball). And if we consider the implications of this we will note that the pattern of black encircled by white that is characteristic of eyes, the pattern that repeatedly fascinates Krapp at all ages, is also the reverse of the pattern of white encircled by black which characterizes not only Krapp's room but also his lifetime project of separating the grain from the husk. Furthermore, we will note that, in that moment in the punt, the encircling world in the light does not become superfluous; it continues to participate in the moment of central darkness. Krapp, now with his eyes in shadow, is in touch with patterns larger than those of his own or the girl's making or understanding: 'I lay down across her with my face in her breasts and my hand on her. We lay there without moving. But under us all moved, and moved us, gently, up and down, and from side to side' (p. 23).

The sexual nature of these movements is evident, but more is at issue here. It is a moment of physical passivity experienced in strong sunlight with darkness at the heart of the moment. And it is a moment that startles many of the commentators on Beckett's work. As Alvarez puts it, 'It is a new tone and a new direction for Beckett's writing. . . . Its subject is not depression but grief, and instead of shying away from its causes, it shows, poignantly and with great beauty, precisely what has been lost.'[28] This estimate of the lyrical power of 'the curiously poignant climax' is shared by Walker, Robinson, and Fletcher and Spurling.[29] But if we look at it more closely we find great difficulty in isolating the features that give it such value. When Alvarez comments that the passage 'shows, poignantly and with great beauty, precisely what has been lost', he is responding appropriately to the power of the incident, but misreading its nature. The passage is, in many ways, bordering on the trite. The scene of a lake, sunshine, a punt, a girl, is only briefly sketched for us. There is little to indicate a peculiarly attractive landscape, an unusually attractive girl, or an idiosyncratic kind of relationship. Indeed, the scene calls upon us to bring into play a set of general responses to such scenes that are commonplace in every romantic novel and every second-rate Hollywood movie. An empirical generalization about its important common features will make it seem more common than important. An attempt to use such features as criteria for separating grain from husk would collapse the distinction between the two. We must recognize that this moment, while related to a well-established class of moments, escapes the commonplace by becoming more than just another member of the class. In Krapp's view and in ours, its differences considerably outweigh its similarities to stock scenarios. But it is the differences in conjunction with the similarities that give it its peculiar power. It is a moment that starts from something well known but points beyond it. It is a moment that speaks to Krapp and us of values not yet understood, but not necessarily beyond the reach of understanding. And it speaks to us, not directly, but via Krapp's responses to an episode that he cannot explain and cannot forget. These are key recognitions, as we will see, for our understanding of the moment and of the play.

When Esslin placed this play in the category of the Theatre of the Absurd, he did so because much of the play stresses the multiplicity of self, the difficulties involved in stabilizing knowledge, and the hopelessness of Krapp's later life. But because he failed to link the negative features that might fit with his key generalizations about Absurd Theatre to more positive ones that do not fit, he gradually lost touch with the play. Generalizations that focus our attention on the negative side of Krapp's life must also accommodate our experience and understanding of moments that transcend that negativeness and, indeed, gain much of their value from that transcendence. If the importance of that moment in the punt was affirmed only by someone young and gullible, it would have nothing like the power it gains from being not only affirmed, but reaffirmed by someone who is old, cynical, internally divided and close to despair. The stage directions at the beginning of the play hammer home the fact of Krapp's age and decrepitude. He is 'very near-sighted' (p. 9), 'hard of hearing' (p. 9), has a 'cracked voice' (p. 10), and a 'laborious walk' (p. 10), is 'unshaven' (p. 9), and wears grimy, ill-fitting clothes (p. 9). There is more than a hint of an aged clown in this 'wearish old man' (p. 9), with his 'white face, purple nose', and large 'white boots' (p. 9). His dominant attitude towards his own past is one of contempt and disgust, an attitude that is frequently apparent in his rejection of things once highly valued. When such a man, at such a time in his life, views anything positively, we greet it with surprise and careful attention. And when such a man, at such a time in his life, views something so positively that he is prepared to contemplate living through all the pain and the failure just to experience it once more, we greet it with even more surprise and more careful attention. And that is precisely what we do, and precisely where we are liable to be misled, if we look to this moment for criteria that will enable us definitively to separate grain from husk.

Throughout the play, the audience in the theatre confronts an on-stage image with light at the centre and dark around the outside and is easily caught up in the task Krapp has set himself and in its persistent failure. If we, like Krapp, seek to generalize from the moments when the grain seems clearly separable from the husks, we are likely to encounter the same frustrations he has encountered. Attempts to generalize about the kinds of incidents that make life worth reliving lead us to a dilemma similar to that of Krapp when he plans a great public statement on the value of his own life. In both cases, particular instances are valued as means towards an end of summarizing empirical generalizations, and those generalizations threaten always to collapse into the trite. Instances, in this context, are placed on the perimeter of concern and given a status subordinate to that of the 'light of understanding' that occupies the well-lit centre. Generalizations, thus used, reduce, disturb, or simply fail to accommodate the value of the particular cases encountered. But if we recall our earlier argument that generalizations can have more than one kind of relationship to the data and more than one kind of relationship to the user, we will see what Krapp has yet to see – that the reverse image, the one of light encircling dark, suggests possibilities for the resolution of his dilemma.

The episode in the punt, we should note, is entered in the ledger under the heading 'Farewell to . . . love' (p. 13). This generalization from the single instance is in keeping with the light/dark distribution in Krapp's room. The lived moment is subordinate to the generalizations about it, and the generalization is a concluding, not an initiating, event. It is led up to, but it leads nowhere. The episode in the punt, at this point viewed in terms of a concern for a subsequent synthesis of key events in Krapp's life, plays a role and earns a value in Krapp's life that is very different from the one that is emergent at the end of the play. But it is important to note that more is being challenged here than this one local error, large though it may be. Whatever the power of that moment in the punt, it is by no means alone in sustaining and accumulating value in his later life and it is by no means alone in challenging the very basis of Krapp's persistent goal of leading from instances to concluding generalizations. What these moments and many of Krapp's responses to them display is the evident value of movement not just from, but towards past events –

events which, while not yet understood, intriguingly invite further under-standing and further experiencing. And that further understanding is, interestingly enough, associated not just with light surrounded by dark, but alternately with dark surrounded by light. When Krapp, recording in his sixties, contemplates what would encourage him to live his life over again, with all its pains and failures, the context is an image with darkness established at the core: Krapp conceives of himself lying 'propped up in the dark' and using that darkness as a base for moving elsewhere:

> Ah finish your booze now and get to your bed. Go on with this drivel in the morning. Or leave it at that. [*Pause*] Leave it at that. [*Pause*] Lie propped up in the dark – and wander. Be again in the dingle on a Christmas Eve, gathering holly, the red-berried. [*Pause*] Be again on Croghan on a Sunday morning, in the haze, with the bitch, stop and listen to the bells. [*Pause*] And so on. [*Pause*] Be again, be again. [*Pause*] All that old misery. [*Pause*] Once wasn't enough for you. [*Pause*] Lie down across her. [*Long pause. He suddenly bends over machine, switches off, wrenches off tape, throws it away, puts on the other, winds it forward to the passage he wants, switches on, listens staring front.*] (pp. 26–7)

The tape of the moment with the girl in the punt runs once more, concluding with the rejection of the moment and of the years which gave rise to such moments. The final line, 'No, I wouldn't want them back', is listened to by Krapp '*motionless, staring before him. The tape runs on in silence*' (p. 28). The physical motion and mental stasis that initiated the action of the play have given way to physical stasis and mental movement. The questions he fails to frame are ours to frame and ours to answer, as the tape recorder runs on in silence.

The years Krapp would not want back are those he readily rejected in his thirties. Now, in his sixties, Krapp's attitude is shifting. No longer moving hopefully from moment to final understanding, he moves from partial understanding to re-experienced moment. Those moments in the dingle on Christmas Eve, walking the bitch on a Sunday morning, and lying with that girl in the punt seem valuable in retrospect, and not just valuable, but valuable enough to warrant living through all that old misery one more time. Their value, however, neither emerges from nor concludes in a generalized synthesis that might replace them or substitute for them. The moment in the punt is the most important of those moments, but it is not the only important moment nor the only kind of important moment. We have learned by the failure of Krapp's own efforts to produce a general synthesis of the value in his life not to seek the features these moments have in common. Their value is not just in them, but also in him, and not just in him, but in him at a particular time in his life in the context of years of unhappy experiences. Their value for us lies not in their intrinsic qualities, but in their joint capacity to make a largely failed life seem almost worth living to the cynical old man staggering sadly around the stage. And if we go back to the important phrase in the play with which Krapp greeted his mother's death, we get an indication of what we are to make of these recurring incidents with no obvious common features. As his mother dies, Krapp comments:

> All over and done with, at last. I sat on for a few moments with the ball in my hand and the dog yelping and pawing at me. [*Pause*] Moments. Her moments, my moments. [*Pause*] The dog's moments. [*Pause*] (p. 20)

Krapp records this moment and others like it on annual tapes which are entered in the ledger as a series of discrete but related moments recorded on a series of discrete but related tapes (box three, spool five etc.). The image of discrete but related moments in the jumble of tape recordings is recapitulated in the image of discrete but related moments in the episode with mother and dog, and also in the fragmented continuity of Krapp's whole life. But at this point it is as important to note the relatedness as to note the fragmentation.

Krapp, we are aware, walks back and forth in his den, from the light at the centre to the darkness in the background, recording and playing back reports on important moments in his life. These activities are, for Krapp, during much of his life, means to an end – the means are the recorded moments, the end a generalized public statement about their common features. But, for the audience, these activities and the images they display have begun to suggest more than Krapp himself understands. And if we look at one further image, that of the tape recorder itself and its mode of dealing with information, we will locate, by comparison and contrast, an important perspective on Krapp's modes of dealing with information. Differences, of course, are immediately evident. Krapp's memory is less reliable and his values change. But further consideration will reveal an important similarity between Krapp and the tape recorder, which, at the end of the play, continues to run. The tape recorder, surrounded by boxes that contain a series of recordings of a series of moments, is not exhibiting a pattern that suggests the emergence or imminence of a synthesizing conclusion. The tape recorder and its tapes contain a record of and display an image of variously related and intermittently valued moments. And that image exemplifies precisely what Krapp's life has been. The tape recordings themselves, not any subsequent pattern to be abstracted from them, offer an image of continuity without overall consistency,[30] but if we link the image of the tape recorder to that of light and dark, the significance of the varied relatedness begins to emerge. As we move beyond Krapp's tendency to equate value with the central core of light, we move also towards a recognition that value is not necessarily absent when it offers no clear set of common features – but neither, we should note, is it only randomly present.

Once we have recognized the importance of this paradox, we can see how many other details fall into place. The light at the core of Krapp's world is misvalued – it indicates Krapp's belief that variety must finally give way to sameness, that particulars are less important than generalizations, that moments are less important than the patterns in which they can be subsumed. The reversed relationship of light and dark in the play, which places dark at the centre and light on the perimeter, is the more instructive arrangement. It indicates *moments valued in the context of, but not subsumed by, any generalized notion of their significance.* The moments in the dingle on Christmas Eve, walking the bitch on a Sunday morning, gazing at the eyes of Bianca, the dark nurse, and the girl in the punt are not in themselves very unusual and share no obvious or necessary common ground. Their value is attested to by the activities of the witness, not by the testimony he seeks to abstract from them. Their value to us emerges not because of their common ground, but because of the fact that, in spite of their diversity, they sustain the attention of a particular valuer, someone who finds them worthy of further contemplation at a time when he is more than ready to turn away from life, towards approaching death. In that context they have value for him, and thence for us. We know little of what led up to the moment in the boat, who the girl was, what else occurred that day, what happened to her afterwards. And we do not need to know. The value of the moment is not to be explained this way. Krapp's life may not make any overall sense, nothing much of it may endure, no empirical generalization may be derivable from his taped moments, but Krapp's mind and its capacity to re-create moments of value to him rescues the play and Krapp from the despair that is always just an arm's length away. The Krapp who seeks to separate generalizable grain from husks is not to be opposed just to earlier selves but to a persisting self who lives his life in the absence of, rather than in the context of, its generalizable grain. We see that Krapp's movement back and forth from dark to light is itself an enactment of a way of living that he engages in without being able to conceptualize – the living of life as a series of discrete but related moments. Krapp's emblematic movement back and forth between domains is one that places light and dark in a dynamic, open-ended relationship, rather than in a static, hierarchical relationship. To give priority to light or to dark is to curtail their potential for interaction. Each provides not just an alternative to the other, but a mode of access to the other, and their ongoing interaction keeps Krapp open to possibilities he is otherwise prone to ignore. Krapp's life consists finally of an aggregate of moments variously remembered and variously valued, but valued, nevertheless – a life summed up in the emblematic tape recorder with its fragments stored up against Krapp's ruin.

To note the alternating relationships between light and dark in the play is to note also the interaction of instance and generalization. The latter is not an appropriate goal but an enabling starting-point; it does not subsume particular instances but provides a channel to them. We thus see Krapp rejecting love, rejecting his earlier dreams and earlier visions, questioning his own beliefs and his own memories. But this filtering activity of the cynical mind is still interrupted, as it has always been interrupted, by moments that refuse to be subsumed, reduced, or definitively explained. They are not moments to be characterized by common-core generalizations, but moments linked, almost inadvertently, by the emergence of a heuristic means of access to them; they are Krapp's moments, valued by Krapp because they continue to suggest more than they reveal, because they invite understanding but never quite satisfy it. In the course of the play they continue to elude the generalizations, cynical or otherwise, that he seeks to hurl at them. 'All that old misery' (p. 26) fits, as a generalization about his life, only where it touches, and there continue to be moments that persistently remain more than and other than mere misery. The tape-recorded recollections, the inverted light/dark images, and the prompting summaries of the ledger continue to provide access, not to the defining core of Krapp's life, but to the multiple moments of persisting value that give it continuity with the past and continuation for the future.

An essay Beckett wrote in his youth about the work of Proust has attracted much critical attention as a possible key to this play. The essay distinguishes between two kinds of memory: voluntary memory, which is a manifestation of habitual awareness, and the more highly valued involuntary memory which, in moments of unexpected perception, offers the possibility of habit-transcending rediscovery. But there are important differences as well as similarities between the issues raised by the play and those raised by the essay.[31] Not the least of these is the complementarity between the general and the particular which in the earlier essay seem rigidly opposed, the general being irredeemably habit-governed. But when Krapp talks of lying propped up *in the dark* and wandering (p. 26), this is an indication of an active mind using its knowledge and its memories to seek to go beyond them. The same holds for his repeated playing of tape-recorded moments. Stored knowledge is a starting-point not for its replication, but for wandering (p. 26), for going on, for exploring further the moments of recollected significance. And this, interestingly enough, is very much in line with a remark often overlooked in the Proust essay. Beckett, for a moment, describes memory not as an instrument for pre-existing reference, but as a potential 'instrument of discovery'.[32] The word 'instrument' implies voluntary use, while the word 'discovery' implies transcendence of habit. It is this linkage that is the more characteristic of the important side of Krapp's psychological activity in the play. The world of light interacts with the world of dark not by subsuming it nor by eliminating it, but by providing the means of access to the multiplicity it enfolds. The world of light offers the generalizations, which if heuristically employed, can provide the starting-points for contact with recollected particularity which is more than and other than the general frameworks addressed to it. The valued moment in the darkness, in contrast to the moment of involuntary memory which is valued 'because it has been forgotten',[33] is valued because it has not yet been fully known. At the play's close, Krapp is valuing such moments, not in the absence of more general knowledge, but in the context of the knowledge he has acquired, the life he has lived, and the person he has become.

When Krapp stares into space at the end of the play, he is physically, but not psychologically inert. The tape recorder runs on to remind us of moments in motion, of movement from the light of understanding *towards* the not yet understood, of generalizations that offer not a means of concluding investigation, but a means of continuing it. The moments on the tape invite and sustain Krapp's attention as his mind moves from the light of understanding towards the darkness of discovery, where it wanders, weighing and wondering. These moments have few visible features in common, but for Krapp and for us, they invite similar kinds of attention and consequently achieve related kinds of value. In an article on Beckett, Kolve suggests that the playwright 'seeks an art that can catch novelty, that can apprehend the moment between the death of an old habit and the birth of a new'.[34] In Krapp's aggregate of such moments, we encounter a lifetime's surviving novelties set against a background of puzzlement and despair that Krapp characterizes as 'All that old misery' (p. 26). These valued moments, in Kolve's phrase, 'sink into the consciousness like stones in a lake'[35] – moments in motion, moving Krapp and us from the enabling light towards the unplumbed depths of entrancing dark.

11 Pinter:
Betrayal

The pursuit of structural novelty in the modern theatre has, as we have noted throughout, a continuity of its own. Such continuity is the consequence of, among other things, a widely shared motive for the creation of new drama structures and new theatre structures. One dramatist after another has registered a recognition of the degree to which the methods chosen for presenting information and sharing experience in the theatre affect the nature of the information presented and the experience shared. Such an attitude towards the language of the theatre compels playwrights who seek to say new things to create the structures that will make new things sayable. This, in turn, reinforces the anti-tradition bias of many modern playwrights, who fear that recourse to traditional forms will lead to nothing but repetition of already established knowledge. A consequent interest in the nature and function of 'other worlds' in the theatre has thus been a recurring concern, one with complex implications for the relationships between old and new worlds, past and present ways of knowing, established conventions and emerging novelties. But these issues of relating old and new take on a peculiar structural and thematic importance in Pinter's *Betrayal*. Both the playwright and the characters seek to locate novelty where many would not expect to find it, to establish originality where many would assume it to be neither plausible nor possible.

It will therefore be useful, at this point, to remind ourselves of the two kinds of value in literature that T. S. Eliot discusses in an essay quoted earlier:

> We are inclined, in our judgements upon the past, to exaggerate the import-
> ance of the innovators at the expense of the reputation of the developers:
> which might account for what will seem, surely, to a later age, our undue
> adulation of Donne and depreciation of Milton. . . . There are times for
> exploration and times for the development of the territory acquired.[1]

And, we might add, those times are not necessarily mutually exclusive. The development of the territory acquired can coexist with the exploration of new territory in the work of a single period, or a single author, or even a single play.

It is important, therefore, to look once more at the persistence of nineteenth-century conventions in the work of many modern playwrights. Shaw, in spite of his attacks on the well-made play, continued to make successful use of its basic structures and typical devices throughout the first half of the twentieth century. Plays by J. M. Barrie, Somerset Maugham and Arthur Wing Pinero were being written for the London stage at the same time in the 1920s when Pirandello was writing *Six Characters in Search of an Author* and *Henry IV*. Indeed, the tradition of the well-made play, alive and functioning in the work of Shaw, Barrie, Maugham and Pinero, continued to thrive in the work of Noel Coward and Terence Rattigan, and it has continued to affect the work of other playwrights to this day. Even the play that is supposed to have marked a great watershed in the modern British theatre, John Osborne's *Look Back in Anger*, now seems very traditional with only one or two innovative features. Furthermore, such highly experimental work as that of Giraudoux is also grounded in the structures and stereotypes of the well-made play,[2] and we could add, for good measure, that no one familiar with the work of such innovative dramatists as Arthur Miller, Edward Albee, David Storey, Trevor Griffiths and Harold Pinter could overlook their extensive reliance on major aspects of the well-made-play format. Indeed, as Taylor has pointed out: 'What else is *The Birthday Party* but a well-made drawing-room drama complete in every detail, even down to the meticulously realistic dialogue, except that the exposition is left out altogether?'[3] Well, the answer must be that it is a great deal else. But the point is otherwise fair: *The Birthday Party* is, among other things, an extension, as well as a revision, of the tradition of the well-made play.

Eliot's concern for recognizing the value of those who develop acquired territory as well as those who explore new territory is thus something of a salutary reminder. Much of considerable importance in the theatre has been achieved by those who continue working extensively with established conventions as well as by those who focus extensively on innovation. The innovators need attention, and they need converts, so they must initially overstate their case both for what they are doing and against what audiences are used to. It remains for subsequent dramatists to see beyond the polemics that introduced innovation and to look for further ways of combining, as well as contrasting, old and new in the theatre. In the work of such playwrights we often see extended attempts to combine major features of the well-made-play tradition with the best of the epistemologically based innovations of the modern theatre.

When Taylor remarked that Pinter's *The Birthday Party* is a well-made drawing-room drama with the Exposition left out, he was making an important point about both the conventionality and the unconventionality of the play. And he went on to focus in more detail on the latter:

> It would be easy to write in the necessary explanations: how Stanley came to be living in this seaside boarding house, what his secret is and why McCann and Goldberg came to get him. But of course this is not what the play is about: it is the process that interests Pinter, the series of happenings, and not the precise whys and wherefores. These are totally incoherent, as necessarily they have to be in so much of life, where no explanations are offered and we must make the best we can of it.[4]

Taylor is undoubtedly on the right track here, but his description of the novelty in the play is not entirely accurate. The whys and wherefores are not 'totally incoherent', they simply cohere in ways other than those that are typical of plays with a well-made format. And the notion that Pinter is interested in 'process', rather than in origins, ends and explanations, again sets up a dichotomy where a connection is just as important as a contrast. The 'process' characteristic of the action in a Pinter play is not the same as the cause/consequence process of the well-made play, but it does involve, nevertheless, a concern for origins, ends and explanations. Instead of these being a) totally incoherent, or b) coherent in the manner of the well-made play (i.e. coherent in the sense of containing one underlying set of consistent truths that it is the function of the action to reveal to characters and audience), they are, instead, coherent in a somewhat different way. And to clarify that form of coherence we will need to look carefully at the dramatic worlds Pinter creates, at their characteristic combinations of conventionality and originality, and at the ways in which Pinter's challenge to one form of explanation leads not to the incoherence of all explanation, but to a reconsideration of the roles explanations play in our lives.

We might thus wish to consider, at this point, why Pinter should make extensive use of well-made-play elements that might encourage us to antici-pate, and then fail to find, a consistent set of explanatory truths. And that question leads to an important recognition about the persisting strength of the well-made play. As all those who have written on the subject would agree, the structure of the well-made play is one that embodies an attitude towards explanation and truth that is not at all untypical of attitudes we frequently bring to bear on our own lives. There is, we usually feel, for any situation in which we find ourselves, a basic explanation. If we have not yet found it, we fault ourselves, not the situation. With more effort and more ingenuity, we could, we feel sure, locate the basic truths that govern a particular context in which we find ourselves. This assumption of available, if not immediately accessible, certainty is one that Pinter wishes both to activate and to challenge. For if the well-made elements of his plays invite one assumption about the conclusiveness of explanations, other elements in the plays require us to consider alternatives.

The disturbing events in Pinter plays characteristically serve to remind us that the explanations we rely on in our daily lives tend often to be incomplete and that we frequently resort to rounding them out with guesses based upon not clearly justifiable assumptions. Consequently, further inspection of a situation is likely to generate not clearer explanations but more confusion, as our guesses and assumptions fail to stand up to further scrutiny. Indeed, as Heisenberg's uncertainty principle in scientific inquiry has made us all uneasily aware, our methods of explanation can in part constitute the data to be explained. This provides an alarming potential for circularity in our explanatory activities.[5] Such circularity is disturbingly embodied, for example, in scientific processes for getting at the ultimate constituents of matter. As atoms and subparticles of atoms are accelerated at ever-increasing speeds in atom-smashers, an apparently endless proliferation of new basic particles of the atom results. Doubt rises with the increasing numbers, and there are now those who feel that what is happening in the atom-smashers is not the analysis of the atom into ever smaller parts, but the synthesis of matter and energy that occurs when the energy involved in the atom-smashing is converted into matter in ways predicted by Einstein's theory of relativity. Thus, it seems, the proliferation of new particles might well result from the methods used to locate them. That which is to be explained in part results from, and is in part constituted by, the method of examining and explaining it.

We need pursue such scientific complexities no further, but for our purposes we must recognize that one of the basic thematic consequences of the well-made-play structure is the reinforcement of an attitude towards the nature of explanation, experience and truth that is easily accepted as the only reasonable one. It is not, however, the only possible attitude, nor the only reasonable attitude, towards such things. And although it provides the basis for one mode of explanation in Pinter plays, it is by no means the dominant one, nor the one that gives the plays their disturbing and disorientating quality. For Pinter, we live somewhere between the poles of objectivity and subjectivity, and we repeatedly find ourselves in worlds that threaten to slide towards one or the other. Consequently, we tend to alternate between, on the one hand, a comforting assumption that somewhere out there, just beyond our current reach, lie ultimate truths and final explanations, and, on the other, an intermittent awareness that a dizzying variety of possible truths and explanations seems to be available. It is the predominance of the former assumption, this expectation that certainty will ultimately be accessible, that Pinter finds most worrying, both in the typical themes of the well-made play and in the typical activities of our daily lives, and he is at pains to establish the importance of the other alternative:

> A character on the stage who can present no convincing argument or information as to his past experiences, his present behaviour or his aspirations,

nor give a comprehensive analysis of his motives is as legitimate and as worthy of attention as one who, alarmingly, can do all these things.[6]

But Pinter's concern is not to dramatize one alternative at the expense of another. Rather it is to explore social interaction in the context of certainty confronting and negotiating with doubt, doubt negotiating with other doubt, and certainty with other certainty.[7]

The well-made format thus offers, for Pinter, a useful means of embodying and activating one set of audience and character expectations about the relationship between event and explanation, which he can then go on to use as a basis for activating others. The subsequent thwarting of initial expectations for characters and audience alike is not, however, the point of conclusion towards which the action moves; rather, it is the starting-point for further exploration of situations and further consideration of the relationships between events and explanations. When Taylor sought to describe Pinter as more interested in 'process' than in explanations, he was thus opposing two things that in the Pinter world, and in much of our world, are inextricably intertwined. The issue is not one of opposing process to explanation, *but one of dramatizing the process of explaining* and clarifying its function in our lives. *This process is not to be contrasted with, but is in fact a contributing component of, the situations that are to be explained.* For the key point about character activity in a Pinter play is that the characters, like the dramatist, are persistently engaged in a struggle not so much to locate the truths that underlie inherited structures, as to create the kinds of structures that will embody acceptable truths.

Explanatory coherence in a Pinter play is thus something rather different from that of the well-made play. It is something to be generated by the characters and *imposed* by them on the action, and its imposition frequently involves desperate competition among a variety of characters, each seeking to impose on events and situations self-enhancing explanations. This is not a matter of uncontrolled subjectivities dreaming up unconstrained, self-serving explanations, but a matter of community-constrained individuals struggling to persuade or coerce others to go along with explanations that seem to them most fitting, as well as most self-enhancing. It is this persisting struggle that makes 'process', in Taylor's terms, seem so important, and it is the consequent lack of an obviously definitive truth in the explanations that leads to the erroneous conclusion that the whys and wherefores are 'totally incoherent'. But they are not incoherent; they are simply more flexible and less firm than those typical of the well-made play. And it is because they are so flexible that they are not necessarily opposed to process, but function as constitutive parts of the interactive process that Pinter seeks to dramatize.

The novelty in much of Pinter's work is thus one that can appropriately (but not indispensably) be grounded in a set of structural/thematic conventions that are derived from the well-made play. These structural/thematic conventions, which embody one set of attitudes towards explanatory possibilities, provide a point of departure for plays which dramatize situations in which the activity of explaining makes a different contribution to the action. Instead of leading us towards a definitive conclusion, the process of explanation leads back towards itself. Initially promising definitive conclusions, it subsequently provides the basis for thwarted expectations, and thus becomes itself something in need of explanation. In terms of our earlier discussion, this can be reformulated as a dramatized recognition of the inescapable interaction for characters, for dramatist and for audience, of things known and the ways of knowing that help generate them. And this is an important reformulation of the issue, for it helps us to locate the importance of Pinter's attempts to combine the much maligned conventions of nineteenth-century theatre with the epistemologically based innovations of the modern theatre. The experience he offers to the audience is not one of predominant conventionality or radical novelty; it is, instead, a calculated mixture by means of which Pinter explores new territory while continuing to develop territory already acquired. Pinter's novelty of stagecraft precisely invokes and carefully transcends specific structural conventions. Such a revision in structure necessarily promotes a revision in the relationship between stage and audience, a change from one kind of connection towards another possibility of connection, and thus towards another mode of meaning. What holds in the theatre between play and audience also holds on Pinter's stage for the relationships between characters. They, too, are caught up in a struggle to establish, in the context of their daily lives, appropriate connections between the known and the unknown, the traditional and the unconventional, the commonplace and the unexpected.

These connections are not always easy to establish, either for characters or for audiences, and the peculiar combination of the commonplace and the novel in Pinter's plays has been, in other contexts, the subject of much discussion. From the beginning of his career, Pinter's work has attracted a puzzled acknowledgement of his capacity to use mundane features of daily life as the unlikely foundation for plays which seem, nevertheless, startlingly unusual. McLaughlin, for example, draws attention to the way Pinter generates 'such atmospherics of menace and dread out of shabby, commonplace elements'.[8] Cohen, with an accompanying negative judgement, notes that in his early plays in particular, 'The most straightforward remarks were invested with frightful implications or made to look like menacing evasions.'[9] And Taylor, in two separate articles, directs our attention to 'the obsessive fascination the most apparently banal exchanges exert in his plays'.[10] I have written at length elsewhere about the peculiar problems Pinter's dialogue seems to present,[11] but it is important to see that similar problems permeate the entire texture and structure of his plays. For our purposes, the key issue in each individual play is the peculiar mode of interaction established between the commonplace and the unusual, the traditional and the experimental, the practical and the epistemological – factors that achieve a startling structural and thematic embodiment in his complex play, *Betrayal*.

The title, *Betrayal*, provides an immediate indication of a central thematic concern in a play that deals with what looks like a much-dramatized, conventional situation – that of an affair between a man and his best friend's wife. The much-worn nature of the theme becomes itself a subject of concern for characters who have to cope with the *commonplace* nature of their own situation, even as they struggle with the *novelty* of finding themselves in it for the first time. This commonplace element in what is, for them personally, a new situation is a key factor in the difficulties they have to cope with. Robert, the wronged husband, on the brink of confronting the unpalatable fact of his wife's affair, says bitterly, but pointedly, that there is not much more to be said about the subject of betrayal. For him, traditional interpretation of a traditional situation provides a sound basis for a traditional condemnation of that situation and of those who participate in it. His wife, Emma, offers a less traditional interpretation of the situation and argues that betrayal is not what she sees as its defining characteristic, or at least, not yet. What they are discussing is, appropriately enough, a novel that Emma is reading, but the implications for their relationship and for the play are clearly there.

> ROBERT: Oh . . . not much more to say on that subject, really, is there?
> EMMA: What do you consider the subject to be?
> ROBERT: Betrayal.
> EMMA: No, it isn't.
> ROBERT: Isn't it? What is it then?
> EMMA: I haven't finished it yet. I'll let you know.
> ROBERT: Well, do let me know.
>   [*Pause*] (p. 78)[12]

Dealing with the typical, the commonplace, the conventional aspect of the affair and with the conventional evaluation that must accompany it constitutes a major problem for all the characters. It is also a problem for the dramatist who cannot afford to write a play that simply reduplicates conventional situations and inherited clichés, even though it may make extensive use of them. For Emma and Jerry, and for the dramatist, novelty must also have its due if there is to be value here. And the major proponent of novelty is Jerry, the husband's best friend and best man, who stresses at the outset of the affair the radical originality of the relationship between himself and Emma.

> JERRY: You're lovely. I'm crazy about you. All these words I'm using, don't you see, they've never been said before. . . . Everyone knows. The world knows. It knows. But they'll never know, they'll never know, they're in a different world. I adore you. I'm madly in love with you. I can't believe that what anyone is at this moment saying has ever happened has ever happened. Nothing has ever happened. Nothing. This is the only thing that has ever happened. (pp. 135–7)

The sheer rhetorical force of the words exemplifies the urgency of the emotions that generate them, but the very claim to novelty is couched in terms often as conventional as the situation itself. Only occasionally does their extremity mark the situation as possibly unusual. The claims that nothing else has ever happened, that a new world has come into being, and that only two people exist in it all speak of strong emotions, but the argument for originality seems not only to invoke, but to rely on the condition of discontinuity with the past and is thus a fragile one. It suggests a need for escape as much as a hope for discovery; indeed, it seems to make the latter dependent on the former. And if novelty requires insulation from conventionality in order to flourish, it is a novelty that is suspect on that basis alone. The image of other worlds that has emerged so often in modern theatre here emerges as an image of wished for, but not yet substantiated, novelty. Emma, sensing the precariousness and the appeal of what Jerry is saying, responds with doubt as well as hope, attitudes that become characteristic of her behaviour throughout.

Jerry's argument, slightly inebriated though it may be, is central to the structure and theme of the play. The emphatic pronouncement that these well-worn clichés could never have been uttered before and the emotional affirmation that this situation is new because all previous situations, resembling it or otherwise, didn't really happen are both grounded in his claim that a 'different world' has indeed come into being, a world based on extensive and essential exclusion. In this new world there are only Jerry and Emma, no husbands or wives, no children, no other responsibilities, no other commitments, no past. Such a present and such a future require not the foundation of the past, but its elimination, and we must give careful thought to the viability of such a strangely constituted novelty. At first glance, Jerry's requirements seem neither practical nor possible, and they seem even less so when we recall that the coming into being of this new world has been grounded in a fantasy that invokes the very past Jerry is seeking to transcend. Just moments earlier, Jerry had been fantasizing about Emma and their new relationship in ways that not only invoke the past, but rely extensively upon it. Recalling Emma's wedding to Robert, Jerry remarks: 'I should have had you, in your white, before the wedding. I should have blackened you, in your white wedding dress, blackened you in your bridal dress, before ushering you into your wedding, as your best man' (p. 135).

Jerry's world of uncontaminated novelty seems thus to emerge from a rather conventional fantasy – a fantasy based not upon the transcendence of convention, but upon its temporary violation. And the importance of convention to the fantasy is only reinforced by our recollection that Emma had just told Jerry she didn't wear white for the wedding. The fantasy is based not so much upon an accurate recollection, but upon a manipulation of memories and conventions that must constrain Jerry even as he violates them. Novelty for Jerry, it appears, is more closely related to conventionality than he wishes to acknowledge, and his refusal to acknowledge that fact registers not just his hopes but also his fears. Fears that conventionality must subsume novelty are the corollary of hopes that novelty might and must escape the past. But these fears serve only to lend urgency to the hopes, and when those hopes are reinforced by Emma's, we are invited to explore further the attractions and the viability of a novelty that relies upon seemingly unsustainable conditions. And the play's structure seems designed to empha- size both sides of the incipient dichotomy between novelty and conven- tionality. The conventional situation of a semi-drunken, ex-best man making a pass at his best friend's wife looms large as a counterweight to Jerry's attempts to establish the unprecedented novelty of this episode in their lives. And the very conventionality of the situation looms large as a counterweight to any claims the play might make about its own originality – until we note that this scene is occurring not as the opening scene from which the play's action will flow, but as its closing scene, the scene towards which the play's development leads. In which ways, and to what extent, we may wonder, is Jerry's claim for the novelty of his situation validated by the action of the play, and in which ways, and to what extent is the play's claim for novelty validated by the structural innovation of depicting the affair and its conse- quences in reverse chronological order?[13]

These are not, of course, easy questions to answer, but the play's action invites us to ask them and we must thus look closely at the significance of the play's peculiar structure. It is, of course, evident that the pattern of reverse chronology offers an accumulating dramatic irony in which audience knowl- edge of the events increases in the same proportion as character knowledge decreases. As the play progresses, we see the characters in chronologically earlier and earlier scenes and they consequently know less about their relationships with each dramatized year. But if we are to work from the notion that how things are said and presented on-stage in part constitutes what is said and presented on-stage, we must look very closely at the ways in which the reversal of conventional sequence contributes to and directs our attention towards whatever novelty Jerry and the play can claim. Such novelty must operate in spite of the conventional nature of the main action and the stock nature of the scenes. The moment of professing love, the secret meetings, the moment of confessing the betrayal of a loved one, the meeting between friends who love the same woman, the acknowledgement that an affair has run its course – all are stock scenes with conventional attitudes and values attached to them. And all have formed the basis of stock plays with a stock structure of Exposition, Complication, Crisis and Resolution. Simply to reverse their sequence of presentation will not suffice to rescue these scenes from their conventionality, and we must go on to note that there are other elements of structure which, when combined with that of reverse chro- nology, serve not just to reverse an established pattern, but to dramatize an ongoing and repeatedly renewed process. The nature of this process will become clearer if we note, at this point, that reversed chronology is a characteristic but by no means consistent factor in the play's sequence and structure. The play certainly goes backward year by year, *but within each year* the scenes go chronologically forward. Thus, Scenes One and Two, in 1977, follow chronologically upon each other. Scene Three chronologically precedes them in 1975, as does Scene Four in 1974. But Scenes Five, Six and Seven, in 1973, follow each other chronologically. Scene Eight chronologically precedes them in 1971, as does Scene Nine in 1968. We thus have two scenes in chronological order followed by two scenes in reversed chronological order, followed by three scenes in chronological order, and then two scenes in reversed chronological order. The structure of the play is thus not by any means one simply based on reverse chronology. And if we look more closely, we see that there is another, much more illuminating structural principle in operation. Scenes One to Four involve the following characters: Scene One: Jerry and Emma; Scene Two: Jerry and Robert; Scene Three: Jerry and Emma; Scene Four: Jerry, Emma and Robert. This sequence of scenes is exactly the same as that followed in Scenes Six to Nine: Scene Six: Jerry and Emma; Scene Seven: Jerry and Robert; Scene Eight: Jerry and Emma; Scene Nine: Jerry, Emma, and Robert. And the missing scene is, appropriately enough, the middle scene of the play, Scene Five. It is the only scene in which Jerry does not appear, the only scene in which Robert and Emma interact alone together, and it is, of course, the scene in which Emma's betrayal of Robert is discovered and acknowledged. The structure of the play is thus constituted by two sets of the same four scenes presented on either side of a pivotal scene of discovery of the play's central betrayal.

The structure of the play might be presented thus:

scene 1:	Jerry and Emma		scene 6:	Jerry and Emma
scene 2:	Jerry and Robert	scene 5:	scene 7:	Jerry and Robert
scene 3:	Jerry and Emma	Robert and	scene 8:	Jerry and Emma
scene 4:	Jerry, Emma, and Robert	Emma	scene 9:	Jerry, Emma, and Robert

Far from being a structure based solely on reversed chronology, the play uses reversed *and* normal chronology as part of a structure which makes use of *repetition* and *renewal* as its governing features. This conjunction of structural repetition and renewal is, of course, no accident. It is one means of manifesting the complex relationship between conventionality and novelty that is central to the play. But it is just as important that we note that when the play moves chronologically forwards as well as chronologically backwards, it focuses our attention less on a narrative sequence than on a series of episodic moments. And this, in turn, is a further structural manifestation of Jerry's concern for the relationship between novelty and convention. For Jerry, novelty requires insulation from convention, the present must be isolated from the past, and consequently renewal must be separated from repetition. Jerry's claims in the final scene that everybody else lives in 'a different world' and that nothing else has ever happened are exaggerated, but they are claims that might flourish, if they can flourish at all, in distinct, episodic moments. They require that he and others persuaded by him narrow their focus of attention, that they construct novelty by isolating current events and current relationships from those of the past. The play seems to offer a series of such moments for a series of characters. But in what respect can we regard other characters as attempting to achieve and sustain, in these episodic events, something analogous to the novelty that Jerry is reaching towards in the final episode of the play? To what extent are Jerry's conflicting needs comparable with those of the other characters? As we shall see, the intermittently episodic nature of this chronologically orientated play provides Pinter with the perfect structure for dramatizing not just Jerry, but two other characters caught between the insistence of the old and the urgency of the new, characters constantly haunted by the incipient conventionality of situations that have been precipitated by their most spontaneous emotions.

Such structural underpinning of thematic concerns is in accord with principles of writing Pinter has followed since the beginning of his career. As he put it in a 1962 speech:

> I think I can say that I pay a meticulous attention to the shape of things, from the shape of a sentence to the overall structure of the play. This shaping, to put it mildly, is of the first importance.[14]

And such shaping is evident not only in the sequence in which the characters are presented to us in *Betrayal*, not only in the patterning that repeats a series of scenes, but also in the sense of fragmentation that disrupted chronology provides. Sequence, pattern and fragmentation are all structural manifestations of renewal in the context of repetition, novelty in the context of conventionality, and exclusion in the context of inclusion. For characters and audience alike, the conflict between chronological continuity and episodic fragmentation is emblematic of two competing perspectives on the action – the one large and all-embracing, the other local and almost self-contained. These competing local and larger perspectives provide conflicting possibilities for making judgements about experiences and also for interpreting and explaining those experiences. And these efforts at interpretation and explanation partly confront and partly contribute to the nature of the situations that emerge – situations whose novelty and value depend very much on the characters' and the audience's readiness to adopt one mode of interpretation rather than another.

When the play begins, the Jerry/Emma affair is in the chronological past and the two characters are enjoying a brief reunion in a pub in London at noon. The stage direction informing us of the precise hour seems gratuitously specific, but the questions it raises must be held temporarily in abeyance. The play's action moves quickly away from calendar and clock time towards psychological time, and towards the changes time has wrought in Emma's and Jerry's memories of their affair and their joint past. 'Just like old times' (p. 12), Emma comments, looking around the pub, but her attempts selectively to reconstruct those times immediately clash with Jerry's competing selective focus. And this conflict over modes of selection provides the first indication in the play of a kind of character interaction that will have major consequences.

'Do you know how long it is since we met?' (p. 13) Emma asks, as a bridge from the present episode to intimate memories of the past. Jerry's response, far from reinforcing that bridge between their present and their former relationship, offers an alternative to it. His reply is in terms of their last social encounter, though she was thinking of their last meeting as a couple. Refusing to be rebuffed, Emma continues to try to use selective elements from their joint past as a means of restoring intimacy to their largely separate present:

EMMA: I thought of you the other day.
         [*Pause*]
         I was driving through Kilburn. Suddenly I saw where I was. I just stopped, and then I turned down Kinsale Drive and drove into Wessex Grove. I drove past the house and then stopped about fifty yards further on, like we used to do, do you remember? (p. 21)

Jerry repeatedly steers the conversation away to other topics, but Emma tries one more time (p. 28) to direct the conversation towards their Wessex Grove past, before abandoning the effort and conceding defeat:

EMMA: Listen, I didn't want to see you for nostalgia, I mean what's the point? I just wanted to see how you were. Truly. How are you?
JERRY: Oh what does it matter?
         [*Pause*]
         You didn't tell Robert about me last night, did you? (pp. 28–9)

Jerry's reply effectively reasserts the no longer intimate nature of their relationship and removes whatever remaining hopes Emma had for finding something more in it. But this reply also underlines Jerry's concern for a rather different aspect of their joint past – his relationship with Emma's husband.

When Emma informs Jerry that she has just learned that Robert has been having affairs for years, Jerry's mind turns immediately to the fact that they betrayed Robert for years (p. 25). And when Emma tells him of the breakup of her marriage to Robert, Jerry's concern is immediately for his relationship with Robert, not hers (pp. 27, 29).

JERRY: You told him everything?
EMMA: I had to.

JERRY: You told him everything . . . about us?
EMMA: I had to.
         [*Pause*]
JERRY: But he's my oldest friend. I mean, I picked his own daughter up in my
         own arms and threw her up and caught her, in my kitchen. He
         watched me do it. (p. 29)

Jerry's example of the trust between himself and Robert indicates that his
concern for Robert is, at this point, stronger than his concern for Emma. But
this recognition is likely to mislead us. We should note that Jerry is not so
uninterested in Emma that he would refuse to meet her this day. Commitments to both Robert and Emma are still in place, but they are commitments
in conflict, and neither Jerry nor Emma can find a way of separating them or
reconciling them.

Emma's subsequent reluctance to discuss aspects of their past that interest
Jerry matches his reluctance to discuss aspects of their past that interest her,
and the scene concludes with a rejection not just of selected aspects of the
past, but of the whole past that gave rise to their competing selective
concerns:

EMMA: It doesn't matter. It's all gone.
JERRY: Is it? What has?
EMMA: It's all all over.
         [*She drinks.*] (pp. 29–30)

The repetition of 'all' in that final line is oddly out of tune with much of the
discussion that has preceded it. Both Emma and Jerry, for their own purposes,
focus insistently on selected aspects of their joint past. And to see them trying
and failing to locate a common ground of selectivity is to note the absence of a
feature that subsequently turns out to have been crucial to the relationship
while it flourished, a feature that is also manifest in the play's episodic
structure – the insulation of some aspects of their lives from others. At any
point at which 'all' intrudes, all is indeed over, for the insulation their
relationship needed from the claims of other relationships is gone. It is
important to note the connection here between the characters' mode of
interaction and the play's mode of structuring its scenes. And it is just as
important to note that the two characters persist in their attempts to control
their lives by selectively acknowledging information in spite of the havoc this
process seems to have wrought. In an important sense, all is thus not over, for
'all' can embrace larger contexts than those they wish to confront at this time,
together.

Jerry's relationship with Robert, however, seems, at this point, more
important to him than what is left of his relationship with Emma or of her
relationship with Robert. Far from rejecting the whole overall situation, he
continues to struggle to control who knows what and when, particularly, but
not only, Robert. And in this struggle to control information, the struggle is

every bit as important as the control. In the very scene which Jerry uses as an example of the importance of trust in his relationship with Robert – the one in which he throws the latter's daughter, Charlotte, up in the air – we encounter the signs of an internal ambivalence that turns out to be fundamental to Jerry's several conflicting relationships, and to the problems he has of living life successfully on the basis of selecting and controlling what knowledge he will share and with whom.

> JERRY: Listen. Do you remember, when was it, a few years ago, we were all in your kitchen, must have been Christmas or something, do you remember, all the kids were running about and suddenly I picked Charlotte up and lifted her high up, high up, and then down and up. Do you remember how she laughed?
> EMMA: Everyone laughed.
> JERRY: She was so light. And there was your husband and my wife and all the kids, all standing and laughing in your kitchen. I can't get rid of it.
> EMMA: It was your kitchen, actually.
> [He takes her hand. They stand. They go to the bed and lie down.]
> Why shouldn't you throw her up?
> [She caresses him. They embrace.] (pp. 100–1)

These words were uttered, of course, much earlier, in 1973, when the affair was well under way. The words occur in the sixth scene of the play, linking, as we would expect from the play's structure, Scene One with Scene Six. The moment had lodged in Jerry's mind by 1973 and had persisted since. Jerry's emphasis on the presence of all members of both families ('your husband and my wife and all the kids') in a moment of family union provides one side of the scene's significance – trust, camaraderie, sharing, public social activity, family happiness. But it is a moment of manifest trust that contains visible seeds of impending betrayal. The hint of sexuality in picking up the daughter and throwing her up and down is reinforced by Emma's repetition of the phrase as she later caresses Jerry on the bed, and also by Jerry's comment, many years later, on Charlotte's beauty and her resemblance to Emma. There is clearly, in this persisting image, the pattern of renewal and repetition that links and grounds the many instances of betrayal that permeate the play. Betrayal and trust are closely intertwined in this recollected scene, and, we will see, in the whole action of the play.

The interdependence of betrayal and trust is also registered in one further aspect of the remembered scene, and this clarifies for us the larger function in the play of Jerry's desire to control situations by selectively sharing knowledge of them. Jerry cannot, he says, 'get rid of it' from his mind. It is a scene that *reveals* to him the intimacy and joy of the relationship between the two families. But it is also a scene that largely *conceals* and only partially *reveals* the latent betrayal of that relationship in an impending affair with Emma. It thus haunts his mind as a signal of more than he is ready to acknowledge about the close links between one relationship and another that betrays it. But the scene reveals to the audience what it conceals from him, both in its sexual overtones, the context in which it arises, and in one further detail – Jerry's tendency to misremember the place where it occurred. Twice (p. 20 and p. 101 – 1977 and 1973) he places the scene in Robert and Emma's kitchen, rather than his own. Emma corrects him both times. The error seems mysterious until we reach the play's final scene and recognize, in Jerry's initial fantasy about seducing Emma in her bridal gown, the interdependence of Jerry's conventionality and his originality. The fantasy of deflowering Emma in the role of his best friend's wife is one that helps explain his locating the memory/fantasy of 'throwing up' Charlotte/Emma in his best friend's kitchen where their role and relationship to Robert can most forcefully be violated. The memory is one that registers the interaction of trust/betrayal and revealing/concealing in Jerry's memory and in the other characters' daily lives, and helps clarify the basis for the endless struggles to control information.

That struggle for control continues in the play's second scene. Jerry has learned from Emma that she betrayed him the night before by telling Robert of their affair. Now Jerry discovers that while Emma has *revealed* to him the fact that she has told Robert, she has *concealed* the fact that she told him, not last night, but years ago. In a few brief hours, Jerry shifts from anger at Emma – for revealing knowledge – to anger at Robert and Emma – for concealing knowledge from him.

> JERRY: Why didn't she tell me?
> ROBERT: Well, I'm not her, old boy.
> JERRY: Why didn't you tell me?
>   [*Pause*]
> ROBERT: I thought you might know.
> JERRY: But you didn't know for *certain*, did you? You didn't *know*!
> ROBERT: No.
> JERRY: Then why didn't you tell me?
>   [*Pause*]
> ROBERT: Tell you what?
> JERRY: That you knew. You bastard. (p. 40)

The ironies here are heavy. The accusations are coming from the sexual betrayer Jerry to Robert the sexually betrayed, rather than the reverse. And Jerry's concern for honesty from Robert registers an expectation that he himself has failed to meet in his dealings with Robert. But the major issue for our purposes is the way in which Jerry can feel betrayed by Emma because she revealed something he wanted concealed, and betrayed by Robert because he concealed something he would rather have had revealed.[15]

We quickly see in the two opening scenes that what is at issue is understanding and control of the processes of concealing and revealing by three people who, long acknowledging the inevitability of betrayal, have grown steadily accustomed to trying to live both by it and with it. And we note in retrospect that two of only three lengthy contributions that Jerry makes to the opening scene are concerned with control of that revealing/concealing process. One long speech registers his puzzlement that Robert could have been having affairs all these years without Jerry knowing (p. 26). The other, ironically enough, concerns the one aspect of his past affair with Emma that seems still to be a matter of pride to him – pride tempered by an accompanying 'irritation' that concealment had, in fact, worked so well that no one was in a position to admire the skill with which the affair was concealed:

> JERRY: We were brilliant. Nobody knew. (p. 23)

We thus begin to see that the play is concerned less with any single act of betrayal and more with repeated instances of betrayal and the procedures for dealing with a world in which it seems a persisting process.

Deception in this play is thus by no means the province solely of inveterate liars. Oddly enough, it seems repeatedly to become part of attempts to establish and maintain many kinds of trust. And the play is directed less towards exposing the moral implications of that paradox and more towards exploring its complex manifestations and consequences.

We listen with particular interest, therefore, when strategies of expla-nation become themselves topics of discussion, topics requiring further explanation. With their affair reaching its close, Emma (indirectly of course) appeals for a moment of honesty between herself and Jerry. As they struggle to explain their inability, or unwillingness, to find time for each other any more, Jerry comes up with what looks like an odd and unrelated comment about Robert.

> JERRY: Nights have always been out of the question and you know it. I have a family.
> EMMA: I have a family too.
> JERRY: I know that perfectly well. I might remind you that your husband is my oldest friend.
> EMMA: What do you mean by that?
> JERRY: I don't *mean* anything by it.
> EMMA: But what are you trying to say by saying that?
> JERRY: Jesus. I'm not *trying* to say anything. I've said precisely what I wanted to say.
> EMMA: I see.
> [*Pause*] (pp. 52–3)[16]

Emma does indeed see, and so do we. The reminder that Robert is Jerry's oldest friend reveals to her a fact she already knows, but prefers not to confront. When Jerry reminds her of it, it functions not just as a reminder, but also as a warning not to allow their affair, or its demise, to damage the ongoing relationship between Jerry and Robert. That warning is what Jerry is 'trying to say by saying that', but he' is not willing to make the warning explicit. For Jerry, the words do indeed say 'precisely what I wanted to say', revealing and concealing simultaneously by manipulating implicit and explicit information. *The local texture of the dialogue, which exhibits the tension between implicit and explicit information, thus recapitulates the larger patterns of the dialogue, which manifest the tension in character interaction between concealing and revealing knowledge. This, in turn, is reflected in the structure of the play, which explores the possibility that novelty can emerge in the context of conventionality if local domains can be insulated from larger domains.*

The clause 'what are you trying to say by saying that' thus directs our attention to the central concern of the play – not just the characters' struggle to control the relationship between revealing and concealing in a world of reciprocal trust and betrayal, *but the way of life that bases itself upon that paradoxical struggle.* We noted earlier the ways in which the epistemological concerns of modern experimental plays are welded by Pinter on to the conventional situations that provided the stock plays of melodrama. And we noted also the way in which this artistic concern merges with character concerns in the praxis of their daily living. In this dramatic world, the ways in which things get said help constitute what is said. The ways in which things are concealed and revealed provide an important part of what is concealed and revealed and thus lived by in a world in which reality is that construction of a situation that characters jointly acknowledge. Jerry's attempt to insulate the novelty from the conventionality of the impending affair with Emma by announcing that 'this is the only thing that has ever happened' (pp. 136–7) would look, if it were occurring at the beginning of the play, like a momentary extravagance. But when we have watched the repeated efforts of characters to control information, we see that it is only an extreme instance of a much more widespread pattern of episodic living: a pattern of living that is grounded in ways of controlling what will and will not be fully explained, what will and will not be mutually acknowledged. *For the central point that relates the epistemological to the practical in these endless struggles is that control over what is revealed and concealed is control of the reality that is lived by.* The basic grounding of the worlds of this play is thus not the ethical or moral abstraction, but the ways of life that exemplify the complex and paradoxical roles of ethical and moral values in daily living. Emma perpetuates her marriage by concealing from Robert her affair with Jerry. After Robert has discovered the affair, both seek to continue their relationships with Jerry by concealing the discovery from him. Jerry, until the last chronological scene, continues his relationship with Robert by concealing (he thinks) the affair from Robert. And, at the chronological end of the action, Jerry is still concerned about preserving relationships with Charlotte and with his wife Judith on the basis of controlling what they know and thus the acknowledged reality they will live by. Explanatory deception is repeatedly adopted as a means of preserving trust. The strategies of coping help contribute to what is to be coped with.

The implications of revealing and concealing that are embodied in the question 'what are you trying to say by saying that?' (p. 53) thus have large implications for the nature of the dialogue and for the way of the life it helps constitute. But the relationship between that way of life and the play's episodic structure has further significance and requires further clarifica-tion. We should note, therefore, that Emma's question about *the point of a statement* is echoed later in a question about *the point of a book* – the book Emma was reading on the day Robert learned about the affair with Jerry:

> ROBERT: Oh . . . not much more to say on that subject, really, is there?
> EMMA: What do you consider the subject to be?
> ROBERT: Betrayal.
> EMMA: No, it isn't. (p. 78)

Uncertainty over the real subject of a book links the notion of concealing/revealing in a conversation to concealing/revealing in writing a book, and concealing/revealing in the process of betrayal. What might seem, at first glance, a merely reinforcing echo takes on further significance when the issue of the ambiguous point of something arises a third time, not just in the context of words, but in the context of daily actions. Oddly enough, the issue under discussion is *the point of a lunch*:

> JERRY: I spoke to Robert this morning.
> EMMA: Oh?
> JERRY: I'm taking him to lunch on Thursday.
> EMMA: Thursday? Why?
> JERRY: Well, it's my turn.
> EMMA: No, I meant why are you taking him to lunch?
> JERRY: Because it's my turn. Last time he took me to lunch.
> EMMA: You know what I mean.
> JERRY: No. What?
> EMMA: *What is the subject or point of your lunch?*
> JERRY: No subject or point. We've just been doing it for years. His turn, followed by my turn.
> EMMA: You've misunderstood me.
> JERRY: Have I? How?
> EMMA: Well, quite simply, you often do meet, or have lunch, to discuss a particular writer or a particular book, don't you? So to those meetings, or lunches, there is a point or a subject.
> JERRY: Well, there isn't to this one.
> [*Pause*] (my emphasis, pp. 94–6)

Jerry stonewalls here as determinedly as in their earlier discussion of the point of a single remark. But the audience knows that this scene is occurring immediately after Robert's discovery of Emma's affair with Jerry, a scene that had led to Robert's barked, penultimate remark:

[*Pause*]

ROBERT: I've always liked Jerry. To be honest, I've always liked him rather more than I've liked you. Maybe I should have had an affair with him myself.
[*Silence*] (p. 87)

The audience is aware that Emma is desperately concerned to know the point of the forthcoming lunch, because she can envisage a scene of massive recrimination between the two men, or a scene in which Robert begins to deal in new ways with Jerry to enact some sort of revenge on her. The fact that they have arranged to have lunch (which might suggest conciliation) seems to heighten, rather than allay, her fears: fears undoubtedly linked to Robert's semi-threat of having an 'affair' with Jerry himself.

There is nothing in the play to suggest any homosexual basis for an 'affair' between Robert and Jerry, and our interpretation of the remark must be directed elsewhere. What seems to matter to Robert in making his counter-threat is the notion of *a competition between relationships, a competition that is based upon patterns of inclusion and exclusion, patterns that help define the nature of relationships in the play and the episodic structure of lives lived in a persistent struggle to control processes of revealing and concealing.* The thematic implications of that episodic structure begin to emerge more clearly when we note that the intimacy of relationships based upon careful inclusion and exclusion is affirmed and tested in interaction, largely *during lunch.* And we have yet to deal with the larger implication of Emma's remark that a lunch, like a book and like an utterance in a conversation, can have not only a substance and a structure but also a point.

The persistence of lunch engagements may seem a surprising factor in the play, but it is undeniably and intrusively there. One of the first things Jerry says when he registers his surprise that Robert has known for years about the affair between Jerry and Emma is: 'But we've seen each other . . . a great deal . . . over the last four years. We've had lunch' (p. 39). The continuation of their lunch engagements seems to indicate to Jerry an affirmation that their relationship continues sound. The irony is that he feels the soundness could survive his participating in the affair with Emma and screening it out when with Robert, but not Robert's knowing of the affair and screening it out when with him. For the audience, however, this screening out, this excluding of certain aspects of reality, is seen as part of a larger pattern in which characters repeatedly screen out certain things in order to hold on to others: a pattern characteristic of so many of the relationships in the play, particularly those built around the daily lunch hour. Chronologically, the first scene that shows Jerry and Emma alone is a lunchtime meeting in the flat they rented (Scene Eight in 1971); so is the second chronological scene where they are alone together (Scene Six in 1973). In the third chronological scene, early one afternoon (Scene Three in 1975), their relationship is disintegrating and Emma tries to revive it by suggesting that they can still meet at lunchtime. An important indication of Jerry's waning interest in their affair is his diminished enthusiasm for making intimate lunches possible:

EMMA: We can meet for lunch.
JERRY: We can meet for lunch but we can't come all the way out here for a quick lunch. I'm too old for that. (p. 52)

And the fourth chronological scene in which they are alone together (1977, the first scene of the play) is a moment of tentative reunion, set in a pub at 'Noon' (p. 11). That stage direction, apparently superfluous as we noted earlier, finds its place in a larger pattern with large implications.

The pattern of meetings focused on (though not restricted to) the lunch hour is unmistakable; so is the recurring indication of intimacy (a form of inclusion/exclusion) that accompanies them. For example, when Emma reports seeing Jerry's wife Judith out at lunch one day (with a lady) she is instantly suspicious about what it might mean that Judith did not report their meeting to Jerry. She wonders whether Judith knows about the affair between Jerry and Emma, and whether Judith may be having an affair herself (pp. 123–8). The closeness of the Jerry/Robert relationship is exemplified in the fact that they have enjoyed lunching together 'for years. His turn, followed by my turn' (p. 95). And lunch quickly becomes an issue when Robert begins to register his suspicions about the Emma/Jerry affair. His suspicions emerge in his irritation that Emma might be working her way into territory and time that used to be his and Jerry's alone, and this sense of invasion manifests itself in a derisive invitation. Reacting to Emma lying on a bed in Venice, clasping and enjoying a book given to her by Jerry, Robert informs her that Jerry 'was telling me about it at lunch last week' (p. 76), and he sarcastically suggests she might wish to join them at future business lunches.

ROBERT: You think it's good, do you?
EMMA: Yes, I do. I'm enjoying it.
ROBERT: Jerry thinks it's good too. You should have lunch with us one day and chat about it.
EMMA: Is that absolutely necessary?
[Pause]
It's not as good as all that.
ROBERT: You mean it's not good enough for you to have lunch with Jerry and me and chat about it?
EMMA: What the hell are you talking about? (p. 77)

Once again, the point of Robert's remark, though not explicit, is clearly there for the audience, if not for Emma. The Robert/Jerry pattern of luncheon inclusion/exclusion is being violated by the Jerry/Emma pattern of inclusion/exclusion, and what is being discussed here in terms of books and critical opinions is registering also with Robert in terms of contrasting relationships, competing intimacies and conflicting loyalties.

The conflict over luncheon loyalties thus becomes a major instance of the conflict over relationship loyalties in the aftermath of Robert's discovery of the Jerry/Emma affair. On returning from Torcello, Robert struggles (Scene Seven) to salvage his relationship with Jerry in a testy lunch together. The lunch environment seems to serve more to remind Robert of a lost intimacy with Jerry than to revive it. And Robert registers his feeling of exclusion from both Jerry and Emma again indirectly and again in terms of their taste in books.

ROBERT: I'm a bad publisher because I hate books. Or to be more precise, prose. Or to be even more precise, modern prose, I mean modern novels, first novels and second novels, all that promise and sensibility it falls upon me to judge. . . . You know what you and Emma have in common? You love literature. I mean you love modern prose literature, I mean you love the new novel by the new Casey or Spinks. It gives you both a thrill. (pp. 115–16)

Robert subsequently apologizes to Jerry for these remarks, but it is clear that he is salvaging the relationship at some cost to himself. And that cost becomes evident when Jerry in the next chronological scene (1974, Scene Four) takes up Robert's invitation, at the end of their lunch, to come by some time and have a drink.

Fifteen months have passed since the invitation, but the issues remain unresolved. And in this scene, which presents the only lengthy conversation between three characters involved in endless subterfuge, the major focus of concern is honesty in literature, honesty in life, and again, oddly enough, honesty about lunch. The endless battles to control what is to be revealed and concealed focus momentarily on the notion of a shared form of honesty. But the concern for honesty and for the renewal of failing relationships is, as always, expressed indirectly. Emma registers her strong feelings about Casey's dishonest writing; Robert suggests lunch with Jerry in the context of a squash game that excludes Emma; Jerry and Robert argue over who will pay for it and (indirectly) control it; Emma, recognizing Robert's effort to exclude her, offers to resolve their problem by coming to watch the game herself and then buying lunch for all three.

The exclusion/inclusion struggle thus becomes a battle between Robert and Emma over Jerry – a battle that is finally rendered irrelevant by Jerry excluding them both:

ROBERT: No, really, we haven't played for years. We must play. You were rather good.
JERRY: Yes, I was quite good. All right. I'll give you a ring.
ROBERT: Why don't you?
JERRY: We'll make a date.
ROBERT: Right.
JERRY: Yes. We must do that.

ROBERT: And then I'll take you to lunch.
JERRY: No, no. I'll take you to lunch.
ROBERT: The man who wins buys the lunch.
EMMA: Can I watch?
          [Pause]
ROBERT: What?
EMMA: Why can't I watch and then take you both to lunch?
ROBERT: Well, to be brutally honest, we wouldn't actually want a woman around, would we, Jerry? I mean a game of squash isn't simply a game of squash, it's rather more than that. You see, first there's the game. And then there's the shower. And then there's the pint. And then there's lunch. After all, you've been at it. You've had your battle. What you want is your pint and your lunch. You really don't want a woman buying you lunch. You don't actually want a woman within a mile of the place, any of the places, really. You don't want her in the squash court, you don't want her in the shower, or the pub, or the restaurant. You see, at lunch you want to talk about squash, or cricket, or books, or even women, with your friend, and be able to warm to your theme without fear of improper interruption. That's what it's all about. What do you think, Jerry?
JERRY: I haven't played squash for years.
          [Pause] (pp. 68–70)

Jerry's pointed remark cuts off the flow of male exclusion of the female, of Robert/Jerry's exclusion of Emma. The male/male ritual with its evocative phrases of 'a date', 'squash', 'a game', 'a battle', and being 'at it',[17] all followed by a drink, a lunch, and some intimate conversation, offers repeated hints of a competing male/female relationship also focused on the lunch hour. These hints are in the audience's mind when it encounters later Robert's semi-threat to have an affair with Jerry (p. 87). But the competing patterns of Robert/Jerry excluding Emma, Emma/Jerry excluding Robert, and Robert/Emma excluding Jerry are all put to one side in this scene, as Jerry rejects Robert's and Emma's various suggestions by indicating that he is about to go off to New York for a week with Casey. After Jerry leaves, 'Robert returns. He kisses her. She responds. She breaks away, puts her head on his shoulder, cries quietly. He holds her' (p. 71). Neither has the Jerry he/she wants and both have sacrificed much of themselves and each other to hold on to their relationships with him. The moment of shared honesty is a silent moment of mutual recognition, but it leads to no lasting renewal. In the ongoing pattern of trust leading to betrayal to new trust and new betrayal, Emma will betray both Robert and Jerry by turning, herself, towards a relationship with Casey.

The play's focus on the lunch hour is thus extensive and informative, and it helps clarify the larger implications of the play's episodic structure. Exemplified in that structure is a way of life based on interludes, episodes, moments – but we are now in a position to see that these are frequently *moments salvaged from one social pattern as the problematic basis for another*. The lunch hours thus link with other such moments – quick drinks after work, secretly shared afternoons and brief holidays – special occasions that provide the basis for relationships endlessly struggling to accommodate betrayal and trust. Relationships based on such a way of life involve constant manipulation to prevent one episode from contaminating another, to reveal only what can sustain (even if only temporarily) a desired relationship, to conceal whatever would undermine the value of those moments. This way of life is based on careful inclusion and exclusion, endless struggles for control of what will and will not be known, participated in, and/or acknowledged. Characters struggle to sustain moments of vitality, originality and idiosyncratic value by insulating them from larger patterns that might betray their mundaneness, their conventionality and their mixed value. The boundaries that have provided the focus of the action in so many modern plays are here manifest in the episodic separateness of moments that depend on their separateness for their novelty and value. The rituals of lunch-hour intimacy are wrenched from competing patterns and competing commitments – patterns and commitments from which they must be temporarily insulated, but with which they must also eventually collide.

But the point the play is making is more subtle yet. The luncheons, evening drinks and summer holidays promise to insulate old relationships from the effects of new ones that threaten to betray them. But the boundaries established by displacement in time and space are never sufficient. As each relationship is forced to accommodate itself to others, each is steadily undermined by the cumulative effect of what also sustains it: explanations that involve compromise, adjustment, disguise and deception. Trust is not suddenly disrupted in a cataclysmic moment of betrayal; rather, trust and betrayal become mutually dependent agents of steady subversion: the former by tending to ask more of a relationship than it can possibly offer, the latter by tending to offer less to a relationship than it needs to survive. We thus encounter instances of relationships that conclude though not yet exhausted (Jerry and Emma), and that persist though no longer fruitful (Jerry and Robert). As we watch the progress of these relationships and the characters' repeated struggles to control competing loyalties, we recognize the basis for Jerry's initial desire for complete novelty in his relationship with Emma and also for his subsequent acceptance of the inevitable limits upon such novelty. Special relationships and special occasions can temporarily be insulated from larger contexts, but the local and larger contexts must steadily come to terms with each other.

Jerry, in his semi-inebriated state at the beginning of his affair with Emma, claimed that 'Nothing has ever happened. Nothing. This is the only thing that has ever happened' (pp. 136–7). In making that claim, he was announcing the only conditions under which the new loyalty to Emma could survive and flourish – conditions that require the new relationship to be insulated from old loyalties to Robert and Judith. This announcement of the necessary conditions includes an unacknowledged indication of the ultimate impossibility of such conditions. At best, a few moments, a few lunches or even a few dozen might survive such requirements, but nothing of lasting value could be located there. To survive and flourish, the new relationship must come to terms with old responsibilities and overcome them. But as it does so, the uncontaminated moments must also come to terms with contamination and may thereby lose their value. And if they survive and become the new dominant pattern of daily life, and long-term loyalties, they must then prove themselves capable of withstanding contamination by future lunch relationships, future short-term intimacies, future moments of potential betrayal.

The pattern of daily life registered in the texture of the play, with its recurring focus on working days interrupted by intimate luncheons, is also one that is registered in the play's basic structure. As we have noted above, the play is structured symmetrically, with two related groups of four scenes distributed on either side of the pivotal fifth scene. It is difficult not to be drawn towards a further recognition of the way in which the structure of the play thus becomes an emblem of its basic theme. The structure of scenes, with four before Scene Five and four after Scene Five, recapitulates the structure of a working day with four hours before lunch and four hours after. And the scene that is set structurally, though not chronologically, at the play's 'noon' hour is, ironically enough, the only scene in the play which is devoted to Robert and Emma, husband and wife, alone together.[18] The play's structure embodies what its action will reveal, that this too is an episode in the larger process of betrayal that the play seeks to dramatize.

In this central scene, Robert and Emma are visiting Venice. They have returned for a holiday to a place that was the scene of their love at a time when it promised enduring loyalty and mutual trust. They return to it now, as Jerry and Emma later return to a pub at noon, encountering 'old times' (p. 12) and new times simultaneously.

> ROBERT: How many times have we been to Torcello? Twice. I remember how you loved it, the first time I took you there. You fell in love with it. That was about ten years ago, wasn't it? About . . . six months after we were married. Yes. Do you remember? I wonder if you'll like it as much tomorrow.
> [Pause] (p. 82)

The memory of love on a previous visit gives way on this visit to the discovery of Jerry and Emma's affair (p. 84). Like the trip to Torcello, the period of mutual love and enduring loyalty turns out to have been only an episode, a period separated in space and time from other patterns of loyalty and betrayal. Holidays, like lunch hours, are separated from the larger patterns of daily living, and what is built on them does not easily survive the return to contaminating conflicts. Robert registers this recognition when he returns to London and to his now damaged relationship with both Emma and Jerry.

ROBERT: I'll tell you what it is, it's just that I can't bear being back in London. I was happy, such a rare thing, not in Venice, I don't mean that, I mean on Torcello, when I walked about Torcello in the early morning, alone, I was happy, I wanted to stay there forever. (p. 117)

But, as he himself recognizes, the latest visit to Torcello was like previous visits to Torcello, like lunch hours with Jerry, and like years of love with Emma: all turn out to be episodes sustained as much by what they exclude as by what they include. And what they exclude undermines in the long run what has been sustained in the short. Only if one of these moments was 'the only thing that has ever happened' (p. 137) could the episode be unbounded, the loyalties unchallenged, and the inevitable betrayal forestalled.

The episodic structure of the play with its non-uniform chronology thus indicates to us the episodic nature of periods of trust and betrayal in a series of relationships. And the location of the Emma/Robert scene at the 'noon' hour of the play ironically confirms what the action reveals – that the seemingly basic relationship of the play, the one that would provide the enduring ground of a well-made play, is simply another episode in a series of episodes of varying duration. A marriage that is to be revived by holidays is as episodic in nature and extent as any affair that grounds itself on lunch-hour intimacies, early evening drinks, and intermittent afternoon assignations. What is repeatedly dramatized in the play is a pattern of ongoing betrayal, and a repeated process of urgent attempts to adjust to it, accommodate it, and control it. The inclusions and exclusions, the revealing and concealing that give these episodic relationships their novelty and value cannot be indefinitely controlled, and the choice repeatedly confronted is how long to try to salvage and when to decide to dispense with relationships that are initially sustained by, and eventually betrayed by, their basis in special occasions.

In this light, the most enduring relationship in the play, the one between Jerry and Robert, becomes not the one that manifests the most enduring trust, but the one that can absorb the most extensive betrayals. Jerry and Robert seem to be inveterate salvagers, committed to a continuity that seems likely to rob their relationships of almost all that could make them worth while. The second scene of this play determined to resist chronology as the primary basis of its structure is also the final chronological scene of the action. It threatens to offer what a well-made-play finale might offer – the ultimate confrontation of the two close friends involved with the same woman. But the scene is not the play's finale, and it simply renews rather than resolves the process of betrayal. What it offers is confirmation that both men had known about the affair for years, had kept their knowledge from each other, had persistently accommodated to the betrayals involved, and now intend to continue them. They will continue, not only in the context of mutual betrayal of trust, but even in the context of mutually acknowledged betrayal of trust.

It is difficult to overlook the intermittent parallels between this episode and the one involving Jerry and Emma in the play's first scene. Jerry seeks to revive something of his earlier relationship with Robert by recalling the reading of Yeats, in whose poetry Robert and Jerry had both been interested when they were undergraduates and editors of poetry magazines at Oxford and Cambridge. When Robert earlier described that period to Emma, he pointed out that they were 'bright young men', 'close friends', 'long before I met you. Long before he met you' (p. 83). Robert's recollection seems designed, in 1973, to indicate to Emma that she is the intruder, the contaminating force, that threatens to undermine a long-lasting relationship. But when reminded of these early days by Jerry's 1977 reference to Yeats, Robert is as non-committal about their joint past as Jerry was in the play's first scene in response to Emma's reminders of her joint past with him. The confrontation between Jerry and Robert ends, not with mutual rejection, nor with mutual reconciliation, but with polite agreement to continue a relationship that has lost almost all of its credibility and value. Ironically, the final words between them, and the final chronological words in the play, are directed towards Jerry's other enduring relationship (with his wife) and a renewal of the special occasions that keep it and so many of the relationships in the play, alive and limping.

> [Pause]
> ROBERT: Where are you going this summer, you and the family?
> JERRY: The Lake District. (p. 46)

The persistence of the Jerry/Robert relationship is thus not a simple measure of its value, but an index of continuity purchased at the cost of diminishing mutual expectations. And Robert's comment to Jerry, after his own experience on holiday with Emma, suggests the recognition of a pattern on his part that is both revealed and concealed by the concluding remark. The Jerry/Judith relationship seems to persist in the same ways that the Jerry/Robert relationship has persisted, and as the Emma/Robert relationship so long persisted – by steadily concealing more than it reveals. Judith never appears in the play, although it focuses extensively on her husband. From early in the affair, 1971, Jerry is worried about her relationship with fellow doctors, but, typically enough, phrases his worries in terms of his recurring concern for control of what is to be concealed and revealed in relationships: 'I don't know exactly what's going on' (p. 127). Emma is consistent enough to query Judith's faithfulness, but Jerry, astonished that Robert would duplicate his (Jerry's) deception of a friend, would doubtless be astonished at Judith's duplication of his and Emma's betrayal of their spouses. Jerry keeps the

relationship with Judith going by refusing to inquire, by disregarding sugges-
tive patterns of behaviour, and by constantly providing explanations that
reconstruct and render temporarily harmless her behaviour and her absence.
'She's too busy' is his recurring phrase: 'She's got lots to do. She's a very good
doctor. She likes her life. She loves the kids' (p. 129). Judith, he wishes to
believe, is always too busy – too busy to suspect him and too busy to emulate
him. But her physical absence from the play reinforces our sense of her
physical absence from much of his life – except of course on special occasions,
like summer holidays in Venice or the Lake District.

The Jerry/Judith relationship seems to persist on the same basis as the
Jerry/Robert relationship: compromised beyond the possibility of major
value, it continues on the strength of extensive exclusion and diminished
expectations. But if Jerry, Robert and Judith can settle for such compromises,
Emma, it seems, cannot.

> [*Pause*]
> EMMA: Tell me . . . have you ever thought . . . of changing your life?
> JERRY: Changing?
> EMMA: Mmnn.
> [*Pause*]
> JERRY: It's impossible.
> [*Pause*] (pp. 127–8)

The words occur in 1971, the first chronological scene of Jerry and Emma's
affair. It leads into a brief consideration, early in the affair, of faithfulness.
Emma wonders if Judith is faithful to Jerry, asks about his faithfulness to her
(Emma), and confirms her own faithfulness to Jerry. But the attempt to
insulate the relationship from betrayal is already hopelessly compromised,
because the rules for faithfulness in their relationship cannot apply to
spouses.

> [*Pause*]
> EMMA: Listen. There's something I have to tell you.
> JERRY: What?
> EMMA: I'm pregnant. It was when you were in America.
> [*Pause*]
> It wasn't anyone else. It was my husband.
> [*Pause*]
> JERRY: Yes. Yes, of course.
> [*Pause*]
> I'm very happy for you. (p. 130)

The dilemma and the compromise are evident to both characters. Their
lunch-hour intimacies and their afternoon assignations are not, and cannot
be, fully insulated from the larger commitments of their lives. The novelty
cannot be kept separate from the consequences of pre-existing conventional
commitments. Emma, recognizing this, suggests 'change' in those larger

commitments; Jerry will not consider it, and the pattern is set. Jerry wishes to make of his relationship to Emma what he makes of his relationship with Robert and his relationship with Judith – commitment based on concealment as the basis of intimacy, compromise as the foundation for truth. Emma, already in the cycle, is in no position to alter it unilaterally. But when, in 1975, she and Jerry confront the impending conclusion of their affair, the issues surface once more in discussion of their hideaway flat.

> [*Pause*]
> EMMA: It's just . . . an empty home.
> JERRY: It's not a home.
> [*Pause*]
> I know . . . I know what you wanted . . . but it could never . . . actually be a home. You have a home. I have a home. With curtains, etcetera. And children. Two children in two homes. There are no children here, so it's not the same kind of home.
> EMMA: It was never intended to be the same kind of home. Was it?
> [*Pause*]
> You didn't ever see it as a home, in any sense, did you?
> JERRY: No, I saw it as a flat . . . you know.
> EMMA: For fucking.
> JERRY: No, for loving.
> EMMA: Well, there's not much of that left, is there?
> [*Silence*]
> JERRY: I don't think we don't love each other.
> [*Pause*]
> EMMA: Ah well.
> [*Pause*] (pp. 54–5)

Jerry, it seems, in spite of their infrequent visits, has kept the flat going, just as he has kept the relationship with Robert and the relationship with Judith going. But Emma, presenting him with the either/or of fucking or loving, confronts in his response the capacity for compromise that keeps Jerry's relationships going while undermining most of what they might stand for. His 'I don't think we don't love each other' is a revelatory line that seeks to sustain what its negations radically undermine. It is a far cry from his initial announcement that nothing else had ever happened in the world but his relationship with Emma, and it reveals how much is compromised by the subsequent need to accommodate so many conflicting loyalties and commitments.

Emma, on the other hand, finally turns away from the compromises of Jerry and Robert. And when she does so, it is to Casey, who, whatever his limitations, has, in 1974, taken the decisive step of ending a compromised relationship. He has left his wife Susannah and their three children and is 'living alone round the corner' (p. 66). Emma has turned to Casey and has decided to end her marriage to Robert. But the possibility that she and Casey might build upon these major decisions a new kind of relationship capable of avoiding the endless manipulations of revealing and concealing is undermined by her very presence at noon in a pub with Jerry. The pattern, if not the personnel, seems likely to continue. The breakup of marriages and friendships involves an honest acknowledgement of betrayed trust – a doubtful basis on which to build future enduring trust. But the alternative contemplated by the play is one of endless degrees of unacknowledged betrayal. Emma's new path looks alarmingly like the path taken by Jerry when he tried to build a relationship with her on the basis of nothing else having ever happened. But something else has always happened and will always happen, and the action of the play moves, not towards a resolution that removes that recurring truth, but towards a poignant recognition of the persistence of the hope that enduring novelty can yet grow out of conventional situations, that love and trust can yet be built upon a past and a present of recurring betrayal. The play's earliest chronological scene is also its final sequential scene, as the play registers structurally what it exemplifies thematically – the conflation of beginnings and endings in a world of endless repetition.

JERRY: As you are my best and oldest friend and, in the present instance, my host, I decided to take this opportunity to tell your wife how beautiful she was.

ROBERT: Quite right.

JERRY: It is quite right, to . . . to face up to the facts . . . and to offer a token, without blush, a token of one's unalloyed appreciation, no holds barred.

ROBERT: Absolutely.

JERRY: And how wonderful for you that this is so, that this is the case, that her beauty is the case.

ROBERT: Quite right.
          [*Jerry moves to Robert and takes hold of his elbow.*]

JERRY: I speak as your oldest friend. Your best man.

ROBERT: You are, actually.
          [*He clasps Jerry's shoulder, briefly, turns, leaves the room. Emma moves towards the door. Jerry grasps her arm. She stops still. They stand still, looking at each other.*] (pp. 137–8)

Jerry moves towards Robert, his best friend, and takes hold of his elbow, and when he leaves, Jerry grasps the arm of Emma, his best friend's wife. The conflict between competing loyalties is enacted in that movement, and the perilous link between betrayal and trust is embodied in the lingering stare of Jerry and Emma at each other.

The moment of hope for Emma and Jerry is also a moment of doubt. Jerry, stressing how lovely he finds Emma, has just announced that 'this is the only thing that has ever happened'. The characters are caught up in the hope that radical novelty can yet occur in a cliché-ridden, conventional situation, in the hope that love and trust can flourish in a context of a renewed betrayal of love and trust. The hope is an enduring one; it has been the subject of romantic literature for hundreds of years. It has also, in various forms of finally expressed love, provided the conclusion to a thousand plays, novels and movies. In such endings, a new beginning is always promised, a new opportunity for a different and not fully charted future. But the major irony of this play is that Jerry's phrase 'this is the only thing that has ever happened' (pp. 136–7) is undercut, for the audience, by the fact that the whole of the rest of the play has already happened. And because of the play's use of reversed chronology, we know how the characters' future is charted, and we know that that future is to re-enact the cycle of trust leading to betrayal, leading to new trust and further betrayal. But that is not all there is to say about the final scene, for though its location in the play invites us to doubt, its existence as a scene nevertheless invites us to hope. And both attitudes must apply for us, as for the characters, when the play's structure exhibits the insulation of the episodic event as well as the insidiousness of a debilitating continuity.

We have noted that the play's structure offers an emblematic mixture of repetition and fragmentation, a mixture that grounds each scene in a conflict between episodic separateness and sequential continuity. Such a conflict has, in the lives of the characters, a clear experiential equivalent, but it is also important to see that it involves the audience, too, in an experiential dilemma. The full impact of the concluding scene strikes us when we find ourselves, as audience, in possession of knowledge *concealed* from the characters (who don't know their own futures) but *revealed* to us by the preceding action of the play. And, oddly enough, we find it impossible, in spite of our knowledge, not to participate, for a moment, in Jerry's and Emma's hopes for what their future together might be. The urgency of Jerry's remarks and the reluctant fascination in Emma's response link with the episodic structure of the play to invite us to share their hopes – to contemplate for a moment an inviting possibility that we know to be, in their case, an impossibility. As we share, however briefly, and however partially, that embryonic hope, we also find ourselves embroiled in the very patterns the play is dramatizing. We hope, *in spite of our knowledge* of their future. Our hope for them, like their hope for themselves, is based upon a refusal, however brief and however partial, to acknowledge the strength and persistence of a conventional pattern of betrayal – even when we have witnessed the recurrence of the pattern before our eyes. Knowledge of the play certainly restricts our sharing their hope, but knowledge of the nature of love, born of special occasions (and frequently destined to die there) enables us to share, for a moment, their moment.

The final emotions between Jerry and Emma could not be more lightly sketched, but the characters' visible belief in the possibility that love and trust can transcend betrayal reactivates our belief, even as our memory of the play stifles it once more. But the moment in which we respond to their responses re-enacts for a moment in our lives the process dramatized in the characters' lives – *the process of instinctive but purposive concealment of knowledge as a means of embracing novelty and value*. Only by giving the scene's local perspective priority over the play's larger perspective can we share what the characters share – a moment of hope that the relationship might flourish. For that brief moment, we participate in Jerry's belief that 'this is the only thing that has ever happened'. But our participation in it and its full implications brings us, more quickly than it does Jerry, to an awareness that the conditions for sustaining their feelings of transcendence and novelty are also the conditions that will surely undermine and finally destroy those same feelings. The question we are left with is whether what the characters fail to resolve, we as individuals may yet resolve on the basis of the momentary hope that we are invited to share with them.

Must trust always lead to betrayal? Must the novel event always be subsumed under conventional processes? Can novelty be linked with conventionality without thereby reducing itself to an instance of what it seeks to transcend? Is it possible to break out of the cycle, to locate alternatives other than those of the inaccessible novelty fully insulated from the conventional and the unsustainable novelty finally reduced to the conventional? The challenge is not only the characters' and the dramatist's, it is also ours. It is a challenge that runs through the play, through the modern genre, and through the modern period. When Paula Tanqueray sadly concluded in *The Second Mrs. Tanqueray* that 'the future is only the past again, entered through another gate',[19] she was announcing a belief that what the action of the play held for her must hold for everyone. The play demonstrated the situational inevitability and also the ethical unacceptability of that conclusion. Subsequent dramatists have sought structurally and thematically throughout the modern period to link the old to the new, the conventional to the experimental, the already discovered to the process of subsequent discovery. The well-made play's structure of Exposition, Complication, Crisis and Resolution, all within the world of the play, has given way to play structures in which conclusions are either ambiguous or absent. Complication and Crisis lead now not to Conclusion, but to the clarification of renewed Complication. In the process, the Complication has crossed the footlights, has moved from the worlds of the plays into the worlds of the audiences. The challenges offered by the plays' actions are ours, not the characters' nor the playwrights', to resolve. The future, as well as the past, is ours to grapple with, come to terms with, and, if possible, control.

Though *Betrayal* offers no instance of a relationship that manages to sustain value and novelty in a world of rediscovered conventionality and repeated betrayal, its episodic structure offers equivocal support to the possibility that life may yet prove otherwise. Emma's noon meeting with Jerry at the start of the play, and her new affair with Casey, both indicate that belief in the possibility of novelty transcending conventional patterns persists even when no enduring instance has yet been encountered. And the full implication of the final scene is located only when we link it to that initial scene and understand that we have indeed encountered, in both places, instances of potentially enduring value. The final scene offers, not, as Jerry wishes, an instance of novelty fully transcending conventionality, but an episode in which newly discovered novelty, embryonic trust, and emerging love play their part in a cycle which, while endlessly inviting betrayal, endlessly seeks to rise beyond it. Betrayal may be the persisting conclusion of this recurring process, but for the characters involved, it is not the central truth of its beginning nor its necessary conclusion. Every new start does indeed posit the possibility of discovering 'a different world' (p. 136). And the play ends with such a beginning, with a moment when the cycle has just begun, when love is in the ascendant, and past and future betrayals have receded to a distance. At such moments it is indeed possible to believe that the novelty of such situations might outweigh their conventionality, that they might provide the basis for new traditions, rather than be subsumed once more by existing traditions. The play dramatizes the appealing possibility of the one and the insidious probability of the other, but by concluding with a new beginning, a new episode of hope, it simultaneously sustains and subverts the hope voiced so determinedly by Jerry that life is starting over again. In such episodic situations, such moments of determined exclusion, the truisms of the contaminating past and the compromised future are held at bay, and something valuable flourishes, for a while.

> ROBERT: Oh . . . not much more to say on that subject, really, is there?
> EMMA: What do you consider the subject to be?
> ROBERT: Betrayal.
> EMMA: No, it isn't.
> ROBERT: Isn't it? What is it then?
> EMMA: I haven't finished it yet. I'll let you know. (p. 78)

12 Conclusion

The marking and merging of horizons, characteristic, as we noted earlier, of the modern theatre, has appeared in a variety of ways in the plays subjected to detailed scrutiny. This variety is an important indication that the principles of continuity suggested in the opening chapters are not principles for mere replication but principles which provide an evolving basis for growth and development in the modern theatre. As we study the field, we encounter borders of many kinds foregrounded for many purposes. Pinero invites us into the little world of St James's parish and leads us steadily towards its limiting moral horizons. We view the action through the eyes of the play's benevolent *raisonneur* and, when his perspective is discredited, we share his emerging recognition of the need to move beyond what his philosophical and moral commitments, reflected in the 'refined' stage set, are able to provide. Ibsen focuses our attention on and guides us beyond the horizons of the doll's house by helping us to see, and also see by means of, an image network. This network enables us to discover more about social relationships than the characters do, to recognize that what is at stake in their limited perspectives and premature certainties is our joint capacity to review, rather than simply replicate or reject, established wisdom, with its dual implications of disease and cure. Strindberg situates us, from the beginning of the play, outside the domain it predominantly dramatizes. The play's inner and outer horizons remind us, in differing ways, of the boundedness of the Earth domain and, from our outside perspective, the Earth-world's limits seem more fundamental than its variety. The implicit promise of alleviated suffering, embodied in the shifting stances of the Daughter of Indra, finally fail to bear fruit, and as a consequence, the play's various modes of inquiry become not just the means of inquiry, but also the subject of inquiry. Brecht makes a virtue of epistemological necessity by focusing on the fact that a mode of knowing is not just a limit upon knowledge but also a condition for knowledge. A social border, likewise, is not only a limit but also a frontier, a bridge to ever-expanding novelty of knowledge in a world which, lacking any fixed core, lacks also any fixed and inbuilt limit. By reminding us of the provisionality of historical worlds, Brecht persuades us of the provisionality of our own, and by demonstrating the cumulative process of complex seeing, of seeing beyond the confines of any subject and any domain, he suggests that learning how to learn in contexts of incipient continuity and discontinuity is as important as any facts we acquire for others or establish for ourselves. Ionesco, constantly in search of the newly typifying rather than the historically typical, sets the edges of his stage set on the frontiers of known reality. Characters from other worlds invade the stage and subsequently the auditorium. An idiosyncratic particular situation offers the means of drawing attention to social and epistemological limitations in our inherited world and provides testimony that leads us beyond what we are frequently prepared to contemplate as useful modes of interaction in the world of the theatre or in the social worlds around it. Beckett divides his stage into an area of light and an area of dark. He then uses contrasting modes of interaction between the domains as a means of exploring the possibility and persistence of value in a human life character-ized by discontinuity as well as continuity. Pinter, recognizing the constant process of construction and reconstruction that is the social consequence of a pluralistic world, offers a play with a partially reversed chronology to embody the qualified and episodic nature of community relationships. The play's episodic structure registers the punctuated equilibrium of lives devoted to controlling the boundaries that divide each social relationship from others that compete with it. Repeated efforts by the characters to create new worlds and to sustain others depend upon precarious attempts to insulate new worlds from old, new loves from pre-existing responsibilities, new opportunities from established commitments. In all of these plays, the complexities of epistemological pluralism hover persistently in the background of domains as varied as the ethical, moral, social, spiritual, psychological and aesthetic.

The marking and merging of theatrical horizons is thus an important element in these and other modern plays which explore for many purposes the viability of domains of many kinds. Such a recognition is not, however, a reason to give the similarities among these plays priority over their differ-ences. By studying modern plays in the major context of each other, we learn appropriate means of access to their diversity and particularity, but it is important to remember that it is a means of access, not a final destination. The marking and merging of horizons in these plays, besides being one of several modes of embodying themes, is also a sophisticated means of orientat-ing audiences towards the action of the plays. As members of an audience, we repeatedly find ourselves situated in particular ways relative to particular horizons of particular domains. The orientation the plays thus offer is often also a means of reorientation, as the plays invite us not just to look for summarizing themes, but also to reconsider our ways of understanding and participating in plays as a first step towards reconsidering our ways of understanding and participating in the social worlds that surround us. Plays once thought to offer us only instruction and entertainment serve also to stimulate inquiries of various but related kinds for various but related purposes. The plays characteristically exhibit and exploit the epistemological consequences of a pluralistic universe in which community constructions function as both persisting problem and putative cure.

This recurring concern in modern plays for the boundaries that separate and connect contrasting worlds, particularly the worlds of the stage and auditorium, is both characteristic of, and of major consequence to, the modern theatre. But an interest in contrasting worlds is not, as we noted earlier, unique to modern drama. Though modern uses of 'theatre' and 'world' motifs are grounded in extensive cultural concern for the consequences of living in a pluralistic universe, the motifs themselves and some of the uses to which modern dramatists put them have a long and honourable history. That history includes preceding examples in the dramatic genre and elsewhere in western literature, and there are, of course, similar developments in other genres in the modern period. A glance at some of those instances will serve to show that current examples are not without ancestry and neither are they mere replications of pre-existing models. Rather, as our general line of argument on convention and innovation has repeatedly shown, related principles of continuity provide the appropriate means of approaching novelty in our literature, in our culture, and in our daily lives. Lines of continuity among modern plays justify a consideration of them, as we noted earlier, in the major, but not exclusive, context of each other. It will thus be useful, at this point, to trace some of the broader patterns of continuity that reach back to the earliest English drama, and beyond.

Drama in the medieval period had its own characteristic use of an other-world format, one that depended on a particular conception of the relationship between space and time in both on-stage and off-stage worlds. This relationship has been illuminatingly explored by Kolve in *The Play Called Corpus Christi*. As many have noted, place in the Corpus Christi drama is subject to sudden puzzling variations (e.g. from Wakefield to Bethlehem in the *Secunda Pastorum*), and it seems that, in some sense, all earthly places are the same place. As Kolve points out, the other world in such medieval drama is not spatially, but temporally, distinct from the everyday world that the drama also portrays. This distinction renders change in earthly location less important than continuity between a temporal world (ours) and a timeless one (God's). The drama attends to the temporal world as a prelude to going beyond it: 'the events chosen for dramatization are those in which God intervenes in human history.'[1] It is ultimately for the sake of those moments when the temporal world encounters the timeless that the drama focuses on events in the temporal world. The temporal world is thus portrayed as one which serves to reveal, by intermittently recapitulating, patterns of the eternal world. In such a context, the past and future are both immanent in the present, and similarities and differences between places and times are less important than similarities and differences between the worlds of temporal and timeless patterns:

> time is displayed as an artifact shaped by God, whose patterns express His eternal truth. Time concerns us because we are alive in it and because God's plan for man's redemption can be worked out only in its terms. But man's real business is eternity, and the drama exists to remind him of that.[2]

The two worlds of the Corpus Christi drama are thus not geographically but temporally distinct, and the temporal world is very much subservient to the timeless world. The connection between the two is less a matter for spatial embodiment in boundary zones than for intermittent replication, by emblematic scenes, of patterns of timeless implication. The movement in the *Secunda Pastorum* from Wakefield to Bethlehem is thus important not for what it tells us about life in either domain specifically, but for what it tells us about the relationship between life on earth, and life in the timeless world beyond it. When a border becomes the focus of attention in medieval drama, the spatial conflict in a temporal domain is likely, as in *The Castle of Perseverance*, to be an allegorical representation of conflict significant to the timeless domain. In that play, the image of a castle under siege is used to represent human life under attack by human vices and defended by Christian virtues. The situation is somewhat different, as we shall see, in the English folk drama that preceded the medieval drama and continued to be performed alongside it. But in the Corpus Christi drama, the temporal world's boundaries register the temporal world's divisions only as a means of redirecting our attention to a larger, enduring unity.

The drama of the Renaissance displays a rather different use of the other-world format. A change in place in the temporal domain regains its importance because time and temporality are relocated in our cultural and conceptual environments. Kolve helpfully cites Poulet on the importance to the Renaissance of rediscovering value in the temporal world: 'Temporality then no longer appeared solely as the indelible mark of mortality; it appeared also as the theatre and field of action where despite his mortality man could reveal his authentic dignity and gain a personal immortality.'[3] When Shakespeare's Antony travels to Cleopatra's Egypt, the change of world involves also a fundamental change of values. When characters in Shakespeare's comedies leave their urban environments and venture into such domains as the Forest of Arden (*As You Like It*), Windsor Forest (*The Merry Wives of Windsor*), and the forest on the frontiers of Mantua (*The Two Gentlemen of Verona*), they move from one distinctive world to another:

beyond the walls of cities known at least by name to the Elizabethans stretches another and magical world: forests where fairies dance by moonlight, the pastoral landscape where shepherds woo their loves, the beautiful mountain where is a lady richly left, awaiting the right hero . . . always it is the world as we wish it were instead of as it is, reality refashioned 'as you like it'.[4]

Frye characterized this other-world of Shakespearian drama as a 'green world', and its implications, for Shakespeare's work and others', has been much discussed, notably by Berger and Hawkins. Frye has made a sustained attempt to characterize in 'green world' terms the basic structural pattern of Shakespeare's major comedies. Their action, Frye suggests, moves 'from normal world to green world and back again'.[5] Hawkins, however, notes that this pattern is visible in only four of the comedies, and suggests that the others register a different kind of structure:

> Against the four comedies of the green world, we can set *The Comedy of Errors, Love's Labor's Lost, Much Ado About Nothing,* and *Twelfth Night.* These belong to what for the present I shall call the 'alternate pattern', whose distinctive mark is unity of place.[6]

To characterize the importance of place in these comedies, he suggests the term 'closed world' as an appropriate descriptive term. Though the action of these plays is restricted to one domain, its implications are not, for the social structure of the 'closed world' is often disrupted by intruders from without. In the comedies as a whole, there is thus either a dramatized or implied 'second world', and Hawkins goes on to assimilate his 'alternate pattern' of Shakespearian comedy to Frye's by suggesting that we replace Frye's normal world/green world contrast with a closed world/green world contrast and thereby incorporate all of the comedies, whether they set their scenes in one domain or two. Various versions of this two-world structure can then be viewed from various stances by characters and audiences in various plays. The second world may be implied or displayed, and it may be seen from the vantage point of an insider or an outsider.[7] Berger, like Hawkins, resists the simplicity of Frye's pattern, but focuses more on the range and complexity of green worlds than on alternative descriptive terms, and, in this context, the larger implications of Shakespeare's two-world pattern begin to appear:

> As a sophisticated literary device, Frye's green world is not the peculiarly Elizabethan phenomenon he claims it to be, and it may have a dangerous or sinister side to it which he is inclined to play down in the Elizabethans. . . . The sophisticated notion of a green world, and of a problematical green world, goes back at least as far as Homer's Phaiakia.[8]

Though the nature of the 'second world' varies from medieval to Renaissance drama, it is interesting to note its persistence, and even more interesting to note how Berger traces it back to classical times. He is not alone in doing so, however, for Frye and Hawkins, too, comment not only on the motif's persistence, but also upon its pervasiveness. Frye first traces Shakespeare's adoption of the green-world motif back to English folk drama, to

> the drama of folk ritual, of the St. George play and the mummers' play, of the feast of the ass and the Boy Bishop, and of all the dramatic activity that punctuated the Christian calendar with the rituals of an immemorial paganism,[9]

and he goes on to link it to mythic patterns of green-world life triumphing over waste-land death. Berger notes the diversity of second worlds and their range of implication:

> More's Utopia, Sidney's golden world and Arcadia, Spenser's Faerie, Shakespeare's green world and stage world, Marvell's poetic gardens, Alberti's picture plane as a window, Leonardo's painted second nature, Filarete's Sforzinda, Castiglione's Urbino, Machiavelli's hypothetical state, Gilbert's magnetic terrella, Galileo's experiment world, the new world described in Descartes' *Discourse*.[10]

Hawkins sets out to trace the second-world pattern from ancient Greece to modern England, moving from country to country and from genre to genre. The closed-world/green-world pattern of interaction goes back, he argues, to 'the fountainheads of Western story-telling',[11] to the *Odyssey*, the *Iliad* and the *Aeneid*. Subsuming the green world under an archetype of quest narrative and the closed world under an archetype of siege narrative, he is able to characterize the narrative pattern of the *Odyssey* as a closed-world/green-world(s)/closed-world structure, that of the *Iliad* as a cycle of siege and counter-siege between two closed worlds, and that of the *Aeneid* as an episodic alternation between closed and green worlds.[12] The two-world pattern then becomes very widespread indeed. In Restoration drama, the sophistication of characters from the town is repeatedly contrasted with the ignorance of characters from the country (with, of course, the incipient thematic possibility of reversing the pattern in a particular case). In subsequent drama, in the context of the Romantic era, the norms themselves could be reversed with emphasis on the town's corruption and the country's innocence; later again there emerged the possibility of exploring the strange worlds of Gothic romance. In the novel, closed worlds and green worlds, siege and quest, and town and country contrasts appear regularly, in texts as diverse as *Don Quixote*, *Tom Jones*, *Pride and Prejudice*, *The Scarlet Letter*, *Heart of Darkness*, and *The Ambassadors*. And in poetry, the green-world/closed-world pattern is used to embody the theme of innocence and experience in poetry from Chaucer to Blake to Yeats.

The technique of contrasting two domains of human experience is thus an enduring one in western culture and is a basic narrative technique that persists when the epic is succeeded by the romance and then by the novel, and it also persists in poetry and drama from classical times to the present. But

Berger's emphasis upon the variety of uses of the second-world motif is as important as any recognition of its persistence as a motif.[13] Hawkins makes a similar point from a different angle when he stresses that an archetype is not a stereotype, that the possibilities of the closed-world/green-world pattern are limited only by the imagination of the artist.[14] To perceive the persistence of this pattern is thus only part of the process of understanding it, for it may have many characteristic kinds of use as well as many particular uses.

It is intriguing to note in these studies of world relationships in classical, medieval and Renaissance times, a repeated use of a 'second-world' or 'double-world' or 'two-world' vocabulary to describe that interaction. If three or more worlds are at issue, they are quickly resolved into two major kinds, so that the several-worlds format is reduced to a two-worlds format. And between these two worlds, there is frequently the potential for a resolvable conflict. The second world, whatever its virtues, whatever its powers, is also, among other things, subordinate to a first world that is either given or emergent and which can either assimilate or reject what the second world has to offer. A two-world conflict holds out the possibility of a conclusive resolution in favour of one world or the other or in terms of a mixture of both. A two-world conflict in a modern context of multiple worlds, however, offers no such possibilities, for the conclusion of one conflict between worlds is only the prelude to the next. And this difference is of major importance in characterizing modern uses of the world motif.

Periods do not, as we noted earlier, fall into neat patterns of sameness and difference. Every literary period is characterized by variety, as well as by recurring configurations. Indeed, Miller has argued that 'periods differ from one another because there are different forms of heterogeneity, not because each period held a single coherent "view of the world".'[15] There are thus only broad distinctions to be made between previous uses of the world motif and those characteristic of the modern period. For our purposes the key issue is not whether the modern world is more or less unified than earlier worlds, but that modern diversity earns characteristic kinds of value and receives characteristic kinds of treatment. To note the prevalence of an earlier two-world conception is thus to note an important basis for contrasting earlier uses with a modern use of the other-world motif – a use which involves not just two worlds, but two or more.

Berger helps us see this point more clearly when he seeks to characterize Renaissance use of the two-world motif by locating it closer to a recoverable unity than to an incipient pluralism.

> The Renaissance heterocosm was more literally a *second* world because it was conceived as being set over against, not *an* other world, nor *a* first world, but *the* first world. This first world is the actual universe of kingdoms, planets, stars and angels. It comprises the natural, historical and spiritual environments of man. Depending on one's viewpoint one could ascribe its created structure to nature

or God or both, and its apparent character to perception or tradition or both. The general Renaissance attitude toward these worlds may be located, in historical terms, somewhere between the positions epitomized in the following two statements. First, St. Augustine: 'there is no principle of unity but that alone from which all unity derives,' namely, God. Second, Cassirer: 'true unity is never to be sought in things as such, but in intellectual constructions, in frames of reference, which we choose according to the peculiarity of the field to be measured.'[16]

In the modern period, we are conceptually, if not spiritually, closer to Cassirer than to Augustine, and the existence of a second world has, for us, a significantly different status. A movement into a second world is a prelude not to a return to the first, but to an entry into a third and a fourth and so on. The very existence of a second world is emblematic of the existence of others. The ancient narrative devices of quest and siege, escape and invasion, expulsion and intrusion, become aspects of a continuing process, not elements of a teleological progression. Our concern is directed not towards the conclusion of the pattern, but towards the implications of the process. The results of escaping from or intruding into a world are accompanied by a recognition that further movement is always an option to be weighed, a possibility to be contemplated. The movement from first world to second world is an instance of a process that reminds us of the provisionality of all worlds, of their constructed nature, of their reconstructive potential.

Concern for an other-world motif in the modern period is thus related to, but is no mere replication of, a two-world motif that is traceable to classical times. In the modern period, a second world is important not just for the relationship it contracts with a first world, but because its very existence as a second world suggests the possibility of others. And this suggestion has large implications for the status of both worlds and for any others that might succeed them. In the modern theatre, these implications are registered in the repeated focusing of attention on the borders, and not just on the centres of domains. Audiences and characters are repeatedly guided towards horizons of domains, towards the points at which what is inside any domain can be seen in the context of what might lie beyond it. The provisionality of all domains is the logical consequence of a recognition that the second world is not emblematic of a privileged alternative, but of a whole series of alternatives of which the first world was only one among many.

This is not, of course, to undervalue the domains we start from. Goodman may well be right to argue that 'reality in a world, like realism in a picture, is largely a matter of habit',[17] but habits are not always without their justifications, and they are not always easy to break. The very use of the world motif in the pluralistic modern period is a means of acknowledging the viability and persistence of what lies within a domain and the potential costs as well as benefits involved in seeking to reconstitute it. Though we live in worlds of community constructs, our worlds are neither easily established nor easily dismantled. The drama of the pluralistic universe is neither a drama of relativistic clichés nor of incipient monism. It is not seeking to show that because everything is relative, anything goes; nor is it seeking to show that differences can easily be transcended in an ultimate, ideal and persisting synthesis. Rather, it seeks to give stability its due in contexts of contingency, to explore the nature of value in worlds of change, the viability of commitment in worlds of provisionality, the persistence of social relationships and social organizations in worlds of social and individual variation. The drama helps us recognize the ways we rescue from the threat of relativistic chaos domains of stability and continuity, domains in which we can establish firm but not final bases for growth, coherence and renewed commitment. A pluralistic universe is one in which we can defer change but not ignore it, control stability and not be controlled by it.

For some, the loss of a 'given' unity is threatening and fearsome, an occasion for anguish, alienation and *Angst*. For others, the loss of a 'given' unity is the loss of what we never had, and recognition of that fact provides a ratification of human creativity and control. The modern drama seeks to give both attitudes their due in modern worlds that have their own characteristic version of traditional conflicts between faith and reason, trust and betrayal, continuity and change, hope and despair. To focus on negative options at the expense of positive ones is to miss an important part of what the modern theatre has to offer us. Driver's otherwise valuable history of the modern theatre is a significant case in point. He rightly refuses to make chronology the sole basis for his historical account, but, when generalizing about the modern period, he makes too much of the negative side of modern pluralism. One of the key features of modernism, he feels, is 'the alienation [modern man] feels from nature, society, himself, and the past'. This precipitates a line of argument about 'the theater's increasing alienation from society' which produces the startling, though tentative, conclusion that 'the theater has virtually ceased to serve as an aesthetic focus for contemporary experience.' This negative view of the modern world and the consequent belief that the modern theatre 'has lost a great degree of social importance' follow logically upon the assumption that

> drama requires . . . a high degree of social cohesion with regard to values, symbols, and myths. . . . The more open and 'advanced' society becomes through industrialization and the growth of many political and intellectual opinions, the more the dramatist feels the uselessness of his task in the face of cultural fragmentation.[18]

These opinions are worth quoting at length because they are widely shared, appear in an otherwise impressive work, and register the clear consequences of focusing on the negative side of a pluralistic universe at the expense of its positive side. The sense of loss looms large, and the recognition of opportunity is dim. Though it differs in degree from text to text, the same problem emerges in several of the 'Theatre of X' books, whose titles and approaches encourage us to give excessive attention to the negative by focusing on such things as protest, revolt and the absurd.

In the modern theatre, we must recognize, most worlds are potentially green and potentially closed, and it is for us to take the responsibility for making them one or the other. Our attitudes shift with our vantage points, and the drama of the modern period thus regularly situates us on the borders of domains. At such locations, we can both become aware of our current vantage points and consider choosing new ones, recognizing, as we do so, the possibility of constructing others for ourselves. From our chosen vantage points, it is for us to decide whether what each world enables is worth the price of what it excludes. To make that decision, to recognize that that is the nature of much of our decision making, is already to have encountered in the local texture of our lives the experiential and pragmatic implications of the pluralistic universe. William James, we recall, pointed out that a key distinguishing feature of a pluralistic universe is that, in it, every domain has, whether we attend to it regularly or not, 'a genuinely "external" environment'.[19] The several worlds of the modern theatre are without final limit, but each is always within its own limits. Whether those limits remain rigid or become flexible is ours to decide. Changes may be speedy or slow, refreshing or painful or both, but in the modern theatre, audiences and characters are rarely far from a boundary, from the point at which the benefits and liabilities of one world are brought into disturbing confrontation with those of another and another and another.

When Brustein suggested that the traditional and the modern theatres might be distinguished by, among other things, 'the engagement of their audiences, and the nature of the worlds they imply and evoke',[20] he was offering a suggestion with greater explanatory power than he realized. World motifs and audience engagement are mutually implicating in a modern theatre that uses its own status as a world as a means of investigating other worlds. The boundaries of the stage, of the set, and of the building offer evocative emblems of the many domains whose horizons are first marked and then, to the appropriate degree, merged. The second world in the modern theatre and the second world of the modern theatre are thus, among other things, reminders of the existence of and significance of other worlds. The traditional closed worlds and green worlds reappear on the modern stage, but their centres are only initially and not finally fixed, their boundaries initially but not finally firm. Whether the audience is located on the same or other side of the boundaries as the characters, whether it is directed or taken beyond the worlds familiar to the characters, the green worlds encountered offer only a qualified paradise, the closed worlds only a provisional prison. The process that brought audience and characters to this domain and this horizon will beckon them on to others.

The drama of inquiry in a pluralistic universe can offer us no final horizon, no ultimate destination, no road back to where we began. The focus of attention is not on conclusion but on clarification. When we encounter fixity and repetition, as in, for example, *A Dream Play*, *Waiting for Godot*, and *The Bald Soprano*, it is often in the closed-world context of disappointed expectations; when we encounter change, it is often in the ambiguous green-world context of both an opportunity to be seized and a danger to be controlled. Traditional closed-world/green-world motifs of escape and invasion are as prevalent as in earlier two-world literature, but our attention is directed beyond them. We see beyond the boundaries of particular worlds that generate either the need for escape or the fear of, or desire for, invasion, and we recognize that such needs, fears and desires are incipient characteristics of every world. Our concern is not finally for escape or invasion, but for developing further our understanding of the ways of living that attend upon the recognition that every world, no matter what its lineage, has a provisional status, that every boundary, no matter how firm, is also a frontier, that every resting place, no matter how attractive, is also the site of a potential new beginning. The drama of inquiry is also an incitement to inquiry, a reminder that learning is as fundamental to our lives as loving, that moving on is not only a process of leaving things behind, but also of keeping up with what we have the capacity to become. As history shows and as the drama of inquiry displays, there is no point at which we can finally stop and rest satisfied with where we have arrived and what we have achieved. If we must repeatedly contemplate the possibility of moving on, it is well to have acquired the knowledge that dramas of inquiry have individually to offer, but it is more important to have mastered the technique they have collectively displayed: the technique of inquiring further for ourselves.

Notes

1 Theatres and worlds

1. As early as 1949, Fergusson was referring to 'the centerless diversity' of the modern theatre. Francis Fergusson, *The Idea of a Theater*, Princeton, NJ, 1949, p. 2.
2. Gascoigne draws attention to one of the dilemmas that confront the makers of frameworks when he tries to reconcile, in his own work, the typical with the actual:

> Readers may be surprised, in the chapters on the various decades, at the failure of certain dramatists to make much of an appearance. . . . The reason is that in dealing with *Subject-matter* I have discussed plays according to how typical they are and not in terms of their aesthetic merit. It is frequently the second rank of serious dramatists who are most typical of their time. Of course, to disregard aesthetic standards of comparison is a dangerous activity which, if carried too far, can lead directly to the ludicrous. I hope I have avoided carrying it too far. (Bamber Gascoigne, *Twentieth Century Drama*, London, 1962, p. 14)

3. J. L. Styan and Eric Bentley have made notable contributions in this regard. See, for example, Styan's *Drama, Stage and Audience*, London, 1975, and Bentley's introduction to *The Theory of the Modern Stage*, Harmondsworth, 1976.
4. Émile Zola, 'Naturalism in the theatre', trans. Albert Bermel, in Bentley (ed.), *The Theory of the Modern Stage*, p. 351.
5. ibid., p. 367.
6. August Strindberg, 'Author's Foreword to *Miss Julie*', *Six Plays of Strindberg*, trans. Elizabeth Sprigge, New York, 1955, p. 73.
7. Henrik Ibsen, *Ibsen: Letters and Speeches*, ed. Evert Sprinchorn, New York, 1964, p. 241.
8. Michel de Ghelderode, as quoted in Ruby Cohn, *Currents in Contemporary Drama*, Bloomington, Ind., 1969, p. 202.
9. Bertolt Brecht, *Brecht on Theatre*, trans. John Willett, New York, 1964, p. 22.

10. Antonin Artaud, *The Theater and Its Double*, trans. Mary Caroline Richards, New York, 1958, p. 86.

11. Anne Paolucci, 'Pirandello and the waiting stage of the absurd', *Modern Drama*, 23, June 1980, p. 102.

12. Peter Brook, reported by Hugh Hunt in Hugh Hunt, Kenneth Richards and John Russell Taylor, *The Revels History of Drama in English*, VII, London, 1978, p. 155.

13. George Lukács, 'The sociology of modern drama', paraphrased by Eric Bentley, *Theatre of War*, New York, 1972, p. 112. An abbreviated version of Lukács's study, trans. Lee Baxandall, appeared in *Tulane Drama Review*, 9 (iv), Summer 1965, pp. 146–70. It was reprinted in Bentley (ed.), *The Theory of the Modern Stage*, pp. 425–50.

14. Robert Brustein, *The Theatre of Revolt: An Approach to the Modern Drama*, Boston, 1964; Martin Esslin, *The Theatre of the Absurd*, New York, 1969; George E. Wellwarth, *The Theater of Protest and Paradox: Developments in the Avant-Garde Drama*, New York, 1971; Gloria Orenstein, *The Theater of the Marvellous: Surrealism and the Contemporary Stage*, New York, 1975; Eric Bentley, *The Theatre of Commitment*, New York, 1967; Bentley, *Theatre of War*.

15. Peter Brook, *The Empty Space*, New York, 1968.

16. Driver suggests that 'the modern theater's rediscovery of itself as *space* has been its single most important achievement' (Tom F. Driver, *Romantic Quest and Modern Query: A History of the Modern Theater*, New York, 1970, pp. 93–4). See also his comment:

> The culmination of the search for the fully three-dimensional stage means that the wheel has come full circle. Modern theater practice touches hands with primitive theater, in which the décor tends to be symbolic, giving only the suggestion of place and mood, while it is the actor and the audience who use the theatrical space and give it its meaning (p. 93).

In his soon-to-be-translated book, Peter Szondi devotes extensive attention to the importance of performance space in the modern theatre (Peter Szondi, *Theorie des Modernen Dramas*, Frankfurt am Main, 1966).

17. Luigi Pirandello, quoted and translated by Claudio Vicentini, 'Pirandello, Stanislavsky, Brecht, and the "opposition principle"', *Modern Drama*, 20, December 1977, p. 381.

18. Eugène Ionesco, *Notes and Counter Notes: Writings on the Theatre*, trans. Donald Watson, New York, 1964, p. 17.

19. Arthur Adamov, quoted and translated by Esslin, op. cit., p. 74.

20. Bentley, *Theatre of War*, p. 112.

21. Wellwarth, op. cit., p. 3.

22. Esslin, op. cit., p. 184.

23. Orenstein, op. cit., pp. 121–2.

24. I take up in the concluding chapter the issue of traditional use of the 'world' motif, particularly Shakespeare's, and relevant critical discussion, such as Frye's notion of Shakespeare's 'green worlds' and Hawkins's notion of Shakespeare's 'closed worlds'. Goldman also has valuable things to say about 'theatre and world' in *The Actor's Freedom*, New York, 1975, pp. 113–61.

25. W. B. Yeats, *The Countess Cathleen*, *The Collected Plays of W. B. Yeats*, New York, 1953, p. 20.

26. Arthur Wing Pinero, *The Second Mrs. Tanqueray*, Boston, 1894, p. 32.

27. Henry Arthur Jones, *The Liars*, *English Drama in Transition*, *1880–1920*, ed. H. F. Salerno, New York, 1968, p. 77.

28. George Bernard Shaw, *Major Barbara*, in *Bernard Shaw's Plays*, New York, 1970, p. 1.

29. James M. Barrie, *The Admirable Crichton*, *English Drama in Transition*, *1880–1920*, pp. 292–3.

30. ibid., p. 329.

31. ibid., p. 324.

32. T. S. Eliot, *The Family Reunion*, in *T. S. Eliot: The Complete Poems and Plays*, *1909–1950*, New York, 1971, p. 252.

33. David Storey, *Cromwell*, London, 1973, p. 66.

34. Trevor Griffiths, *Comedians*, London, 1980, p. 64.

35. John Osborne, *Look Back in Anger*, London, 1959, p. 17.

36. A system now extended, of course, to include the Third World of developing nations, particularly those of Africa and Asia. Note that I do not here address the issue of whether the modern world is more or less heterogeneous than those of the past. As we will see, the important issue is one of differing attitudes towards manifest diversity.

37. Bertolt Brecht, *Life of Galileo*, trans. Wolfgang Sauerlander and Ralph Manheim, in *Bertolt Brecht: Collected Plays*, V, ed. Ralph Manheim and John Willett, New York, 1972, pp. 6 and 21.

38. Strindberg, *A Dream Play*, in op. cit., p. 260.

39. Driver provides an extended discussion of the implications of historicism for the modern theatre, but his outline of the path of influence does not lead him to recognize the complexity and variety of its subsequent impact. See Driver, op. cit., pp. x–xviii.

40. E. D. Hirsch Jr, *The Aims of Interpretation*, Chicago, 1976, p. 38. The quotation from F. Meinecke is from his *Die Entstehung des Historismus*, Munich, 1947.

41. Wilhelm von Humboldt, as quoted in Cassirer, Ernst, *Language and Myth*, trans. Susanne K. Langer, New York, 1953, p. 9.

42. Stuart Chase, foreword to Benjamin Lee Whorf, *Language, Thought, and Reality*, ed. John B. Carroll, Cambridge, Mass., 1969, p. x.

43. Basil Bernstein, 'A socio-linguistic approach to social learning', in Basil Bernstein, *Class, Codes and Control*, I, London, 1971, pp. 122–3.

44. Edward Albee, *The Zoo Story*, in *'The American Dream' and 'The Zoo Story'*, New York, 1961, p. 37.

45. Walter H. Pater, *The Renaissance*, New York, 1961, p. 221.

46. H. Hoijer, 'The relation of language to culture', in Tax, Sol (ed.), *Anthropology Today: Selections*, Chicago, 1962, p. 262. The 'worlds' metaphor is also a favourite of Sapir:

> The fact of the matter is that the 'real world' is to a large extent unconsciously built up on the language habits of the group. No two languages are ever sufficiently similar to be considered as representing the same social reality. The worlds in which different societies live are distinct worlds, not merely the same

world with different labels attached. (Edward Sapir, 'The status of linguistics as a science', *Selected Writings of Edward Sapir*, Berkeley, 1949, p. 162)

47. Nelson Goodman, *Ways of Worldmaking*, Indianapolis, 1978, p. x.
48. Stephen Toulmin, *Human Understanding*, Princeton, 1972, p. 41.
49. ibid., p. 42. The issue here, it should again be noted, is not whether the modern world is more or less unified than the worlds of the past, but whether existing diversity receives one kind of attention or another. I examine in the final chapter some contrasting ways of dealing with social heterogeneity.
50. Peter Handke, *Kaspar*, in *'Kaspar' and Other Plays*, trans. Michael Roloff, New York, 1975, p. 137.
51. Samuel Beckett, *All that Fall*, in *'Krapp's Last Tape' and Other Dramatic Pieces*, New York, 1960, p. 80.
52. *Krapp's Last Tape*, in ibid., pp. 10 and 14–15.

2 Marking and merging horizons

1. Antonin Artaud, *The Theater and Its Double*, trans. Mary Caroline Richards, New York, 1958, pp. 68–9. See also Friedrich von Schiller, 'Prologue to *The Bride of Messina*', *Works of Schiller*, IV, ed. N. H. Dole, New York, 1910, pp. 223–33.
2. George Lukács. 'The sociology of modern drama', paraphrased by Eric Bentley, *Theatre of War*, New York, 1972, p. 112.
3. Bennett provides a wealth of useful information on the evolution of this trend in German drama and dramatic theory. However, it is difficult to agree that 'the attempt to create, in the theater, a world that is somehow more authentic than the real world outside' is something that enters German and European dramatic traditions with Goethe's *Faust* acting as its 'most conspicuous vehicle' (pp. 154, 155). The notion of a privileged theatre world is a staple of medieval drama which uses its capacity to embody a more authentic world for purposes other than those envisaged by Bennett in the German tradition, and other than those characteristic of modern drama in general (see V. A. Kolve, *The Play Called Corpus Christi*, Stanford, 1966; Anne Righter, *Shakespeare and the Idea of the Play*, London, 1962; James L. Calderwood, *Shakespearean Metadrama*, Minneapolis, 1971; J. L. Styan, *Drama, Stage and Audience*, London, 1975). On this issue, Bennett seems closer to the truth when he acknowledges in his introduction 'a continuous intellectual tradition from Elizabethan poetics to the dramatic theory and practice of the eighteenth century German Renaissance' (p. 19). Excessive claims for the source value of German drama tend unnecessarily to undermine fully justifiable claims for its more local importance. The relationship between German and European drama is (to borrow a phrase Kolve uses in another context) 'one not of parentage but of cousinship' (Kolve, op. cit., p. 2). Bennett makes the case for that more local importance intelligently and comprehensively, and he reminds us that 'if the relationship between stage and auditorium does not have a necessary function in expressing the work's meaning, then it is hard to see how the form of drama is aesthetically justified' (p. 149). He is also right to stress that when, in the process of interpreting a particular play, 'we speak of the "situation in the theater", we are referring not to any real theater or

audience but rather to the situation implied and (ideally) generated by the text' (p. 150). Benjamin Bennett, *Modern Drama and German Classicism: Renaissance from Lessing to Brecht*, Ithaca, NY, 1979.

4. Artaud, op. cit., p. 13.

5. Thornton Wilder, 'Some thoughts on playwriting', in Gallup, Donald (ed.), *American Characteristics and Other Essays*, New York, 1979, p. 123.

6. Bertolt Brecht, *Brecht on Theatre*, trans. John Willett, New York, 1964, p. 122.

7. Eugène Ionesco, *Notes and Counter Notes*, trans. Donald Watson, New York, 1964, p. 80.

8. ibid., p. 102.

9. Peter Handke, 'Introduction to *Kaspar*', '*Kaspar*' and Other Plays, trans. Michael Roloff, New York, 1975, p. 60.

10. Luigi Pirandello, *Six Characters in Search of an Author*, in *Naked Masks: Five Plays*, ed. Eric Bentley, New York, 1952, p. 247. See also Pirandello's comment on this creation, pp. 372–3.

11. Jean Genet, *The Balcony*, trans. Bernard Frechtman, New York, 1966, p. 96.

12. As we will see later, metatheatrical features have important relationships with and are not just opposed to the mimetic features of modern drama. June Schlueter, who wishes to focus on the interplay between reality and illusion, nevertheless thinks it valuable to distinguish two traditions in the drama, the realistic tradition and 'the other tradition' of metatheatre (June Schlueter, *Metafictional Characters in Modern Drama*, New York, 1979, p. 2). Metaplays, for Abel, on the other hand, 'belong to a special genre', not uniquely modern, but the dominant genre of the last 300 years (Lionel Abel, *Metatheatre: A New View of Dramatic Form*, New York, 1963, p. 59). The notion of a distinctive metatheatrical genre or tradition has to come to terms with the point acknowledged by Schlueter and rendered emphatically by Ruby Cohn: 'Almost as soon as there was a theatre, the world was compared to a stage, and its inhabitants to role-players' (Ruby Cohn, *Currents in Contemporary Drama*, Bloomington, 1969, p. 198). The analogy is not new, and formal manifestations of the theatricality of the theatre have a long history (see Righter, op. cit., and Calderwood, op. cit.). What is important is not to bracket these features in a special genre, nor to consign them to an independent tradition, but to establish the functions they serve in different plays in different periods, and to see in the modern period whether any change in their function can account for what Schlueter calls 'the great outpouring' (p. 4) of works exhibiting such features in that period. This is not then a matter of isolating them for idiosyncratic attention, but of scrutinizing their interaction with other traditional and novel features of the drama in the modern period.

13. Craig approvingly attributes this notion to Eleanora Duse: Edward Gordon Craig, *On the Art of the Theatre*, Chicago, 1912, p. 79. Elsewhere, however, he spelled out more clearly his interests in both continuity and change in the theatre: 'Never copy the old but *never forget the old* – for there is always some good to be found in it' (quoted in Edward Anthony Craig, *Gordon Craig: The Story of His Life*, New York, 1968, p. 289). The younger Craig also points out that his father considered it 'essential to establish a library and a museum in which would be preserved everything that they could find relating to the theatre's past history' (p. 289).

14. Adolphe Appia, as quoted in James Roose-Evans, *Experimental Theatre: From Stanislavsky to Today*, New York, 1973, p. 69.

15. Styan's observations on the Haymarket Theatre are very much to the point:

> In 1880 Squire Bancroft advertised his renovated Haymarket Theatre with this description: 'A rich and elaborate gold border, about 2 ft. broad, after the pattern of a picture-frame, is continued all round the proscenium, and carried even below the actor's feet – there can be no doubt the sense of illusion is increased'. . . . As the apron receded behind the proscenium arch, the actor retreated into the picture-frame. The house-lights gradually went out with the advent of gaslight after 1849 and the spectator was shut off from the actor by a curtain of darkness (Styan, op. cit., p. 170).

16. It is curious to read Styan's interpretation of this flexibility as an indication of artistic uncertainty. In an otherwise impressive study of the relationship between plays, periods and theatres, Styan cites the varied structures of modern theatres as proof that the modern theatre 'is everywhere in search of its physically appropriate mode'. He thus concludes that 'the decision of the British National Theatre to have two [sic] stages, one a picture-frame and the other an open stage, suggests that the final choice is not yet made'. There are, of course, three auditoriums in the National Theatre, but Styan would presumably regard this as further proof of modern uncertainty. It is surely not uncertainty that is at issue here, but a demand for flexibility, for the opportunity to make the most of whatever theatre architecture can make possible. In a period of exploration, the search is not directed necessarily towards eliminating alternatives, but towards locating them and exploiting them. This is not a manifestation of uncertainty but of pluralistic interests and goals. Though I disagree with some aspects of Styan's interpretation of the modern theatre, his book contains a wealth of valuable information and opinion on the relationships between plays and their performance arenas. And his estimate of the significance of that link seems to me entirely right:

> Playing in a frame or in a circle affects the whole discipline of the actor and the choice of play he makes; but the decision will radically determine the kind of experience that audiences expect of their theatre-going, and therefore the skills of the playwright, the role of the manager, the function of the theatre in society and the whole future of the drama.

If we can but agree that the future is not single, and that it is unlikely to be any more homogeneous than the past, then Styan's comment seems very persuasive (ibid., p. 138).

17. Peter Brook, reported by Hugh Hunt in Hugh Hunt, Kenneth Richards and John Russell Taylor, *The Revels History of Drama in English*, VII, London, 1978, p. 155.

18. Brecht, op. cit., p. 30.

19. Walter Sokel provides a brief summary of the impact of philosophy on the status of art as it evolves from classical times to the Romantic era. From Aristotle, Plato and Kant, he notes we derive 'three basic principles of artistic creation: mimesis, revelation, and free creation or autonomous art'. The notion of autonomous art he traces to Kant's *Critique of Judgement* (Walter H. Sokel, *The Writer in Extremis: Expressionism in Twentieth-Century German Literature*, Stanford, 1959, p. 13).

20. Nelson Goodman, *Ways of Worldmaking*, Indianapolis, 1978, p. 22.

21. Artaud, op. cit., p. 61.
22. When Sokel traces the evolution of expressionism and modernism from Kant's doctrine of autonomous art, he notes the extremes to which it can lead:

> In the pure abstraction of the modernist, as in the formless shriek of the naive Expressionist, lies the same basic indifference to the world in its twofold aspect as model and audience. As the naive Expressionist is unconcerned about his offenses to public taste and morals, the true modernist is equally callous as to whether or not the public can understand him.

He goes on to remind us that the non-naïve wing of the expressionist movement foundered because it was unable to reconcile its competing goals: (1) to reform social life by means of art, and (2) to reform art by setting it free from social constraints: 'Shortly after 1920 the two goals of Expressionism – attachment to an objective reality and free creation of surreality – appeared distinct and irreconcilable' (Sokel, op. cit., pp. 20 and 227).
23. F. H. Bradley, *Appearance and Reality*, New York, 1906, p. 346.
24. Ionesco, op. cit., p. 115.
25. ibid., p. 184.
26. Eugène Ionesco, *The Chairs*, in *Four Plays by Eugène Ionesco*, trans. Donald M. Allen, New York, 1958, p. 139.
27. Brecht, op. cit., p. 9.
28. ibid., p. 190.
29. Artaud, op. cit., p. 81.
30. ibid., pp. 82–3.
31. ibid., p. 86.
32. Throughout this discussion I avoid the term 'dialectic' because of its limited ideological implications, and because it would create what would be, in the context of this discussion, misleading assumptions that contrasting domains are: (a) opposites; (b) susceptible to synthesis; (c) interacting in the context of a teleological scheme. In a given case, any or all of these may apply, but also they may not. As we shall see in discussion of the work of William James, a pluralistic universe and a dialectical universe are by no means the same thing. Difficulties that arise from equating the two are evident from time to time in Bennett's otherwise impressive *Modern Drama and German Classicism*, and they render problematic some of his arguments for a direct line of development from German classicism to modern drama via Lessing, Goethe, Schiller, Hegel and Nietzsche. For Bennett, modern theatre is what German classical theatre was, 'essentially *a dialectical theater*', one which captures '*a dialectical sense of life*, a sense of existence as unrelieved flux and vertigo in which everything immediately implies its negation'. Bennett argues that

> the importance of a dialectical sense of life in the shaping of modern drama . . . has been demonstrated by critics who do not even mention Hegel. Guthke, for example, shows very clearly that an important segment of modern drama derives its form from the attempt not merely to combine the comic and the tragic but to synthesize these opposed forces in such a way that each implies the other. (pp. 231–3)

Though Bennett, seeing part of the problem with which the term 'dialectic' presents him, seeks to separate the word 'dialectic' from its implication of 'linear or circular progress' (p. 234), the implications of oppositeness, synthesis and a teleological scheme come up repeatedly in his argument and are inseparable from any useful application of the term. If we allow the word 'dialectical' to become interchangeable with the word 'contrasting' we are likely to find ourselves seriously misled. Contrasting domains are not necessarily opposite, do not necessarily imply each other, are not necessarily susceptible to synthesis, and do not necessarily participate in any larger scheme with demonstrable origins and ascertainable ends. In a given case, of course, any of these factors may indeed apply.

33. Arthur Miller, *After the Fall*, New York, 1964, p. 2.

34. Genet, op. cit., p. 96.

35. See my article 'Creativity and commitment in Trevor Griffiths's *Comedians*', *Modern Drama*, 24, December 1981, pp. 404–23. Thomas R. Whitaker, in a thought-provoking book (*Fields of Play in Modern Drama*, Princeton, 1977), explores audience/stage interaction from another angle. Describing a play as 'a form of attentive playing', he argues that 'its full meaning must therefore include the fact of our participation in it' (p. 6).

36. Styan, op. cit., p. 150. Edward Braun provides a valuable survey of the major theatre directors of the modern era in *The Director and the Stage: From Naturalism to Grotowski*, London, 1982.

37. An innovation of another kind was the 'relief stage' of the 1908 Munich Artists' Theatre. The theatre used a shallow stage to enable actors and relevant stage properties to function in the same visual plane. Georg Fuchs outlines the concerns of the Munich Theatre's work in *Revolution in the Theatre: Conclusions Concerning the Munich Artists' Theatre*, trans. Constance Connor Kuhn, Ithaca, NY, 1959. See, in particular, his chapter on 'Stage and auditorium':

> The objective is not the painting with depth of perspective but the flat relief. By purely architectural means we created three planes: a forestage, or proscenium; a middle stage, which is usually used as the playing space; and an inner stage. (p. 89)

Fuchs, like others, notes the interdependence of experiments in the drama and experiments in the theatre:

> The Artists' Theatre plans to rebuild the stage from the ground up. It is not just a matter of the stage and what is on the stage. Instead, the entire problem of design as it touches the drama and the spectators should be considered, both on the stage and in the auditorium. The theatre is an organic whole. (p. 79)

38. Ruby Cohn, 'The fabulous theater of Edward Bond', in Bock, Hedwig and Wertheim, Albert (eds), *Essays on Contemporary British Drama*, Munich, 1981, p. 194. See also her comment:

> Lear's quest is strongly theatrical. He has to find his way through two walls – the first cruelly visible and the second a metaphor for well-wishers and sympathetic strangers. It is only when Lear can tear down the metaphoric wall that he acquires the resolution to assault the physical wall . . . the play begins and ends at the wall. (pp. 193–4)

39. Tennessee Williams, *The Two-Character Play*, in *The Theatre of Tennessee Williams*, V, New York, 1976, p. 365.
40. Richard N. Coe, *The Vision of Jean Genet: A Study of His Poems, Plays and Novels*, New York, 1968, pp. 213–14.
41. Maurice Valency, Introduction to *Jean Giraudoux: Four Plays*, New York, 1959, p. xiii.
42. ibid.
43. Ruby Cohn, *Currents in Contemporary Drama*, Bloomington, Ind., 1969, p. 154.
44. Luigi Pirandello, *Six Characters in Search of an Author*, in *The Nobel Prize Library: Perse, Pirandello, Pontoppidan, Quasimodo*, trans. Eric Bentley, New York, 1971, pp. 120 and 124. Pirandello remarks on the importance of '*lighting the two groups in contrasting colors*' (p. 122).
45. ibid., p. 124.

3 Reconciling worlds

1. Eugène Ionesco, *Notes and Counter Notes*, trans. Donald Watson, New York, 1964, p. 80.
2. ibid., p. 17.
3. Luigi Pirandello, *On Humor*, ed. and trans. Antonio Illiano and Daniel P. Testa, Chapel Hill, NC, 1974; see particularly Part I, Chapter V, and Part II, Chapter V.
4. Antonin Artaud, *The Theater and Its Double*, trans. Mary Caroline Richards, New York, 1958, p. 39.
5. ibid., p. 41.
6. ibid., p. 72.
7. ibid., p. 111.
8. Peter Handke, 'Introduction to *Kaspar*', in '*Kaspar*' *and Other Plays*, trans. Michael Roloff, New York, 1975, p. 60. Compare Edward Bond, *The Pope's Wedding*, London, 1971, p. 9: the opening stage direction advises us that 'The objects are very real, but there must be no attempt to create the illusion of a "real scene".'
9. This contamination can, of course, be regarded as distracting conflict, and can give rise to attempts to change the actor into a fully theatrical phenomenon by converting him into a puppet or a marionette. See Driver's discussion of this issue in the context of theatrical space: 'A Craig in some of his pronunciamentos or a Meierhold in his Moscow theater might all too literally turn the actor back into an acrobat or a marionette' (Tom F. Driver, *Romantic Quest and Modern Query: A History of the Modern Theater*, New York, 1970, p. 92).
10. Jean-Paul Sartre, *No Exit*, in '*No Exit*' *and Other Plays*, New York, 1955, p. 47.
11. Jean Genet, *The Balcony*, New York, 1966, p. 89.
12. ibid., p. 32.
13. ibid., p. 35.
14. ibid., p. 65.
15. ibid., p. 70.
16. ibid., p. 57.
17. Nelson Goodman, *Ways of Worldmaking*, Indianapolis, 1978, p. 2. See also Goodman's comment: 'The monist can always contend that two versions need only

be right to be accounted versions of the same world. The pluralist can always reply by asking what the world is like apart from all versions' (p. 96).

18. William James, *A Pluralistic Universe*, New York, 1909, p. 321. In seeking to characterize the separateness and relatedness of given and created worlds, Dürrenmatt provides an example of this alternating sense of multiple and single worlds:

> A writer's work does not mean copying the world, but creating it anew, setting up new worlds of his own that in themselves give a picture of the world, because their building materials are taken from present times. . . . A logical particular world cannot depart from our world at all. (Friedrich Dürrenmatt, quoted and translated by Timo Tiusanen, *Dürrenmatt: A Study in Plays, Prose, Theory*, Princeton, 1977, p. 216)

19. James, *A Pluralistic Universe*, pp. 321–4.
20. William James, *The Principles of Psychology*, II, New York, 1950, pp. 291–3.
21. ibid., p. 291.
22. Alfred Jarry, *Ubu Roi*, trans. Cyril Connolly and Simon Watson Taylor, in *The Ubu Plays*, ed. Simon Watson Taylor, New York, 1969, p. 21.
23. Richard Gilman, *The Making of Modern Drama*, New York, 1974, p. 69.
24. George Bernard Shaw, 'A talk with Mr. Bernard Shaw about his new play', *Pall Mall Budget*, 19 April 1894, reprinted in *Arms and the Man*, ed. Louis Crompton, New York, 1969, p. 80. Shaw, who is noted more for the conviction than for the consistency with which he presents his views, also argues the case for rejecting verisimilitude; see *Our Theatres in the Nineties*, I, London, 1932, pp. 91–2. See also Kennedy's comment on Shaw's similarly ambivalent approach to language:

> It is really the case that Shaw was, simultaneously, drawn to verisimilitude and driven to all the known forms of eloquence in dialogue by a contrary impulse. The linguistic gap that separates 'the natural that is mainly the everyday' and 'the free use of all the rhetorical and lyrical arts' fairly epitomises the duality found in all the plays. That is why one finds a hesitancy under the seemingly robust critical statements; and we are enabled, as if reading a code, to see how, whenever Shaw makes the attempt to come near to everyday speech, the dialogue is soon transposed into quite another key. (Andrew K. Kennedy, *Six Dramatists in Search of a Language*, London, 1975, pp. 56–7)

25. John Harold Wilson (ed.), *Six Restoration Plays*, Boston, Mass., 1959, p. xii.
26. Terry Eagleton, *Marxism and Literary Criticism*, London and Berkeley, 1976, p. 49.
27. Earl Miner, 'On the genesis and development of literary systems', *Critical Inquiry*, 5, Winter 1978, p. 349.
28. 'The aim of the poet is either to benefit, or to amuse, or to make his words at once please and give lessons of life' (Horace, 'Art of poetry', in Adams, Hazard (ed.), *Critical Theory Since Plato*, New York, 1971, p. 73).
29. Having distinguished western poetics, based originally on the drama, from Asian poetics, based originally on the lyric, Miner goes on to outline the long-term consequences of a system of poetics for a society's treatment of other genres: 'In spite of the encounter with drama after a great narrative achievement, Indian poetics produced an essentially lyric system, one affective and expressive' whereas, in

western poetics, 'the preexistent mimetic tradition, had by Horace perhaps third-hand from Aristotle and from other sources, precluded a full affective component in the system' (Miner, op. cit., p. 352). (After contrasting a drama-based poetics with a lyric-based poetics, Miner confesses his puzzlement at the apparent 'absence of a critical system defined from narrative' (p. 35ɔ).)

30. René Girard, 'To Double Business Bound': Essays on Literature, Mimesis, and Anthropology, Baltimore, Md, 1978, p. viii. It is the multiplicity of mimetic possibilities that enables us to make sense of the fact that though Plato and Aristotle conceived of art as imitative, reliable critics can nevertheless argue that, from the perspective of the present, classical drama was non-illusory, non-realistic, and non-mimetic. We can recognize that such either/or choices are not appropriate here and that the issue is one involving kinds of illusion, kinds of realism, and kinds of mimesis. Likewise, when Esslin suggests that 'from the vantage point of today, it is the brief episode of photographic realism in the theatre that stands out as a deviation from the mainstream of the development of drama' (Martin Esslin, Reflections: Essays on Modern Theatre, New York, 1969, p. 190), we can see that it is neither a brief episode nor a deviation; it is one of many variations on an ongoing theme of mimesis that offers many kinds of grounds for many kinds of imitation. Photographic realism, verisimilitude, imitation, holding a mirror up to nature, instructing, entertaining and so forth are lingering components of a long tradition; but it is as important to note that they linger as to note that forces are at work to revise or overthrow them.

31. Mihai Spariosu, 'Editor's introduction', Mimesis in Contemporary Theory: An Interdisciplinary Approach, Philadelphia (forthcoming).

32. Styan seeks to contrast the anti-illusory theatre of the present with the non-illusory theatre of the past (J. L. Styan, Drama, Stage and Audience, London, 1975, p. 183). Valency suggests that some of the excesses and obscurities of the modern theatre follow upon 'the breaking of the chain of imitation' (Maurice Valency, The Flower and the Castle: An Introduction to Modern Drama, New York, 1975, p. 11).

33. Eugène Ionesco, The Bald Soprano, in Four Plays by Eugène Ionesco, trans. Donald M. Allen, New York, 1958, p. 7. (In some translations this play is given the title The Bald Prima Donna.)

34. Eugène Ionesco, in Conversations with Eugène Ionesco, trans. Jan Dawson, ed. Claude Bonnefoy, London, 1970, pp. 141–9. There is, of course, no reason to believe that earlier kinds of theatre were limited to what critical assumptions of those periods could encompass. The epistemological challenges of the modern theatre serve to extend our awareness of possibilities we might otherwise overlook in earlier theatre.

35. ibid., p. 145.

36. Jerzy Grotowski, Towards a Poor Theatre, New York, 1968, p. 130.

37. Trevor Griffiths, 'Author's preface', 'Through the Night' and 'Such Impossibilities', London, 1977, p. 12.

38. William James, A Pluralistic Universe, p. 321.

39. Goodman, op. cit., p. 20.

40. Wolfgang Iser, The Act of Reading: A Theory of Aesthetic Response, Baltimore, Md, 1978, p. 73. In this book, Iser offers a fascinating discussion of the functions of literature in general in our psychological and social lives, and he extensively explores its norm-challenging and norm-creating roles.

41. It is important to note here that it would be less than adequate to try to distinguish modern theatre from earlier theatres on the basis of simple contrasts between inquiry and instruction or between the mimetic and the anti-mimetic. Modern theatre is strongly characterized by a particular kind of inquiry, as I have outlined above, but this should be recognized as a change in priority among, and use of, related options at a particular point in theatre history. Innovation is often a matter of renovation, and the novelties of the present can, of course, serve to remind us of forgotten or overlooked characteristics of the past. The important contrasts between differing theatre periods would vary from case to case, but the appropriate distinctions would often be between one kind of inquiry and another, between one kind of instruction and another, between one kind of entertainment and another, and between one kind of mimesis and another. Contrasts between periods are, however, rarely simple, and the various theatres of the past were usually more complex than critical assumptions of the past might suggest. Experiments in the modern theatre should thus serve to extend our awareness of the possibilities of the theatre and send us back to the past with our interests renewed and our sensibilities sharpened.

42. Goodman, op. cit., p. 102.

43. John Hodgson, *The Uses of Drama: Acting as a Social and Educational Force*, London, 1972, p. 11.

4 Generalizing about worlds

1. In this respect, the views of T. S. Eliot on originality and conventionality remain as valuable as ever. He explains how original individual work helps reconstitute a prior tradition, warns against our 'tendency to insist, when we praise a poet, upon those aspects of his work in which he least resembles anyone else', and points out that 'it would not be desirable, even if it were possible, to live in a state of perpetual revolution. . . . There are times for exploration and times for the development of the territory acquired' (T. S. Eliot, 'Tradition and the individual talent' and 'The music of poetry', *T. S. Eliot: Selected Prose*, ed. John Hayward, Harmondsworth, 1965, pp. 22 and 60). If 'development' were regarded as another kind of exploration, the point would seem precisely right. It is certainly the case that many important writers produce one or two startlingly new works, but for most of them, most of the time, there is the equally important task of making new and illuminating use of inherited structures and/or structures that the individual writer may have invented earlier.

2. Eric Bentley, *The Theatre of Commitment*, New York, 1967, p. 224.

3. ibid.

4. Martin Esslin (ed.), *Absurd Drama*, Harmondsworth, 1974, p. 9. The problem for the Theatre of the Absurd seems particularly evident. If one of the goals of such plays is 'an integration between the subject matter and the form in which it is expressed' (Martin Esslin, *The Theatre of the Absurd*, New York, 1969, p. 7), then generalizations that draw attention to some parts of the plays at the expense of others must surely be counterproductive. Brustein, on the other hand, seeks intriguingly to make a virtue of necessity by arguing that, in retrospect, his Theatre of Revolt seems

to be unified more by what the playwrights commonly reject than by what they commonly share:

> In order to emphasize similarities rather than differences among the various playwrights, I have primarily examined the negative side of their revolt: inclined to disagree about what they are for, these playwrights are generally agreed about what they are against. My emphasis sounds like special pleading – but it is an emphasis very frequently made by the playwrights themselves. (Robert Brustein, *The Theatre of Revolt*, Boston, 1964, p. 415)

5. Ludwig Wittgenstein, *Philosophical Investigations*, trans. G. E. M. Anscombe, New York, 1969, pp. 31–2.

6. Eric Bentley sought to establish a similar point about literary categories several decades ago: 'The trouble with literary terms is that in proportion as they become impressive they become useless, in proportion as they become exact they become inapplicable' (Eric Bentley, *The Playwright as Thinker: A Study of Drama in Modern Times*, New York, 1946, p. 24).

7. Wittgenstein, op. cit., pp. 50–1. William James makes a related point:

> As the sciences have developed farther, the notion has gained ground that most, perhaps all, of our laws are only approximations. . . . Their great use is to summarize old facts and to lead to new ones . . . ideas (which themselves are but parts of our experience) become true just in so far as they help us get into satisfactory relation with other parts of our experience, to summarize them and get about among them by conceptual short-cuts instead of following the interminable succession of particular phenomena. Any idea upon which we can ride, so to speak; any idea that will carry us prosperously from any one part of our experience to any other part, linking things satisfactorily, working securely, simplifying, saving labor; is true for just so much, true in so far forth, true instrumentally. ('Pragmatism: A new name for some old ways of thinking', in *'Pragmatism' and 'The Meaning of Truth'*, Cambridge, Mass., 1978, pp. 33–4).

See also Nelson Goodman's comment: 'truth must be otherwise conceived than as correspondence with a ready-made world' (*Ways of Worldmaking*, Indianapolis, 1978, p. 94).

8. E. D. Hirsch Jr, *The Aims of Interpretation*, Chicago, 1976, p. 41. Though Szondi tends to overemphasize the negative side of modern variety and thus to alternate between nostalgia for a unified past and hopes for a reunified future, his discussion of the historical dimension of the theatre experience is always thought-provoking (Peter Szondi, *Theorie des Modernen Dramas*, Frankfurt am Main, 1966).

9. Bertolt Brecht, *Brecht on Theatre*, trans. John Willett, New York, 1964, p. 276. Michel Foucault has written extensively on similarity and difference, continuity and discontinuity in *The Archeology of Knowledge*, trans. A. M. Sheridan Smith, New York, 1972. The dilemmas of expressionism are also relevant here, for they register the dangers that emerge when an interest in difference is pursued at the expense of renewed continuity. As Sokel puts it: 'Both Existentialism and Expressionism are concerned with describing the ineffable. They seek to do justice to that which lies "beyond" or "beneath" conceptual understanding; both seek to define the "feel" of

experience which is by definition incommunicable.' Sokel links this goal to Kant pronouncing "the divorce not only between art and logical discourse, but also between art and empirical experience, from which logic abstracts its concepts' (Walter H. Sokel, *The Writer in Extremis: Expressionism in Twentieth-Century German Literature*, Stanford, 1959, p. 53 and p. 10). For many modern playwrights, the persisting task is to give difference its due without insisting on differences so radical that art becomes incomprehensible, unsharable, and consequently useless. For them, art and life, aesthetics and ethics, epistemology and pragmatics are initially distinguishable but not finally separate. For a helpful discussion of the relationship between aesthetic and instrumental theories of literature, see John M. Ellis, *The Theory of Literary Criticism: A Logical Analysis*, Berkeley, 1974, pp. 233–47.

10. Paul Ricoeur, *The Philosophy of Paul Ricoeur*, ed. Charles E. Reagan and David Stewart, Boston, 1978, p. 144. Note once more that this process of human development is not a dialectical activity of the kind envisaged by Hegel and developed by Nietzsche. We do not need to assent to the notion that 'human nature is based on an utterly unresolvable internal antithesis' or that 'man is . . . a dialectical entity whose very being is the tension between antitheses, and who thus always has yet to *become what he is*' (Benjamin Bennett, *Modern Drama and German Classicism*, Ithaca, NY, 1979, pp. 236–7). A pluralistic universe does not make the growth of knowledge dependent on a 'primal contradiction' in human nature; a pluralistic universe allows for change, but does not necessarily require it for some programme for social or individual fulfilment: change may occur or it may not, and the results in either case may make us more or less happy, more or less fulfilled.

11. Goodman, op. cit., p. 20.

12. Wolfgang Iser argues that the point of 'realism' is, in fact, not just to copy reality but to teach us new modes of vision. He is thus quick to recognize and explore the larger implications of Shaw's line in *Major Barbara*: 'You have learnt something. That always feels at first as if you had lost something.' Iser's excellent work on the role of the reader in the literary event has supplied invaluable perspectives to modern poetics. See Wolfgang Iser, *The Implied Reader*, Baltimore, Md, 1974, and *The Act of Reading*, Baltimore, Md, 1978.

13. Modern movements in literary theory have registered the difficulties involved in linking similarity with difference, continuity with discontinuity. Structuralism, in spite of an initial concern for difference, has tended, via its interest in wholeness and homologies, to give priority to features of similarity and continuity: post-structuralism has responded by giving priority to difference and discontinuity. In a pluralistic world, it is difficult, but indispensable, to give both sets of features their due. Otherwise, structuralist interpretations will remain incipiently reductive, and post-structuralist interpretations incipiently endless.

Mixtures of similarity and difference also pose problems for generic classification of texts, both modern and otherwise, and the relevant issues for genre theory have been illuminatingly explored by Ralph Cohen ('On the interrelations of eighteenth-century literary forms', in Harth, Phillip (ed.), *New Approaches to Eighteenth Century Literature*, New York, 1974, pp. 33–78) and by E. D. Hirsch Jr (*Validity in Interpretation*, New Haven, Conn., 1967, pp. 68–126).

5 Pinero: *The Second Mrs. Tanqueray*

1. Clayton Hamilton (ed.), *The Social Plays of Arthur Wing Pinero*, I, New York, 1917, p. 3. Hamilton has in mind Sheridan's *The School for Scandal* as the last play of any consequence in the English theatre. Note also Burns's claim in 1948:

> *The Second Mrs. Tanqueray* held a supreme place in the theatre for many years. It has been produced more times than any other modern English play and has been more widely translated. Paula Tanqueray – as an acting role – has attracted some of the greatest actresses of the modern stage. (Winifred Burns, 'Certain women characters of Pinero's serious drama', *Poet Lore*, 54, Autumn 1948, p. 218)

Nicoll's praise is slightly more qualified:

> Today, of course, we see the weaknesses of this drama more clearly than contemporaries saw them. . . . Yet, with all this recognition of its failings, none of us may deny the fact that in *The Second Mrs. Tanqueray* the English drama at the close of the nineteenth century first surely found itself. (Allardyce Nicoll, *A History of English Drama, 1660–1900*, V, Cambridge, 1959, p. 181).

But even in the 1940s Pinero's work in general was not wearing well, and Dunkel, writing a critical biography of Pinero, was forced to argue that 'his career is no less interesting because of the present eclipse of his reputation' (Wilbur D. Dunkel, *Sir Arthur Pinero: A Critical Biography with Letters*, Chicago, 1941, p. 2).

2. Stephen S. Stanton (ed.), *'Camille' and Other Plays*, New York, 1957, p. x.

3. See John Russell Taylor, *The Rise and Fall of the Well-Made Play*, New York, 1967; Maurice Valency, *The Flower and the Castle: An Introduction to Modern Drama*, New York, 1975; Stanton, op. cit.

4. Valency, op. cit., pp. 66–7. Valency also reminds us of the well-known story of Sardou's training as a dramatist: 'He had schooled himself . . . in the method of Scribe by reading the first Act only of the master's plays in order to see how close he could come to working out Scribe's solution in the succeeding Acts' (pp. 77–8).

5. ibid., p. 67. In Stanton's version, the structure of the well-made play is more narrowly defined:

> True examples of such drama display seven structural features: 1) a plot based on a secret known to the audience but withheld from certain characters (who have long been engaged in a battle of wits) until its revelation (or the direct consequence thereof) in the climactic scene serves to unmask a fraudulent character and restore to good fortune the suffering hero, with whom the audience has been made to sympathize; 2) a pattern of increasingly intense action and suspense, prepared by exposition (this pattern assisted by contrived entrances and exits, letters, and other devices); 3) a series of ups and downs in the hero's fortunes, caused by his conflict with an adversary; 4) the counter-punch of peripeteia and *scène à faire*, marking, respectively, the lowest and the highest point in the hero's adventures, and brought about by the disclosure of secrets to the opposing side; 5) a central misunderstanding or *quiproquo*, made

obvious to the spectator but withheld from the participants; 6) a logical and credible dénouement; and 7) the reproduction of the overall action pattern in the individual acts. (op. cit., pp. xii–xiii)

6. ibid., p. xiii. See also Stanton's comment:

> The subject matter of English drama at mid-century could hardly have been more insipid, but Scribe's inexhaustible vitality and resourcefulness, more than any other single factor, at least restored the compact dramatic form that had distinguished the work of the best eighteenth-century playwrights. (p. xxxvi)

7. ibid., p. xiii.
8. Valency, op. cit., p. 67.
9. Taylor, op. cit., p. 16; Valency, op. cit., p. 66.
10. Taylor, op. cit., p. 17.
11. Stanton, op. cit., p. vii.
12. ibid., p. viii.
13. ibid., p. xi.
14. Taylor, op. cit., p. 163.
15. ibid., p. 48.
16. Stanton, op. cit., p. xv.
17. Valency, op. cit., pp. 92–3.
18. ibid., p. 92.
19. Taylor, op. cit., p. 139. See also Gilman's argument that the well-made play was 'pre-eminently a bourgeois mode in having been designed for the amusement and edification of an affluent, newly cultured class and in reflecting that class's values and self-estimation, its sense of the world' (Richard Gilman, *The Making of Modern Drama*, New York, 1974, p. 69).
20. Taylor argues that:

> The aesthetic conventions of the well-made play depended on the moral conventions of the society it was written about and for. All the drama arose from the conflicts which occurred when these social conventions were transgressed and the transgressor had in some way to be brought to book. If the dramatist accepted for a moment that the conventions were at best a polite fiction, at worst a monstrous imposition stifling all true social progress, and in either case that they were not as immutable as one of nature's laws, then he was cutting the ground from under his own feet. (op. cit., p. 85)

Taylor goes on to note that, as the work of Wilde, Shaw, and Maugham demonstrates, the well-made format is well-suited to light comedy if not to more serious drama (ibid., p. 91). But even more interesting is his later argument that, in the work of Rattigan, new possibilities for synthesizing old and new in drama emerge (ibid., p. 160), and that

> if the old-fashioned well-made drama is really dead and gone a brand new, 1960s sort is just round the corner: one which accepts the continuing validity of certain basic prerequisites in the sort of play-making advocated by Archer, *while radically modifying the way in which they are applied.* (ibid., pp. 162–3) (emphasis mine)

21. Arthur Wing Pinero, *The Second Mrs. Tanqueray*, Boston, 1894. All page references are to this edition.

22. For discussion of these general points, see Cecil W. Davies, 'Pinero: The drama of reputation', *English*, 14, Spring 1962, p. 15; Burns, op. cit., pp. 203 and 199; Walter Lazenby, *Arthur Wing Pinero*, New York, 1972, p. 124; Taylor, op. cit., pp. 64–5; Erika Meier, *Realism and Reality*, Bern, Switzerland, 1967, p. 69; Meisel summarizes and elaborates on Shaw's criticism of the play in Martin Meisel, *Shaw and the Nineteenth-Century Theater*, Princeton, NJ, 1963, pp. 79–80 and 153–7; Booth provides a useful survey of contemporary response to the play in Michael R. Booth (ed.), *English Plays of the Nineteenth Century*, II, Oxford, 1969, pp. 333–40; Shaw's critique of the play, particularly its process of exposition, is in George Bernard Shaw, *Our Theatres in the Nineties*, I, London, 1932, pp. 45–6.

23. Cecil F. Armstrong, among others, discusses the convention of the early and mid-Victorian happy ending and notes that 'it recurred after anything and every-thing' (*Shakespeare to Shaw: Studies in the Life's Work of Six Dramatists of the English Stage*, Freeport, NY, 1968, p. 228). Attempts to use the well-made format for more serious thematic exploration naturally put at risk the assured happy ending and made 'old-fashioned' those audience members who could not do without it.

24. It is important to note that when Aubrey's past catches up with him, it is not the conventional 'past' of a wayward sexual life, but the past of a virtuous, if not always successful, relationship with wife and daughter.

25. To the original audience, the St James's Theatre in which the play was performed offered a local emblem for the little world of St James's parish.

26. Hamilton Fyfe takes issue with the play on this point, suggesting that the coincidence is forced and that its consequences could have been avoided (*Sir Arthur Pinero's Plays and Players*, New York, 1930, p. 133).

27. See in particular, Taylor, op. cit., pp. 64–6. Donohue, who finally concludes that the play breaks no important new ground, notes with interest Pinero's novel combination in Paula of 'two conventional and previously mutually exclusive guises' for the fallen woman – those of 'the professional courtesan' and 'the domestic sinner' (Joseph Donohue, 'Character, genre, and ethos in nineteenth-century British drama', *Yearbook of English Studies*, 9, 1979, p. 96).

28. Meier, op. cit., p. 69.

29. Valency, op. cit., p. 79.

30. ibid., p. 79. Cecil W. Davies discusses the function of Pinero's *raisonneurs* in op. cit., p. 17.

31. Meier, op. cit., p. 69.

32. Paula sadly observes that 'the future is only the past again, entered through another gate' (p. 168). She is, of course, discussing her past and the ways in which its consequences seem inescapable. But we should note that her attempt to generalize the issue has larger consequences for the play's basic themes. The past reasserts itself perpetually because public social values are not open to change. Instead of being allowed to interact with and adjust to the demands of recalcitrant facts, established values are insulated from them by being temporarily suspended when serious-ly challenged. A prime example is the 'double standard' of sexual behaviour which suspends (sometimes indefinitely) for some men the rules applied to all women.

33. Lazenby is on the right track here when he claims that 'the tragedy grows out of

. . . three varieties of rightness and the complications of chance and circumstance' (op. cit., p. 128).

34. Note that Aubrey's relationship with his former wife recapitulates the pattern of other relationships. A staunch Roman Catholic, she judges him adversely when she fails 'to stir up in him some sympathetic religious belief' (p. 20) and puts their child in a convent to protect her. When she (the first Mrs Tanqueray) was dying, she forgave her husband his limitations and there was a reconciliation. But this was merely a suspending of the rules she lived by, because she continued to insist that the child complete her convent education. Thus, after his wife's death, when Aubrey 'attempted to gain his girl's confidence and affection he was too late; he found he was dealing with the spirit of the mother' (p. 21). The dead mother's values, temporarily suspended in his case, continue to flourish in the child Ellean. Ironically, it is this very child who, at the end of the play, has advanced only as far as Drummle's (and her mother's) limited and limiting philosophy of forgiveness.

35. The technique of discrediting the *raisonneur* is not unique to Pinero's work. It occurs for example in Ibsen's and Shaw's plays and bears interesting resemblance to the novel's use of an unreliable narrator.

36. Meisel provides a valuable summary of the conventions of Courtesan and Magdalen plays upon which *The Second Mrs. Tanqueray* is clearly based. An interest in establishing the originality of Shaw's work leads him, however (as it led Shaw), to focus primarily on the conventionality of the work of other playwrights. In an otherwise impressive work, Meisel thus adopts, without exploring it further, Shaw's evaluation of Drummle, accepts Aubrey's condemnation of the 'double standard' as if it were the concluding speech of the play, and assumes that if Pinero is invoking the convention of the acceptable death of the tainted heroine, he must be following it rather than challenging it: 'one of the curiosities for our time of a nineteenth-century artistic sensibility is the complete acceptability of the perfectly gratuitous deaths of so many sympathetic heroines who had gone astray' (op. cit., pp. 75–80 and 141–59).

37. In a speech on 'The modern British drama' delivered to the Royal Academy in 1895, Pinero characterized thus the task of the contemporary dramatist: '[to give] back to the multitude their own thoughts and conceptions illuminated, enlarged, and, if needful, purged, perfected, transfigured . . . during recent years the temper of the times has been changing; it is now a period of analysis, of general, restless inquiry' (Arthur Wing Pinero, 'The modern British drama', *The Theatre*, June 1895, pp. 347–8).

6 Ibsen: *A Doll's House*

1. Michael Meyer, *Ibsen: A Biography*, New York, 1971, p. 454.

2. F. L. Lucas, *The Drama of Ibsen and Strindberg*, New York, 1962, p. 149. Note that reaction to the play was not as instantly widespread as it sometimes appears in retrospect. Meyer points out that although the play was published in Copenhagen in 1879, two years passed before it was performed outside Scandinavia and Germany, and ten years before a recognizably faithful version appeared in England or America; France did not see the play until 1894 (op. cit., p. 458).

3. Benedetto Croce, *European Literature in the Nineteenth Century*, trans. Douglas Ainslie, London, 1924, p. 341.

4. All page references are to A Doll's House in The Oxford Ibsen, V, trans. and ed. James W. McFarlane, London, 1961.

5. Rolf Fjelde, Ibsen: The Complete Major Prose Plays, New York, 1978, p. 121.

6. Einar Haugen, Ibsen's Drama: Author to Audience, Minneapolis, 1979, p. 103.

7. Meyer, op. cit., p. 426.

8. Northam and Meyer disagree on the direct role of Scribe's work in influencing Ibsen's, but influence is a somewhat dated issue (John Northam, 'Ibsen's search for the hero', Ibsen: A Collection of Critical Essays, ed. Rolf Fjelde, Englewood Cliffs, NJ, 1965, pp. 93–4; Meyer, op. cit., p. 117).

9. Haugen, op. cit., p. vii. Gilman, on the other hand, stresses the limiting conventionality of many of Ibsen's plots: 'their plots keep crowding out their perceptions' (Richard Gilman, The Making of Modern Drama, New York, 1974, p. 71).

10. John Northam, Ibsen's Dramatic Method: A Study of the Prose Dramas, London, 1953, p. 37.

11. George Bernard Shaw, The Quintessence of Ibsenism, New York, 1957, p. 175. It should not be overlooked that the so-called 'discussion' scene was already present in Ibsen's earlier play, Love's Comedy – a point Raymond Williams draws attention to in Drama from Ibsen to Eliot, Harmondsworth, 1964, p. 56.

12. ibid., pp. 76–8.

13. ibid., p. 78.

14. Hermann J. Weigand, The Modern Ibsen, New York, 1960, p. 68. See also F. L. Lucas, 'I do not think that [Ibsen] would have regarded Nora's ultimate return as improbable' (op. cit., p. 148).

15. Northam, Ibsen's Dramatic Method, pp. 16–31. Northam also offers us a comparative study of various drafts of the play on the grounds that 'if a great writer takes pains to make adjustments to an early draft of a play before he is content to let it go as a finished work of art, then the alterations will tend to be significant' (ibid., p. 31). It is difficult to understand why this notion persists in literary criticism. If something is in the final draft, it is significant no matter when it first appeared in the earlier drafts, and its significance is not changed in the slightest by the fact that it first occurred in an early or late draft. The item has only the significance the rest of the final draft bestows upon it. Arguments about the status of draft information can, as Northam in fact concedes, be mounted in favour of early draft material as easily as they can be made in favour of late draft material: e.g. 'it may be that certain ideas were so fundamental to the play that they found their place in the earliest jottings and were never displaced' (ibid., pp. 31–2). Northam, in spite of having thus undermined his own procedure, persists in it anyway on the flimsy grounds that dealing with a lot of draft changes makes up for the theoretical inadequacy of dealing with only one or two.

16. Discussing the image of the orphanage in Ghosts, Williams concludes that it is merely 'an illustrative analogy' whose 'quality rests solely on the quality of the experience to which it is related'. Only in Ibsen's final plays does Williams acknowledge something that Northam perceives intermittently in A Doll's House, the use of symbolic material to provide 'an external framework for examination of a pattern of experience' (Williams, op. cit., pp. 85 and 107).

17. Arthur Wing Pinero, The Second Mrs. Tanqueray, Boston, 1894, p. 1.

18. Note, in this respect, Ibsen's well-known attack on the excesses of naturalism:

'Zola goes down into the sewer to take a bath; I, in order to cleanse it.' Quoted in Halvdan Koht, *The Life of Ibsen*, trans. Ruth L. McMahon and Hanna R. Larsen, London, 1931, p. 173. The point is not quite fair to Zola, who believed it possible to write plays of everyday life with something approaching a certain grandeur of style.

19. Rolf Fjelde, Introduction to *Ibsen: A Collection of Critical Essays*, p. 5.

20. Northam, *Ibsen's Dramatic Method*, pp. 19–21.

21. Weigand, op. cit., p. 27. Evidence for this would include Nora's saving up of her 'secret' for the day when her wiles and charms might no longer entrance Torvald: 'When Torvald isn't quite so much in love with me as he is now, when he's lost interest in watching me dance, or get dressed up, or recite. Then it might be a good thing to have something in reserve' (p. 215). See also her attempt to use flesh-coloured silk stockings to captivate Dr Rank (p. 247). This aspect of Nora's behaviour would stand comparison with that of Blanche Dubois: 'I want to *deceive* him enough to make him want me' (Tennessee Williams, *A Streetcar Named Desire*, New York, 1972, p. 81).

22. *The Compact Edition of the Oxford English Dictionary*, II, New York, 1971, p. 3237.

23. Henrik Ibsen, speech to the Norwegian League for Women's Rights, 1898, in *Ibsen: Letters and Speeches*, ed. Evert Sprinchorn, New York, 1964, p. 337.

24. The more precise function of Rank in the play has, however, puzzled many, including Northam who also quotes Henning Kehler: 'Rank's illness only accounts for Rank's character, but it has no connection with the leading idea of the play', and William Archer: 'The entrance of Dr. Rank in the last act of *A Doll's House* is a wholly unnecessary interruption to the development of the crisis between Nora and Helmer' (Northam, *Ibsen's Dramatic Method*, pp. 29 and 31).

25. See Valency's extended discussion of this figure in Maurice Valency, *The Flower and the Castle*, New York, 1975, p. 79.

26. Such certainty is frequently satirized in the behaviour of Shaw's type-characters. See, for example, Stephen in *Major Barbara*: 'how can [people] differ about right and wrong? Right is right; and wrong is wrong; and if a man cannot distinguish them properly, he is either a fool or a rascal' (*Major Barbara*, in *Bernard Shaw's Plays*, ed. Warren S. Smith, New York, 1970, p. 6).

27. Brustein largely overlooks the degree to which Ibsen dramatizes the necessity for, as well as the dangers of, inherited views. But his generalization about Ibsen plays, which seems less applicable elsewhere, is largely on the right track as far as one aspect of *A Doll's House* is concerned:

> Ibsen has no illusions about the permanence of truth; for him, all intellectual postulates, no matter how persuasive, are invariably reduced to lifeless conventions in time. For Ibsen, therefore, the ultimate Truth lies only in the perpetual conflict of truths, and even the rebel must be careful not to institutionalize his revolt.

Had Brustein managed to discover the subtlety with which the interaction between institutional truth and individual truth is dramatized in this play, he might have qualified his generalization and have refrained from dismissing the play as an 'experimental bungle' (Robert Brustein, *The Theater of Revolt*, Boston, 1964, pp. 48 and 67).

28. Many have been puzzled by Ibsen's evident reliance upon many of the conventions of the well-made play, in spite of his frequent public attacks on it: e.g. 'Ibsen's attitude towards the well-made play, like all his attitudes, is ambiguous. He used the French techniques – and he also despised them' (ibid., p. 67). Brustein, in his concern to make Ibsen into a committed rebel ('the real quintessence of Ibsenism is total resistance to whatever is established' (ibid., p. 48)), has overlooked the possibility of Ibsen's using well-made-play techniques both for their strengths *and* for their limitations. Certainly Ibsen, early in his career, was ready to reject the one with the other. As Williams puts it, 'Ibsen, writing in 1851 in the periodical *Andhrimner (Manden)*, had severely criticized Scribe's dramatic methods, finding in the whole tendency of French drama too great a reliance on "situation", at the expense of "psychology"' (Williams, op. cit., p. 53). Later in his career, Ibsen was to find ways of fusing the well-made play's strength in manipulating 'situation', with the interpretative analogies' strength in the sphere of exploring psychology. He was then able to make use of both to dramatize the breadth and the narrowness of his characters' intellectual and emotional horizons.

7 Strindberg: *A Dream Play*

1. August Strindberg, *A Dream Play*, in '*A Dream Play*' and *Four Chamber Plays*, trans. Walter Johnson, Seattle, Wash., 1973. All page references are to this edition.
2. J. L. Styan, *The Dark Comedy: The Development of Modern Comic Tragedy*, New York, 1968, p. 68.
3. It is often pointed out that the Prologue was added more than four years after the rest of the play was completed. Though Dahlström and others urge us not to forget this point, it is difficult to assign any persuasive significance to it. (See Carl Dahlström, *Strindberg's Dramatic Expressionism*, New York, 1965, p. 176.) Some plays and some parts of plays are written more quickly than others; some plays are extensively revised, some are not. In every case it is the completed work with which we must deal.
4. See, for example, Martin Lamm, *August Strindberg*, ed. and trans. Harry G. Carlson, New York, 1971, p. 398; John Ward, *The Social and Religious Plays of Strindberg*, London, 1980, pp. 214 and 226; Walter Johnson, '*A Dream Play*: Plans and fulfillment', *Scandinavica*, 10, November 1971, p. 108; Alice N. Benston, 'From naturalism to the Dream Play: A study of the evolution of Strindberg's unique theatrical form', *Modern Drama*, 7, February 1965, p. 394.
5. ibid., p. 382.
6. As Valency puts it: 'Four trends . . . have principally affected the course of modern drama: naturalism, impressionism, symbolism, expressionism. These words are not only embarrassingly imprecise, but, beyond a certain point, their associations are meaningless' (Maurice Valency, *The Flower and the Castle: An Introduction to Modern Drama*, New York, 1975, p. 363). Terms as imprecise as these can, if relied on for distinctive classification, confuse the very issues they are intended to clarify; they consequently tend to become not just the instruments of study, but also the objects of study. See, for example, Styan's recent three-volume work: *Modern Drama in Theory and Practice*, New York, 1981.
7. Madsen offers a useful survey of Zola's naturalism, of Strindberg's interest in it,

and of some of the internal pressures that are characteristic of the movement. His summary of Zola's ideas is as follows:

> In his theoretical writings Zola established the following principles for the naturalistic novel and drama: The naturalistic novelist and playwright must observe reality closely and render it in a carefully documented way. In his portrayal of character the naturalist, using a scientific approach, should point out how character is determined by the forces of heredity and environment – to make his characterization scientifically valid, he should utilize the results of physiological and psychological research. In the naturalistic drama a realistically rendered décor should have the same determining function as the realistically depicted milieu in the novel. In the naturalistic drama, furthermore, Zola called for extreme simplicity and concentration of structure, attacking the lengthy expositions and involved intrigues of the romantic drama and the well-made play. He recommended that naturalistic playwrights model themselves, in some respects, on the classical French drama by adopting its psychological portrayal of character, its simplicity of structure, and 'grand' conflicts. Finally Zola insisted on naturalness of staging, acting, and diction. His definition of the so-called *nouvelle formule* for the naturalistic drama can be summarized in the three principles of *faire vrai*, *faire grand* and *faire simple*. (Børge Gedsø Madsen, *Strindberg's Naturalistic Theatre: Its Relation to French Naturalism*, Seattle, 1962, pp. 13–14)

8. Valency, op. cit., p. 104.
9. Martin Esslin, *Reflections: Essays on Modern Theatre*, New York, 1969, pp. 13–14.
10. Émile Zola, Preface to *Thérèse Raquin* (1873), quoted in Esslin, op. cit., p. 13. Esslin also quotes Otto Brahm, a critic, director and enthusiastic advocate of German naturalist drama: 'We swear by no formula and would not dare to chain into the rigid compulsion of rules that which is in eternal flux – life and art' (ibid., p. 16).
11. ibid., pp. 25–6.
12. Émile Zola, 'Naturalism in the theatre', trans. Albert Bermel, in Eric Bentley (ed.), *The Theory of the Modern Stage*, Harmondsworth, 1976, p. 359. (Bermel's text consists of essays Zola wrote 1875–80.) This inconsistency on Zola's part can be attributed, in part, to a widely held naturalist belief that, though no truths hold for all time, some truths are fundamental to particular eras. Characters determined by heredity and environment are implicitly determined by their era. The question that then arises is whether an era, upon careful consideration, might best be thought of as a moment or as a millennium. The value of formulae will fluctuate with the scale.
13. Zola, 'Naturalism in the theatre', p. 369.
14. August Strindberg, 'Author's Foreword to *Miss Julie*', in *Six Plays of Strindberg*, trans. Elizabeth Sprigge, New York, 1955, pp. 71–2.
15. ibid., p. 71.
16. August Strindberg, 'On modern drama and modern theatre' (1889), in Toby Cole (ed.), *Playwrights on Playwrighting*, New York, 1961, p. 17. Gilman points out that

> almost as soon as Strindberg had been identified as one of the leaders of naturalism he hastened to call himself a *nyanaturalist*, a 'new' one. . . . Strindberg's plays . . . of this period resembled those of the movement's

acknowledged leaders . . . but the differences were more important. (Richard Gilman, *The Making of Modern Drama*, New York, 1974, pp. 90–1)

The differences, I would suggest, indicate Strindberg's ability to do with naturalism what he subsequently did with expressionism: push an evolving movement very quickly to the limits implicit in its conventions.

17. This recognition helps explain why arguments about modernism being a continuation of naturalism or a reaction against it seem always to be inconclusive. Modernism builds upon some aspects of naturalism and rejects others; naturalism participates in the same range of tensions that characterize the rest of modernism, and is best thought of as an instance of modernism rather than as a rejected alternative.

18. Walter H. Sokel, *The Writer in Extremis: Expressionism in Twentieth-Century German Literature*, Stanford, 1959, p. 9.

19. ibid., pp. 9–10.

20. ibid., p. 38.

21. ibid., p. 20.

22. ibid., p. 21.

23. ibid., p. 162.

24. Sokel also points out that expressionism (like naturalism) can lay claim to a tradition:

> [Expressionism] is an extreme development of tendencies inherent in the Elizabethan and Baroque drama and especially of the Shakespearean form with its rapid changes of scene and narrative-historical rather than analytic structure. In some respects the 'dream play' represents the culmination of the theatrical tradition descended from the miracle and Passion plays, Baroque drama and Baroque opera, *Faust*, *Peer Gynt*, Romanticism, and the Wagnerian *Gesamtkunstwerk*. Strindberg's conception of and preface to his *Dream Play*, in which he compares the whole world to a dream of the divine dreamer, suggest echoes of Calderón, the whole Spanish Baroque, Grillparzer, and, above all, the dramas of Shakespeare's late or 'Baroque' period, *The Tempest* and *King Lear*. 'We are such stuff as dreams are made [on]' is not very far from the assumptions of the dream play, and the heath scenes in the third act of *King Lear*, in which nature becomes a dynamic projection of a raving mind, are very close to Expressionism. (ibid., p. 39)

25. Madsen makes a case for the continuity of Strindberg's experimentation in op. cit., p. 158.

26. Zola, 'Naturalism in the theatre', p. 369.

27. Though others' do not, Johnson's translation of the play prominently indicates its three distinct sections. His introduction also provides a chart listing the play's fifteen scenes and the points at which the divisions occur (pp. 4–5).

28. For relevant discussion, see Raymond Jarvi, 'Ett drömspel: A symphony for the stage', *Scandinavian Studies*, 44, Winter 1972, pp. 28–42, and Evert Sprinchorn, 'The logic of A Dream Play', *Modern Drama*, 5, December 1962, p. 354.

29. Meyer, in his introduction to the play, describes a 1974 production in which the Daughter was played by three different actresses. The play was directed by Michael Ockrent in Edinburgh. 'Ockrent employed the unusual device of having three

actresses play Agnes simultaneously on three different physical levels and in different characterizations, to suggest her various aspects. Cordelia Oliver in the *Guardian* described the performance as "gripping the imagination from the first moment when, one by one, on different levels like hallucinations, the intense faces of the women float, disembodied, in the blackness"' (*August Strindberg, The Plays*, II, ed., intr. and trans. Michael Meyer, London, 1975, p. 552).

30. Brandell draws attention to Strindberg's tendency 'to invest [past works] with new value by bringing them in line with his most recent efforts' (Gunnar Brandell, *Strindberg in Inferno*, trans. Barry Jacobs, Cambridge, Mass., 1974, p. 264). Strindberg's interpretation of his own work is regularly coloured by whichever new idea has become dominant in his mind. A striking example is his claim in a diary entry for 18 November 1901, that he has discovered a revelatory Buddhist meaning in his almost completed *A Dream Play*. 'Now the "Indian Religion" has given me the explanation of my dream play, and of the meaning of Indra's daughter, the secret of the Door=Nothingness – All day I read about Buddhism' (quoted in Gunnar Ollén, *August Strindberg*, trans. Peter Tirner, New York, 1972, pp. 89–90). Steene argues that 'Strindberg's chance reading in Indian philosophy brought about a confirmation of ideas he had already dramatized in the play rather than a new revelation' (Birgitta Steene, *The Greatest Fire: A Study of August Strindberg*, Carbondale and Edwardsville, 1973, p. 98). Sprinchorn notes the play's local references to Indian philosophy but concludes that 'Buddha has little to do with the rest of the play' (op. cit., p. 355).

31. Paulson's decision to vary the phrase in translation suggests a misplaced concern for the needs of actresses at the expense of the needs of the play:

> The phrase 'Mankind is to be pitied' can . . . easily become laughable in the mouths of unseasoned or uninspired actors [sic] because of its frequent repetition in the play. For that reason I have thought it important to vary it somewhat in translating the play. (Arvid Paulson (ed. and trans.), *Eight Expressionist Plays (Strindberg)*, New York, 1972, p. 340)

32. Strindberg, 'Author's Foreword to *Miss Julie*', p. 64.

33. Johnson develops this point at some length in his Introduction to the play (pp. 11–12).

34. The unchanging nature of this world and the steady state of its events are both fully in accord with the tenets of naturalism. As Valency points out: 'the naturalist plays of the Théâtre Libre . . . had no reversals of fortune, because in life there is no escape from oneself, and their principle of progression was simply a gradual intensification of what was clear from the start' (op. cit., p. 112).

35. Raymond Williams, *Drama from Ibsen to Eliot*, Harmondsworth, 1964, p. 136.

36. Lamm offers a warning on this point: 'To conclude [from the play's prefatory note] that the play depicts the dreams of one individual, and that one character can be singled out as the dreamer would be a mistake' (op. cit., p. 392). Williams takes the issue further and argues that 'the unifying consciousness of the dreamer is not so much the substance of the play as its machinery' (op. cit., p. 135). And Valency suggests that the play has 'the enigmatic character of a work of art, and not at all the enigmatic character of a dream' (op. cit., p. 327).

37. Quoted in Ollén, op. cit., p. 90. Strindberg's accompanying claim that a Buddhist revelation is available in the play is less helpful than his indication of which features of the play stand most in need of explanation.

38. Rolf Fjelde, Introduction to *Ibsen: A Collection of Critical Essays*, ed. Rolf Fjelde, Englewood Cliffs, NJ, 1965, p. 5.

8 Brecht: *Life of Galileo*

1. All page references are to the *Life of Galileo* in *Bertolt Brecht: Collected Plays*, V, trans. Wolfgang Sauerlander and Ralph Manheim, ed. Ralph Manheim and John Willett, New York, 1972. This text also provides an interesting comparison of the three major versions of the text, which Brecht revised extensively over a period of almost twenty years (see pp. 265–305). The three major versions are the first version of 1938–43, the American (Laughton) version of 1944–7, and the Berlin version of 1953–6. The text used in the Manheim and Willett edition is a translation of the Berlin version of 1953–6.

2. More accurately, his confirmation and elaboration of those of Copernicus.

3.   Werfel's attack on Wagner revealed the fundamental contradiction lurking in German Expressionism from its beginning. German Expressionism sought to be two things in one: a revolution of poetic form and vision, and a reformation of human life. . . . Shortly after 1920 the two goals of Expressionism – free creation of a surreality and attachment to an objective reality – appeared distinct and irreconcilable. The aesthetic and ethical wings of Expressionism divorced and this divorce spelled the end of the movement. (Walter H. Sokel, *The Writer in Extremis: Expressionism in Twentieth-Century German Literature*, Stanford, 1959, p. 227)

(Note that I have slightly altered the word order in this abbreviated quotation to keep the aesthetic and ethical references in parallel.)

4. The similarities and differences between Brecht's work and that of German expressionists set up the by now familiar problem of classification: do we focus on similarity at the expense of difference or vice versa? Do we view Brecht as an expressionist or not? The dilemma is evident in Gilman's comment:

> Brecht, by common agreement the greatest of the German expressionist writers, was not one. Sharing in its ambience, particularly its violent repudiation of what it considered bourgeois spirit and mentality, and participating in some of its procedures, its architectural looseness and general movement away from naturalism, he was nevertheless temperamentally and in his artistic aims at an opposite pole from most of expressionism's practitioners. . . . Brecht was never interested in the 'soul', even as a concept, or in the self apart from its situation among others. (Richard Gilman, *The Making of Modern Drama*, New York, 1974, p. 195)

5. Gray's comment on this term is worthy of note:

> The word 'epic' here, translating the German 'episch', is unfortunate. 'Episch' has, in this context, none of the associations with heroism and greatness that 'epic' often has, as in 'an epic tale'; it is merely a literary category, and in German this category includes not only narrative poetry, but also novels, and is often used to distinguish these from the lyric and the drama. In speaking of an

'epic' theatre, Brecht meant to imply a theatre which would not be exciting, 'dramatic', full of tensions and conflicts, but slower-paced, reflective, giving time to reflect and compare. (Ronald D. Gray, *Brecht the Dramatist*, Cambridge, 1976, pp. 71–2)

6. Szczesny argues that Brecht's aim is 'the replacement of the societal enforcement of the individual's social role under capitalism by the societal enforcement of the individual's social role under communism' (Gerhard Szczesny, *The Case Against Bertolt Brecht, with Arguments Drawn from his 'Life of Galileo'*, trans. Alexander Gode, New York, 1969, p. 4).

7. Lüthy suggests that Brecht has never 'been able to indicate by even the simplest poetic image or symbol what the world for which he is agitating should really look like' (Herbert Lüthy, quoted in Gilman, op. cit., p. 192).

8. Bertolt Brecht, 'In praise of doubt', *Poems 1913–1956*, ed. and trans. John Willett and Ralph Manheim, London, 1976, pp. 333–6. Elsewhere in the poem, Brecht compares 'the thoughtless who never doubt' and 'the thoughtful who never act' (p. 335).

9. Ronald D. Gray, *Bertolt Brecht*, New York, 1961, p. 73.

10. Müller describes Korsch as 'the only person to whom Brecht consistently conceded the honorable title of teacher' (Klaus-Detlef Müller, 'Me-Ti', in Weber, Betty Nance and Heinen, Hubert (eds), *Bertolt Brecht: Political Theory and Literary Practice*, Athens, Georgia, 1980, p. 44). On the relationship between Brecht and Korsch, see Douglas Kellner's essay in ibid., 'Brecht's Marxist aesthetic: The Korsch connection' (pp. 29–42), and Edward Berckman's essay 'The function of hope in Brecht's pre-revolutionary theater', in Fuegi, John (ed.), *Brecht Heute: Brecht Today*, Frankfurt am Main, 1971, pp. 11–26. See also Alfred D. White, *Bertolt Brecht's Great Plays*, London, 1978.

11. ibid., p. 17. Note that Dickson is able to quote both Marx and Engels as favouring, at times, an open-ended rather than a teleological approach to social progress: Keith A. Dickson, *Towards Utopia: A Study of Brecht*, Oxford, 1978, p. 8.

12. White, op. cit., p. 16. White also offers a useful summary of orthodox Hegelian and Marxist views:

> Marx's characteristic thought as relevant to us may be summarised (following his sketch in the Preface to *A Contribution to the Critique of Political Economy*) as involving the tenets (1) 'that legal relations as well as forms of state are to be grasped neither from themselves nor from the so-called general development of the human mind, but rather have their roots in the material conditions of life'; (2) that the economic structure of society is based on relations of production which men enter into with each other – relations corresponding to the stage of development of production and not dependent on men's free will; (3) that the economic structure of society is 'the real foundation, on which rises a legal and political superstructure and to which correspond definite forms of social consciousness'; (4) that material life conditions social, political and intellectual life – 'it is not the consciousness of men that determines their being, but, on the contrary, their social being that determines their consciousness'; (5) that material productive forces, as they develop, demand changes in the relations of production and property between men; (6) that these changes

come about in a social revolution, whereby the new material conditions, having developed within the existing society, change the economic foundation and consequently the whole superstructure; (7) that 'the bourgeois relations of production are the last antagonistic form of the social process of production; at the same time the productive forces developing in the womb of bourgeois society create the material conditions for the solution of that antagonism'.

This world-view is a materialist use of historical dialectics as developed by Hegel, for whom history is a flux of contradictions seen as analogous to philosophical concepts (theses). Theses are to Hegel not independent, but automatically engender their opposites (antitheses). From thesis and antithesis proceeds a synthesis, which combines them without really superseding them. In history, the universal synthesis is the self-realisation of the harmonious world spirit. Marx interprets the flux of contradictions as a succession of kinds of society which alienate man – that is, force people to sell their labour and renounce the values it creates, thus alienating them and inhibiting their free self-development as individuals. The synthesis he replaces by the concept of man's freeing himself from alienation by revolutionary practice which removes contradictions. (pp. 16–17)

13. Though I quote, where useful, from all of Brecht's writings, my own general comments about Brecht's plays are directed throughout to his major plays. Brecht's lesser work was frequently more diverse in structure and function.

14. Anthony Tatlow, 'Critical Dialectics', in Weber and Heinen, op. cit., p. 23.

15. ibid., pp. 23–6.

16. ibid., pp. 25 and 26.

17. Kellner, op. cit., p. 30.

18. Müller, op. cit., p. 47.

19. Bertolt Brecht, *Brecht on Theatre: The Development of an Aesthetic*, ed. and trans. John Willett, New York, 1964, p. 43. See also Brecht's comment:

The new alienations are only designed to free socially-conditioned phenomena from that stamp of familiarity which protects them against our grasp today. . . . For it seems impossible to alter what has long not been altered. We are always coming on things that are too obvious for us to bother to understand them . . . and who mistrusts what he is used to? (ibid., p. 192)

20. Stephen S. Stanton (ed.), *'Camille' and Other Plays*, New York, 1957, p. vii.

21. Brecht, *Brecht on Theatre*, p. 37.

22. ibid.

23. ibid., p. 39.

24. ibid., p. 85.

25. ibid., p. 183.

26. ibid., p. 45.

27. ibid., p. 201.

28. ibid., p. 203.

29. ibid.

30. ibid., p. 57.

31. ibid., p. 44.

32. ibid.

33. Bertolt Brecht, *The Messingkauf Dialogues*, trans. John Willett, London, 1965, p. 103.

34. There has been much critical debate about the place of emotion in Brecht's theatre. Initially opposing empathy and emotion in favour of cultivating an intellec-tual response, Brecht subsequently accepted that there was, of course, room for emotion and entertainment in the theatre. But the actor who displays and encour-ages emotion in the theatre can do so without inviting uncritical empathy: 'The alienation effect intervenes, not in the form of absence of emotion, but in the form of *emotions which need not correspond to those of the character portrayed*' (*Brecht on Theatre*, p. 94). The emotions shown must be shown to be shown so that an audience can both participate in and distance itself from the emotions of the characters, and thus consider them in the context of other concerns.

35. ibid., p. 122. See also Brecht's remark that the kind of theatre he envisages 'will have to acknowledge certain limits to imitation. It must be able to justify any outlay in terms of its purpose' (ibid., p. 123).

36. ibid., p. 60. Such division in the audience is one manifestation of Brecht's concern for method in preference to message. Note also his comment on Shaw's work:

> As for Shaw's own ideas, I cannot at the moment recollect a single one that could be called typical of him, though I know of course that he has a lot; but I could name a great deal that he has found to be typical of other people. *He himself may well think that his way of viewing things is necessarily more important than his actual views.* That says much for a man of his sort. (my emphasis) (ibid., pp. 12–13)

37. Note Brecht's comment that 'fate is no longer a single coherent power; rather there are fields of force which can be seen radiating in opposite directions' (ibid., p. 30).

38. Note also Brecht's expressed interest in 'Alienation effects in Chinese acting', and his comment that

> stylistically speaking, there is nothing all that new about the epic theatre. Its expository character and its emphasis on virtuosity bring it close to the old Asiatic theatre. Didactic tendencies are to be found in the medieval mystery plays and the classical Spanish theatre, and also in the theatre of the Jesuits. (ibid., pp. 91–9 and pp. 75–6).

Gray suggests a more recent tradition, regarding Brecht's theatre as an 'affirmation of the tradition represented by such dramatists as Lenz, Büchner, the early Hauptmann, and Wedekind' (Gray, *Bertolt Brecht*, p. 20).

39. Martin Esslin, *Brecht: The Man and His Work*, New York, 1971, pp. 267–8.

40. White draws attention to three other problems that confront those who wish to see the play in such black and white terms: it is unlikely that a single act of one man would change three centuries of history; it is neither plausible nor historically accurate to claim that Galileo in the play or in the Italy of 1633 held the balance of power; it is perverse for us, as it would be perverse for Galileo, to disregard the example of Bruno, who, as the play reminds us, was burned for espousing the views

Galileo now shares, and whose martyrdom for the sake of truth seems to have been quite useless. (White, op. cit., p. 66).

41. As many have pointed out, Brecht's use of the term 'Aristotelian' to characterize the drama that preceded his serves mainly to draw attention to his readiness to invest in polemical simplifications. What he treats as defining givens are often somewhat selective, and they might best be treated as recurring trends rather than as omni-present facts. See, for example, Weideli's comment on Brecht's term 'non-Aristotelian' to characterize his own theatre. For Weideli, Brecht

> came to neglect, through his interest in demonstration, the didactic aspects of ancient Greek tragedy, which is not founded solely on *catharsis* (or purification of the passions by identification with the hero) but on *anagnorisis* (the act of becoming conscious of something) as well. (Walter Weideli, *The Art of Bertolt Brecht*, trans. Daniel Russell, New York, 1963, p. 71)

See also Gray's comments on the same issue in *Brecht the Dramatist*, pp. 81–4. Gray also points out that theatre audiences have often been anything but the passive, hypnotized mass that Brecht suggests they have been:

> In the eighteenth century it was common practice in some theatres to supply blinds or curtains for the boxes, inside which actresses could provide better entertainment than they could on the stage. In the same period, riots in the audience might be provoked in order to obtain a change of play, or in protest at the price of tickets: at Drury Lane, the actors, far from being regarded as beyond reach, had to be protected from assault from the pit by spiked railings. (ibid., p. 73).

42. Dickson, op. cit., p. 86. See also Hill's comment: 'The highest praise . . . must be reserved for the characterization of Galileo's adversaries, the dignitaries of the Church, who are not shown as mean or stupid men but as intelligent, even sympathetic representatives of the authorities of the time' (Claude Hill, *Bertolt Brecht*, Boston, 1975, p. 120).

43. Sokel offers valuable comments on Brecht's treatment of character in Walter H. Sokel, 'Brecht's concept of character', *Comparative Drama*, V, Spring 1971, pp. 177–92.

44. Esslin, op. cit., pp. 267–8.

45. We should not overlook, in this respect, the irony of Cardinal Barberini's borrowing from Voltaire: 'If God did not exist, we should have to invent Him' (p. 52). Galileo discovers, as Barberini has discovered, that some source of ethical guidance is a social (and scientific) necessity.

46. Brecht, *Brecht on Theatre*, p. 193.

47. ibid., p. 204.

48. ibid., p. 37.

49. ibid., p. 86.

50. ibid., p. 184. See also *Mother Courage*: 'Virtue isn't rewarded, only wickedness, the world needn't be like this, but it is' (*Brecht: Collected Plays*, V, trans. Ralph Manheim, New York, 1972, p. 199).

51. Brecht, *Brecht on Theatre*, p. 193. On this point, we should note, as Dickson reminds us, that it is important to look carefully at Marx's thinking on the

relationship between the individual and society, which is often narrowly construed as deterministic control, by abstract forces, of the individual's consciousness and behaviour. Quoting Marx's comment: 'there must be no attempt to define society as an abstraction over against the individual', Dickson points out that, for Marx,

> Society must on no account be 'reified' . . . i.e. treated as though it exists independently of the individuals who compose it. Thus, if it true that the individual is exclusively defined in terms of society, it is equally true that society is defined in terms of the individual. (op. cit., p. 45)

52. Brecht, *Brecht on Theatre*, p. 175.

9 Ionesco: *The Chairs*

1. Eugène Ionesco, *Notes and Counter Notes: Writings on the Theatre*, trans. Donald Watson, New York, 1964, p. 29.
2. ibid., p. 44.
3. It is by now widely recognized that Ionesco's views of Brecht's theatre are based more upon a popular misunderstanding of Brecht's work that upon a close examination of the plays themselves. Julian Wulbern reports on a discussion with Ionesco of this issue:

> [Ionesco] admitted quite openly that his direct experience of Brecht's works was limited, since he neither read nor spoke German. He had seen a few of the plays in French, such as *Three Penny Opera*, *The Caucasian Chalk Circle*, *The Exception and the Rule*, and *A Man's a Man*, and he had seen the Berliner Ensemble's production in German of *Mother Courage* during the Paris International Theatre Festival in the summer of 1954. He had never read any of Brecht's theoretical writings; his criticism of such theoretical concepts as the *Verfremdungseffekt* was based entirely on his own reaction to the French Marxist writers such as Bernard Dort and René Wintzen who had sought to introduce Brecht's works to the French theater public. Singularly unabashed by these admissions of ignorance, M. Ionesco persisted in his vehement criticism of Brecht. (Julian H. Wulbern, *Brecht and Ionesco: Commitment in Context*, Urbana, Ill., 1971, pp. 4–5)

4. Ionesco, *Notes and Counter Notes*, p. 80. We should not overlook in this quotation Ionesco's comment that 'solitude ends or may end by identifying itself with the community'. Ionesco, like Brecht, wants the theatre to discover and embody new kinds of reality which can then interact with community realities. But the new modes of interaction contemplated are open to misinterpretation in both cases – as Ionesco's attitude towards Brecht's theatre and (as we shall see) Tynan's attitude towards Ionesco's theatre demonstrate.
5. ibid., p. 36; Bertolt Brecht, *Brecht on Theatre*, ed. and trans. John Willett, New York, 1964, pp. 24 and 72. For both playwrights the theatre is philosophical in its pursuit of discovery and change. Neither writer favours using the theatre to illustrate inherited systems of abstract thought.
6. Brecht, op. cit., p. 122.

7. Ionesco, *Notes and Counter Notes*, p. 26.
8. ibid., pp. 87–108.
9. Kenneth Tynan, in ibid., p. 94.
10. Eugène Ionesco, 'Mes pièces ne prétendent pas sauver le monde', *L'Express*, 15/16 October 1955, p. 8.
11. Ionesco, *Notes and Counter Notes*, p. 106.
12. ibid., p. 102.
13. ibid., p. 48.
14. ibid., p. 93.
15. Tynan, with support from Esslin, argues that Ionesco seems to believe that language has been radically devalued, that words are meaningless, and that communication is impossible (Kenneth Tynan in ibid., p. 88; Martin Esslin, *The Theatre of the Absurd*, New York, 1969, pp. 7, 117, 157). Ionesco pointedly replies that 'the very fact of writing and presenting plays is surely incompatible with such a view', and that what interests him is the difficulty, not the impossibility, of making oneself understood (*Notes and Counter Notes*, p. 90).
16. Wulbern, op. cit., p. 8.
17. See, for example, how Ionesco moves from one kind of statement to the other in his remarks on the capacity of imaginative reality to change the world:

> I have always considered imaginative truth to be more profound, more loaded with significance, than everyday reality. Realism, socialist or not, never looks beyond reality. It narrows it down, diminishes it, falsifies it, and leaves out of account the obsessive truths that are most fundamental to us: love, death and wonder. It presents man in a perspective that is narrow and alien; truth lies in our dreams, in our imagination: every moment of our lives confirms this statement. . . . Everything we dream is 'realizable.' Reality does not have to be: it is simply what is. It is the dreamer, the thinker or the scientist who is the revolutionary; it is he who tries to change the world. (Ionesco, *Notes and Counter Notes*, p. 16)

18. One such comment runs as follows: 'All history is contained in each moment of history: any moment in history is valid when it transcends history; in the particular lies the universal' (ibid., p. 21).
19. 'Several times I have said that it is in our fundamental solitude that we rediscover ourselves and that the more I am alone, the more I am in communion with others; whereas in organized society, which is an organization of functions, man is merely reduced to his function, which alienates him from the rest' (ibid., p. 78; see also pp. 91, 107, 108).
20. ibid., p. 181. We see in this quotation some evidence of Ionesco's tendency to confuse the issues he is seeking to clarify. His argument that the 'particular meaning' hides its essential significance is not compatible with his arguments elsewhere for the importance of the particular as a privileged mode of access to the general. His distinction between 'apparent content or subject' and 'genuine subject' is analogous to the distinction I use between topic and theme. Because Ionesco seems at times ready to use content, subject and theme interchangeably, he finds himself forced to restore such distinctions by relying upon a contrast between 'apparent' and 'genuine' manifestations of them.

21. ibid., p. 80.
22. Richard Schechner, 'The Bald Soprano and The Lesson: An inquiry into play structure', in Lamont, Rosette C. (ed.), Ionesco: A Collection of Critical Essays, Englewood Cliffs, NJ, 1973, p. 22.
23. The general viability of this category will be considered in chapter 10.
24. Eugène Ionesco, Conversations with Eugène Ionesco, ed. Claude Bonnefoy, trans. Jan Dawson, London, 1970, p. 142.
25. ibid., p. 143. Ionesco's intermittent readiness to give both novelty and repetition a role in his theatre (not just novelty alone) is also reflected in his intermittent readiness to give both new methods and old methods their due, and in his readiness to confer upon both new truths and rediscovered truths the status of revelation:

> I believe that as one invents, one discovers, and that invention is discovery or rediscovery. . . . An extension of the frontiers of known reality depends upon a rediscovery of method and a rejuvenation of idiom. A genuine avant-garde movement can only be of value if it is more than a fashion. It can only spring from intuitive discovery, followed by a reassessment of neglected models from the past, which require constant rediscovery and rejuvenation. (Ionesco, Notes and Counter Notes, p. 35).

26. Ionesco, Conversations with Eugène Ionesco, p. 46. For Ionesco, imagination must at some point become revelation, which is social and sharable, and not slide into illusion, which is individual and private. When he seeks in moments of revelatory imagination to 'broaden the frontiers of known reality' (Notes and Counter Notes, p. 102), this must be done in such a way as to enable the audience to share the experience by linking old with new.
27. ibid., p. 81.
28. ibid., p. 38. When discussing his theatre, Ionesco is thus at pains to point out the retrospective and non-prescriptive nature of his comments on the theatre:

> What I have just said is not a preconceived theory of dramatic art. It has not come before, but after my own personal experience of the theatre. Thinking about my own plays, good or bad, has provoked these few ideas. The reflections came afterward. I have no ideas before I write a play. I have them when I have finished it, or while I am not writing any at all. I believe that artistic creation is spontaneous. It is for me. Once again, all this is chiefly valid for me; but if I could believe I had discovered instinctively in myself the basic framework and permanent character of the objective reality of drama, or thrown even a little light on what the essence of the theatre is, I should be very proud. (ibid., p. 34)

29. Some have been tempted, nevertheless, to turn to philosophies of Nothingness or Absence as a means of dealing with the play. See, for example, Schechner's discussion of Sartre's Being and Nothingness and Ionesco's 'world of the Not'. Having made the Not transcendent, Schechner is soon forced to the conclusion that 'it transcends any purely social interpretation we may give it' (Richard Schechner, 'The enactment of the "Not" in Ionesco's Les Chaises', Yale French Studies, 29, 1962, pp. 69 and 72).

30. Wilhelm Von Humboldt, as quoted in Cassirer, Ernst, *Language and Myth*, trans. Susanne K. Langer, New York, 1953, p. 9.

31. Ionesco, *Notes and Counter Notes*, p. 191.

32. ibid., pp. 188–9.

33. Eugène Ionesco, *The Chairs*, in *Four Plays by Eugène Ionesco*, trans. Donald M. Allen, New York, 1958. All page references in the text are to this edition.

34. Ionesco rejects any play which instead of having 'evidence to *offer*' has 'a thesis to *prove*', and criticizes those who believe 'that writing a play should be like presenting a thesis in which problems find their solution on the stage' (Ionesco, *Notes and Counter Notes*, pp. 32 and 24).

35. ibid., p. 191.

36. ibid., p. 93.

37. ibid., p. 102.

10 Beckett: *Krapp's Last Tape*

1. All pages references are to Samuel Beckett, *'Krapp's Last Tape' and Other Dramatic Pieces*, New York, 1960.

2. James Knowlson, *Light and Darkness in the Theatre of Samuel Beckett*, London, 1972, p. 11.

3. Commenting on the tape made in Krapp's thirties, Webb argues: 'Evidently light had represented to him consciousness, activity, individuality, the burden of being himself, and the darkness had seemed to him to offer a retreat into the freedom of unawareness. The present Krapp seems to feel the same way.' He then seeks to link these distinctions to Krapp's relationships with women, who attract him alternately towards manhood and developed individuality or towards childhood and diminished individuality: 'Either path frightens him: forward into light and a full life, or backward into darkness and spiritual or psychological death. Half in life and half out of it, he can choose neither one direction nor the other.' As he himself acknowledges, these distinctions run into trouble once we see that some of the women in Krapp's life seem to share his problems rather than cause them. And Webb, like Knowlson, eventually moves beyond these attempts to establish definitive distinctions and choices in the light/dark images and towards attempts to deal, as the play demands, with their interaction (Eugene Webb, *The Plays of Samuel Beckett*, London, 1972, pp. 71–4). See also Knowlson, op. cit., p. 22.

4. Ronald Hayman, *Samuel Beckett*, New York, 1973, p. 72.

5. Arthur K. Oberg, 'Krapp's Last Tape and the Proustian vision', *Modern Drama*, IX, December 1966, p. 333.

6. Michael Robinson, *The Long Sonata of the Dead: A Study of Samuel Beckett*, New York, 1969, p. 284.

7. Martin Esslin, *The Theatre of the Absurd*, New York, 1969, p. 56: 'In *Krapp's Last Tape*, the self at one moment in time is confronted with its earlier incarnation only to find it utterly strange.'

8. Bernard F. Dukore, 'Krapp's Last Tape as tragicomedy', *Modern Drama*, 15, March 1973, p. 351.

9. Ruby Cohn, *Samuel Beckett: The Comic Gamut*, New Brunswick, NJ, 1962, p. 249.

10. Hayman, op. cit., pp. 77 and 76.

11. A heuristic generalization might well become merged with an empirical gener-alization about common ground if the data are similar and the task dictates that similarity be isolated at the expense of difference. And all three might merge if a historically grounded generalization about announced authorial aim could be shown to have produced extensive and central common ground and if the aim of the critical task were to locate such common ground. But the three kinds of generalization remain distinguishable, particularly where the data are diverse and where no authorial programme is claimed to be operating. Heuristic aims also vary according to the critical task at hand, e.g. – preference for one kind of heuristic generalization rather than another will depend on relative interest in author, period, genre and reader/audience.

12. See, for example, Walter Kerr, 'Making a cult of confusion', *Horizon*, 5 (i), September 1962, pp. 33–41, and Esslin's reply, 'Walter Kerr and the Absurd', *Tulane Drama Review*, 7 (iii), Spring 1963, pp. 13–17. See also Letitia Dace, 'On Jean Genet and Martin Esslin, or here Absurdist, there Absurdist, every-where . . .', *Kansas Quarterly*, 3 (ii), Spring 1971, pp. 110–16, and Esslin's reply in the same issue pp. 116–17. See also Lionel Abel, 'The Theatre and the "Absurd"', *Partisan Review*, Summer 1962, p. 454; Bamber Gascoigne, 'Shoot the audience', *Spectator*, 15 June 1962, p. 800; C. W. E. Bigsby, *Confrontation and Commitment*, Columbia, Missouri, 1968, p. xvii; Arnold P. Hinchliffe, *The Absurd*, London, 1969, p. 37. Some of these exchanges have become rather heated, and my concern here is not to side with any particular party in the dispute but to try to clarify the causes of the confusion. Such clarification has consequences, as we will see, for our understanding of both Krapp's difficulties in the play and our own in dealing with it.

13. He does, however, reject from the first the notion of a 'self-proclaimed school' (*The Theatre of the Absurd*, p. 4) and is both puzzled and annoyed when sections of the book persuade some readers to revive it. See Martin Esslin, *Reflections: Essays on Modern Theatre*, New York, 1969, p. 183.

14. If Esslin quotes from playwrights, as he does, to validate his assignment of their work to the Theatre of the Absurd, it is not surprising that many set out to obtain counter-quotations to invalidate what appears to be a genetic claim. If Esslin claims, as he does, that plays of the Absurd have 'a good deal in common' (*The Theatre of the Absurd*, p. 4), it is not surprising that many respond by demonstrating that what they have in common is not always extensive and not always central.

15. ibid., p. x.

16. Martin Esslin (ed.), *Absurd Drama*, Harmondsworth, 1974, p. 9.

17. Martin Esslin, *Reflections: Essays on Modern Theatre*, p. 183.

18. Esslin's argument seeks to give the Theatre of the Absurd general historical parameters (running roughly from the late 1940s to the early 1960s (*The Theatre of the Absurd*, pp. 378–82), a major theme based on a philosophical position of the period ('metaphysical anguish at the absurdity of the human condition is, broadly speaking, the theme of the plays of Beckett, Adamov, Ionesco, Genet, and the other writers discussed in this book' (p. 5)), a specific structural goal ('striving for an integration between the subject matter and the form in which it is expressed' (p. 7)), a firm social basis ('the reflection of what seems to be the attitude most genuinely representative of our own time' (p. 4)), and an origin in a specific geographical location ('It is no

coincidence that, like . . . so many of the efforts to create new forms of expression in all the arts, the Theatre of the Absurd should be centered in Paris' (p. 8)). These efforts to give the plays of the Theatre of the Absurd a social, temporal and geographical basis, as well as a thematic and structural common ground, are given further historical reinforcement by discussion of the playwrights' lives and by attempts to establish the Absurd as itself a distinctive historical force ('As regards the new generation of playwrights who have emerged since the Theatre of the Absurd made its first astonishing impact, their work also clearly cannot remain unaffected by it. Whether they are themselves influenced by the Theatre of the Absurd or whether they react against it, one thing is certain: this is an approach to drama that of necessity must have left its mark on the theatre' (p. 380)). All of this seems a far cry from subsequent heuristic claims that the category of the Theatre of the Absurd is simply 'a working hypothesis', which is valid only in so far as it helps us gain insight into a work of art, and which was never meant to have anything approaching 'a reality as concrete and specific as a branded product of the detergent industry'.

19. Esslin, *The Theatre of the Absurd*, p. x.

20. Ludwig Wittgenstein, *Philosophical Investigations*, trans. G. E. M. Anscombe, New York, 1969, p. 33. For Wittgenstein, categories, explanations, descriptions and interpretations are always from one point of view or another inexact, but he is quick to remind us that '[inexact] does not mean "unusable"' (p. 41). The mistake is to assume that our descriptive activities are justified only if they encapsulate the essential core of things to be described. Such an approach to description unnecessarily narrows its possible function, addresses itself to a prematurely categorized world, and loses touch quickly with the temporal and changing aspects of things in the world and our interaction with them: 'we feel as if we had to *penetrate* phenomena: our investigation, however, is directed not towards phenomena, but, as one might say, towards the *possibilities* of phenomena' (p. 42).

21. Scientists do, of course, make use of both empirical and heuristic generalizations.

22. Esslin, *Reflections: Essays on Modern Theatre*, pp. 183–4. See also Esslin's puzzling claim that plays of the Absurd '*resemble* each other in certain *basic* structural respects' (*The Theatre of the Absurd*, p. x; my emphases). This uncertain mingling of similarity and difference has led some, including Hinchliffe, to argue that it is capricious to separate Absurd Theatre from the rest of modern theatre (Hinchliffe, op. cit., p. 78). It might, however, be argued that Hinchliffe overlooks the importance of a major point Esslin tries to make by contrasting Absurd Theatre and Existentialist Theatre – 'It is [the] striving for an integration between the subject-matter and the form in which it is expressed that separates the Theatre of the Absurd from the Existentialist theatre' (Esslin, *The Theatre of the Absurd*, p. 7). But such striving for integration between theme and structure is, of course, characteristic of a wide variety of modern plays. The feature of the Theatre of the Absurd that Esslin uses to distinguish it from Existentialist Theatre could thus be used by Hinchliffe to support his argument that Absurd drama should not be isolated from larger trends in the modern theatre.

23. The natural consequence of these uncertain claims is that more heat than light will emerge from debate over the existence of a Theatre of the Absurd. An inconsistent argument allows one prop to be knocked away without necessary disturbance to another.

24. The play draws our attention in a variety of ways to the differences between the current Krapp and his former selves. Krapp fails to recognize phrases he entered in a ledger in earlier years to summarize the contents of each tape. References to a 'black ball' and to a 'memorable equinox' (p. 13) puzzle him, yet one refers to the moment when he realized his mother was dead, and the other to a moment of seemingly decisive intellectual insight. The confident rejection of happiness by Krapp in his thirties rings hollow to Krapp in his sixties (p. 28), and so does the rejection of youth by Krapp in his twenties to Krapp in his thirties (p. 17). Even the vocabulary of an earlier self has been lost by the later Krapp. The word 'viduity', recorded by Krapp in his thirties, sends Krapp in his sixties in search of a dictionary. But if the discontinuities in Krapp's life are apparent enough, so also are the continuities. While listening to the tape recording, the older Krapp at times laughs in unison and closes his eyes in communion with his earlier self. A near addiction to bananas and alcohol, and a persisting problem with constipation reveal physical continuities over the years; a fascination with women's eyes, and a persisting commitment to the annual task of separating grain from husk reveal spiritual and psychological continuities. But the basic issue for Krapp and for us is not just noting these puzzling phenomena, but ordering and understanding them.

25. Knowlson notes that 'there is also throughout the play a consistent attempt made to mingle the light and the dark, expressing Krapp's desire to reconcile and promote a kind of union between sense and spirit' (op. cit., p. 22). Webb, seeking to link the light/dark images to the importance of women to Krapp in their roles as lover and mother, argues:

> To enter into the kind of relationship to which women call him, Krapp would have to accept a life in which the light of reason and the darkness of the nonrational stood side by side, reached out to one another, and interpenetrated. This, however, is something he dreads as though it were a threat to his very being. (op. cit., p. 72)

These attempts to relate, and not just distinguish, light and dark overlook the importance, as we shall see, of light circumscribing dark and vice versa. Unless that point is noted and developed, a difficult problem leads directly to the more difficult dilemma of reconciling opposites.

26. 'The first woman mentioned in the play, apart from his mother, is Bianca, whose name, significantly, means white in Italian, and whose setting was Kedar Street. Kedar means "dark" in Hebrew' (ibid., p. 73). See also Knowlson's comment: 'Bianca is white by name, but they live together in Kedar (or, in Hebrew, Black) Street' (James Knowlson, 'Krapp's Last Tape: The evolution of a play, 1958–75', Journal of Beckett Studies, 1, Winter 1976, p. 60).

27. For an interesting series of notes on Beckett's adjustments to stage setting, props and action in recent productions of the play, see ibid., pp. 50–65. Knowlson concludes that 'if Beckett has had few second thoughts concerning the actual text of Krapp's Last Tape, the various productions with which he has been associated show him working towards an interpretation in which every element of the production will be dramatically and thematically justified' (p. 64). Changes worth noting include the tossing of the banana skin into the wings, rather than into the audience, and a conclusion which involves dimming all stage light until only the operating light on the tape recorder can be seen.

28. Alfred Alvarez, *Beckett*, London, 1973, pp. 100–1.

29. Roy Walker, 'Samuel Beckett's double bill: Love, chess and death', *Twentieth Century*, 164, November 1958, p. 536; Robinson, op. cit., pp. 285–6; John Fletcher and John Spurling, *Beckett: A Study of His Plays*, New York, 1972, pp. 88–9.

30. Discussion of the tape recorder has usually involved treating it as a local image which invites textural rather than structural generalization. Parkin notes that the recordings on the machine suggest the passing of time: 'Past and future revolve like the spinning tapes' (Andrew Parkin, 'Monologue into monodrama: Aspects of Samuel Beckett's plays', *Éire-Ireland*, 9 (iv), Winter 1974, p. 37). Hayman argues that 'the tape on Krapp's machine is an image of the mind, coiling backwards and forwards in time, endlessly repeating itself' (Hayman, op. cit., p. 76). The image of the tape recorder must interact with the image network of the play as a whole if it is to be appropriately interpreted.

31. Samuel Beckett, *Proust*, New York, 1931. It is dangerous to overlook the fact that the subject of this essay is Proust's work not Beckett's philosophy, and it should not be assumed that Beckett's earlier views on Proust and on philosophical matters have necessarily remained unchanged. The transcendence of Habit in the essay is linked to the rejection of the general in any form:

> when the object is perceived as particular and unique and not merely the member of a family, when it appears independent of any general notion and detached from the sanity of a cause, isolated and inexplicable in the light of ignorance, then and only then may it be a source of enchantment. (ibid., p. 11)

Habit may be suspended when involuntary memory takes over, but 'involuntary memory is an unruly magician and will not be importuned. It chooses its own time and place for the performance of its miracle' (pp. 20–1). Such linking of Habit and generalization has the twin effects of limiting all uses of generalization to one use (reduction) and all transcendence of habitual reduction to involuntary events. Whatever the virtues of such an approach to the work of Proust, it is not an adequate approach to the events in *Krapp's Last Tape*. Krapp voluntarily records his tapes, voluntarily plays back specifically searched-for passages, and considers them in the context of generalizations and summaries located in the ledger. What is on the tapes nevertheless surprises him from time to time, and his responses to the tapes mingle the habitual and the unexpected. The tapes thus share features of both voluntary and involuntary memory (as distinguished in the Proust essay) and what is at issue here is not the separation of habit and generalization on one side from novelty and the particular on the other, but a complex mode of interaction among them. (Oberg, op. cit., pp. 333–8, points out a series of similarities and differences between the play and the essay.)

32. Beckett, *Proust*, p. 17. The notion of an 'instrument of discovery' is not readily compatible with that of 'involuntary memory'. The notion of an involuntary instrument is, potentially at least, a contradiction in terms. This contradiction is of no great consequence in the Proust essay, but it provides opportunities for viewing *Krapp's Last Tape* as an extension of, rather than an illustration of, positions established in the essay.

33. Beckett, *Proust*, p. 54.
34. V. A. Kolve, 'Religious language in *Waiting for Godot*', *The Centennial Review*, 11, Winter 1967, p. 107.
35. ibid., p. 107.

11 Pinter: *Betrayal*

1. T. S. Eliot, 'The music of poetry', in *Selected Prose*, ed. John Hayward, Harmondsworth, 1965, p. 60.
2. Maurice Valency, Introduction to *Jean Giraudoux: Four Plays*, ed. Maurice Valency, New York, 1959, p. xviii.
3. John Russell Taylor, *The Rise and Fall of the Well-Made Play*, New York, 1967, p. 163.
4. ibid.
5. Stanley Fish (among others) has made the case for the similarly problematic status of perception and interpretation. He argues that 'perception (and reading is an instance of perception) always occurs within a set of assumptions that preconstrains what could possibly be perceived', and that such assumptions tend to '*produce* the phenomena [they] purport to describe' (Stanley Fish, 'Why no one's afraid of Wolfgang Iser', *diacritics*, XI (i), Spring 1981, pp. 11 and 7). See also Iser's response in the same volume: 'Talk like whales: A reply to Stanley Fish', *diacritics*, XI (iii), Fall 1981, pp. 82–7.
6. Harold Pinter, quoted in John Russell Taylor, *Anger and After: A Guide to the New British Drama*, London, 1978, p. 339.
7. For further discussion of this point, see Austin E. Quigley, '*The Dumb Waiter*: Undermining the tacit dimension', *Modern Drama*, 21, March 1978, pp. 1–11. Van Laan offers an interesting further response to the play and to the issues raised in my article: Thomas F. Van Laan, '*The Dumb Waiter*: Pinter's play with the audience', *Modern Drama*, 24, December 1981, pp. 494–502.
8. John McLaughlin, 'Harold Pinter and PBL', *America*, 118, 10 February 1968, p. 193.
9. Marshall Cohen, 'Theater 67', *Partisan Review*, 34, Summer 1967, pp. 440–1.
10. John Russell Taylor, *The Angry Theatre: New British Drama*, New York, 1962, p. 261; see also 'Pinter's game of happy families', in John Lahr (ed.), *A Casebook on Harold Pinter's 'The Homecoming'*, New York, 1971, p. 64.
11. Austin E. Quigley, *The Pinter Problem*, Princeton, NJ, Princeton University Press, 1975.
12. All page references are to Harold Pinter, *Betrayal*, London, 1978.
13. Such disruption of chronology is not, of course, unique to Pinter's play. J. B. Priestley, for example, was experimenting with chronology on the British stage in the 1930s. His 'time-plays' – *Dangerous Corner* (1932), *Time and the Conways* (1937), *I Have Been Here Before* (1937) and *An Inspector Calls* (1945) – sought, not entirely successfully, to give structural embodiment to the varied nature of time.
14. Harold Pinter, 'Between the lines', *The Sunday Times* (London), 4 March 1962, mag. section, p. 25.

15. *The American Heritage Dictionary of the English Language*, ed. William Morris, Boston, 1979, provides two synonyms for the word 'betray': (1) reveal – 'making known and thereby breaking a trust or pledge'; (2) deceive – 'faithlessness or treachery that brings another to grave disadvantage or into danger'. It is clear that the latter can include the former, and that betrayal can involve revealing and/or concealing.

16. This passage from *Betrayal* is an interesting dramatization of an important distinction, the linguistic implications of which are extensively explored in *The Pinter Problem*. See particularly chapter II, and discussion of the ways in which what is being done with the words helps constitute what is said.

17. In *The Homecoming*, Lenny uses this phrase to describe his parents' activities the night they were conceiving him: '[Young people] often ruminate, sometimes singly, sometimes in groups, about the true facts of that particular night – the night they were made in the image of those two people *at it*' (Harold Pinter, *The Homecoming*, New York, 1966, p. 36).

18. See also Pinter's comment in the published text: '*Betrayal* can be performed without an interval, or with an interval after Scene Four' (p. 8). It should be noted, however, that for the film version of the play, as for filmed versions of his other plays, Pinter approved the interpolation of a few brief scenes.

19. Arthur Wing Pinero, *The Second Mrs. Tanqueray*, Boston, 1894, p. 168.

12 Conclusion

1. V. A. Kolve, *The Play Called Corpus Christi*, Stanford, 1966, p. 119.

2. ibid., pp. 122–3.

3. George Poulet, *Studies in Human Time*, trans. Elliott Coleman, Baltimore, Md, 1956, p. 10; quoted in Kolve, op. cit., p. 102.

4. Sherman Hawkins, 'The two worlds of Shakespearean comedy', *Shakespeare Studies*, 3, 1967, p. 64.

5. Northrop Frye, 'The argument of comedy', in *Modern Shakespearean Criticism: Essays on Style, Dramaturgy, and the Major Plays*, ed. Alvin B. Kernan, New York, 1970, p. 170.

6. Hawkins, op. cit., p. 65.

7. ibid., pp. 69–74.

8. Harry Berger, 'The Renaissance imagination: Second world and green world', *The Centennial Review*, 9, 1965, p. 49.

9. Frye, op. cit., pp. 169–70.

10. Berger, op. cit., p. 47. Berger also raises and sheds intelligent light upon the issue of whether the second world is a term for a domain within a text or for the domain of the text itself: 'the second world *in* a fiction and the second world *as* a fiction' (p. 48).

11. Hawkins, op. cit., p. 76. Felperin provides a valuable study of the other-world basis of romance and its wide dissemination through our culture: 'although we associate classical Greece with epic, tragedy, and comedy, it is actually the birthplace of romance in all its subsequent forms. The *Odyssey* is not only an epic but the first romance' (Howard Felperin, *Shakespearean Romance*, Princeton, NJ, 1972, p. 8).

12. Hawkins, op. cit., pp. 75–6. As Hawkins pursues his analysis further, the

green-world/closed-world distinction becomes a matter of perspective and presentation and not just a matter of the intrinsic qualities of a world. Thus, he argues,

> for Olivia or Adriana, who live there, Illyria or Ephesus is about as magical as Boston. Rosalind is enchanted by the pastoral world of Arden; for Corin, Arden is a place to tend sheep, where one's present master is stingier than the last. . . . Audience perspective finally determines which is a green world and which is closed. Whatever Corin thinks of Arden, we see it as Rosalind does; for us Ephesus is a closed world, since we see the humdrum causes for the bewitchment of Antipholus. But, of course, we are dealing with the continuum of a creative imagination, not the rigid oppositions of a system. (pp. 74–5)

13. Berger reminds us that 'models exist to be emulated, not imitated' (op. cit., p. 78).
14. Hawkins, op. cit., pp. 77–8.
15. J. Hillis Miller, 'Deconstructing the deconstructers', *diacritics*, V (ii), Summer 1975, p. 31.
16. Berger, op. cit., p. 51. Again, what we are dealing with here are characteristic features of periods, not exclusive features. There are always interesting examples of heterogeneity in every period. Robert Herrick's poem 'Dreames', for example, runs as follows: 'Here we are all, by day; by night w'are hurl'd/By dreames, each one, into a sev'rall world' (*The Poems of Robert Herrick*, ed. L. C. Martin, London, 1965, p. 21). The notion that we share one world while awake but have worlds of our own while asleep goes back at least as far as Heraclitus. What is important, however, is not whether those in other periods conceived of multiple worlds, but how they conceived of their status, their relationships and their implications.
17. Nelson Goodman, *Ways of Worldmaking*, Indianapolis, 1978, p. 20.
18. Tom F. Driver, *Romantic Quest and Modern Query: A History of the Modern Theater*, New York, 1970, pp. viii, 469, 462, 461, 457–8.
19. William James, *A Pluralistic Universe*, New York, 1909, p. 321.
20. Robert Brustein, *The Theatre of Revolt*, Boston, 1964, p. 4.

Selected bibliography

To keep the bibliography to a reasonable length I have excluded all editions of plays, except for those plays given extended attention in the text, and all journal articles, except those referred to in the text and notes. The bibliography includes all books cited, books which, though not cited, have had some impact on my approach to the issues discussed, and a selection of the many books that might provide the interested reader with useful lines of further inquiry.

Abel, Lionel (1962) 'The Theatre and the "Absurd"', *Partisan Review* (Summer), 454–9.

Abel, Lionel (1963) *Metatheatre: A New View of Dramatic Form*, New York, Hill & Wang.

Abrams, Meyer H. (1953) *The Mirror and the Lamp: Romantic Theory and the Critical Tradition*, New York, Oxford University Press.

Adams, Hazard (ed.) (1971) *Critical Theory Since Plato*, New York, Harcourt, Brace, Jovanovich.

Alvarez, Alfred (1973) *Beckett*, London, Fontana.

Appia, Adolphe (1962) *Music and the Art of the Theatre*, trans. Robert W. Corrigan and Mary Douglas Dirks, Coral Gables, Fla, University of Miami Press.

Armstrong, Cecil F. (1968) *Shakespeare to Shaw: Studies in the Life's Work of Six Dramatists of the English Stage*, Freeport, NY, Books for Libraries Press.

Artaud, Antonin (1958) *The Theater and Its Double*, trans. Mary Caroline Richards, New York, Grove Press.

Artaud, Antonin (1968–74) *Collected Works*, I–IV, trans. Victor Corti, London, Calder & Boyars.

Auerbach, Erich (1957) *Mimesis: The Representation of Reality in Western Literature*, trans. Willard Trask, Garden City, NY, Doubleday.

Beckett, Samuel (1931) *Proust*, New York, Grove Press.

Beckett, Samuel (1960) *Krapp's Last Tape*, in *'Krapp's Last Tape' and Other Dramatic Pieces*, New York, Grove Press.

Bennett, Benjamin (1979) *Modern Drama and German Classicism: Renaissance from Lessing to Brecht*, Ithaca, NY, Cornell University Press.

Benston, Alice N. (1965) 'From naturalism to the Dream Play: A study of the evolution of Strindberg's unique theatrical form', *Modern Drama*, 7 (February), 382–98.

Bentley, Eric (1946) *The Playwright as Thinker: A Study of Drama in Modern Times*, New York, Reynal & Hitchcock.

Bentley, Eric (1967) *The Theatre of Commitment and Other Essays on Drama in Our Society*, New York, Atheneum.

Bentley, Eric (1972) *Theatre of War: Comments on 32 Occasions*, New York, Viking Press.

Bentley, Eric (ed.) (1976) *The Theory of the Modern Stage*, Harmondsworth, Penguin.

Berger, Harry, Jr (1965) 'The Renaissance imagination: Second world and green world', *The Centennial Review*, 9, 36–78.

Bernstein, Basil (1971–5) *Class, Codes and Control*, I–III, London, Routledge & Kegan Paul.

Bigsby, C. W. E. (1968) *Confrontation and Commitment: A Study of Contemporary American Drama, 1959–66*, Columbia, Mo., University of Missouri Press.

Bock, Hedwig and Wertheim, Albert (eds) (1981) *Essays on Contemporary British Drama*, Munich, Max Hueber Verlag.

Bonnefoy, Claude (ed.) (1970) *Conversations with Eugène Ionesco*, trans. Jan Dawson, London, Faber & Faber.

Booth, Michael R. (ed.) (1969–76) *English Plays of the Nineteenth Century*, I–VI, Oxford, Oxford University Press.

Bradbrook, M. C. (1948) *Ibsen the Norwegian*, London, Chatto & Windus.

Bradley, F. H. (1906) *Appearance and Reality: A Metaphysical Essay*, New York, Macmillan.

Brandell, Gunnar (1974) *Strindberg in Inferno*, trans. Barry Jacobs, Cambridge, Mass., Harvard University Press.

Brandes, Georg (1964) *Henrik Ibsen*, trans. Jesse Muir and William Archer, New York, Benjamin Blom.

Braun, Edward (1982) *The Director and the Stage: From Naturalism to Grotowski*, London, Methuen.

Brecht, Bertolt (1964) *Brecht on Theatre: The Development of an Aesthetic*, ed. and trans. John Willett, New York, Hill & Wang.

Brecht, Bertolt (1965) *The Messingkauf Dialogues*, trans. John Willett, London, Methuen.

Brecht, Bertolt (1972) *Life of Galileo*, trans. Wolfgang Sauerlander and Ralph Manheim, in *Bertolt Brecht: Collected Plays*, V, ed. Ralph Manheim and John Willett, New York, Vintage.

Brecht, Bertolt (1976) *Poems 1913–1956*, ed. and trans. John Willett and Ralph Manheim, London, Methuen.

Brook, Peter (1968) *The Empty Space*, New York, Atheneum.

Brook, Peter (1968) *US*, Indianapolis, Bobbs-Merrill.

Brustein, Robert (1964) *The Theater of Revolt: An Approach to the Modern Drama*, Boston, Little, Brown.

Burns, Winifred (1948) 'Certain women characters of Pinero's serious drama', *Poet Lore*, 54 (Autumn), 195–219.

Calderwood, James L. (1971) *Shakespearean Metadrama*, Minneapolis, University of Minnesota Press.

Carpenter, Charles A. (1969) *Bernard Shaw and the Art of Destroying Ideals*, Madison, University of Wisconsin Press.

Cassirer, Ernst (1953) *Language and Myth*, trans. Susanne K. Langer, New York, Dover.

Clark, Barrett H. (ed.) (1947) *European Theories of the Drama*, New York, Crown.

Coe, Richard N. (1968) *The Vision of Jean Genet: A Study of His Poems, Plays and Novels*, New York, Grove Press.

Cohen, Marshall (1967) 'Theater 67', *Partisan Review*, 34 (Summer), 436–44.

Cohen, Ralph (1974) 'On the interrelations of eighteenth-century literary forms', in Harth, Phillip (ed.) *New Approaches to Eighteenth Century Literature*, New York and London, Columbia University Press, pp. 33–78.

Cohn, Ruby (1962) *Samuel Beckett: The Comic Gamut*, New Brunswick, NJ, Rutgers University Press.

Cohn, Ruby (1969) *Currents in Contemporary Drama*, Bloomington, Indiana University Press.

Cohn, Ruby (1981) 'The fabulous theatre of Edward Bond', in Bock, Hedwig and Wertheim, Albert (eds) *Essays on Contemporary British Drama*, Munich, Max Hueber Verlag.

Cole, Toby (ed.) (1961) *Playwrights on Playwrighting: The Meaning and Making of Modern Drama from Ibsen to Ionesco*, New York, Hill & Wang.

Craig, Edward Anthony (1968) *Gordon Craig: The Story of His Life*, New York, Knopf.

Craig, Edward Gordon (1912) *On the Art of the Theatre*, Chicago, Browne's.

Craig, Edward Gordon (1983) *Craig on Theatre*, ed. J. Michael Walton, London, Methuen.

Croce, Benedetto (1924) *European Literature in the Nineteenth Century*, trans. Douglas Ainslie, London, Chapman & Hall.

Dace, Letitia (1971) 'On Jean Genet and Martin Esslin, or here Absurdist, there Absurdist, everywhere . . .', *Kansas Quarterly*, 3 (ii) (Spring), 110–16.

Dahlström, Carl (1965) *Strindberg's Dramatic Expressionism*, 2nd edn, New York, Benjamin Blom.

Davies, Cecil W. (1962) 'Pinero: The drama of reputation', *English*, 14 (Spring), 13–17.

De Man, Paul (1971) *Blindness and Insight: Essays in the Rhetoric of Contemporary Criticism*, London, Oxford University Press.

Demetz, Peter (1962) *Brecht: A Collection of Critical Essays*, Englewood Cliffs, NJ, Prentice-Hall.

Dickson, Keith A. (1978) *Towards Utopia: A Study of Brecht*, Oxford, Clarendon Press.

Donohue, Joseph (1979) 'Character, genre, and ethos in nineteenth-century British drama', *Yearbook of English Studies*, 9, 78–101.

Downer, Alan S. (1950) *The British Drama: A Handbook and Brief Chronicle*, New York, Appleton-Century-Crofts.

Driver, Tom F. (1970) *Romantic Quest and Modern Query: A History of the Modern Theater*, New York, Delacorte Press.

Dukore, Bernard F. (1973) 'Krapp's Last Tape as tragicomedy', *Modern Drama*, 15 (March), 351–4.

Dunkel, Wilbur Dwight (1941) *Sir Arthur Pinero: A Critical Biography with Letters*, Chicago, University of Chicago Press.

Eagleton, Terry (1976) *Marxism and Literary Criticism*, London, Methuen, and Berkeley, University of California Press.

Elam, Keir (1980) *The Semiotics of Theatre and Drama*, London, Methuen.

Eliot, T. S. (1965) *Selected Prose*, ed. John Hayward, Harmondsworth, Penguin.

Ellis, John M. (1974) *The Theory of Literary Criticism: A Logical Analysis*, Berkeley, University of California Press.

Esslin, Martin (1963) 'Walter Kerr and the Absurd', *Tulane Drama Review*, 7 (iii) (Spring), 13–17.

Esslin, Martin (1969) *Reflections: Essays on Modern Theatre*, Garden City, NY, Doubleday.

Esslin, Martin (1969) *The Theatre of the Absurd*, revised edn, Garden City, NY, Anchor Books.

Esslin, Martin (1971) *Brecht: The Man and His Work*, New York, Anchor Books.

Esslin, Martin (1971) 'Reply to Letitia Dace', *Kansas Quarterly*, 3 (ii) (Spring), 116–17.

Esslin, Martin (ed.) (1974) *Absurd Drama*, Harmondsworth, Penguin.

Esslin, Martin (1982) *Pinter the Playwright*, London, Methuen.

Felperin, Howard (1972) *Shakespearean Romance*, Princeton, NJ, Princeton University Press.

Fergusson, Francis (1949) *The Idea of a Theater*, Princeton, NJ, Princeton University Press.

Fish, Stanley (1981) 'Why no one's afraid of Wolfgang Iser', *diacritics*, X1 (i) (Spring), 2–13.

Fjelde, Rolf (ed.) (1965) *Ibsen: A Collection of Critical Essays*, Englewood Cliffs, NJ, Prentice-Hall.

Fjelde, Rolf (trans. and introd.) (1978) *Ibsen: The Complete Major Prose Plays*, New York, Farrar, Straus & Giroux.

Fletcher, John and Spurling, John (1972) *Beckett: A Study of his Plays*, New York, Hill & Wang.

Foucault, Michel (1972) *The Archeology of Knowledge*, trans. A. M. Sheridan Smith, New York, Pantheon Books.

Fuchs, Georg (1959) *Revolution in the Theatre: Conclusions Concerning the Munich Artists' Theatre*, trans. Constance Connor Kuhn, Ithaca, NY, Cornell University Press.

Fuegi, John (ed.) (1971) *Brecht Heute: Brecht Today*, Frankfurt am Main, Athenäum.

Fyfe, Hamilton (1930) *Sir Arthur Pinero's Plays and Players*, New York, Macmillan.

Gale, Steven H. (1977) *Butter's Going Up: A Critical Analysis of Harold Pinter's Work*, Durham, NC, Duke University Press.

Gascoigne, Bamber (1962) 'Shoot the audience', *Spectator* (15 June), 800–1.

Gascoigne, Bamber (1962) *Twentieth-Century Drama*, London, Hutchinson.

Gassner, John (1956) *Form and Idea in Modern Theatre*, New York, Dryden.

Geertz, Clifford (1973) *The Interpretation of Cultures: Selected Essays*, New York, Basic Books.

Genet, Jean (1967) *The Thief's Journal*, trans. Bernard Frechtman, Harmondsworth, Penguin.

Gill, Brendan (1980) 'Looking back', *New Yorker* (14 January), 55–6.

Gilman, Richard (1974) *The Making of Modern Drama*, New York, Farrar, Straus & Giroux.

Girard, René (1978) *'To Double Business Bound': Essays on Literature, Mimesis, and Anthropology*, Baltimore, Md, Johns Hopkins University Press.

Goldman, Michael (1975) *The Actor's Freedom: Toward a Theory of Drama*, New York, Viking.

Goodman, Nelson (1978) *Ways of Worldmaking*, Indianapolis, Hackett Publishing.

Gosse, Edmund (1908) *Henrik Ibsen*, New York, Scribner.

Gray, Ronald D. (1961) *Bertolt Brecht*, New York, Grove Press.

Gray, Ronald D. (1976) *Brecht the Dramatist*, Cambridge University Press.

Griffiths, Trevor (1977) 'Author's preface', *'Through the Night' and 'Such Impossibilities'*, London, Faber & Faber.

Grossvogel, David I. (1958) *The Self-conscious Stage in Modern French Drama*, New York, Columbia University Press.

Grotowski, Jerzy (1968) *Towards a Poor Theatre*, New York, Simon & Schuster.

Guicharnaud, Jacques and Beckelman, June (1961) *Modern French Theatre from Giraudoux to Beckett*, New Haven, Conn., Yale University Press.

Hamilton, Clayton (ed. and intro.) (1917–1922) *The Social Plays of Arthur Wing Pinero*, I–IV, New York, Dutton.

Handke, Peter (1975) 'Introduction to *Kaspar*', in *'Kaspar' and Other Plays*, trans. Michael Roloff, New York, Farrar, Straus & Giroux.

Haugen, Einar (1979) *Ibsen's Drama: Author to Audience*, Minneapolis, University of Minnesota Press.

Hawkins, Sherman (1967) 'The two worlds of Shakespearean comedy', *Shakespeare Studies*, 3, 62–80.

Hayman, Ronald (1973) *Samuel Beckett*, New York, Ungar.

Hill, Claude (1975) *Bertolt Brecht*, Boston, Twayne.

Hinchliffe, Arnold P. (1969) *The Absurd*, London, Methuen.

Hirsch, E. D. Jr (1967) *Validity in Interpretation*, New Haven and London, Yale University Press.

Hirsch, E. D. Jr (1976) *The Aims of Interpretation*, Chicago, University of Chicago Press.

Hodgson, John (1972) *The Uses of Drama: Acting as a Social and Educational Force*, London, Eyre Methuen.

Hoijer, H. (1962) 'The relation of language to culture', in Tax, Sol (ed.) *Anthropology Today: Selections*, Chicago, University of Chicago Press, pp. 258–77.

Horace (1971) 'Art of poetry', in Adams, Hazard (ed.) *Critical Theory since Plato*, New York, Harcourt, Brace, Jovanovich. pp. 68–75.

Hudson, Lynton A. (1951) *The English Stage, 1850–1950*, London, George Harrap.

Hunt, Hugh, Richards, Kenneth and Taylor, John Russell (1978) *The Revels History of Drama*, vii, London, Methuen.

Ibsen, Henrik (1961) *A Doll's House*, in McFarlane, James W. (trans. and ed.) *The Oxford Ibsen*, V, London, Oxford University Press.

Ibsen, Henrik (1964) *Ibsen: Letters and Speeches*, ed. Evert Sprinchorn, New York, Hill & Wang.

Ionesco, Eugène (1955) 'Mes pièces ne prétendent pas sauver le monde', *L'Express* (15/16 October), 8.

Ionesco, Eugène (1958) *The Chairs*, in *Four Plays by Eugène Ionesco*, trans. Donald M. Allen, New York, Grove Press.

Ionesco, Eugène (1964) *Notes and Counter Notes: Writings on the Theatre*, trans. Donald Watson, New York, Grove Press.

Iser, Wolfgang (1974) *The Implied Reader*, Baltimore and London, Johns Hopkins University Press.

Iser, Wolfgang (1978) *The Act of Reading: A Theory of Aesthetic Response*, Baltimore and London, Johns Hopkins University Press.

Iser, Wolfgang (1981) 'Talk like whales: A reply to Stanley Fish', *diacritics*, X1 (iii) (Fall), 82–7.

Jacobsen, Josephine and Mueller, William R. (1964) *The Testament of Samuel Beckett*, New York, Hill & Wang.

James, Henry (1948) *The Scenic Art: Notes on Acting and the Drama 1872–1901*, New Brunswick, NJ, Rutgers University Press.

James, William (1909) *A Pluralistic Universe*, New York, Longmans, Green.

James, William (1950) *The Principles of Psychology*, 2 vols, New York, Dover.

James, William (1978) *'Pragmatism' and 'The Meaning of Truth'*, Cambridge, Mass., Harvard University Press.

Jarvi, Raymond (1972) '*Ett drömspel*: A symphony for the stage', *Scandinavian Studies*, 44 (Winter), 28–42.

Johnson, Walter (1963) *Strindberg and the Historical Drama*, Seattle, Wash., University of Washington Press.

Johnson, Walter (1971) '*A Dream Play*: Plans and fulfillment', *Scandinavica*, 10 (November), 103–11.

Jones, David E. (1960) *The Plays of T. S. Eliot*, Toronto, University of Toronto Press.

Kennedy, Andrew K. (1975) *Six Dramatists in Search of a Language*, London, Cambridge University Press.

Kenner, Hugh (1961) *Samuel Beckett*, New York, Grove Press.

Kermode, Frank (1970) *The Sense of an Ending: Studies in the Theory of Fiction*, New York, Oxford University Press.

Kernan, Alvin B. (ed.) (1970) *Modern Shakespearean Criticism: Essays on Style, Dramaturgy, and the Major Plays*, New York, Harcourt, Brace & World.

Kerr, Walter (1962) 'Making a cult of confusion', *Horizon*, 5 (i) (September), 33–41.

Kitchin, Laurence (1962) *Mid-Century Drama*, London, Faber & Faber.

Knowlson, James (1972) *Light and Darkness in the Theatre of Samuel Beckett*, London, Turret Books.

Knowlson, James (1976) '*Krapp's Last Tape*: The evolution of a play, 1958–75', *Journal of Beckett Studies*, 1 (Winter), pp. 50–65.

Koht, Halvdan (1931) *The Life of Ibsen*, trans. Ruth L. McMahon and Hanna R. Larsen, London, Allen & Unwin.

Kolve, V. A. (1966) *The Play Called Corpus Christi*, Stanford, Stanford University Press.

Kolve, V. A. (1967) 'Religious language in *Waiting for Godot*', *The Centennial Review*, 11 (Winter), 102–27.

Krutch, Joseph Wood (1966) 'Modernism' in Modern Drama: A Definition and an Estimate, Ithaca, NY, Cornell University Press.

Lahr, John (ed.) (1971) *A Casebook on Harold Pinter's 'The Homecoming'*, New York, Grove Press.

Lamm, Martin (1952) *Modern Drama*, trans. Karin Elliott, Oxford, Blackwell.

Lamm, Martin (1971) *August Strindberg*, ed. and trans. Harry G. Carlson, New York, Benjamin Blom.

Lamont, Rosette C. (ed.) (1973) *Ionesco: A Collection of Critical Essays*, Englewood Cliffs, NJ, Prentice-Hall.

Lazenby, Walter (1972) *Arthur Wing Pinero*, New York, Twayne.

Leacroft, Richard (1973) *The Development of the English Playhouse*, London, Methuen.

Lucas, F. L. (1962) *The Drama of Ibsen and Strindberg*, New York, Macmillan.

Lukács, George (1965) 'The sociology of modern drama', trans. Lee Baxandall, *Tulane Drama Review*, 9 (iv) (Summer), 146–70; reprinted in Eric Bentley (ed.) (1976) *The Theory of the Modern Stage*, Harmondsworth, Penguin, pp. 425–50.

McLaughlin, John (1968) 'Harold Pinter and PBL', *America*, 118 (10 February), 193.

McLuhan, Marshall (1967) *The Gutenberg Galaxy: The Making of Typographic Man*, London, Routledge & Kegan Paul.

McMahon, Joseph H. (1963) *The Imagination of Jean Genet*, New Haven, Conn., Yale University Press.

Madsen, Børge Gedsø (1962) *Strindberg's Naturalistic Theatre: Its Relation to French Naturalism*, Seattle, University of Washington Press.

Magarshack, David (1980) *Chekhov the Dramatist*, London, Methuen.

Marx, Karl and Engels, Friedrich (1970) *The German Ideology*, ed. C. J. Arthur, New York, International Publishers.

Meier, Erika (1967) *Realism and Reality*, Bern, Francke Verlag.

Meinecke, F. (1947) *Die Entstehung des Historismus*, Munich, Leibniz.

Meisel, Martin (1963) *Shaw and the Nineteenth-Century Theater*, Princeton, NJ, Princeton University Press.

Meserve, Walter J. (ed.) (1965) *Discussions of Modern American Drama*, Boston, Heath.

Meyer, Michael (1971) *Ibsen: A Biography*, New York, Doubleday.

Meyer, Michael (ed., trans. and intro.) (1975) *August Strindberg: The Plays*, I–II, London, Secker & Warburg.

Miller, Arthur (1978) *The Theater Essays of Arthur Miller*, ed. Robert A. Martin, New York, Viking Press.

Miller, J. Hillis (1975) 'Deconstructing the deconstructers', *diacritics*, V (ii) (Summer), 24–31.

Miner, Earl (1978) 'On the genesis and development of literary systems', *Critical Inquiry*, 5 (iv) (Winter), 339–53.

Mortensen, Brita M. E. and Downs, Brian W. (1949) *Strindberg: An Introduction to His Life and Work*, Cambridge, Cambridge University Press.

Nicoll, Allardyce (1952–9) *A History of English Drama, 1660–1900*, I–VI, Cambridge, Cambridge University Press.

Northam, John (1953) *Ibsen's Dramatic Method: A Study of the Prose Dramas*, London, Faber & Faber.

Oberg, Arthur K. (1966) '*Krapp's Last Tape* and the Proustian vision', *Modern Drama*, 9 (December), 333–8.

Ollén Gunnar (1972) *August Strindberg*, trans. Peter Tirner, New York, Ungar.

Orenstein, Gloria (1975) *The Theater of the Marvellous: Surrealism and the Contemporary Stage*, New York, New York University Press.

Paolucci, Anne (1980) 'Pirandello and the waiting stage of the absurd (with some observations on a new "critical language")', *Modern Drama*, 23 (June), 102–11.

Parkin, Andrew (1974) 'Monologue into monodrama: Aspects of Samuel Beckett's plays', *Éire-Ireland*, 9 (iv) (Winter), 32–41.

Pater, Walter H. (1961) *The Renaissance*, New York, World Publishing Co.

Paulson, Arvid (ed. and trans.) (1972) *Eight Expressionist Plays (Strindberg)*, New York, New York University Press.

Pinero, Arthur Wing (1894) *The Second Mrs. Tanqueray*, Boston, W. H. Baker & Co.

Pinero, Arthur Wing (1895) 'The modern British drama', *The Theatre* (June), 346–8.

Pinter, Harold (1962) 'Between the lines', *The Sunday Times* (London) (4 March), mag. section, p. 25.

Pinter, Harold (1978) *Betrayal*, London, Eyre Methuen.

Pirandello, Luigi (1952) 'Preface to *Six Characters in Search of an Author*', in *Naked Masks: Five Plays*, ed. Eric Bentley, New York, Dutton, pp. 363–75.

Pirandello, Luigi (1974) *On Humor*, ed. and trans. Antonio Illiano and Daniel P. Testa, Chapel Hill, NC, University of North Carolina Press.

Poulet, George (1956) *Studies in Human Time*, trans. Elliott Coleman, Baltimore, Md, Johns Hopkins University Press.

Pronko, Leonard C. (1963) *Avant Garde: The Experimental Theater in France*, Berkeley, Calif., University of California Press.

Quigley, Austin E. (1975) *The Pinter Problem*, Princeton, NJ, Princeton University Press.

Quigley, Austin E. (1978) '*The Dumb Waiter*: Undermining the tacit dimension', *Modern Drama*, 21 (March), 1–11.

Quigley, Austin E. (1981) 'Creativity and commitment in Trevor Griffiths's *Comedians*', *Modern Drama*, 24 (December), 404–23.

Raymond, Agnes (1966) *Jean Giraudoux: The Theatre of Victory and Defeat*, Amherst, Mass., University of Massachusetts Press.

Reynolds, Ernest (1965) *Early Victorian Drama (1830–1870)*, New York, Benjamin Blom.

Ricoeur, Paul (1978) *The Philosophy of Paul Ricoeur*, ed. Charles E. Reagan and David Stewart, Boston, Beacon Press.

Righter, Anne (1962) *Shakespeare and the Idea of the Play*, London, Chatto & Windus.

Robinson, Michael (1969) *The Long Sonata of the Dead: A Study of Samuel Beckett*, New York, Grove Press.

Roose-Evans, James (1973) *Experimental Theatre: From Stanislavsky to Today*, New York, Discus/Avon.

Roy, Emil (1972) *British Drama Since Shaw*, Carbondale, Ill., Southern Illinois University Press.

Sapir, Edward (1949) *Selected Writings of Edward Sapir*, Berkeley, University of California Press.

Sartre, Jean-Paul (1963) *Saint Genet: Actor and Martyr*, trans. Bernard Frechtman, New York, Braziller.

Schechner, Richard (1962) 'The enactment of the "Not" in Ionesco's *Les Chaises*', *Yale French Studies*, 29, 65–72.

Schiller, Friedrich von (1910) 'Prologue to *The Bride of Messina*', in Dole, N. H. (ed. and trans.) *Works of Schiller*, IV, New York, pp. 223–33.

Schlueter, June (1979) *Metafictional Characters in Modern Drama*, New York, Columbia University Press.

Scott, Nathan A. (1965) *Samuel Beckett*, London, Bowes & Bowes.

Shaw, George Bernard (1894) 'A talk with Mr. Bernard Shaw about his new play', *Pall Mall Budget* (19 April); reprinted as 'Interview in the *Pall Mall Budget*' in *Arms and the Man*, ed. Louis Crompton, New York, Bobbs-Merrill, 1969, pp. 77–80.

Shaw, George Bernard (1932) *Our Theatres in the Nineties*, I–III, London, Constable.

Shaw, George Bernard (1957) *The Quintessence of Ibsenism*, New York, Hill & Wang.

Shaw, George Bernard (1958) *Shaw on Theatre*, ed. E. J. West, London, MacGibbon & Kee.

Sokel, Walter H. (1959) *The Writer in Extremis: Expressionism in Twentieth-Century German Literature*, Stanford, Stanford University Press.

Sokel, Walter H. (1971) 'Brecht's concept of character', *Comparative Drama*, V (Spring), 177–92.

Southern, Richard (1961) *The Seven Ages of the Theatre*, New York, Hill & Wang.

Spariosu, Mihai (ed. and intro.) *Mimesis in Contemporary Theory: An Interdisciplinary Approach*, Philadelphia, John Benjamins (forthcoming).

Sprigge, Elizabeth (1949) *The Strange Life of August Strindberg*, New York, Macmillan.

Sprinchorn, Evert (1962) 'The logic of *A Dream Play*', *Modern Drama*, 5 (December), 352–65.

Stanislavski, Constantin (1961) *Stanislavski on the Art of the Stage*, ed., trans. and intro. David Magarshack, New York, Hill & Wang.

Stanislavski, Constantin (1980) *My Life in Art*, trans. J. J. Robins, London, Methuen.

Stanton, Stephen S. (ed. and intro.) (1957) *'Camille' and Other Plays*, New York, Hill & Wang.

Starkie, Walter F. (1965) *Luigi Pirandello, 1867–1936*, Berkeley, Calif., University of California Press.

Steene, Birgitta (1973) *The Greatest Fire: A Study of August Strindberg*, Carbondale, Ill., Southern Illinois University Press.

Strindberg, August (1889) 'On modern drama and modern theatre', in Cole, Toby (ed.), *Playwrights on Playwrighting*, New York, Hill & Wang, 1961, pp. 15–22.

Strindberg, August (1955) 'Author's Foreword to *Miss Julie*', in *Six Plays of Strindberg*, trans. Elizabeth Sprigge, Garden City, NY, Doubleday, pp. 61–73.

Strindberg, August (1973) *A Dream Play*, in *'A Dream Play' and Four Chamber Plays*, trans. Walter Johnson, Seattle, Wash., University of Washington Press.

Styan, J. L. (1968) *The Dark Comedy: The Development of Modern Comic Tragedy*, New York, Cambridge University Press.

Styan, J. L. (1975) *Drama, Stage and Audience*, London, Cambridge University Press.

Styan, J. L. (1981) *Modern Drama in Theory and Practice*, I–III, New York, Cambridge University Press.

Szczesny, Gerhard (1969) *The Case Against Bertolt Brecht, with Arguments Drawn from his 'Life of Galileo'*, trans. Alexander Gode, New York, Ungar.

Szondi, Peter (1966) *Theorie des Modernen Dramas*, Frankfurt am Main, Suhrkamp.

Taylor, John Russell (1962) *The Angry Theatre: New British Drama*, New York, Hill & Wang.

Taylor, John Russell (1967) *The Rise and Fall of the Well-Made Play*, New York, Hill & Wang.

Taylor, John Russell (1978) *Anger and After: A Guide to the New British Drama*, London, Eyre Methuen.

Tiusanen, Timo (1977) *Dürrenmatt: A Study in Plays, Prose, Theory*, Princeton, NJ, Princeton University Press.

Toulmin, Stephen (1972) *Human Understanding: The Collective Use and Evolution of Concepts*, Princeton, NJ, Princeton University Press.

Toulmin, Stephen and Goodfield, June (1965) *The Discovery of Time*, New York, Harper & Row.

Valency, Maurice (ed. and intro.) (1959) *Jean Giraudoux: Four Plays*, New York, Hill & Wang.

Valency, Maurice (1975) *The Flower and the Castle: An Introduction to Modern Drama*, New York, Macmillan.

Valency, Maurice (1980) *The End of the World: An Introduction to Contemporary Drama*, New York, Oxford University Press.

Van Laan, Thomas F. (1970) *The Idiom of Drama*, Ithaca, NY, Cornell University Press.

Van Laan, Thomas F. (1981) '*The Dumb Waiter*: Pinter's play with the audience', *Modern Drama*, 24 (December), 494–502.

Vicentini, Claudio (1977) 'Pirandello, Stanislavsky, Brecht, and the "opposition principle"', *Modern Drama*, 20 (December), 381–92.

Wagner, Richard (1964) *Wagner on Music and Drama*, ed. Albert Goldman and Evert Sprinchorn, trans. H. A. Ellis, New York, Dutton.

Walker, Roy (1958) 'Samuel Beckett's double bill: Love, chess and death', *Twentieth Century*, 164 (November), 533–44.

Ward, John (1980) *The Social and Religious Plays of Strindberg*, London, Athlone Press.

Webb, Eugene (1972) *The Plays of Samuel Beckett*, London, Peter Owen.

Weber, Betty Nance and Heinen, Hubert (eds) (1980) *Bertolt Brecht: Political Theory and Literary Practice*, Athens, Ga, University of Georgia Press.

Weideli, Walter (1963) *The Art of Bertolt Brecht*, trans. Daniel Russell, New York, New York University Press.

Weigand, Hermann J. (1960) *The Modern Ibsen: A Reconsideration*, New York, Dutton.

Wellwarth, George E. (1971) *The Theater of Protest and Paradox: Developments in the Avant-Garde Drama*, revised edn, New York, New York University Press.

Whitaker, Thomas R. (1977) *Fields of Play in Modern Drama*, Princeton, NJ, Princeton University Press.

White, Alfred D. (1978) *Bertolt Brecht's Great Plays*, London, Macmillan.

Whorf, Benjamin Lee (1969) *Language, Thought, and Reality*, ed. John B. Carroll, Cambridge, Mass., MIT Press.

Wilde, Oscar (1927) *The Works of Oscar Wilde*, New York, Black's Readers Service.

Wilder, Thornton (1979) 'Some thoughts on playwriting', in Gallup, Donald (ed.) *American Characteristics and Other Essays*, New York, Harper & Row, pp. 115–26.

Willett, John (1977) *The Theatre of Bertolt Brecht*, London, Methuen.

Williams, Raymond (1954) *Drama in Performance*, London, Frederick Muller.

Williams, Raymond (1964) *Drama from Ibsen to Eliot*, revised edn, Harmondsworth, Penguin.

Williams, Raymond (1968) *Drama from Ibsen to Brecht*, London, Chatto & Windus.

Wilson, John Harold (ed. and intro.) (1959) *Six Restoration Plays*, Boston, Mass., Houghton Mifflin.

Wittgenstein, Ludwig (1969) *Tractatus Logico-Philosophicus*, trans. D. F. Pears and B. F. McGuinness, New York, The Humanities Press.

Wittgenstein, Ludwig (1969) *Philosophical Investigations*, trans. G. E. M. Anscombe, New York, Macmillan.

Worth, Katharine (1973) *Revolutions in Modern English Drama*, London, G. Bell & Sons.

Worth, Katharine (1978) *The Irish Drama of Europe from Yeats to Beckett*, Atlantic Highlands, NJ, Humanities Press.

Wulbern, Julian H. (1971) *Brecht and Ionesco: Commitment in Context*, Urbana, Ill., University of Illinois Press.

Zola, Émile (1893) *The Experimental Novel, and Other Essays*, trans. B. M. Sherman, New York, Cassell.

Index

Abel, Lionel, 268n, 297n
Abrams, Meyer H., 48–9
Adamov, Arthur, 7, 297n; *The Invasion*, 20
Adams, Hazard, 273n
Albee, Edward, 222; *The Zoo Story*, 18
Alberti, Leon Battista, 258
alienation, 152, 163
Alvarez, Alfred, 213–14
anti-play, 49–50
Antoine, André, 45
Appia, Adolphe, 26
Archer, William, 279n, 283n
Aristotle, 47, 269n, 274n
Armstrong, Cecil F., 280n
Artaud, Antonin, 5–8, 13, 22–5, 27–9, 31, 38, 43, 45, 49, 51; Theatre of Cruelty, 6, 31
l'art pour l'art, 177
Augustine, 260
Austen, Jane, 258

Balzac, Honoré de, 72, 121
Bancroft, Squire and Marie, 26, 269n
Barrie, James M., 222; *The Admirable Crichton*, 10, 33; *Peter Pan*, 25
Beckett, Samuel, 25, 299n; *All That Fall*, 20; *Embers*, 34; *Endgame*, 33; *Happy Days*, 58; *Krapp's Last Tape*, 20, 199–220; *Proust*, 219, 300n; *Waiting For Godot*, 3, 12, 32, 35
Bennett, Benjamin, 267–8n, 270n, 277n

Benston, Alice N., 119–20, 122–4, 284n
Bentley, Eric, 5, 7, 264n, 268n, 276n, 285n; Theatre of Commitment, ix, 6, 58–9; Theatre of War, 6
Berckman, Edward, 289n
Berger, Harry, 257–9, 302–3n
Bernstein, Basil, 17
Bigsby, C. W. E., 297n
Blake, William, 258
Bond, Edward, *Lear*, 33–4, 271n; *The Pope's Wedding*, 272n; *Saved*, 58; *The Worlds*, 15
Bonnefoy, Claude, 274n, 295n
Booth, Michael R., 280n
Bradley, F. H., 28–9, 44
Brahm, Otto, 285n
Brandell, Gunnar, 287n
Braun, Edward, 271n
Brecht, Bertolt, 5, 8, 13, 15, 24–6, 31, 45, 49, 51, 55, 58, 63, 172–4, 176–9, 253, 288n, 290–1n, 293n; *The Caucasian Chalk Circle*, 293n; complex seeing, 152–4, 156–7, 163, 254; Epic Theatre, 6, 145–54, 158–60, 163, 167–8, 174, 180, 288–9n; *The Exception and the Rule*, 293n; *The Good Woman of Setzuan*, 20; *Life of Galileo*, 142–71, 253–4; *A Man's a Man*, 25, 293n; Marxism, 145–7, 154; *Mother Courage*, 3, 58, 292n, 293n; *Three Penny Opera*, 293n
Brook, Peter, 5, 7, 26

Brustein, Robert, 262, 283–4n; Theatre of
　Revolt, x, 6, 57, 59, 262, 275–6n
Büchner, Georg, 291n; *Woyzeck*, 69
Burns, Winifred, 278n, 280n

Calderón, Pedro, 286n
Calderwood, James L., 267n
Cassirer, Ernst, 260, 266n, 296n
Castiglione, Baldassare, 258
Castle of Perseverance, The, 256
Cervantes, Miguel de, 258
Chase, Stuart, 17
Chaucer, Geoffrey, 258
Chekhov, Anton, 51, 55, 83; *The Cherry
　Orchard*, 20, 34, 39; *The Sea Gull*, 3;
　The Three Sisters, 20, 34; *Uncle Vanya*,
　20
closed worlds, 257–63, 265n, 303n
Coe, Richard N., 34
Cohen, Marshall, 226
Cohen, Ralph, 277n
Cohn, Ruby, 35, 200, 264n, 268n, 271n
coincidence, 80
comprehensiveness, xii–xiv, 148–9, 151,
　154, 225
Conrad, Joseph, 258
continuity, xi–xiv, 15, 30, 40–5, 47,
　50–1, 54, 55–65, 149, 167–70, 174,
　176, 181, 193, 200–1, 204–8, 217–21,
　253–5, 261, 276–7n
convention, x–xi, xiv, 24, 26, 35, 49, 52,
　56, 69–74, 88, 91, 94–6, 113, 116,
　120–1, 125–8, 147, 158, 182, 221–6,
　227–31, 237, 247, 249–52, 255, 275n,
　279n, 281n
convergence, 150–1
Cook, Capt. James, 19
Coward, Noel, 222
Craig, Edward Anthony, 268n
Craig, E. Gordon, 26, 268n, 272n
Croce, Benedetto, 281n

Dace, Letitia, 297n
Dahlström, Carl, 284n
Davies, Cecil W., 280n
Descartes, René, 258
dialectics, 32, 146–7, 168, 270–1n, 277n
Dickson, Keith A., 289n, 292–3n
difference, x, 20, 36, 50, 54, 55–65, 149,
　159, 168, 174, 181, 183, 200, 204–5,
　214, 217, 254, 261, 276–7n, 288n
Dilthey, Wilhelm, 62

discontinuity, 41–5, 47, 50, 55–65, 151,
　200–1, 206, 208–9, 254, 276–7n
discovery, xiv, 4–7, 23–5, 42, 50–4, 59,
　64–5, 154, 156–7, 173, 176, 180–1,
　198, 219–20, 251–2, 254, 295n
discussion play, 95, 111, 113, 125, 127,
　134–6, 139–40, 180
divergence, 150–1
diversity, x–xiv, 3–7, 15–21, 54, 59–60,
　124–5, 198, 200–7, 218, 254, 259,
　261, 264n, 266–7n, 275n
Donohue, Joseph, 280n
Driver, Tom F., 261, 265–6n, 272n
Dukore, Bernard F., 200
Dumas, Alexandre, *fils*, 70, 72, 110; *Le
　Demi-monde*, 82; *L'Étrangère*, 83
Dunkel, Wilbur D., 278n
Dürrenmatt, Friedrich, 273n; *The Visit*,
　35, 58
Duse, Eleanora, 268n

Eagleton, Terry, 47
Einstein, Albert, 224
Eliot, T. S., 221–2, 275n; *The Cocktail
　Party*, 83; *The Family Reunion*, 11
Ellis, John M., 277n
Engels, Friedrich, 289n
entertainment, 47–8, 50, 53, 64, 255,
　274–5n
Esslin, Martin, 8, 120, 122, 274n,
　291–2n; Theatre of the Absurd, ix, xi,
　6, 57–9, 174, 180, 201–5, 214, 262,
　275n, 294n, 296–8n
existentialism, 276n, 298n
expressionism, ix, 27, 98, 119–20, 122–7,
　130, 132–5, 139–140, 144, 153, 170,
　174, 178, 202, 270n, 276n, 284n,
　286n, 288n

Felperin, Howard, 302n
Fergusson, Francis, 98, 264n
fiction, 49, 185–8, 192–4, 198
Fielding, Henry, 258
Filarete, 258
Fish, Stanley, 301n
Fjelde, Rolf, 93, 98, 140, 282n
Fletcher, John, 214
Foucault, Michel, 276n
Frisch, Max, *The Firebugs*, 20, 39
Frye, Northrop, 257–8, 265n
Fuchs, Georg, 271n
Fuegi, John, 289n
Fyfe, Hamilton, 280n

Galileo (Galilei), 258
Gasgoigne, Bamber, 264n, 297n
Gelber, Jack, *The Connection*, 25, 32
generalization, x–xiv, 3–7, 55–65, 77–9, 178, 180, 201–7, 209, 214–20, 261, 297n, 300n
Genet, Jean, 34, 55, 297n; *The Balcony*, 3, 8, 20, 25, 32, 39–40, 58; *The Blacks*, 45; *The Maids*, 25
Ghelderode, Michel de, 5; *The Death of Doctor Faust*, 20
Gilbert, William, 258
Gilman, Richard, 273n, 279n, 282n, 285n, 288n
Girard, René, 274n
Giraudoux, Jean, 20, 34–5, 222
Goethe, Johann W. von, 5; *Faust*, 69, 267n, 270n, 286n
Goldman, Michael, 265n
Goodman, Nelson, 19, 27, 41, 51, 53, 64, 260, 272n, 276n
Gray, Ronald D., 145, 288–9n, 291–2n
Gray, Simon, 53
green worlds, 257–63, 265n, 303n
Griffiths, Trevor, 51, 222; *Comedians*, 13, 33; *Such Impossibilities*, 274n; *Through the Night*, 274n
Grillparzer, Franz, 286n
Grotowski, Jerzy, 51, 271n; *Poor Theatre*, 33

Hamilton, Clayton, 69
Handke, Peter, *Kaspar*, 20, 25, 38, 49
Haugen, Einar, 93–4, 282n
Hauptmann, Gerhardt, 291n
Hawkins, Sherman, 257–9, 265n, 302–3n
Hawthorne, Nathaniel, 258
Hayman, Ronald, 200, 300n
Hegel, G. W. F., 32, 146–7, 270n, 289–90n
Heiberg, Gunnar, 94
Heidegger, Martin, 64
Heisenberg, Werner K., 224
Heraclitus, 303n
Herder, Johann G. von, 16–17, 28, 62, 123
Herrick, Robert, 303n
heterocosm, 259
Hill, Claude, 292n
Hinchliffe, Arnold P., 297–8n
Hirsch, E. D., 16, 62, 277n
Hodgson, John, 53
Hoijer, H., 18

Homer, 120, 257–8, 302n
Horace, 48, 273–4n
Humboldt, Wilhelm von, 17, 182
Hunt, Hugh, 265n, 269n

Ibsen, Henrik, xiii, 5, 51, 55, 83, 108, 115–16, 140, 146, 172, 281n, 283–4n; *A Doll's House*, xvi, 33, 91–114, 118, 135–6, 143, 253; *Ghosts*, 20, 34, 39, 282n; *Hedda Gabler*, 3; *The Lady from the Sea*, 34; *Love's Comedy*, 282n; *The Master Builder*, 57; *Peer Gynt*, 286n; *The Wild Duck*, 20
ideology, 148, 173–6, 181, 194, 198
image network, 98–101, 104, 107–8, 110–11, 112–13, 118, 125, 135, 253
impressionism, 27, 284n
innovation, ix, xi, xiv, 25–7, 49, 221–2, 255, 275n
inquiry, 50–4, 60–5, 114–16, 118, 125–7, 131, 133, 137, 140–1, 146–54, 169–70, 255, 262–3, 275n, 281n
instruction, 47–8, 50, 64, 115, 173, 176, 181, 194, 197, 255, 274–5n
interpretative analogy, 97, 100, 104–5, 107–8, 113, 135, 284n
Ionesco, Eugène, 7, 24, 37–8, 45, 49–51, 55, 293–7n; *The Bald Soprano*, 3, 25, 30, 45, 49, 179, 274n; *The Chairs*, 20, 30–1, 35, 172–98, 254; *The Lesson*, 179; *Rhinoceros*, 39
Iser, Wolfgang, 52, 274n, 277n, 301n

James, Henry, 258
James, William, 41–3, 262, 270n, 276n
Jarry, Alfred, 7–8; *Ubu Roi*, 45
Jarvi, Raymond, 286n
Johnson, Walter, 284n, 286–7n
Jones, Henry A., *The Liars*, 10

Kant, Immanuel, 19, 27, 123, 269n, 277n
Kehler, Henning, 283n
Kellner, Douglas, 147, 289n
Kennedy, Andrew K., 273n
Kerr, Walter, 297n
Knowlson, James, 199, 296n, 299n
Koht, Halvdan, 283n
Kolve, V. A., 220, 255–6, 267n
Korsch, Karl, 145–7, 289n

Labiche, Eugène, 71
Lahr, John, 301n
Lamm, Martin, 284n, 287n

Lamont, Rosette C., 295n
Lazenby, Walter, 280–1n
Lenz, Jacob, 291n
Leonardo (da Vinci), 258
Lessing, Gotthold E., 123, 270n
Lewis, C. I., 19
Lucas, F. L., 91, 282n
Lukács, George, 5, 23
Lüthy, Herbert, 289n

Machiavelli, Niccolò, 258
McLaughlin, John, 226
McLuhan, Marshall, vi
macrocosm, 15
Madsen, Børge Gedsø, 284–6n
Manheim, Ralph, 288n
Marvell, Andrew, 258
Marx, Karl, 289–90n, 292–3n
Maugham, Somerset, 72, 222, 279n
Meier, Erika, 82–3, 280n
Meierhold, Vsevolod, 272n
Meinecke, Friedrich, 16
Meisel, Martin, 280–1n
metatheatre, 25, 268n
Meyer, Michael, 91, 94, 281–2n, 286–7n
microcosm, 15
Miller, Arthur, 222; After the Fall, 32–3, 58; Death of a Salesman, 25
Miller, J. Hillis, 259
mimesis, 45–54, 98, 123–5, 144, 153, 269n, 273–5n
Miner, Earl, 47, 273–4n
modernism, 261, 286n
monism, 41–2, 141, 261, 272–3n
More, Thomas, 258
Müller, Klaus-Detlef, 147, 289n
mummers' play, 258

naturalism, ix, 24, 46, 119–27, 132–5, 139–40, 144, 153, 174, 180, 202, 282–8n
Nicoll, Allardyce, 278n
Nietzsche, Friedrich W., 270n
Northam, John, 95, 97–9, 282–3n
novelty, x–xiv, 23–5, 30, 36, 42–4, 49–54, 63–5, 69, 95, 106, 115, 119, 124, 148–53, 156, 166–71, 173–81, 193–4, 198, 220–3, 226–31, 237, 243–4, 249–52, 262–3, 268n, 275n, 300n

Oberg, Arthur K., 200
obscurity, 29–36, 56, 117, 123–4, 175, 223, 270n, 274n
O'Casey, Sean, The Plough and the Stars, 25
Ockrent, Michael, 286–7n
Oliver, Cordelia, 287n
Ollén, Gunnar, 287n
O'Neill, Eugene, Anna Christie, 34; The Emperor Jones, 45; The Iceman Cometh, 25; Long Day's Journey Into Night, 39, 58
Orenstein, Gloria, 8; Theatre of the Marvellous, ix, 6, 57
originality, x, 25, 49, 69–70, 94, 113, 173, 221–3, 227–9, 243, 275n, 281n
Osborne, John, The Entertainer, 25, 33; Look Back in Anger, 13, 222; The World of Paul Slickey, 15

Paolucci, Anne, 5
Parkin, Andrew, 300n
Pater, Walter H., 18
Paulson, Arvid, 287n
performance space, ix, 5–7, 12–14, 23–36, 38–45, 55, 57, 72, 253–4, 260–3, 265n, 267–72n; Betrayal, 230–3, 237, 242–5, 250–2; The Chairs, 172, 180–4, 188–98; A Doll's House, 91–4, 97–100; A Dream Play, 116–18, 126, 133–5, 138–41; Krapp's Last Tape, 199, 207–8, 215–18; Life of Galileo, 142–4, 149–55, 162, 168–71; The Second Mrs. Tanqueray, 83–90
Pinero, Arthur Wing, xiii, 51, 96–7, 116, 146, 172, 222, 278n, 281n; The Second Mrs. Tanqueray, 9, 69–90, 91, 94, 98, 113, 118, 143, 158, 251, 253, 278n; Trelawney of the 'Wells', 57
Pinter, Harold, 231; Betrayal, 221–52, 254; The Birthday Party, 222; The Caretaker, 20, 25; The Collection, 33; The Dumb Waiter, 301n; The Homecoming, 302n; The Lover, 58
Pirandello, Luigi, 7, 37–8, 45, 53, 55, 222; Henry IV, 3, 222; Six Characters in Search of an Author, 20, 25, 35–6, 58, 69, 222; Tonight We Improvise, 33
Plato, 47, 269n, 274n
pluralism, 9–21, 27–36, 40–4, 51–4, 55, 60, 63, 254–5, 259–63, 269–70n, 273n, 277n; Betrayal, 221, 224–5, 231, 237, 242–3, 251–2; The Chairs, 181–2, 188, 193–4, 198; A Doll's House, 100,

112–14; *A Dream Play*, 116–18, 125–7, 133–5, 140–1; *Krapp's Last Tape*, 200–2, 208, 217–20; *Life of Galileo*, 143–6, 150–6, 162–3, 170–1; *The Second Mrs. Tanqueray*, 77–9, 88–90
poststructuralism, 277n
Poulet, George, 256
Priestley, J. B., *Dangerous Corner*, 301n; *An Inspector Calls*, 301n; *I Have Been Here Before*, 301n; *Time and the Conways*, 301n
problem play, 95, 113

Quigley, Austin E., 271n, 301–2n

raisonneur, 82, 86, 89, 100, 104, 109–11, 113, 118, 253, 280–1n
Rattigan, Terence, 222, 279n; *Harlequinade*, 25
realism, 64, 119–21, 124, 173–4, 222, 260, 274n, 277n, 294n
relativism, 19, 29, 55, 89, 141, 261
Ricoeur, Paul, 64, 277n
Righter, Anne, 267n
Robinson, Michael, 200, 214
Roose-Evans, James, 268n

St George play, 258
Sapir, Edward, 17, 266–7n
Sardou, Victorien, 70–1, 278n
Sartre, Jean-Paul, 295n; *No Exit*, 39, 58
Schechner, Richard, 179, 295n
Schiller, Friedrich von, 267n, 270n
Schlueter, June, 268n
Scribe, Eugène, 70–2, 82, 110, 278–9n, 282n, 284n
second world, 257–60
Secunda Pastorum, 255–6
Shakespeare, William, 256–8, 265n, 280n; *Antony and Cleopatra*, 256; *As You Like It*, 256; *The Comedy of Errors*, 257; *King Lear*, 286n; *Love's Labour's Lost*, 257; *The Merry Wives of Windsor*, 256; *Much Ado About Nothing*, 257; *The Tempest*, 280n; *Twelfth Night*, 257; *Two Gentlemen of Verona*, 256
Shaw, George Bernard, 46, 55, 72, 95, 222, 273n, 279–81n, 291n; *Major Barbara*, 10, 33, 39, 277n, 283n; *Man and Superman*, 3, 39, 57; *Saint Joan*, 25
Sheridan, Richard B., *A School for Scandal*, 278n
Sidney, Philip, 258

similarity, 36, 50, 55–65, 153, 155, 159, 168, 174, 183, 200, 204–5, 214, 217, 254, 276–7n, 288n
Sokel, Walter H., 123–4, 144, 269–70n, 276–7n, 286n, 288n, 292n
solipsism, 175–7
Spariosu, Mihai, 48
Spenser, Edmund, 258
Sprinchorn, Evert, 286–7n
Spurling, John, 214
Stanislavsky, Konstantin, 33
Stanton, Stephen S., 70–3, 148, 278–9n
Steene, Birgitta, 287n
Stoppard, Tom, 53; *Night and Day*, 58; *The Real Inspector Hound*, 45; *Rosencrantz and Guildenstern Are Dead*, 12, 25
Storey, David, 222; *Cromwell*, 13; *In Celebration*, 58
Strindberg, August, 25, 45, 51, 55, 137, 146, 172, 287n; *A Dream Play*, 15, 28, 115–41, 143–4, 150, 153, 253; *The Father*, 20, 57; *The Ghost Sonata*, 3; *Miss Julie*, 5, 121–2; *To Damascus*, 69
structuralism, 277n
Styan, J. L., 33, 264n, 267n, 269n, 274n, 284n
symbolic naturalism, 119–25, 139–40, 284n
Synge, John M., *Playboy of the Western World*, 15, 25, 57; *Riders to the Sea*, 34
Szczesny, Gerhard, 289n
Szondi, Peter, 265n, 276n

Tatlow, Anthony, 146
Taylor, John Russell, 72–4, 222, 225–6, 278–80n, 301n
testimony, 24–30, 45, 176, 178, 181, 197–8, 254
theatricality, 4–7, 23–36, 37–40, 43–54, 63–5, 119–25, 138, 149–53, 174, 177, 183, 192, 268n, 272n, 275n
thesis play, 95
Tiusanen, Timo, 273n
Toulmin, Stephen, 19
tradition, 35, 51–4, 69, 82–3, 95, 109–10, 113, 116, 118, 158, 194, 200, 221–3, 226–7, 251–2, 262–3, 268n, 274–5n, 286n
Tynan, Kenneth, 30, 174–6, 293–4n

unity, x, xii, 55, 61, 63, 149, 151, 200–1, 207, 256–7, 259–61, 267n, 276n

Valency, Maurice, 34–5, 70–1, 73, 82–3,
   274n, 278n, 283–5n, 287n, 301n
Van Laan, Thomas F., 301n
Vicentini, Claudio, 265n
Vico, Giambattista, 62
Virgil, 258
Voltaire, François M. A., 292n

Wagner, Richard, 288n
Walker, Roy, 214
Ward, John, 284n
Webb, Eugene, 296n, 299n
Wedekind, Frank, 291n; Spring
   Awakening, 35
Weideli, Walter, 292n
Weigand, Hermann J., 103, 282n
Weiss, Peter, Marat Sade, 25, 33
well-made play, 46, 70–5, 80–3, 89–91,
   95–8, 100–1, 104, 110–1, 113, 116,
   124, 126, 144, 148, 157–8, 160, 166,
   174, 180, 222–5, 245, 251, 278–80n,
   284n

Wellwarth, George E., 7; Theatre of
   Protest and Paradox, ix, xi, 6, 57, 262
Werfel, Franz, 288n
Whitaker, Thomas R., 271n
White, Alfred D., 145, 289n, 291–2n
Whorf, Benjamin Lee, 17–18
Wilde, Oscar, 53, 279n
Wilder, Thornton, 24, 45, 53, 55
Willett, John, 288n
Williams, Raymond, 95–6, 109, 136,
   282n, 284n, 287n
Williams, Tennessee, A Streetcar Named
   Desire, 39, 283–4n; The Two Character
   Play, 34
Wilson, John H., 46
Wittgenstein, Ludwig, 60–2, 64, 204, 298n
Wulbern, Julian H., 293–4n

Yeats, W. B., 258; The Countess Cathleen,
   8, 11

Zola, Émile, 5, 7, 55, 120–2, 125,
   283–5n; Thérèse Raquin, 285n